"Jenson's opening vision of catholicity provides an ideal foundation for winning over an audience that may not be wholly convinced of the value of tradition. His conversational style will draw readers in for a journey with some of the most important theologians of the Christian tradition in a way that is both engaging and accessible. This book will be deeply valued in the classroom."

—**Mary Veeneman**, North Park University

"Today the church and her theology can frequently seem rather thin and immature, whereas the Bible calls us to wholeness and maturity. Jenson adeptly shows that learning from our elders—more specifically from the Triune God's work in and through this 'great cloud of witnesses'—plays a crucial role in growing into that fullness. This book introduces eleven brilliant figures, surveys their work and influence, introduces significant secondary literature, and helps guide readers not merely to know them but to think with them. I wish everyone could be in the classroom with this master teacher; now his classroom expands, and all of us can follow his guidance."

—**Michael Allen**, Reformed Theological Seminary, Orlando

# THEOLOGY
# IN THE
# DEMOCRACY
# OF THE DEAD

# THEOLOGY
# IN THE
# DEMOCRACY
# OF THE DEAD

*A Dialogue with the Living Tradition*

# MATT JENSON

**B**
**Baker Academic**
*a division of Baker Publishing Group*
Grand Rapids, Michigan

© 2019 by Matt Jenson

Published by Baker Academic
a division of Baker Publishing Group
PO Box 6287, Grand Rapids, MI 49516-6287
www.bakeracademic.com

Printed and bound by CPI Group (UK) Ltd, Croydon, CR0 4YY

Library of Congress Cataloging-in-Publication Data
Names: Jenson, Matt, 1976– author.
Title: Theology in the democracy of the dead : a dialogue with the living tradition / Matt Jenson.
Description: Grand Rapids : Baker Academic, a division of Baker Publishing Group, 2019. |
    Includes bibliographical references and index.
Identifiers: LCCN 2019003749 | ISBN 9780801049439 (pbk.)
Subjects: LCSH: Theology—History.
Classification: LCC BR118 .J46 2019 | DDC 230.09—dc23
LC record available at https://lccn.loc.gov/2019003749

ISBN 978-1-5409-6239-3 (casebound)

19   20   21   22   23   24   25      7   6   5   4   3   2   1

To the faculty, students, and staff
of the Torrey Honors Institute,
past and present

# CONTENTS

Acknowledgments    xi

Abbreviations    xiii

Introduction    1

1. A King or a Fox? *Irenaeus of Lyons and the Theology of Scripture*    5
2. The Word Who Became Flesh: *The Center and Circumference of Athanasius's Theology*    33
3. "The Lovely Things Kept Me Far from You": *The Wayward Loves of Augustine*    63
4. "That Most Biblical of Theologians": *Denys the Areopagite and the Brilliant Darkness of God*    85
5. Faith Seeking Understanding—or Understanding Seeking Faith? *Anselm of Canterbury and the Logic of God*    107
6. "St. Thomas of the Creator": *Aquinas and the Beginning and End of All Things in God*    129
7. "One Little Word Shall Fell Him": *The Word of God and the Faith of Martin Luther*    165
8. "What Do You Have That You Did Not Receive?": *John Calvin on Having God as Father*    193
9. The Beauty of Holiness: *Jonathan Edwards's Religion of the Heart*    221
10. A Pietist of a Higher Order: *Schleiermacher, Jesus, and the Heart of Religion*    247

11. "The Happiest Theologian of Our Age": *Karl Barth on the One Word of God That We Have to Hear*   275

Bibliography   305
Scripture Index   321
Subject Index   325

# ACKNOWLEDGMENTS

This book has been hard work and a long time in coming. With each chapter, I have known the joyful disorientation of diving down the rabbit hole of one of the church's great minds. Frequently, I wondered if I would be able to make sense of them, much less help others do the same. Fred Sanders and Doug Sweeney came along just at the right time at a couple of points in the project, believing in me and nudging me ahead. Bob Hosack and I began meeting together years ago; he has been a patient, gracious, and clear editor. He handed off the project to Julie Zahm, who has capably and kindly overseen the process of bringing the manuscript to book form. Thanks to her, to Paula Gibson, Brandy Scritchfield, Jeremy Wells, and my anonymous, eagle-eyed copyeditor.

My research assistants—Hannah Grady, Miranda Hess, and Sophia Johnson—have been massively helpful. Hannah and Miranda closely read the book and offered many suggestions of felicitous phrasing, cuts, queries about matters of interpretation, and the perspective of that elusive "target audience." Sophia helped with the bibliography and indexes. Biola University has provided much-needed space to research and write through financial support, including a sabbatical in the spring of 2014 and a course release in the fall of 2017.

I am deeply grateful for the time each of these people took to read and respond to portions of the book and am happy to now call many of them friends: Khaled Anatolios, Uche Anizor, John Behr, Sarah Brown, Julie Canlis, John Cavadini, Oliver Crisp, Christine Helmer, Joe Mangina, Dave Nelson, Paul Rorem, Fred Sanders, Kate Sonderegger, Chelle Stearns, Doug Sweeney, Terry Tice, Diane Vincent, Joseph Wawrykow, David Wilhite, Thomas Williams, and Sarah Hinlicky Wilson. They pushed me, kept me honest, blew wind into my sails, wondered with me, confirmed my intuitions, and corrected me. Not only would this book be much weaker without their good help, but there are places where I would have been a questionable guide. There may still be some of those, and the old saw gets it right—the mistakes are all mine.

I could fill a book telling you of the friendships that have sustained, enriched, illuminated, and directed me over these years. To name only a few: the people of Fountain of Life Covenant Church—my family in the deepest sense; the Spears, Mikasa, and Sato families; my wonderful parents, Ron and Mary; my sister Molly, who becomes a closer friend each year; and now Sarah.

The Torrey Honors Institute at Biola University has been my academic home for a dozen years now. I know of nothing quite like it. My job is to discuss the greatest books of the West for hours on end with students eager to grow in the likeness of Christ. I have the best students and the brightest colleagues—colleagues who are dear friends. Most of these chapters began as lectures in Torrey, and I gladly dedicate this book to its students, faculty, and staff.

# ABBREVIATIONS

AH    *Against Heresies*. By Irenaeus of Lyons. Edited by Alexander Roberts, James Donaldson, and A. Cleveland Coxe. N.p.: Ex Fontibus, 2010.

CD    *Church Dogmatics*. By Karl Barth. Edited and translated by G. W. Bromiley and T. F. Torrance. 13 vols. Edinburgh: T&T Clark, 1956–75.

CH    *Celestial Hierarchy*. By Pseudo-Dionysius. In *Pseudo-Dionysius: The Complete Works*. Translated by Colm Luibheid and Paul Rorem. New York: Paulist Press, 1987.

Comm.    *Calvin's Commentaries*. By John Calvin. Translated by the Calvin Translation Society. Edited by John King et al. 22 vols. Edinburgh, 1843–55. Reprint, Grand Rapids: Baker, 2009. (*Comm. Romans* = *Calvin's Commentaries: Romans*; *Comm. Psalms* = *Calvin's Commentaries: Psalms*; etc.)

Dem.    *On the Apostolic Preaching* (= *The Demonstration of the Apostolic Preaching*). By Irenaeus. Translated by John Behr. Crestwood, NY: St. Vladimir's Seminary Press, 1997.

DN    *The Divine Names*. By Pseudo-Dionysius. In *Pseudo-Dionysius: The Complete Works*. Translated by Colm Luibheid and Paul Rorem. New York: Paulist Press, 1987.

EH    *The Ecclesiastical Hierarchy*. By Pseudo-Dionysius. In *Pseudo-Dionysius: The Complete Works*. Translated by Colm Luibheid and Paul Rorem. New York: Paulist Press, 1987.

Ep.    *Epistles* (Letters). By Pseudo-Dionysius. In *Pseudo-Dionysius: The Complete Works*. Translated by Colm Luibheid and Paul Rorem. New York: Paulist Press, 1987.

Inst.    *Institutes of the Christian Religion*. By John Calvin. Translated by Ford Lewis Battles. Edited by John T. McNeill. 2 vols. Louisville: Westminster John Knox, 1960.

LW    *Luther's Works*. By Martin Luther. American ed. Edited by J. Pelikan and H. Lehmann. 55 vols. St. Louis: Concordia; Philadelphia: Fortress Press, 1955–86.

MT      *Mystical Theology.* By Pseudo-Dionysius. In *Pseudo-Dionysius: The Complete Works.* Translated by Colm Luibheid and Paul Rorem. New York: Paulist Press, 1987.

Or.     *On God and Christ: The Five Theological Orations and Two Letters to Cledonius.* By Gregory of Nazianzus. Translated by Lionel Wickham. New York: St. Vladimir's Seminary Press, 2002.

SCG     *Summa contra gentiles.* By Thomas Aquinas. Translated by Anton C. Pegis, James F. Anderson, Vernon J. Bourke, and Charles J. O'Neil. 5 vols. Notre Dame, IN: University of Notre Dame Press, 1975.

ST      *Summa theologica.* By Thomas Aquinas. Translated by Fathers of the English Dominican Province. 5 vols. Allen, TX: Christian Classics, 1981.

WJE     *The Works of Jonathan Edwards.* By Jonathan Edwards. Edited by Perry Miller, John E. Smith, and Harry S. Stout. 26 vols. New Haven: Yale University Press, 1957–2008.

WJEO    *The Works of Jonathan Edwards Online.* By Jonathan Edwards. http://edwards.yale.edu.

# INTRODUCTION

You may be wondering about the macabre title of this book. It's a bit spooky, this reference to a "democracy of the dead." It conjures graveyards, evokes underworlds. The words come from G. K. Chesterton, who writes:

> I have never been able to understand where people got the idea that democracy was in some way opposed to tradition. It is obvious that tradition is only democracy extended through time. It is trusting to a consensus of common human voices rather than to some isolated or arbitrary record. . . . Tradition may be defined as an extension of the franchise. Tradition means giving votes to the most obscure of all classes, our ancestors. It is the democracy of the dead. Tradition refuses to submit to the small and arrogant oligarchy of those who merely happen to be walking about. All democrats object to men being disqualified by the accident of birth; tradition objects to their being disqualified by the accident of death. Democracy tells us not to neglect a good man's opinion, even if he is our groom; tradition asks us not to neglect a good man's opinion, even if he is our father. I, at any rate, cannot separate the two ideas of democracy and tradition; it seems evident to me that they are the same idea. We will have the dead at our councils. The ancient Greeks voted by stones; these shall vote by tombstones.[1]

The marriage of democracy and tradition makes for an odd couple. They are more often portrayed locked in battle, with the traditional fighting to preserve the glory of the past, while the democratic seeks to liberate the many who were passed over and pushed aside in that purportedly glorious age. Democracy liberates *from* tradition, we might think; it gives a voice and a vote to all of us. Finally.

But Christians believe in the communion of the saints. We believe that God is not the God of the dead but the God of the living, and that the city

---

1. Chesterton, *Orthodoxy*, in *Collected Works*, 1:250–51.

1

in which we vote is a heavenly one. And so, as Chesterton quips, we would be insufficiently democratic if we restricted the franchise to "the small and arrogant oligarchy of those who merely happen to be walking about."

This is an issue of catholicity. To speak of the church's wholeness (*catholic* derives from Greek *kata holos*, "according to the whole") is to evoke the fullness of the deposit of faith, as well as all those who by faith have come to know and love the God and Father of our Lord Jesus Christ. To be catholic is to treasure the truth of the Triune God in the company of all his people, living and dead. Given our innate tendencies toward the parochial, however, we have to work to hold in mind and heart those Christians in other times and places; so consider this book a complement to the many recent forays into a more globally informed theology.[2] Whereas those efforts champion a catholicity in space, this seeks and celebrates a catholicity in time.

Karl Barth wrote at the end of his life that "in order to serve the community of today, theology itself must be rooted in the community of yesterday."[3] And yet, what he wrote much earlier is no less true: "Galvanized father-piety is exactly what we do *not* need. . . . But the founders, in their seeking, questioning, confusion, and affliction, who stood in the boundless difficulty and need of the human before the Lord, could challenge us to become founders *ourselves*, also responding to *our* time."[4] To give the dead a vote, then, is not to give the dead *my* vote. It is not to abdicate responsibility to seek understanding. "Let us know; let us press on to know the LORD," Hosea exhorts us (6:3). And if knowing the Lord is about more than theology, it is not about *less* than theology! Theology requires us to think for ourselves, even if never by ourselves and only after and as we learn to think with the mind of Christ under the tutelage and in the company of others.[5]

This book is not an overview of eleven theologians or a survey of their positions on key doctrines. Nor is it theological journalism. Instead, it is an invitation to apprenticeship. Imagine that Irenaeus, say, is a master painter at work in his studio. You and I are standing just over his shoulder, and I am pointing out brushstrokes, color choices, surprising juxtapositions, figural arrangement. I have struggled at times to know how and when to register

2. This is only one of many such attempts, I hasten to add, stretching back to the *ressourcement* movement of the early twentieth century and often flying under the banner of "retrieval theology." See, in particular, the proposal of Allen and Swain, *Reformed Catholicity*, and the survey in Webster, "Theologies of Retrieval."

3. Barth, *Evangelical Theology*, 42.

4. Barth, *Word of God and Theology*, 216. Here and throughout, emphasis in quotations is as set in the original unless otherwise noted.

5. Tom Smail speaks of the Spirit enabling us to respond for ourselves, but never by ourselves, in *Giving Gift*, 27.

disagreement or even disappointment with these theologians. I most want to hold them up as master craftsmen, to suggest that we would do well to imitate their theological concerns and style. But sometimes, because of bad lighting or fatigue, poor judgment or a lack of vision, their work is marred. And sometimes I will say so.

I want you to see what they are doing and why they are doing it. So I will cite primary texts generously, with only occasional forays into the secondary literature. This mirrors my own apprenticeship to these theologians. I have read as much as I can of their primary work, notated it, pored over it, and tried to make sense of what they were doing on their own terms.

I do so as a systematic theologian whose day job is to teach great books in a Socratic style. So my questions are systematic more than they are historical; I am less interested in the sources of Luther's thought than I am in how it holds together and what it implies for the church here and now. And I trust that these primary texts can teach us quite a lot—about how Luther and the others thought, about how we should think, and above all, about who the Triune God is and how he loves the world.

A colleague of mine asked a trenchant question: Is this a democracy or a meritocracy? Do I really mean to extend theological suffrage to "the people," or only to the best and brightest? We might ask further whether this isn't an aristocracy, with only people of a certain status gaining the right to vote. Perhaps this is a faux catholicity after all.

One obvious reason for asking is that all eleven of these theologians are men. Now, I don't think that these are the only possible candidates for inclusion in a book of great theologians. I can quickly think of another half-dozen who could just as easily have been included, and a couple of those I have included are highly contestable. All but one of these eleven are on the booklist in the Torrey Honors Institute, where I teach; to some extent this is an accident of biography. But I stand by the list, nonetheless.

The fact is, few women wrote formal theology at a high level before the last couple centuries. Far more women have written mystical and devotional theology, both of which can be as probing as the more second-order discourse that I consider in this book. There are many material and social reasons that women have seldom written formal theology until relatively recently. To write formal theology requires education and sufficient leisure (often in a monastery). Women rarely had either. Add to this stricter societal expectations and limitations than we are familiar with in the West these days, and the dearth of female theologians should not surprise us.

But perhaps the most significant reason is sin. For blocking women from reading and writing theology, we in the church can only repent and lament.

While I am suspicious of attempts to include certain second-tier theologians out of a desire to rewrite or redress this sinful history, I am heartily eager to see things change. My hope is that the next millennium will yield as many, if not more, great theologians who are women. It is an auspicious sign that some of the most rigorous and creative theologians working today are women. The work of Sarah Coakley, Katherine Sonderegger, Kathryn Tanner, and Frances Young is stimulating, surprising, and searching—and each is so different from the next, giving the lie to the belief that there is something called "the woman's perspective"! Some of the sharpest students who have graduated from the Torrey Honors Institute and gone on to do graduate theological work are women, and I hope to count these women as colleagues and interlocutors in the years to come.

Let me conclude with two metaphors for the craft of writing that describe what I have attempted to do and how I have done it. The first is from Annie Dillard, who describes the experience of writing in the dark, curiously, carefully, almost blindly, only discerning the way as you go: "You write it all, discovering it at the end of the line of words. The line of words is a fiber optic, flexible as wire; it illumines the path just before its fragile tip. You probe with it, delicate as a worm."[6] Some writers know just what they'll say before they begin saying it; I can't begin to understand them.

The second metaphor comes from the Irish poet Seamus Heaney. Really, it is a transformation of metaphor. Descended from men who farmed potatoes and cut peat, Heaney finds himself in a very different vocation; he is a writer. He begins his poem "Digging" like this:

> Between my finger and my thumb
> The squat pen rests; snug as a gun.

Heaney sits at a window and hears his father digging outside, like his father before him. He marvels at the work of these men—but it is *their* work, not his. Then it occurs to him: he may not have a spade, but he does have a pen. Heaney concludes: "I'll dig with it."[7]

A weapon of war has become a tool with which to till the earth so that it might bring forth life. The work of writing connects Heaney to these men who worked the land after all. All three dig; all three cultivate the soil, in which lie buried the past and the future. Consider *Theology in the Democracy of the Dead* an exercise in digging.

---

6. Dillard, *Writing Life*, 7.
7. Heaney, "Digging," in *Poems, 1965–1975*, 3–4.

# 1

# A KING OR A FOX?

*Irenaeus of Lyons and the Theology of Scripture*

When I was a boy, I had a strategy for avoiding things I did not want to hear and see. I would put my hands over my ears, close my eyes, chew my tongue, and drone, confident that this, too, would pass. Really, it's a perfect approach to the scary bits in movies, and it correctly estimates the formative power of images and sounds for good or ill. It cannot, though, be applied to all appearances of evil. Some must be faced head on. Otherwise, one may meet the fate of Pliny's ostriches, who "imagine, when they have thrust their head and neck into a bush, that the whole of their body is concealed."[1] The problem is not so much the parochialism of buried heads but the comical—and dangerous—illusion that the rest of one's body is safe from attack.

So it is as one encounters theological disagreement (leaving aside for the moment whether that disagreement is legitimate or heretical). One may bury one's head or, like the younger me, stop one's ears and close one's eyes, but that response serves only to expose one's flank to attack. What, then, are we to make of the apostle Paul's counsel to Timothy? "O Timothy, guard the deposit entrusted to you. Avoid the irreverent babble and contradictions of what is falsely called 'knowledge,' for by professing it some have swerved from the faith" (1 Tim. 6:20–21). The metaphors seem at first glance to work at cross-purposes. Timothy is to "guard" the deposit of faith, to defend it

---

1. Pliny the Elder (AD 23–79), as cited in Kruszelnicki, "Ostrich Head in Sand." Apparently, the ostrich's practice of burying its head is a myth.

against attackers and ensure its safekeeping in the church. Surely this means a fight, should false teachers seek to rob the church of its treasure. Yet Paul suggests it is best to "avoid" the fatuous volleys of these teachers, perhaps on the principle that the best way to get false teachers to go away is to ignore them.

Therapists speak of fight and flight as default mechanisms for handling conflict. While Paul's counsel of avoidance may often be the tack to take, the church can avoid false teachers for only so long; at some point, direct engagement is called for, with flight being exchanged for fight. In what follows, we'll consider Irenaeus, a second-century bishop and apologist, and his approach to false teaching in the church. Irenaeus saw a change in the weather and battened down the hatches of the faith against a Gnosticism threatening to sink the church's ship. But in guarding the faith, he neither pretended the threat was illusory nor reduced the faith to the size of an answer to the Gnostics' question. Every apologist knows the temptation to fit the defense of the faith to the mold of one's opponent, but a temptation it is, and a Procrustean one resulting in a curtailed faith. Irenaeus's tack is different. He confidently begins his response to the Gnostics by laying bare their variegated myths, trusting that exposition alone will do much of his work. From there, he elegantly lays out a vision of the Christian faith and, indeed, the world as seen through the lens of the apostolic preaching. In the end, "his chief concern is positive; the response far exceeds the stimulus."[2]

### A Very Brief Life

Though this summary of his life is brief, Irenaeus himself lived to a ripe old age (as, so he strangely thought, did Jesus).[3] Born around AD 130, he died around the turn of the century. The details about his life, though, are scant. We know he knew Polycarp (d. 155/156) in his youth, and he may have been from Smyrna (İzmir, in modern Turkey), where Polycarp was bishop.[4] Given that Polycarp knew the apostles and had been appointed bishop by them, Irenaeus stands only one generation removed from the apostles, which grants him significant authority as he demonstrates the apostolic preaching.

From Smyrna, Irenaeus went west, likely spending time in Rome receiving instruction. He may have been taught by Justin Martyr, whose thought Irenaeus followed at a number of points. He eventually arrived in the region

2. Osborn, *Irenaeus of Lyons*, 7.
3. See "Irenaeus," in *Oxford Dictionary of the Christian Church*, 851–52.
4. On Irenaeus and Polycarp, see Behr, *Irenaeus of Lyons*, 50–52, 57–66.

of Gaul, in Lyons, a major city at the meeting of the Rhone and Saône Rivers.[5] The church was young there, having first emerged mid-century, but it had quickly come under attack. In 177 Irenaeus went on a mission to Rome, carrying a letter to Pope Eleutherus from Lyons on behalf of a group of Montanists from Asia Minor. When he returned, the ninety-year-old bishop Pothinus was in prison, where he died. Irenaeus succeeded him, becoming bishop of Lyons and Vienne.[6]

Aside from his answer to Marcion and the Gnostics, to which we will return, the other major event in Irenaeus's bishopric was the Quartodeciman controversy, a debate between the churches in Asia Minor and Rome regarding the dating of Pascha (or Easter). The churches in Asia Minor kept it on Nisan 14, following Jewish custom; but Victor, bishop of Rome (189–198), demanded it be kept the following Sunday, the day of the resurrection, threatening excommunication to those who disobeyed.[7] Irenaeus intervened, pointing out to Victor that the practice in Asia Minor was ancient and that previous Roman bishops had lived peaceably with Asia Minor despite disagreement on this point.[8] Irenaeus certainly lived up to his name as a peacemaker.[9]

Emil Brunner rightly judges that "Irenaeus may be described as the first great theologian of the Early Church; indeed, he has a greater right than any other to the title of the founder of the theology of the Church. All the others build on the foundation which he has laid."[10] His theological vision is truly stunning in scope and detail and almost miraculously mature, given how soon he was writing after the death of the apostles.[11] To move from, for instance, Justin Martyr to Irenaeus is to move from candles to light bulbs, from quills to printing press.

All this can be said, despite his not having written all that much. Besides a few (mostly disputed) fragments, we have only two extant works by Irenaeus (though a handful of other works are known to have existed). The brief

---

5. Osborn, *Irenaeus of Lyons*, 94.

6. "Irenaeus names Polycarp as the dominant influence of his youth. As a bishop, Irenaeus was closer to the collegiate pattern of Polycarp than to the monarchical pattern of Ignatius" (Osborn, *Irenaeus of Lyons*, 3).

7. "Quartodecimanism," in *Oxford Dictionary of the Christian Church*, 1364–65. It is easy to laugh off this dispute as an absurdly scrupulous fight over a calendar, but it is as much a test case in the continuing struggle to navigate the relationship between Judaism and Christianity.

8. John Behr, introduction to Irenaeus, *On the Apostolic Preaching* (= *The Demonstration of the Apostolic Preaching*), 2–3.

9. Osborn, *Irenaeus of Lyons*, 4–6. "Irenaeus" comes from the *eirēnē*, the Greek word for "peace."

10. Brunner, *Mediator*, 249, cited in Canlis, *Calvin's Ladder*, 1.

11. Osborn, *Irenaeus of Lyons*, 1. Osborn dates Irenaeus's writing in the last two decades of the second century.

*Demonstration of the Apostolic Preaching* was discovered only in 1907, in an Armenian translation from the sixth century. In it, Irenaeus lays out the apostolic preaching and then demonstrates it from the prophets. In the much longer *Against Heresies*, whose full title is *The Unmasking and Overthrow of So-Called Knowledge*, he details and critiques the Gnostic systems of the day and sets forth "one and the same" God who created and redeemed the world. To better understand Irenaeus's theology, we will next consider the heretics he was writing against.

### Against Whom? Marcion and the Gnostics

One must take care in reading a secondhand account of beliefs and behaviors, particularly when the account is offered only to be countered. As Giovanni Filoramo notes, "The statements of heresiologists allow us to reconstruct the visible part of an iceberg."[12] Still, among apologists, Irenaeus stands out for his patient care in attending to the tangle of Gnostic myths. The sheer size of his exposition suggests a man intent on answering a real threat to the church, one who recognizes that lazy dismissals are insufficient.[13] This is not to say that Irenaeus provides a fully reliable account of the variety of Gnosticisms in his day, but only that his is a detailed description that seems to be broadly accurate. Our interest, in any case, is less in the historical Gnostics than in the way in which Irenaeus discerned, diagnosed, and deconstructed threats to the church's faith.[14]

It is difficult to sketch the contours of Irenaeus's opponents' views, and not only because of the extravagance of their myths. For one thing, according to

12. Filoramo, *History of Gnosticism*, 169. Even such a modest claim is too sanguine for many. Karen King begins her consideration of Gnosticism by suggesting that "a rhetorical term has been confused with a historical entity" (*What Is Gnosticism?*, 1). If Filoramo would suggest that there's more than meets the eye when Irenaeus reports about the Gnostics, King draws attention to the artificiality of Irenaeus's construction of his opponents' views in light of his own commitments. We do well to follow Richard Norris's advice to "follow him in an attempt to ascertain not so much what Gnosticism looked like to a Gnostic but what it looked like to its opponents" (*God and World*, 75).

13. Two of the five books of *Against Heresies* are devoted to exposition and internal critique of Gnostic mythology.

14. The 1945 discovery of a Gnostic library at Nag Hammadi in Egypt led to a revival of interest in ancient Gnostic texts and fueled a fascination with early Christian "heterodoxy" (or, as some would now prefer, "diversity"). The diversity of sources has led some scholars to wonder whether it is even helpful to speak of such a thing as "Gnosticism." See M. Williams, *Rethinking "Gnosticism."* For a keen-eyed synthesis of the revisionist arguments that keeps orthodox concerns in view, see the chapters on Marcion and the Gnostics in Wilhite, *Gospel according to Heretics*, 21–39, 61–85.

Irenaeus's report, the heresies were varied and incoherent,[15] a loose and loud quilt of poorly patched-together scraps of older opinions. Heresy is problematic insofar as it is a manufactured novelty that fails the test of continuity with orthodox teaching—though pretending to be venerable, it is really innovative (and innovation is a cardinal sin for the church fathers). In another sense, though, heresy *is* old, a tired, incoherent mess of leftover impieties.[16] Of course, precisely as *heresy* rather than simply paganism, it is related to, and parasitic of, Christian truth. One way to think of heretical groups is as "offshoots of official religion, sometimes breaking the umbilical cord."[17]

Before we sketch some of the errors Irenaeus discerns among various Gnostics, we need to consider Marcion. At first part of the Roman church, Marcion parted ways with the church in 144 over his heretical views.[18] Author of a work called *Antitheses*, he could not conceive of justice and mercy embracing. For Marcion, the Creator God of the Old Testament was not the one revealed in Christ; he was ignorant, immoral, and inconsistent.[19] Jesus revealed an utterly new, good God.[20] As a consequence, Irenaeus complains, Marcion's followers "directly blaspheme the Creator, alleging him to be the creator of evils."[21] The world-denigrating character of this position is apparent: it severs the unity of creation and redemption, a unity Irenaeus reasserts. Unsurprisingly, it also suggests that the human body is irrelevant, perhaps even evil. Salvation is for souls, not bodies.[22]

Marcion had the courage of his convictions. Unlike the more subtle Gnostics, he was "the only one who . . . dared openly to mutilate the Scriptures."[23] He "dismembered" much of Scripture, rejecting outright the Old Testament, slashing Luke's Gospel, and eliminating everything in Paul that suggested that the God who made the world was the Father of Jesus Christ.[24] Marcion

15. Irenaeus, *AH* 5.20.1.
16. Irenaeus, *AH* 2.14.2; 3.12.5.
17. Filoramo, *History of Gnosticism*, xvii. Scholars debate whether it is more apt to speak of Gnosticism as a Christian heresy or an independent religion flowing from an Eastern source, possibly older than and maybe even influencing the Christian gospel (*History of Gnosticism*, 10–13).
18. It is difficult to know whether Marcion was expelled or left of his own accord. Irenaeus reports that, when Marcion asked Polycarp, "Recognize us," the bishop responded: "Yes, I recognize you; I recognize the first-born of Satan!" (*AH* 3.3.4).
19. Tilby, "Marcionism," 76. "Nothing is clearer about Marcion's teaching than his complete distaste for the God of Jewish Scripture" (M. Williams, *Rethinking "Gnosticism,"* 24).
20. Filoramo, *History of Gnosticism*, 164.
21. Irenaeus, *AH* 3.12.12.
22. Irenaeus, *AH* 1.27.3.
23. Irenaeus, *AH* 1.27.4; 3.12.12.
24. Irenaeus, *AH* 1.27.2. Wilhite places a caveat on Irenaeus's claim: "There is some debate as to whether Marcion selected and edited *the* canon (as Irenaeus and Tertullian thought he

attacked the unity of God, and he attacked the unity of God's church. After separating from the church, he founded a church of his own, complete with scriptures, bishops, priests, and deacons. He set himself up as a rival, and his shrewd strategy paid off; Tertullian tells us that Marcion's church "filled the entire world."[25]

In one sense, Irenaeus saw the Gnostics—who flourished in the second century, became embattled in the third, and declined in the fourth—as emblematic of heresy.[26] He could write of the Valentinians (a significant form of Gnosticism) that "their doctrine is a recapitulation of all the heretics." They represent all those who tout what is "falsely called 'knowledge'" (1 Tim. 6:20) and lead people astray, and "they who overthrow them, do in fact overthrow every kind of heresy."[27]

To begin with, the Gnostics blaspheme the Creator.[28] They affirm that there is "another god above the Creator."[29] In subordinating the Creator to this other god, they cleave the unity of "the God and Father of our Lord Jesus Christ" (Eph. 1:3; cf. Col. 1:3). The maker was universally known, they claim, a lesser being born of a defect; but the Father was not known until Jesus revealed him in parables and, after his resurrection, more directly to his disciples.[30] There is thus one god or Creator and another god who is Father.[31] In fact, they suggest that the prophets were inspired by different gods, citing the various Hebrew terms designating "God" as evidence.

Second, they blaspheme Christ. They split both God and Christ and claim they were the result of a defect.[32] They affirm "another" only begotten Word, Christ, and Savior—as well as "another" Holy Spirit.[33] Marcion denies that Christ made the world; the Gnostics insist the world was made by angels rather than God's Word; and Valentinus claims the demiurge was responsible for creation.[34] Furthermore, "according to the opinion of no one of the heretics [not Marcion or the Gnostics or Valentinus] was the Word of God made

---

did), or whether he simply made logical conclusions from a 'canon' he had received" (*Gospel according to Heretics*, 27).

25. Filoramo, *History of Gnosticism*, 163.

26. Filoramo, *History of Gnosticism*, 171. Nor were Christians the only critics of Gnosticism; Celsus and Plotinus joined the chorus (7).

27. Irenaeus, *AH* 4.preface.2.

28. Irenaeus, *AH* 5.26.2.

29. Irenaeus, *AH* 2.19.9.

30. Irenaeus, *AH* 1.19.1; 1.20.3.

31. Irenaeus, *AH* 2.27.2; 3.11.1.

32. Irenaeus, *AH* 4.preface.3.

33. Irenaeus, *AH* 2.19.9.

34. Irenaeus, *AH* 3.11.2.

flesh."[35] Unable to countenance the Word made flesh, they likewise recoil at "the salvation of their flesh," thereby "despising the handiwork of God."[36]

This third form of blasphemy—the blasphemy of God's creation—can be seen in the Gnostic claim that only spirit, never matter, is capable of salvation. A dualism of spirit and matter gets fleshed out in the conception of three types of people: spiritual, material, and animal (or psychical).[37] The basic point here is that some things (and people) are capable of salvation, and others are not. "For, just as it is impossible that material substance should partake of salvation (since, indeed, they maintain that it is incapable of receiving it), so again it is impossible that spiritual substance (by which they mean themselves) should ever come under the power of corruption, whatever the sort of actions in which they indulged."[38] Such an "aristocracy of the spirit," with its scheme of salvation by secret knowledge, is a damning doctrine for a huge swath of humanity, and a far cry from Jesus's universal regard for the unlikely and unworthy.[39] In reality, "the truth is unsophisticated . . . being easy of comprehension to those who are obedient."[40]

The Gnostics seek purification *from* matter,[41] while the church teaches purification *in* matter. Escapist soteriologies, where salvation entails a move away from creation, are out of bounds for a church that confesses the resurrection and exaltation of Jesus as Lord, in which the Father vindicates his Son and, in him, all of creation. "Before God raised Jesus from the dead, the hope that we call 'gnostic,' the hope for redemption *from* creation rather than for the redemption *of* creation, might have appeared to be the only possible hope. 'But in fact Christ has been raised from the dead' ([1 Cor.] 15:20)."[42] Implicitly, then, in espousing an escapist soteriology, the Gnostics denigrate both Christ and creation.

Finally, the Gnostics blaspheme the Scriptures. Though taking their cues from "other sources than the Scriptures," the Gnostics seek to give their views an "air of probability" by conscripting the Scriptures in their effort. But "they

35. Irenaeus, *AH* 3.11.3. Wilhite focuses on docetism, the claim that Christ only *appeared* to have a body, in describing the Gnostic heresy (*Gospel according to Heretics*, 76–79).

36. Irenaeus, *AH* 5.31.1.

37. Irenaeus, *AH* 1.7.5.

38. Irenaeus, *AH* 1.6.2. What of the animal, or psychical, people, which include Christians? These *may* be saved on the basis of good works, whereas the spiritual will "entirely and undoubtedly" be saved.

39. Filoramo, *History of Gnosticism*, 170. Filoramo notes, though, that the Gnostics were broadly egalitarian internally and anti-institutional (173–74, 176).

40. From fragment 36 (see Irenaeus, *AH*, p. 673).

41. Filoramo, *History of Gnosticism*, 73.

42. O'Donovan, *Resurrection and Moral Order*, 14.

disregard the order and the connection of the Scriptures, and so far as in them lies, dismember and destroy the truth." Irenaeus explains:

> Their manner of acting is just as if one, when a beautiful image of a king has been constructed by some skilful artist out of precious jewels, should then take this likeness of the man all to pieces, should rearrange the gems, and so fit them together as to make them into the form of a dog or of a fox, and even that but poorly executed; and should then maintain and declare that this was the beautiful image of the king which the skilful artist constructed, pointing to the jewels which had been admirably fitted together by the first artist to form the image of the king, but have been with bad effect transferred by the latter one to the shape of a dog, and by thus exhibiting the jewels, should deceive the ignorant who had no conception what a king's form was like, and persuade them that that miserable likeness of the fox was, in fact, the beautiful image of the king. In like manner do these persons patch together old wives' fables, and then endeavour, by violently drawing away from their proper connection, words, expressions, and parables whenever found, to adapt the oracles of God to their baseless fictions.[43]

Whereas Marcion amputates Scripture, convinced that the Old Testament is a useless appendage, the Gnostics preserve the limbs but distort the form. Both do equal violence to the oracles of God; both seek to silence the divine voice testifying to the coming King. Notice that the Gnostics rearrange the gems into the form of "a dog or a fox"—they cannot even decide among themselves on Scripture's form. Though the church is scattered throughout the world, its faith is one, "as if occupying but one house," "just as if she had but one soul, and one and the same heart . . . [and] one mouth."[44] But the heretics are inconsistent in their individual opinions and with one another.[45] Far from singing in unison, their voices jangle in dissonance and confusion. In all this, they twist the Scriptures "from a natural to a non-natural sense."[46] Their fanciful allegorization directs attention away from God and his economy, seeking "to prosecute inquiries respecting God by means of numbers, syllables, and letters."[47] Scripture, and the history to which it witnesses, is not a site of God's revelation but a code to be deciphered by the Gnostic elite.[48]

43. Irenaeus, *AH* 1.8.1.
44. Irenaeus, *AH* 1.10.2.
45. Irenaeus, *AH* 1.11.1.
46. Irenaeus, *AH* 1.9.4.
47. Irenaeus, *AH* 2.25.1.
48. Filoramo, *History of Gnosticism*, 123. Even the cross and resurrection are reduced to the level of the symbolic.

If the heretics sought to conquer by dividing, Irenaeus defended the faith by illuminating its unity, a unity evidenced in the church. Irenaeus offers weighty practical proof of heresy's corrosion. Heretics scatter God's people and mislead them, while the church edifies them.[49] Only the church has martyrs[50]— who is willing to die for the demiurge?[51] The proof is in the dying.

## Handing On the Faith

In the mid-second century, forces pressured the church's teaching from two sides. On the one hand, Marcion sought to narrow Scripture, eliminating the Old Testament and reducing the New Testament to an edited version of Luke and ten of Paul's epistles (carefully edited to eliminate their Jewishness). On the other hand, the Gnostics sought to expand the scope of Scripture by proliferating writings, supplementing or interpreting Jesus's words with additional accounts like the Gospel of Thomas. These pressures hastened the inevitable process of canonization, in which the apostolic writings were gathered together and a final list of authoritative writings drawn up.[52]

From its earliest days, the church had worked with various shorthand accounts of its faith. Even the tiny phrase "Jesus is Lord" can be seen as a summary of Christian confession. Or consider Paul's words to Timothy:

> Great indeed, we confess, is the mystery of godliness:
> He was manifested in the flesh,
>    *vindicated* by the Spirit,
> seen by angels,
> proclaimed among the nations,
>    believed on in the world,
> taken up in glory. (1 Tim. 3:16)

Paul reminds Timothy of the faith he had handed down to him, so that Timothy might know how one ought to live in "the household of God, which is the church of the living God, a pillar and buttress of the truth" (1 Tim. 3:15).

For a long time, such short confessions worked. Furthermore, they quickly took on definition and became codified in various rules of faith. Robert Jenson

49. Irenaeus, *AH* 2.31.3.
50. Irenaeus, *AH* 4.33.9.
51. Parallel is Athanasius's claim in *On the Incarnation* (27 31, 48) that martyrdom is a proof of resurrection.
52. Bergquist, "Gnosticism," 109.

explains: "The rule of faith, the *regula fidei*, was a sort of communal linguistic awareness of the faith delivered to the apostles, which sufficed the church for generations. This gift of the Spirit guided missionary proclamation, shaped instruction, identified heresy, and in general functioned wherever in the church's life a brief statement of the gospel's content was needed."[53] The rule of faith and its slightly expanded younger cousin, the creed, were not quite the Scriptures in miniature. They said little about Israel, little about Jesus's life, little about the things that preoccupied Paul.[54] But they did provide a hermeneutic for reading Scripture and receiving the faith. Irenaeus writes that we are to "keep the rule of faith unswervingly."[55] This is the rule received in baptism, and by it we are able to read the Scriptures aright and recognize in them the image of the king.[56]

Even with the rule of faith, over time the church faced what Jenson calls "the telephone-game problem"—a problem that became a crisis as the church sailed between Marcion and the Gnostics and that exposed the need for a new Scriptures.[57] In Irenaeus we have the first theologian "to speak unequivocally of a 'New' Testament parallel to the Old."[58] In *Demonstration of the Apostolic Preaching*, Irenaeus sets out the teaching of the apostles as it had been handed down in the church (in part 1) but establishes it on the basis of the prophets (in part 2). It is "a 'demonstration' both in the sense of an 'exposition' as well as a 'proof.'"[59] While the *Demonstration* concerns itself explicitly with upholding the apostolic teaching by appeal to the Hebrew Scriptures and thus only implicitly affirms the scriptural status of the apostolic writings, in *Against Heresies* Irenaeus clearly and robustly considers the apostolic writings as Scripture on par with the prophets.[60] The whole of Scripture is perspicuous and unified, since "the entire Scriptures, the prophets, and the Gospels, can be clearly, unambiguously, and harmoniously understood by all."[61] The

---

53. R. Jenson, *Canon and Creed*, 15.

54. R. Jenson, *Canon and Creed*, 40–41.

55. Irenaeus, *Dem.* 3.

56. Irenaeus, *Dem.* 1.9.4. Variously elaborated summaries of the rule of faith or truth (or, simply, the faith or the truth) can be found in *Dem.* 6–7 and *AH* 1.10.1; 1.22.1; 2.25.2; 2.30.9; 3.4.1–2 (where it is "the tradition"); 3.15.3; 4.33.8 (where it is "true knowledge").

57. R. Jenson, *Canon and Creed*, 34.

58. Kelly, *Early Christian Doctrines*, 56. Kelly adduces Irenaeus, *AH* 4.9.1, for support, and notes that "in teaching that [the New Testament] was inspired Scripture he was by no means an innovator."

59. Behr, introduction to Irenaeus, *Dem.* 17.

60. Irenaeus was the first father "to make full use of the apostolic writings as Scripture" (Behr, introduction to Irenaeus, *Dem.* 15).

61. Irenaeus, *AH* 2.27.2.

Scriptures are united in proclaiming one God;[62] though there are many utterances, there is but one harmonious melody.[63]

The unity of Scripture is grounded in one and the same God: Father, Son, and Holy Spirit. The Scriptures are "perfect, since they were spoken by the Word of God and His Spirit."[64] Against any tendency to malign Israel's God as passé, derivative, or evil, Irenaeus writes that "the prophets were not from one God, and the apostles from another; but, [proceeding] from one and the same," they each exercised their function in God's one economy.[65] The Bible evinces a trinitarian dynamic: "Thus, the Spirit demonstrates the Word, and, because of this, the prophets announced the Son of God, while the Word articulates the Spirit, and therefore it is He Himself who interprets the prophets and brings man to the Father."[66] As we saw above, the Scriptures are about King Jesus.[67] Just as the church needs many members to exhibit him, so were many prophets needed to prefigure him.[68] Both bodies—the body of Christ and the body of truth—are a harmonious unity.[69] Similarly, there is a fourfold gospel. "The Word . . . has given us the Gospel under four aspects, but bound together by one Spirit."[70] Note the singularity of the good news as well as its pluriform articulation.[71]

Recall Paul's description of the church as "a pillar and buttress of the truth." First, consider what the church is *not*. It is not the cornerstone of the truth's temple; that is Jesus. Nor is the church the foundation of truth; that is the apostles and prophets (Eph. 2:20). But the church *is* a "pillar" and "buttress"—that is, a key structural support in the temple of truth.

This is the best vantage from which to consider the question of episcopal succession. The church, in Irenaeus's eyes focused in the bishops and presbyters (or priests), serves the rule of faith by handing on the teaching of the apostles. His clergy-centered account of this process of transmission is grounded in the first bishops as disciples and their role as teachers.[72] Because Irenaeus can count from bishop to bishop back to the apostles, he is in a

62. Irenaeus, *AH* 2.27.2.
63. Irenaeus, *AH* 2.28.3.
64. Irenaeus, *AH* 2.28.2.
65. Irenaeus, *AH* 4.36.5.
66. Irenaeus, *Dem.* 5.
67. He is "the treasure hid in the Scriptures" (Irenaeus, *AH* 4.26.1). "He is both subject and object of prophecy" and the apostolic preaching (Osborn, *Irenaeus of Lyons*, 88).
68. Irenaeus, *AH* 4.33.10.
69. See Irenaeus, *AH* 2.27.1; *Dem.* 1.
70. Irenaeus, *AH* 3.11.8.
71. R. Jenson, *Canon and Creed*, 39.
72. See Irenaeus, *AH* 1.10.1.

position to demonstrate the spurious character of Gnostic claims that Jesus imparted secret knowledge to his disciples, especially in a prolonged tutorial season after his resurrection. The mystery of godliness is indeed great, but it is no longer hidden; it is revealed, a mystery made public through the proclamation of the gospel.[73] The succession of bishops back to the apostles, in which the tradition of the church's teaching has been preserved, is "most abundant proof that there is one and the same vivifying faith."[74] And "the apostles, like a rich man [depositing his money] in a bank, lodged in her hands most copiously all things pertaining to the truth: so that every man, whosoever will, can draw from her the water of life. For she is the entrance of life; all others are thieves and robbers."[75] Two points follow. First, the bank metaphor speaks to the church as a preserver of truth rather than the provider of an interest-bearing account. The truth does not grow.[76] Second, all may come and withdraw from this bank. Against Gnostic elitism, Irenaeus echoes the final notes of Revelation and invites all who desire to "take the water of life without price" (22:17). Such water is at once priceless and free. That Jesus applies this to himself (John 7:37) rather than the church does not compromise Irenaeus's statement but merely underscores the object of the church's faith, which is Christ.

The church is a pillar and buttress of the truth, and God has given the church apostles, prophets, and teachers (1 Cor. 12:28). "Where, therefore, the gifts of the Lord have been placed, there it behooves us to learn the truth, [namely,] from those who possess that succession of the Church which is from the apostles, and among whom exists that which is sound and blameless in conduct, as well as that which is unadulterated and incorrupt in speech."[77] We are to obey the presbyters and bishops, then, who "have received the certain gift of the truth" from the apostles.[78] It is worth highlighting the importance of holy conduct and truthful speech; Irenaeus is not sponsoring a blind submission to ecclesiastical elites, who can do whatever they want. Or rather, Irenaeus

---

73. "For if the apostles had known hidden mysteries, which they were in the habit of imparting to 'the perfect' apart and privily from the rest, they would have delivered them especially to those to whom they were also committing the Churches themselves"; "nor did they teach one set of doctrines in private, and another in public" (Irenaeus, *AH* 3.3.1; 3.15.1).

74. Irenaeus, *AH* 3.3.3.

75. Irenaeus, *AH* 3.4.1.

76. "For the faith being ever one and the same, neither does one who is able at great length to discourse regarding it, make any addition to it, nor does one, who can say but little diminish it" (Irenaeus, *AH* 1.10.2). Such statements have significant bearing on the question of doctrinal development, though Osborn suggests that Irenaeus's own practice gives the lie to his theory (*Irenaeus of Lyons*, 86).

77. Irenaeus, *AH* 4.26.5.

78. Irenaeus, *AH* 4.26.2.

can hardly imagine that those who have been entrusted with the truth from the apostles would be anything but morally upright and devoted to the truth. Because they are these things, and because God has given them to the church for its edification, we ought to "diligently read the Scriptures in company with those who are presbyters in the Church, among whom is the apostolic doctrine."[79] The church is unified in its confession of the truth heard in the Scriptures and taught by the successors of the apostles.[80]

That is, the faith is *catholic*, "everywhere consistent," receiving "testimony from the prophets, the apostles, and all the disciples," being received from and preserved in the church, and ever "renewing its youth" by the Spirit of the living God.[81] It is catholic insofar as it is *apostolic*, and it is apostolic insofar as it is *one*.

## One and the Same

We turn now to consider the unity of the church's faith, grounded in one and the same God. Where Marcion and the Gnostics see division, Irenaeus sees unity. It is easy to psychologize such a statement. The heretics are fighters, perhaps prophetic types who make judgments and draw lines in sand. Irenaeus, true to his name, is more irenic, eager to make and anxious to keep peace. But this understanding is to miss the ontological depth of Irenaeus's vision. The unity at the heart of Irenaeus's theological vision and the front line of his battle with the heretics is the unity of the Triune God and his ways with the world. There is one and the same God the Creator and Father of our Lord Jesus Christ.[82] Irenaeus directs his polemic against those who claim that God is not the Creator (instead positing some sort of derivative, lesser demiurge) and those who claim that Scripture speaks of diverse divine beings. These "are not the names and titles of a succession of different beings, but of one and the same, by means of which the one God and Father is revealed, He who contains all things, and grants to all the boon of existence."[83] God is one, and all that we ascribe to divinity belongs to him; it is not parsed out

79. Irenaeus, *AH* 4.32.1. On the development of the episcopacy and the necessity of something like a "bishop," though not an episcopal polity, for every local church, see M. Jenson and Wilhite, *Church*, 27–35.

80. This confirms Kelly's suggestion that, for Irenaeus, "Scripture and the Church's unwritten tradition are identical in content, both being vehicles of the revelation" (*Early Christian Doctrines*, 39).

81. Irenaeus, *AH* 3.24.1.

82. Irenaeus, *AH* 2.2.5; 2.11.1; 2.35.2–4; 3.1.2; 3.10.5; 3.11.7; 4.10.1.

83. Irenaeus, *AH* 2.35.3.

among a pantheon of more and less divine beings. Others allege that "the Creator was one, but the Father of the Lord another."[84] On the contrary, "God and the Father are truly one and the same," according to the prophets, the gospel, and our worship.[85]

When Marcion split God into two, the Judge and the Savior, he rendered the justice and goodness of God unintelligible. The result is deicide. "For he that is the judicial one, if he be not good, is not God, because he from whom goodness is absent is no God at all; and again, he who is good, if he has no judicial power, suffers the same [loss] as the former, by being deprived of his character of deity."[86]

One and the same God the Creator and Father has given the Scriptures,[87] and the prophets, apostles, and the Lord himself all testify of "our Lord Jesus Christ being one and the same."[88] The Scriptures are not only about Christ, and so testify to him, but they are spoken by Christ, and so are his own testimony.[89] "He who chose the patriarchs and those [who lived under the first covenant], is the same Word of God who did both visit them through the prophetic Spirit, and us also who have been called together from all quarters by His advent."[90] Christ is the Word who "produced both covenants . . . [and] spake with both Abraham and Moses."[91] Irenaeus asserts that the Word, or Son of God, is the subject of the Old Testament theophanies.[92] In the retrospective light of the incarnation, we know that it is fitting for the second person of the Trinity—and not the Father or Spirit—to be made flesh and render the invisible visible. If we are to appropriate the theophanies to one of the persons of the Trinity, then, we do well to appropriate them to the Son.

"But there are some who say that Jesus was merely a receptacle of Christ," to whom Irenaeus preaches "one and the same Jesus Christ."[93] His criterion is clear: "Who is a liar, but he that denieth that Jesus is the Christ? This is the Antichrist."[94] The heretics compromise the incarnation on either end of the gospel accounts. On the one hand, they allege that Christ only descended on

---

84. Irenaeus, *AH* 3.11.1.
85. Irenaeus, *AH* 3.10.5.
86. Irenaeus, *AH* 3.25.3.
87. Irenaeus, *AH* 4.10.1.
88. Irenaeus, *AH* 3.17.4. The law and the gospel have the same author, after all (4.12.3).
89. "The writings [*literae*] of Moses are the words of Christ" (Irenaeus, *AH* 4.2.3).
90. Irenaeus, *AH* 4.36.8.
91. Irenaeus, *AH* 4.9.1.
92. Irenaeus, *Dem.* 44–47.
93. Irenaeus, *AH* 3.16; also see 3.1.2; 3.9.3; 3.16.6; 3.17.4; 4.9.1–2.
94. 1 John 2:22, quoted in Irenaeus, *AH* 3.16.5.

Jesus at his baptism. Irenaeus staunchly denies any form of adoptionism.[95] The Word was made flesh in the virgin conception and birth, not in a later moment of divine sponsorship or promotion. As one fifteenth-century carol puts it: "In this rose containèd was / Heaven and earth in little space." The Son does not crown an already existing human being; the man Jesus just is the Son's incarnate form of existence. On the other hand, some heretics refuse to countenance the death of Christ, claiming that he did not suffer but did instead "fly away from Jesus." Again, this position denies that the man Jesus is simply the Son's incarnate form of existence. It also renders absurd Jesus's command that his disciples take up their cross *and follow him*.[96]

Though Irenaeus has less to say directly about the Holy Spirit as "one and the same," his demonstration of the unity of the apostolic preaching with the prophets is founded on the work of the Spirit, who, as the Nicene Creed has it, "spoke by the prophets" and who binds together the fourfold gospel.[97]

One and the same God—the Father, Son, and Spirit—has created and redeemed the world. The Creator of all is the God of Israel is the God and Father of our Lord Jesus Christ. Irenaeus can even say, bluntly, that "the Holy One of Israel is Christ."[98] Marcion recoils at the thought that the just God of the Old Testament could be identified with the saving God we meet in Christ; the Gnostics shudder to think that created flesh would be redeemed and made fit to bear the Spirit. Irenaeus, though, rejoices that the Word who formed the world was made flesh and even died that flesh might bear the Spirit and see God. Recapitulation (on which more will be said later) is a useful trope through which to teach and remember that creation and redemption are of a piece. To speak of Christ "summing up," "bringing to a head," "uniting," or "recapitulating" humanity in himself is to hold together conceptually God's creating, our sinful scattering, and God's redemptive regathering. The coming of Christ is not an alien invasion, but the belated arrival of the Lord of the land.

No naive reader of Scripture, Irenaeus recognizes that a shift occurs in the biblical drama. With the advent of Christ, God's people are no longer slaves but sons, having received "the greater gift of paternal grace."[99] At times this leads Irenaeus in a supersessionist direction,[100] with the church playing Jacob to Israel's Esau and "snatching away" the Father's blessings.[101] He reads the parable of the wicked tenants to imply that God has rejected the Jews and

95. Irenaeus, *AH* 3.9.3.
96. Irenaeus, *AH* 3.18.5.
97. Irenaeus, *AH* 3.11.8.
98. Irenaeus, *Dem.* 91.
99. Irenaeus, *AH* 4.36.4; also see 4.18.2.
100. Irenaeus, *AH* 4.4.1.
101. Irenaeus, *AH* 4.21.3.

given the blessings of the vineyard to the Gentiles.[102] These are moves made, or at least suggested, within the New Testament itself; in any case, it is "one and the same householder [who] produced both covenants, the Word of God, our Lord Jesus Christ."[103]

More often than he evokes the replacement of Israel by the church, Irenaeus appeals to the unity of God's ways with his people. The church and Abraham share one and the same faith;[104] "God has recapitulated in us the faith of Abraham."[105] The Decalogue is extended and increased, not abrogated, by the coming of the Lord.[106] We are no longer in the law's custody (Gal. 3:24; 5:18) but only because it has now been written on our hearts.[107] Of sacrifices, "the species alone has been changed"; we still offer sacrifices to God, but they are the sacrifices of freed persons, not slaves.[108] Abraham and Moses knew the Father in the Son.[109] Though the law of Moses and the grace of Christ were "fitted for the times," they were given "by one and the same God for the benefit of the human race."[110] One and the same God has one and the same end, even if he works differently during the course of history. There may not be uniformity, but there is certainly consistency of action. Irenaeus can even claim that "there is but one vineyard, since there is also but one righteousness, and one dispensator, for there is one Spirit of God who arranges all things; and in like manner is there one hire."[111] For there is one Spirit—it is one and the same God who grounds the unity of salvation history. This one God, the Creator of all, is the Savior of the world, and it is his unity that ultimately established and sustains "one and the same vivifying faith."[112]

### The Maker and the Made: A Basic Ontological Distinction

To emphasize one and the same God and assign all the work of creation and redemption to him is to espouse a robust monotheism. Irenaeus's refrain in

102. Irenaeus, *AH* 4.36.2.
103. Irenaeus, *AH* 4.9.1.
104. Irenaeus, *AH* 4.21.1.
105. Irenaeus, *Dem.* 95.
106. Irenaeus, *AH* 4.16.4.
107. Irenaeus, *Dem.* 96.
108. Irenaeus, *AH* 4.18.2.
109. Irenaeus, *AH* 4.5–7.
110. Irenaeus, *AH* 3.12.11.
111. Irenaeus, *AH* 4.36.7.
112. Irenaeus, *AH* 3.3.3. "The faith of all is one and the same, since all receive one and the same God the Father. . . . And undoubtedly the preaching of the Church is true and steadfast, in which one and the same way of salvation is shown throughout the whole world" (5.20.1).

the face of the Gnostics' motley pantheon is that God did not need any help in creation. "The origin of all is God, for He Himself was not made by anyone, but everything was made by Him." "He Himself in Himself" made all there is out of nothing,[113] "contains all and is alone uncontainable."[114] We may be able to make something only out of something, but God's superiority to us lies in his ability to make something out of nothing.[115] "And in this respect God differs from man, that God indeed makes, but man is made."[116] In deploying this basic ontological distinction, Irenaeus bleaches talk of God and creation. That the one is not the other frees each to be itself in a manner appropriate to it. God is utterly self-sufficient and wants nothing, "for He is always full of all good."[117] He is not cold toward his creation, but is in his very antecedent fullness free to create and enter into fellowship with his creation without care. It is no slight to evoke creation's utter contingency; that is simply what it means to be the creation that God judged "very good."[118] It is just this "very good" that the Gnostics are unable to affirm.[119]

## God Uses His Hands

God did not need the help of anyone other than God to create, but that does not mean he created on his own. In all of God's works, the Father uses his two hands, the Son and the Spirit. "For God did not stand in need of [angels] . . . as if He did not possess His own hands. For with Him were always present the Word and Wisdom, the Son and the Spirit, by whom and in whom, freely and spontaneously, He made all things, to whom also He speaks, saying, 'Let us make man after Our image and likeness'; He taking from Himself the substance of the creatures [formed], and the pattern of things made, and the type of all the adornments in the world."[120]

Notice the careful monotheism of this passage; God is taking everything needed for creation from himself and working freely and spontaneously with his own two hands. This is "a peculiarity of the pre-eminence of God," that the Father has no need to use a tool.[121] Nor is he in any way inspired or compelled.

113. Irenaeus, AH 2.2.4.
114. Irenaeus, Dem. 4; also see AH 2.1.2; 2.30.9; 4.20.2.
115. Irenaeus, AH 2.10.4. Frances Young argues that the doctrine of creatio ex nihilo was "the fundamental factor in the development of Christian distinctiveness" ("Creatio Ex Nihilo," 140).
116. Irenaeus, AH 4.11.2.
117. Irenaeus, AH 4.14.3.
118. For the details of the basic ontological distinction, see Irenaeus, AH 3.8.3.
119. Gunton, Triune Creator, 47–50.
120. Irenaeus, AH 4.20.1; also see 2.16.3.
121. Irenaeus, AH 2.2.5.

One cannot even speak of an internal compulsion, such that God's liveliness meant he just *had* to create. No, this is spontaneous, a loving decision to make something other than himself; it is not an eruption of heretofore subterranean ferment.

Above all, it was not a loneliness that moved God to create.[122] The creation of Adam does not provide God at last with a companion, as the Word and Wisdom were with the Father from before creation.[123] This is a *trinitarian* monotheism, after all. God works with his hands to mold creation.[124] At times, Irenaeus will specify: the Word "makes," "establishes," "confers existence," while the Spirit, who is Wisdom, "adorns" and "arranges."[125] Irenaeus seems to base this way of assigning tasks in the efficacy of the divine Word in creation and the way in which wisdom orders (or sees the order in) things. We ought not to lean too heavily into this way of distinguishing the work of Son and Spirit, though. After all, Wisdom can as easily evoke the Son's work, as in certain patristic readings of Proverbs 8 and Paul's identification of Christ as the wisdom of God in 1 Corinthians 1. Still, the twofold task of God's hands in creation serves to remind us that the Spirit has a work of his own.

God uses his hands in our re-creation, too. In fact, "never at any time did Adam escape the *hands* of God."[126] The Father did not create humanity and then wash his hands of us, but he intended always to sustain and lead humanity into mature fellowship with God.[127] The Word and Spirit spoke the perfect Scriptures,[128] and the Son is the hand and voice of God.[129] In the fullness of time, "His hands formed a living man, in order that Adam might be created [again] after the image and likeness of God."[130] The Father gives the Son and Spirit to humanity, and the Son and Spirit bring humanity back to the Father.[131] The work of the Son and Spirit in salvation involves an accustoming of God and humanity to one another, a preparation for their mutual indwelling.[132] In the incarnation, the Spirit becomes accustomed to dwell in

122. It is not even proper to speak of the God who possesses all fullness in himself being "moved."

123. Irenaeus, *AH* 4.20.3; also see 4.14.1.

124. Irenaeus, *AH* 4.preface; also see 5.28.4.

125. Irenaeus, *Dem.* 5; *AH* 4.20.2; 4.20.4. More problematically, Irenaeus can speak of being adorned with works of righteousness in order that the Spirit might rest on us (*AH* 4.36.6).

126. Irenaeus, *AH* 5.1.3.

127. Irenaeus, *AH* 5.5.1.

128. Irenaeus, *AH* 2.28.2.

129. Irenaeus, *AH* 5.15.2; 5.16.1; 5.17.2. Jesus heals the man born blind in order "that He might show forth the hand of God, that which at the beginning had moulded man" (5.15.2).

130. Irenaeus, *AH* 5.1.3.

131. Irenaeus, *AH* 3.17.2.

132. Irenaeus, *AH* 3.20.2. On "accustoming," see Osborn, *Irenaeus of Lyons*, 80–82.

humanity as God's temple.[133] The incarnation is a uniting or communion of man with God for the sake of man's participation in God's incorruptibility.[134] This is the fitting end of humanity.

In the next two sections, we will look in more detail at how God uses his hands in our salvation.

## *Adam Redux*: The Logic of Recapitulation

In that longest of Greek sentences that opens Ephesians, Paul rhapsodizes about all the blessings that are ours in Christ. Christ is "the Beloved" in whom we are chosen, predestined for adoption, redeemed, forgiven, lavished with grace, and sealed with the Spirit as a down payment on our inheritance (Eph. 1:3–14). The climax of all this is the revealed mystery of God's will, which is the Father's plan "to unite [*anakephalaiōsasthai*] all things in [Christ], things in heaven and things on earth" (Eph. 1:10). The Greek word translated here as "unite" can also be translated as "sum up," "bring together under one head," or "recapitulate." The will of God is the recapitulation of all things in Christ. John Behr draws attention to the fact that recapitulation is a "well-defined" Hellenistic rhetorical device that "provides a résumé which, as a succinct synopsis, is clearer and therefore more effective."[135]

In two senses, Christ sums up all things. First, he is the treasure hidden in the field of Scripture that is brought to light by his cross.[136] The gospel, therefore, is "the recapitulation of Scripture in a 'concise word'" and just so is "its fulfilment."[137] Christ crucified enables us to return to Scripture and recognize its subject matter, precisely because the crucified Lord recapitulated Scripture. Second, Christ also recapitulates humanity. In Romans 5:12–21, Paul portrays Adam as a type of Christ, and the two are connected by the logic of "just . . . so": just as sin, condemnation, and death came to humanity in Adam, so in Christ come grace, righteousness, and life. He is the one whom Paul elsewhere calls the *eschatos Adam*—the final Adam (1 Cor. 15:45). We might think that Christ takes his bearings from Adam, but in his recapitulation of Adam, Christ reveals for the first time a humanity fully alive.[138]

---

133. Irenaeus, *AH* 3.17.1.

134. Irenaeus, *Dem*. 31.

135. Behr, *Irenaeus of Lyons*, 136–37.

136. Irenaeus, *AH* 4.26.1. Behr writes that the cross is "*the* definitive event in the revelation of God" (*Irenaeus of Lyons*, 134).

137. Behr, *Irenaeus of Lyons*, 138.

138. "In Adam, the Word sketched out in advance what would be revealed and established in the Son of God, Christ himself" (Behr, *Irenaeus of Lyons*, 146).

The incarnation is the Son of God's recapitulation of humanity.[139] In it, Christ replays humanity. "The saviour includes all men in himself compendiously (*summatim*) and repeats the life of the first man, correcting that life at each point."[140] He repeats Adam's life in perfect obedience, summarizing in himself God's will for those made in his image. In so doing, he brings everything under one head, ordering all of humanity and all of creation to the Son. Whereas Adam had been at the head of creation, destining the world to futility and humanity to death in his sin, Christ "commenced afresh the long line of human beings, and furnished us, in a brief, comprehensive manner, with salvation; so that what we had lost in Adam—namely, to be according to the image and likeness of God—that we might recover in Christ Jesus."[141] No longer does Adam summarize our past and future; now past and future are summed up in Christ. Once again, humanity is made in the image of God who is the Son.[142]

Christ is Maker and made, the Word "recapitulating in Himself His own handiwork."[143] In the incarnation, the Son descends to seek a lost humanity that he might return to his Father with humanity found.[144] Glossing God's reminder in the covenant with Noah that he made humanity in the image of God, Irenaeus writes that "the image of God is the Son, according to whose image was man made; and for this reason, He appeared in the last times, to render the image like himself."[145] In this, the incarnate Son both completed and reformed his creation. God created humanity perfect, but immature.[146] From this childlike innocence Adam and Eve were to have grown into the maturity of those who reflect the glory of God. They did not, of course. And in the incarnation, Christ, the image of the invisible God, *completed* humanity, bringing it to maturity in his faithful obedience. We have beheld his glory, the glory of the only begotten of the Father, the glory of God that is humanity alive.[147]

139. See, e.g., *AH* 3.18.7; 4.40.3; 5.1.3; 5.14.1; 5.18.3; 5.19.1; 5.20.2; *Dem.* 6, 30–33, 37, 53, 95, 99.
140. Osborn, *Irenaeus of Lyons*, 99. Recapitulation speaks to how Christ "corrects and perfects" humanity and "inaugurates and consummates a new humanity" (97; see the entire discussion on pp. 97–140).
141. Irenaeus, *AH* 3.18.1.
142. Irenaeus, *Dem.* 22.
143. Irenaeus, *AH* 3.22.1; also 3.22.2; 5.14.2. And, beautifully, "But in every respect, too, He is man, the formation of God; and thus He took up man into Himself, the invisible becoming visible, the incomprehensible being made comprehensible, the impassible becoming capable of suffering, and the Word being made man, thus summing up all things in Himself" (3.16.6).
144. Irenaeus, *AH* 3.19.3; 3.22.1.
145. Irenaeus, *Dem.* 22.
146. Though placed as lord over creation, he was as yet "very little, since he was an infant, and it was necessary for him to reach full-development by growing in this way" (Irenaeus, *Dem.* 12).
147. See Irenaeus, *AH* 4.20.7.

In the incarnation, Christ, the image of the invisible God, also *reformed* humanity; he cast it in his mold yet again and shaped it into his likeness. "Reform" connotes both the repair of something broken and the beginning of something again. Recapitulation is reformation, as the hands of God again mold a disfigured humanity after the likeness of God. In reforming his handiwork, Christ destroys our adversary.[148] Consequently, reformation is not a smooth path of development but the fight of Christ's faithfulness.[149] The Word became flesh "that He might fight for the fathers and vanquish in Adam that which had struck us in Adam."[150] The crucifixion is thus not accidental to recapitulation, but its heart. Christ did not just become a man; he "became a man subject to stripes."[151] Christ's obedience on Calvary's tree undoes Adam's disobedience at Eden's tree by replaying it aright.[152] "He was man contending for the fathers, and through obedience doing away with disobedience completely: for He bound the strong man, and set free the weak, and endowed His own handiwork with salvation, by destroying sin."[153] The correspondence between the two is detailed: Christ's obedience "dissolved the old disobedience."[154] Like Adam, Jesus suffered death on the sixth day.[155] Even in the grave, Christ kept to his correspondence to humanity.[156] Though we "went down to death through a vanquished man," we "may ascend to life again through a victorious one."[157]

Stunning in its capacity to gather together the strands of Scripture into a coherent vision, Irenaeus's understanding of recapitulation reflects the unity of Scripture, which itself testifies to the one, true God.[158] It discerns the divine economy—displaying, for instance, the fittingness of the virgin birth[159] and providing justification for believing in the final salvation of Adam himself.[160]

148. Irenaeus, *AH* 4.24.1.
149. Irenaeus's read of the work of Christ might suggest a certain read of the *pistis Christou* debate. See Hays, *Faith of Jesus Christ*; Bird and Sprinkle, *Faith of Jesus Christ*; Allen, *Christ's Faith*.
150. Irenaeus, *Dem.* 31.
151. Irenaeus, *AH* 4.33.1; also see 4.26.1; *Dem.* 38–39.
152. Irenaeus, *AH* 5.19.1; also see 5.18.3; *Dem.* 34.
153. Irenaeus, *AH* 3.18.6.
154. Irenaeus, *Dem.* 37.
155. Irenaeus, *AH* 5.23.2.
156. Irenaeus, *AH* 5.31.2.
157. Irenaeus, *AH* 5.21.1; also see *Dem.* 45. See Trevor Hart's persuasive critique of Adolf von Harnack's argument that Irenaeus offers an account of physical redemption in his "Irenaeus, Recapitulation and Physical Redemption."
158. "Now the Lord would not have recapitulated in Himself . . . if He had come from another Father. But as He is one and the same . . ." (Irenaeus, *AH* 5.21.2).
159. Irenaeus, *AH* 3.21.10; *Dem.* 32.
160. Irenaeus, *AH* 3.23.2.

At times, though, the schematic symmetry becomes the cart that drives the horse. For instance, Irenaeus speaks of Christ recapitulating Adam and Mary recapitulating Eve, rather than Christ recapitulating humanity per se.[161] Whereas Eve was deceived by the word of an angel, Mary obeys the word of another angel. Led into death by a virgin, humanity is "rescued by a virgin; virginal disobedience having been balanced in the opposite scale by virginal obedience."[162] Though one might be able to salvage this language,[163] it too easily lends itself to the image of Mary as coredemptrix, a popular but not yet dogmatic description of the Blessed Virgin Mary in Roman Catholicism. Irenaeus can even call her "the cause of salvation, both to herself and the whole human race."[164]

Another example is Irenaeus's claim that Jesus lived beyond the age of fifty, "not despising or evading any condition of humanity . . . but sanctifying every age, by that period corresponding to it which belonged to Himself."[165] Jesus need not have experienced everything that each human being experiences firsthand (he was not, after all, a woman, or a Gentile); it is enough that he experienced a fully human life in which he was "tempted as we are, yet without sin" (Heb. 4:15).[166] A less-than-human life could not have been a life lived in our place, but it is neither possible nor necessary for Jesus to have directly encountered every possible human scenario.

Two final brief notes to conclude our discussion of recapitulation are in order. First, one regarding the end of recapitulation. The incarnation is a uniting or communion of man with God for the sake of man's participation in God's incorruptibility.[167] As a consequence of the incarnation, we are united to Christ. In (not merely through) that union we attain immortality and what Irenaeus calls "the greater glory of promotion."[168] Irenaeus can even speak

---

161. Irenaeus, *Dem.* 33.

162. Irenaeus, *AH* 5.19.1.

163. At times, Irenaeus can use recapitulation language as a literary trope without any soteriological content. The antichrist, e.g., is said to recapitulate all wickedness (*AH* 5.29.2).

164. Irenaeus, *AH* 3.22.4.

165. He continues: "For He came to save all through means of Himself—all, I say, who through Him are born again to God—infants, and children, and boys, and youths, and old men. He therefore passed through every age" (*AH* 2.22.4; also see 3.18.7). Here we have a specious anticipation of Gregory of Nazianzus's maxim: "The unassumed is the unredeemed" ("The First Letter to Cledonius the Presbyter," in *On God and Christ*, 158). For a charitable account of Irenaeus's move here, see Behr, *Way to Nicaea*, 130–31.

166. C. S. Lewis suggests that Jesus's sinlessness in temptation, rather than nudging Jesus toward nonhumanity ("to err is human . . ."), evinces Jesus's utter humanity (Lewis, *Mere Christianity*, 109–10).

167. Irenaeus, *Dem.* 31.

168. Irenaeus, *AH* 3.20.2.

of believers as "gods" and of our "pass[ing] into God."[169] What all of this really means is that we have become sons and daughters of God. We ought to be careful of finding that language of sonship deflating. If we do, that is surely a sign that we have missed the shape and size of the blessings that are ours in Christ, the only begotten Son of God. "He has, by means of His advent, poured upon the human race the greater gift of paternal grace."[170] In the earliest references to deification, the fathers did not look to 2 Peter 1:4 ("partakers of the divine nature") as much as to Psalm 82:6 ("I said, 'You are gods, sons of the Most High, all of you'"). While we needn't reject *tout court* the language of deification, we do well to follow church fathers such as Irenaeus who saw in adoption the deepest truths of deification.[171]

A second note concerns the manner of our inclusion in Christ, the *eschatos Adam* (final Adam). One might suppose that to be human is just to be part of the set of humanity recapitulated in Christ. The glory of Christ's work could elicit a doxologically motivated universalism. But such is not the case; those who do not receive the Word do not obtain "the antidote of life."[172] Irenaeus offers a simple free-will defense here, one difficult to question, even if not fully satisfying in light of later discussions of the volitional effects of sin: "His Father has made all in a like condition, each person having a choice of his own, and a free understanding."[173] Those who choose not to love God will suffer a blindness and the ensuing ruin of separation from him.[174] Some "betake themselves to the light, and by faith unite themselves with God, but others shun the light, and separate themselves from God."[175] We are born again, says Irenaeus, in baptism by faith;[176] and it is faith that effects "so great" a change in us and conserves our salvation.[177] This is, above all, to say that without the work of the Spirit, the work of Christ avails nothing.[178] We might say that the Spirit recapitulates Christ's recapitulation in us.[179] It is to this second hand of God that we now turn.

169. Irenaeus, *AH* 4.33.4.
170. Irenaeus, *AH* 4.36.4; also see 3.6.1.
171. Irenaeus affirms that "there is none other called God by the Scriptures except the Father of all, and the Son, and those who possess the adoption" (*AH* 4.preface.4). Also see *AH* 4.1.1; 4.38.4. See Mosser, "Earliest Patristic Interpretations of Psalm 82."
172. Irenaeus, *AH* 3.19.1.
173. Irenaeus, *AH* 5.27.1.
174. Irenaeus, *AH* 5.27.2.
175. Irenaeus, *AH* 5.28.1.
176. Irenaeus, *AH* 1.21.1; 3.17.1.
177. Irenaeus, *Dem.* 61, 3.
178. Irenaeus, *AH* 3.17.2.
179. "The Spirit is God the Recapitulator, who makes the achieved work of Christ present in every age" (O'Donovan, *Word in Small Boats*, 48).

## The Spirit as Innkeeper and Ladder

In a stirring sentence, Irenaeus writes that "the glory of God is a living man; and the life of man consists in beholding God."[180] The glory of God and the flourishing of humanity are directly related, such that the one entails the other. This striking Christian humanism flies in the face of a critic such as Friedrich Nietzsche, who sees in the celebration of divine glory the destruction of humanity. According to Nietzsche, the gods were invented and then used for "the self-crucifixion and self-violation of man."[181] Christianity is nihilism.[182] For Irenaeus, though, God is in no way threatened by human flourishing; rather, it is his fitting counterpart. And it is the Spirit's task to bring about a humanity filled with God's glory. He is the Lord and giver of life, and "where the Spirit of the Father is, there is a living man."[183]

Consider two images Irenaeus uses for the Spirit's work—the Spirit as innkeeper and as ladder.[184] First, he speaks of "the Lord commending to the Holy Spirit His own man, who had fallen among thieves, whom He Himself compassionated, and bound up his wounds, giving two royal *denaria*; so that we, receiving by the Spirit the image and superscription of the Father and the Son, might cause the *denarium* entrusted to us to be fruitful, counting out the increase [thereof] to the Lord."[185] Jesus is the good Samaritan who has rescued us, restored to us the image and likeness by the power of the Holy Spirit (the two royal *denaria*), and given us to the care of the same Spirit. We are rescued from death and brought into the house of healing. Then the Son ascends, leaving our long-term care in the Spirit's capable hands until the Son returns. Our innkeeper uses the means of grace to tend our wounds and nurse us back to health. He is the Lord our Healer (Exod. 15:26).

Our healing comes about as the Spirit refashions us in the image and likeness of God. Irenaeus distinguishes between our abiding possession of the image of God and our having lost the likeness of God.[186] Since we could not see the image, it being invisible, we "did easily lose the similitude." When the Word became flesh, he "confirmed" both image and likeness: he "showed

180. Irenaeus, *AH* 4.20.7.
181. Nietzsche, *Genealogy of Morals*, 2.23.
182. Nietzsche, *Genealogy of Morals*, 2.24; 3.28.
183. Irenaeus, *AH* 5.9.3. Note Irenaeus's care to distinguish between the breath of life and the "vivifying Spirit" (5.12.2). Also note that a gloriously alive humanity is one whose life consists in beholding God. Irenaeus can even say that "this is the glory of man, to continue and remain permanently in God's service" (4.14.1).
184. "The exuberant images are not a cadenza, a flourish within the main work, but the origin of ideas" (Osborn, *Irenaeus of Lyons*, 13).
185. Irenaeus, *AH* 3.17.3.
186. Irenaeus, *AH* 5.6.1.

forth the image truly, since He became Himself what was His image; and He re-established the similitude after a sure manner, by assimilating man to the invisible Father through means of the visible Word."[187] God's intention is "that the Church may be fashioned after the image of His Son."[188] The Father entrusts this fashioning to the Spirit.[189] In Kathryn Tanner's words, "The Son is the shape of the Spirit's working."[190] The Father makes and remakes people who look like his Son in the power of their Spirit. The Son restores the image, and the Spirit paints the image on each believer.[191] Thus Irenaeus can write that a person is "saved altogether because of the communion of the Spirit."[192]

In giving the Spirit, the Lord gave God to humanity, just as in the incarnation, he attached humanity to God.[193] The point here is the union and communion of God and humanity that are established and sustained by the Son and Spirit. The Spirit nurses humanity back to health by uniting us to Christ and fostering our communion with him. He is "the [means of] communion with Christ" given in the church and (our second image) "the ladder of ascent to God."[194]

To speak of the Spirit as the ladder of ascent to God is not to suggest that the Spirit leads us up and away from the flesh. In sharpest contrast to the Gnostics, Irenaeus argues that "flesh is not the antithesis of the Spirit but is his magnum opus."[195] After all, in creation the Spirit adorned the whole person, not a part, and it is the whole person who was made in the image and likeness of God.[196] It is the flesh and blood of Jesus that have saved us and that "procure for us life,"[197] and the Eucharist involves and anticipates "the fellowship and union of the flesh and Spirit."[198] The end of the Spirit's work is not the destruction of the flesh but its salvation.[199]

187. Irenaeus, *AH* 5.16.2.

188. Irenaeus, *AH* 4.37.7.

189. Irenaeus, *AH* 5.8.1.

190. Tanner, *Christ the Key*, 173. Tanner suggests that generally one can speak of the Son giving form and the Spirit giving power (power as "loving inclination and impulse") to the Father's will (174–75).

191. See the comment on Ephrem the Syrian in Rogers, *After the Spirit*, 153.

192. Irenaeus, *AH* 5.11.1.

193. Irenaeus, *AH* 5.1.1.

194. Irenaeus, *AH* 3.24.1. For more on this, see Canlis, *Calvin's Ladder*, 173–228.

195. Canlis, *Calvin's Ladder*, 211.

196. Irenaeus, *AH* 5.6.1. Irenaeus espouses a holistic tripartite anthropology (5.6.1; 5.9.1), though only in a qualified sense (see Osborn, *Irenaeus of Lyons*, 17).

197. Irenaeus, *AH* 5.14.4.

198. Irenaeus, *AH* 4.18.5. "But our opinion is in accordance with the Eucharist, and the Eucharist in turn establishes our opinion" (4.18.5). Geoffrey Wainwright explains: "Doctrinal appeal can be made to the eucharist because in the eucharist the faith comes to focal expression" (Wainwright, *Doxology*, 234).

199. Irenaeus, *AH* 5.12.4.

How does this happen, if we consider salvation from the vantage point of the Spirit? First, the Spirit prepares humanity for salvation in the incarnate Son.[200] The Son leads us to the Father. When we see God, we will be made incorruptible, as the very splendor of God gives us life.[201] This is the process, but it happens gradually in accordance with what we can bear.

Where does it happen? In the church. "For where the Church is, there is the Spirit of God; and where the Spirit of God is, there is the Church, and every kind of grace."[202] If the Spirit is the innkeeper, the church is the inn. If the Spirit is the means of our communion with God in Christ, the church is the context of that communion. In fact, the church just is that company of people who receive the Spirit.[203] The Holy Spirit is the fountain of the church's youth.[204] The eternally young church is our mother who brings us up and nourishes us on the Scriptures. She is also a garden, whose trees are the Scriptures, which the Lord has given us to eat.[205]

Irenaeus conceives the Christian life as growth into maturity. God created humanity good, but immature; human beings were "unaccustomed to, and unexercised in, perfect discipline."[206] The Christian life is an accustoming of humanity to the things of God, a preparation to receive God in full.[207] This process takes time, as God refuses to use coercion with us, instead seeking to persuade us in keeping with the freedom he gave us at creation.[208] This persuasion occurs as we are nourished on the Scriptures in the bosom of the church. There is a pattern of creation, growth, strengthening, abounding, recovery from sin, glorification, and the vision of God.[209] "But we do now receive a certain portion of His Spirit, tending towards perfection, and preparing us for incorruption, being little by little accustomed to receive and bear God."[210] Again, this is not because of an inherent deficiency in the flesh, but instead

200. "The Spirit must dwell in Jesus's own humanity in order to dwell more widely in ours" (Tanner, *Christ the Key*, 168).

201. Irenaeus, *AH* 4.20.5. We ascend "through the Spirit to the Son, and through the Son to the Father" (5.36.2).

202. Irenaeus, *AH* 3.24.1.

203. Irenaeus, *AH* 4.36.2.

204. Irenaeus, *AH* 3.24.1.

205. "For the Church has been planted as a garden [*paradisus*] in this world; therefore says the Spirit of God, 'Thou mayest freely eat from every tree of the garden,' that is, Eat ye from every Scripture of the Lord" (*AH* 5.20.2).

206. Irenaeus, *AH* 4.38.1.

207. Irenaeus, *AH* 4.38.2.

208. Irenaeus, *AH* 5.1.1. Humanity's freedom is a frequent theme in Irenaeus's writing. See 4.4.3; 4.15.2; 4.37.1; 5.1.1; 5.27.1.

209. Irenaeus, *AH* 4.38.3.

210. Irenaeus, *AH* 5.8.1.

because of a need for flesh to be made fit and capable of bearing God. The millennial kingdom will involve our being "accustomed gradually to partake of the divine nature."[211] As the righteous reign on earth, their vision of the Lord will strengthen them and accustom them to "partake in the glory of God the Father."[212] Then they will be fully alive.

## A Concluding Criticism and Commendation

By way of conclusion I offer a criticism and a commendation. My criticism is simple: Irenaeus has an insufficient and inconsistent doctrine of sin. The insufficiency can be seen when Irenaeus turns to the question of the origin of sin. For Genesis, sin is not natural, necessary, or inevitable. It is someone's fault, even if temptation provides the occasion. Passing the buck will not do; despite Adam's blaming of Eve and Eve's blaming of the serpent, the consequences are dire for each.

In contrast, Irenaeus is too hesitant to acknowledge the full responsibility of Adam and Eve. His developmental anthropology, elsewhere such a fruitful way of considering humanity, here compromises his reading of Scripture. One gets the impression that Adam was nothing but a rascal, a little kid who needed scolding but who could hardly have known better: "But the man was a young child, not yet having a perfect deliberation, and because of this he was easily deceived by the seducer."[213] The angel who became the apostate, or devil, envied God's gifts to humanity and so "ruined himself and made the man a sinner" and "caused him to be cast out of the Paradise." It is this angel who is "the head and originator of sin."[214] When Eve protests that "the devil made me do it!," Genesis asks us to hear a sinfully evasive maneuver; Irenaeus, though, suspects she might be right.[215]

Irenaeus's developmental account of anthropology thus obscures the Genesis account, saying too little explicitly about arrested development.[216] Nor does he say much about humanity's subsequent sin, about the baleful state of people whose development has taken a wrong turn. Indeed, it can only be

---

211. Irenaeus, *AH* 5.32.1.
212. Irenaeus, *AH* 5.35.1; also see 5.35.2.
213. Irenaeus, *Dem.* 12.
214. Irenaeus, *Dem.* 16, also 17.
215. And so, Irenaeus gets the Eve–Mary comparison exactly wrong. He fails to see in Eve the cause of sin's entrance into the world, even as he sees in Mary the cause of sin's undoing in the world.
216. One can learn quite a bit about humanity in its sin from *Arrested Development*, a television show in which every character consistently forgoes any acknowledgment of personal responsibility and points a blaming finger at anyone but herself.

ambiguously called a wrong turn on Irenaeus's account, as even the fall is cast as a step toward maturity. It may be a false step, but Irenaeus veers close to positing it as a *necessary* step in humanity's development. While the light of the resurrection thrown back on Adam might bathe the fall in a hopeful light and even justify the pious reference to a *felix culpa*, such an approach can be only an eschatological judgment and must not be used to justify or minimize the ugliness of Adam's sin.[217]

My brief commendation relates to recapitulation. Even given my critique, Irenaeus's account of Jesus's gathering together of humanity and all of creation in himself might just be the most biblically rooted, theologically rich, and comprehensively compelling account of God and his world I have read. It recognizes the deep and complex unity of creation and redemption, of the old and new covenants, of God's ways with Israel and with the church. And it grounds them in Christ without flattening the story. In Irenaeus's story, which is Scripture's, we see Jesus as the climax of the covenant, yes, but as such the climax of history itself.[218] In Christ we meet the same God who created and redeemed the world and the same humanity as we possess, finally fulfilling its vocation as the light of the world.

217. Irenaeus approaches the positing of a necessary, if *felix*, fall in *AH* 4.38–39.
218. The reference is to N. T. Wright, *Climax of the Covenant*.

# 2

# THE WORD
# WHO BECAME FLESH

*The Center and Circumference*
*of Athanasius's Theology*

## The Life of Athanasius of Alexandria

Some theologians are known for the panoramic scope of their vision. Irenaeus's grasp of the whole of the faith, its internal logic and sweeping implications, is breathtaking. Other theologians are known for their commitment to an intellectual cause, for their dogged insistence on a particular point for the good of the church. Athanasius is one of the latter. He is something of a one-trick pony, though his particular trick is, arguably, the most important one for a theologian to get right. Furthermore, in his resolute focus on the full divinity of the Son of God, Athanasius's vantage opened onto the broad terrain of the Christian faith. By looking to the center of things, he managed to see just about everything.

Born in the last few years of the third century, Athanasius was still a teenager when the Roman Empire's persecution of Christians ended with the conversion of Emperor Constantine and the adoption of an imperial policy of toleration in the Edict of Milan (in AD 313). If external hostilities ceased, however, internal strife escalated. A fairly stabilized canon of Scripture, liturgical forms, and various rules of faith had shaped and authorized Christian teaching and witness; peacetime, however, proved ripe for hammering out the precise implications of Scripture's textured account of God.

We might consider the Constantinian Era not so much as a golden age of church-state synergy or the first and fatal step into state-sponsored apostasy (call these the Eusebian and Anabaptist narratives) but rather as a time of Christian expansion—a gold rush, if you will, in which prospectors raced one another West in search of ecclesial and political pay dirt.[1] The Constantinian settlement resembled a frontier town with an at-best-fragile rule of law rather than an established city with a stable infrastructure. The fourth century thus represents a transitional period on the way to Emperor Theodosius's codifying of Nicene Christianity as the official imperial religion in 380 and the affirmation of the Nicene Creed at the Council of Constantinople in 381. While a victory for the church catholic over Arianism, this must have seemed a Pyrrhic one in hindsight; only forty years later Augustine lamented the fall of Rome as it was sacked by Alaric and the *Arian* Goths.[2]

But we are getting ahead of ourselves. Who was Arius? The Arian controversy, a debate about the precise nature of the Son and his relation to the Father in which it was proposed that "there was when the Son was not," began around 319. A few years later, in 325, a young Deacon Athanasius accompanied Bishop Alexander of Alexandria to the Council of Nicaea as secretary (and possibly theological expert). Nicaea condemned the Arian heresy as "alien and strange to the faith of the Church."[3] In his defense of the Nicene definition, Athanasius summarizes the key Arian teachings rejected at Nicaea:

> They say then what the others held and dared to maintain before them; "Not always Father, not always Son; for the Son was not before his generation, but, as others, came to be from nothing; and in consequence God was not always Father of the Son; but, when the Son came to be and was created, then was God called his Father. For the Word is a creature and a work, and foreign and unlike the Father in essence; and the Son is neither by nature the Father's true Word,

---

1. Eusebius writes an ecclesiastical history that climaxes in the peaceful reign of a Christian emperor Constantine (see his *History of the Church* 10), whereas Anabaptists consider the very notion of a Christian emperor an oxymoron. Such an integration of church and state signals, according to the Anabaptist witness, a fatal compromise of the gospel of peace, which forbids Christians to wield the world's weapons of violence. See article 6 of the Schleitheim Confession (1527) in Leith, *Creeds of the Churches*.

2. Timothy Barnes makes the case for the Constantinian circumstances that created what we are describing as a frontier situation in *Athanasius and Constantius*. Rowan Williams quickly narrates the complex and alternating fortunes of Arians and Catholics in *Arius*, 1.

3. Athanasius, *Arian History* 66, in *Select Works and Letters*. All references to Athanasius's works other than *On the Incarnation* and *Letters to Serapion on the Holy Spirit* are drawn from *Select Works and Letters*.

nor his only and true Wisdom; but being a creature and one of the works, he is improperly called Word and Wisdom; for by the Word which is in God was he made, as were all things. Wherefore the Son is not true God."[4]

While he did not hold sway at the council, Athanasius did observe the fight firsthand, including the relative intellectual imprecision and the sizable majority of Nicene fathers who were not up to the theological task of parsing the issues. Little did he know that he would succeed his mentor Alexander only three years after the council, ascending to one of the most important bishoprics in the world on June 8, 328, still in his twenties. The Arian party—really, we ought to say "parties," as it was a loose confederation (itself probably too strong a word) of like-minded dissenters, most of them pious in intent and not necessarily genetically linked to Arius's own theology[5]—quickly muddied the waters after Nicaea and challenged its conclusions. It would be left to Athanasius, and often seemingly *only* Athanasius, to exegete and defend the council against various Arian parties for nearly a half century, during which he would be exiled five times. "Like a beloved but incommodious friend the Council of Nicaea constantly shadowed Athanasius, and that association dictated the course of his theological career and his ecclesial life."[6]

If the Arian parties are the Constantinian frontier's outlaws, its sheriff must be Athanasius. While Timothy Barnes displays a penchant for tabloid headlines in likening Athanasius to a "modern gangster" surrounded by an "ecclesiastical mafia," the rough-and-tumble of the fourth-century frontier suggests why Athanasius "could not have cut such an impressive figure had he not been conspicuously lacking in the Christian virtues of meekness and humility."[7] We should avoid the kind of gritty realism that despairs of the very

4. Athanasius, *Defence of the Nicene Council* 6. See also the summaries of Arian beliefs in Anatolios, *Athanasius*, 85–93; and Leithart, *Athanasius*, 2–5.

5. Khaled Anatolios notes that "despite the rather tendentious remark [by Timothy Barnes] that Athanasius called 'Arian' anyone who disagreed with him, the case is rather that Athanasius called 'Arian' anyone who could be understood to mean that the Son is a creature" (Anatolios, *Athanasius*, 96). Anatolios's remark reflects a recent history of scholarship that follows a Hegelian pattern of universal approbation of Athanasius, a reactionary apologetic on behalf of Arius, and a more subtle synthesis. This synthesis recognizes the diversity and fluidity of fourth-century theology, the biblical concerns of the various "Arian" parties, and the pugnacity of Athanasius but nevertheless offers a pro-Nicene account. Especially helpful for the complexity they add to the picture are Ayres, *Nicaea and Its Legacy*, and R. Williams, *Arius*. According to Williams, Arius was a "conservative" intellect in that he didn't say anything new, but an equally "radical and individual" one who reworked, recombined, and pressed old ideas to their logical conclusions (see 175–78). David Gwynn has recently tried to put all the pieces of Athanasius back together in *Athanasius of Alexandria*.

6. Weinandy, *Athanasius*, 2.

7. Barnes, *Constantine and Eusebius*, 230; Barnes, *Athanasius and Constantius*, 1.

possibility of the long arm of the law adopting a posture of meekness in a one-horse town overrun by outlaws—that seems to have been Jesus's way, after all—but we can still acknowledge the need for backbone and even bravado in such a context. And yet, if we needn't dismiss Athanasius's account of his contest in the name of Jesus with the Arians, we likewise needn't assume that such a heroic apologist thereby escapes the need to apologize, to confess his sins even in defense of the incarnate Son.

The rise of Arianism urgently pressed the need for the church to clarify its language about the one believers had been worshiping for nearly three hundred years. Who is this one, Jesus Christ? Is he God, in the absolute sense that the God of Israel, the one before whom Israel was to have no other gods, is God? Is he some sort of quasi-divine being? If he *is* God, can he possibly be a man? Is it right to think of the perfectly transcendent God being so, not aligned, but *identified* with a man?

We will return to these questions. But for now, we must begin at the heart of the matter. Athanasius, after all, was no speculative theologian but a soteriological one.[8] He started at the point of our salvation, working backward and forward from what God has done in becoming man "for us and our salvation."[9]

### The Word Became Flesh

Anselm, centuries later, asked what seemed an obvious enough question: *Cur Deus homo?* Why *did* God become man? It all depends on how you ask the question: If one seeks the necessity of the incarnation, the occasion that called for such a remedy, one's gaze turns retrospective. "For us and our salvation" he was made man: this was Nicaea's answer, and it was Athanasius's.[10] By virtue of being created out of nothing, humanity is "mobile by nature" and "essentially impermanent."[11] Despite human beings' native mutability, God

8. The centrality of soteriology for Athanasius is the burden of Weinandy, *Athanasius*.
9. The Nicene Creed.
10. See especially Athanasius, *On the Incarnation* 4.
11. Athanasius, *Against the Heathen* 4.3; *On the Incarnation* 3. Hence Adam and Eve would have "naturally" died had they not cleaved to the Word (*On the Incarnation* 3, 5). Thus our first parents were not naturally immortal, or at least not naturally immortal apart from dependence on God. Compare Kathryn Tanner: "Our faculties were made to operate as they should, to operate well, only when incorporating what remains alien to them, the very perfection of Word and Spirit themselves." Being in the image of God suggests that "the presence of Word and Spirit becomes an ingredient of our very constitution." From this she constructs an "apophatically-focused anthropology" with its elaboration of humanity's open-ended plasticity and self-*insufficiency* (Tanner, *Christ the Key*, 28, 54).

"graciously bestowed on them his own life by the grace of the Word." While they *could* die, they need not, "the grace of their union with the Word [having] made them capable of escaping from the natural law" of corruption.[12] But they turned, exchanging the contemplation of God for a fascination with "things nearer to themselves," falling into a "lust of themselves." They turned "from eternal things to things corruptible, by counsel of the devil," and "made themselves at home in these things."[13] In the process, they "lost existence."[14]

Might it not have been enough had Adam and Eve simply repented? Yes, if the problem were only one of sin, but the problem was one of corruption.[15] Repentance doesn't "recall men from what is according to their nature; all that it does is to make them cease from sinning."[16] Upon sinning, humanity fell headlong into its native corruptibility and welcomed death in.[17] "The human race was in process of destruction. Man . . . was disappearing, and the work of God was being undone." This was "both monstrous and unfitting."[18]

There was a problem, and only God could help. Furthermore, God being God, he *had* to solve it. "Such indifference to the ruin of his own work before his very eyes would argue not goodness in God but limitation, and that far more than if he had never created men at all. It was impossible, therefore, that God should leave man to be carried off by corruption, because it would be unfitting and unworthy of himself."[19] More specifically, it was fitting that the Word be the one who rescued humanity from corruption, as he was the one through whom the Father made the world in the first place. "*The renewal of creation has been wrought by the Self-same Word Who made it in the beginning.* There is thus no inconsistency between creation and salvation; for the One Father has employed the same Agent for both works, effecting the salvation of the world through the same Word Who made it in the beginning."[20] Thus, the Father demonstrates his constancy and commitment

12. Athanasius, *On the Incarnation* 5.

13. The previous two sentences draw from Athanasius, *Against the Heathen* 3.1–4; *On the Incarnation* 5.

14. Athanasius, *On the Incarnation* 4.

15. Athanasius skates past the problem of guilt at this point, rather naively; here we do well to listen to Anselm's elaboration of the weighty debt of sin requiring Christ's death in order for us to be reconciled to God. The guilt of sin was problem enough. But Athanasius is right that death is equally a problem.

16. Athanasius, *On the Incarnation* 7.

17. Athanasius, *On the Incarnation* 5.

18. Athanasius, *On the Incarnation* 6.

19. Athanasius, *On the Incarnation* 6.

20. Athanasius, *On the Incarnation* 1. And in *On the Incarnation* 3: "He made all things out of nothing through his own Word, our Lord Jesus Christ."

to creation in sending his Son to save the world and, finally, in raising his Son from the dead.[21]

Athanasius describes the renewal of creation using two images. Creation is a city founded by a king that is "attacked by robbers" "through the carelessness of its inhabitants" and then avenged and saved from destruction by the king himself.[22] Or it is a portrait "obliterated through external stains" that the painter refuses to throw away. Rather, he has the subject sit again, "and then the likeness is re-drawn on the same material."[23] Notice Athanasius's emphasis on the unity of creation and redemption. One can sense, too, in these images his conception of sin leading to dissolution, a careening toward nothingness brought on by corruption. The portrait image serves Athanasius's purposes particularly well, evoking Jesus as the image of God (the "subject" in the analogy), according to whom humanity (the "portrait") was made.

The image of God, its proper function and its compromise as a result of sin, plays a central role in Athanasius's account of the fall (and throughout his theology).[24] The image is a mirror "by which alone [the soul] had the power of seeing the Image of the Father," and our first parents were to preserve the divine likeness within them "through constant contemplation."[25] To speak of humanity being made in the image of God is to call to mind the Son, who "only is Image true and natural of the Father."[26] He is "the exact imprint of his nature" (Heb. 1:3).[27] Our being made in the image of God functioned to reveal the Word, God's own Image, to us, that through him we might "apprehend the Father; which knowledge of [our] Maker is for men the only really happy and blessed life."[28] To know God is to live. As long as Adam and Eve were with

21. In the song "Was It a Morning Like This?" Sandi Patty sings of the way in which creation's bondage to decay is caught up with, and reversed by, the resurrection of the crucified Lord: "Did the grass sing? / Did the earth rejoice to feel you again?" Even the ground was jubilant in sensing that its Maker wasn't dead but alive.

22. Athanasius, *On the Incarnation* 10.

23. Athanasius, *On the Incarnation* 14.

24. For the image's broader function in Athanasius's theology, see Anatolios, *Retrieving Nicaea*, 107–8, 130–31, 136, 148–49.

25. Athanasius, *Against the Heathen* 8.2 (see also *Against the Heathen* 30); *On the Incarnation* 4.

26. Athanasius, *Against the Arians* 3.10.

27. As Gregory of Nazianzus would put it later in the same century, "Beings with no complexity to their nature have no points of likeness or unlikeness. They are exact replicas, identical rather than like" (*Or.* 30.20).

28. Athanasius, *On the Incarnation* 11. God impressed his image on us and gave us "a share in the reasonable being of the very Word Himself, so that, reflecting Him and themselves becoming reasonable and expressing the Mind of God even as He does, though in limited degree, they might continue for ever in the blessed and only true life of the saints in paradise" (*On the Incarnation* 3).

the Word, who imaged forth the Father, they would live, but in sinning they at once forgot God and invited their banishment from his presence—that is, they welcomed death in. "The presence and love of the Word had called them into being; inevitably, therefore, when they lost the knowledge of God, they lost existence with it."[29] In the incarnation of the same Word who had called them into being, God "renew[ed] his Image in mankind, so that through it men might once more come to know him."[30] Restoration to life and renewal of the knowledge of God go hand in hand. The Word became flesh "that they may have life and have it abundantly" (John 10:10b). And "this is eternal life, that they know you, the only true God, and Jesus Christ whom you have sent" (John 17:3).

Another way to consider the question of why God became a man is to ask about the telos of the incarnation, in which case one's gaze looks forward. Christ "did two things: he put an end to the law of death which barred our way; and he made a new beginning of life for us, by giving us the hope of resurrection."[31] The resurrection is "the supreme object of His coming," a "monument" to death's vanquishing and the "assurance" that we, too, will share in his incorruption.[32] Not that Athanasius minimizes the cross, which "has not been a disaster, but a healing of Creation."[33] In fact, Christ's death is "the very centre of our faith," and he will return "no longer to suffer but to bestow on us all the fruit of his cross—the resurrection and incorruptibility."[34] The Word became flesh "so that in his death all might die" and be raised to incorruptible life in him.[35]

That leaves us with the hazardous question of the Son's "becoming." We might think this issue to be fairly straightforward. Here we have clear Johannine language, perfectly suited to articulate—well, let's call it what *happens* to the Word when he becomes flesh (John 1:14). Ah, but already we find ourselves

29. Athanasius, *On the Incarnation* 4.
30. Athanasius, *On the Incarnation* 13. "And how could this be done save by the coming of the very Image himself, our Saviour Jesus Christ?"
31. Athanasius, *On the Incarnation* 10. Compare *On the Incarnation* 16 (where the two things are [1] banishing death and renewing us and [2] making himself visible to us), 20.
32. Athanasius, *On the Incarnation* 22.
33. Athanasius, *Against the Heathen* 1.4.
34. Athanasius, *On the Incarnation* 19, 56.
35. Athanasius, *On the Incarnation* 8. "Athanasius understands the Incarnation in terms of the Passion: the Savior takes a body to die, for it is only through death itself that death is overthrown and life resurrected." Similarly, the Savior must be born of a virgin, "herself pure and spotless," to "guarantee that Christ freely offered his body to death." His body is mortal like ours, but in the sense that "it is capable of death, so that he could die as we do, rather than subject to death" (Behr, *Nicene Faith*, 197, 198, 202). That the incarnation is ordered to the crucifixion is one of Behr's chief burdens in his account of Athanasius.

in trouble. What *happens* to the Word? The one who made everything that is, the one who has life in himself, the one Thomas Aquinas would later call *actus purus* ("pure act")—how can anything be said to happen *to* him? Is he not the one who makes things happen? And if he is already perfect in himself, can something happening to him do anything other than degrade him? After all, "becoming" carries with it connotations of change, of discontinuity. Whatever else happens to me, in "becoming" something, I become something *else*. And if God were to become something else, he could only become less, and thus less than God.

How does Athanasius navigate these waters? He insists on three points, all of which can be seen in his statement that "[the Word] has become flesh not by being changed into flesh, but because he assumed on our behalf living flesh, and has become Man."[36]

First, the Word really does become flesh.[37] If it is difficult for Athanasius to speak of the real enfleshing of the Word without also reminding us of the Word's still greater reality, we ought not to miss the former point. While Athanasius has not achieved the conceptual clarity of Chalcedonian two-natures Christology, his "partitive exegesis" allows us to "conceptually distinguish which properties applying to him are divine and which are human," even while he insists on their unity in one subject such that "we cannot separate these categories into two subjects of predication."[38] So Athanasius: "The properties of the flesh are said to be His, since He was in it, such as to hunger, to thirst, to suffer, to weary, and the like, of which the flesh is capable; while on the other hand the works proper to the Word Himself, such as to raise the dead, to restore sight to the blind, and to cure the woman with an issue of blood, He did through His own body."[39] What is true of him in the flesh really is true, "since he was in it," even though these attributes are "predicated of him in different manners (one as who he is, the other as what he has accepted to do)."[40] The Word really did hunger and thirst. Such is the extent of God's identification with humanity in its plight.

36. Athanasius, *Epistle* 59.8.
37. Keep in mind that "flesh" is often a holistic concept in Scripture, as it is for Athanasius. The Son assumed a body and a soul. "They confessed also that the Saviour had not a body without a soul, nor without sense or intelligence . . . nor was the salvation effected in the Word Himself a salvation of body only, but of soul also" (Athanasius, *Synodal Letter to Antioch* 7). On the hotly contested question of the role of Christ's human soul in Athanasius's thought, see Weinandy, *Athanasius*, 91–96.
38. Behr, *Nicene Faith*, 212, 220.
39. Athanasius, *Against the Arians* 3.31.
40. Behr, *Nicene Faith*, 224. Anatolios argues that Athanasius construes the unity of Christ "much more along the lines of a model of predication than of organic unity," with divine and

It is in this vein that we ought read Athanasius's description of Christ's body as "instrument": "His body was for Him not a limitation, but an instrument, so that He was both in it and in all things, and outside all things, resting in the Father alone. At one and the same time—this is the wonder—as Man He was living a human life, and as Word He was sustaining the life of the universe, and as Son He was in constant union with the Father."[41] As "not a limitation, but an instrument," the flesh of Christ allowed God to be profoundly immanent while remaining transcendent over his creation. Anatolios explains: "It is precisely in virtue of this unrestrained activity that the presence and action of the Logos in the body is to be differentiated from the normal activity of the soul. For the soul, while active with regard to the body, is 'bound' to the body in the sense that its sphere of activity is restricted to the body."[42] The incarnate Son, however, can assume flesh, can be "in" creation and in a particular body (can even "be" in some sense that body) without ceasing to be Lord of all creation and all bodies.[43] Thus Athanasius "maintain[s] the extreme condescension of the Word as consistent with his unmitigated lordliness."[44]

Of course, there are those whose prior metaphysical commitments might lead them to suggest that embodiment entails profanation. But Athanasius turns the tables on them: "Not even His birth from a virgin, therefore, changed Him in any way, nor was He defiled by being in the body. Rather, He sanctified the body by being in it."[45] In his majestic becoming, the Son does not himself undergo change but rather changes the flesh by hallowing it in his coming. God's presence always sanctifies, and in the case of the incarnation his hallowing presence renders the body a temple. The prophet Ezekiel saw God's glory leave the temple (Ezek. 10:18) and foresaw its return to the temple (43:1–12). In the incarnation, God reestablishes the temple, showing forth Christ as the place where his people will worship him in spirit and truth. Christ "Himself prepared this body in the virgin as a temple for Himself, and took it for his

---

human characteristics "predicated of a single grammatical subject." And "the appropriation of the body by the Word legitimates the application of human predications to the subject of 'God the Word'" (*Athanasius*, 80).

41. Athanasius, *On the Incarnation* 17. Comments such as these suggest that the *extra Calvinisticum*—the notion that, even as the incarnate Word who dwelt in space and time, this one transcended space and time "uphold[ing] the universe by the word of his power" (Heb. 1:3)—is not as exclusively Calvinist as its Lutheran detractors suggest. See further McGinnis, *Son of God Beyond the Flesh*.

42. Anatolios, *Athanasius*, 77.

43. For a programmatic exploration of this claim, see T. Torrance, *Space, Time and Incarnation*.

44. Anatolios, *Athanasius*, 76.

45. Athanasius, *On the Incarnation* 17.

very own, as the instrument through which He was known and in which He dwelt."[46] Christ's body is no *mere* instrument, but the Holy of Holies. Thus it is, too, that the church, the body of Christ, is also the temple of the Holy Spirit, as are the bodies of individual believers.[47]

In clarifying that "we do not conceive the whole Word himself to be flesh, but to have put on flesh and become man," Athanasius does not back away from his claim that the Word really does become flesh. Instead, he insists—and this is our second point—that, in becoming flesh, the Word is "not . . . changed into flesh" but remains himself.[48] "For he was not anything which he is not now, nor is he what he was not; but he is as he ever was, and in the same state and in the same respects; otherwise he will seem to be imperfect and alterable."[49]

To say that he is *really* human need not imply that Jesus is *merely* human; he can still be God.[50] He does not become something other than himself but, speaking somewhat crudely, expands himself so that he can be something additional to what he was, is, and ever shall be—God the Son. Flesh does not change him, "but, being the same as before, he was robed in it."[51] "He was not lessened by the envelopment of the body, but rather deified it and rendered it immortal."[52] "Becoming" describes the Son's ministry in the economy of salvation, not his eternal substance.[53]

## The Impassible One

It is self-evident for Athanasius that God is impassible—that is, he cannot be affected in any way. He does not suffer the acts of another. This is more than to say that he feels no pain, either physically or emotionally. It is also to say that he is not marked or acted upon in such a way as to affect him. Surely an austere doctrine, divine impassibility speaks to the absolute priority, changelessness, and transcendence of God vis-à-vis his creation. Paul Gavrilyuk notes that divine impassibility "was first of all an ontological term, expressing God's

46. Athanasius, *On the Incarnation* 8. Similarly, in *Epistle* 60.7, Athanasius writes of "the Lord Who is in the flesh as in a temple."

47. See Minear, *Images of the Church*, 173–220; Beale, *Temple and the Church's Mission*.

48. Athanasius, *Against the Arians* 2.47.

49. Athanasius, *Against the Arians* 4.12.

50. See Oliver Crisp's discussion of this distinction in his *Divinity and Humanity*, 167; Crisp, *God Incarnate*, 23–25. Crisp follows Thomas V. Morris's use of the distinction in *Logic of God Incarnate*.

51. Athanasius, *Against the Arians* 2.8.

52. Athanasius, *Defence of the Nicene Council* 3.14.

53. Athanasius, *Against the Arians* 1.62.

unlikeness to everything created . . . rather than a psychological term implying the absence of emotions." Hence the church fathers' willingness to countenance the strong emotional language applied to God in Scripture, provided the "apophatic qualifier" of impassibility is in place.[54] God's emotional ways are higher than ours (cf. Isa. 55:9).[55] So Augustine confesses to God, "You love without burning, you are jealous in a way that is free of anxiety, you 'repent' (Gen. 6:6) without the pain of regret, you are wrathful and remain tranquil."[56] Here we can begin to see why David Bentley Hart insists that

> divine impassibility is not simply apophatic, a limit placed upon our language . . . but is in fact very much part of the ground of Christian hope, central to the positive message of the evangel. . . . God's *apatheia* is that infinite refuge from all violence and suffering that is the heart's rest. . . . For Christian thought, divine impassibility is the effect of the fullness of trinitarian charity, rather than a purely negative attribute logically implied by the thought of divine simplicity and bodilessness, and so is properly synonymous with "infinite love."[57]

Only a God who cannot be bothered can love.[58]

Athanasius speaks in the same breath of "the impassibility of the Word's nature" and "the infirmities ascribed to Him because of the flesh," which are "not proper to the very Word by nature, but proper by nature to the very flesh." No proto-Nestorian, Athanasius does not posit a pair of subjects, one divine and one human, but insists that "these things are ascribed to him, since they are proper to the flesh, and the body itself is proper to the Saviour." Our infirmities belong to the incarnate Son; they are "proper" to him. But while he therefore suffers in the flesh, he does so as the impassible God, precisely thereby saving us. "Though God [is] impassible, he had taken a passible flesh."[59]

---

54. Gavrilyuk, *Suffering of the Impassible God*, 48, 16.

55. "By calling God 'impassible' Justin and the other Apologists were clearing the decks of popular theological discourse in order to make space for God-befitting emotionally coloured characteristics such as mercy, love, and compassion. . . . The divine impassibility meant first of all that God is in total control of his actions and that morally objectionable emotions are alien to him" (Gavrilyuk, *Suffering of the Impassible God*, 51).

56. Augustine, *Confessions* 1.4.4.

57. D. Hart, *Beauty of the Infinite*, 355. He refers to "that loveliest (and most widely misunderstood) 'attribute,' *apatheia*" (157).

58. See Frances Young's moving account of her change of mind about divine *apatheia* in *God's Presence*, 381–85.

59. Athanasius, *Against the Arians* 3.55; also see 3.31. See the discussions in Anatolios, *Athanasius*, 82–83; Leithart, *Athanasius*, 134–45. Again though, "when the flesh suffered, the Word was *not external* to it; and therefore is *the passion said to be His*: and when He did divinely His Father's works, the flesh was *not external* to Him, but *in the body* itself did the

At times, Athanasius seems to back away from such a strong claim. Of Jesus's prayer in Gethsemane, Athanasius writes that "it was not the Word, considered as the Word, who wept and was troubled, but it was proper to the flesh," and "neither can the Lord be forsaken by the Father, who is ever in the Father, both before he spoke, and when he uttered this cry."[60] Rather than retreating from the mystery of the suffering of the impassible God in the flesh, though, Athanasius guards the mystery by reminding us that he remains the impassible God even in his fleshly suffering. Furthermore, he does so with our salvation in mind. "And while he himself, being impassible in nature, remains as he is, not harmed by these affections, but rather obliterating and destroying them, men, their passions as if changed and abolished in the Impassible, henceforth become themselves also impassible and free from them for ever."[61] How does this work? Athanasius remains frustratingly silent to modern ears on the question of the interaction of divinity and humanity in Christ. Their integrity in Christ rather than their interaction was his chief concern, and he can hardly be blamed for failing to answer a question that we would like answered. Gavrilyuk suggests something of how we might conceive the matter: "Because of his impassibility the Logos enabled the human nature to undergo freely what were otherwise involuntary human experiences. The Logos, as Athanasius put it, 'permitted his body to weep and hunger,' and 'let his own body suffer.' The Logos temporarily suspended his power, allowing human nature to endure these experiences in a real way. The presence of the Logos secured Christ's freedom and control over these otherwise uncontrollable human experiences."[62]

Doesn't this make it all look too easy for Jesus, the one who "learned obedience through what he suffered" and "offered up prayers and supplications, with loud cries and tears, to him who was able to save him from death, and he was heard because of his reverence" (Heb. 5:7–8)? On the contrary. One could argue that the very nonnecessity of Christ's sufferings marks them as uniquely painful. Sinners suffer because of a tangled complex of inner disorder and outer attack. Jesus suffered despite his perfect inner order. As the incarnate Son, he remained free in the face of pain and so gave himself for us even as he suffered. We suffer in part because of ourselves. He suffered because of us, too. He suffered in spite of himself, though, in spite of his innocence and holiness—or rather, he suffered, too, because of himself, because he was none other than the Word who became flesh for us and our salvation. Gavrilyuk

Lord do them" (Athanasius, *Against the Arians* 3.32; emphasis added). The suffering belongs to the Word, who entered *into* it.

60. Athanasius, *Against the Arians* 3.56.
61. Athanasius, *Against the Arians* 3.34.
62. Gavrilyuk, *Suffering of the Impassible God*, 133–34.

explains: "The Word made human experiences his very own by transforming them from within: that which was violent, involuntary, tragically purposeless, and fatal for an ordinary human being was made voluntary, soteriologically purposeful, and life-giving in the ministry of the Word. The Word who is above suffering in his own nature suffered by appropriating human nature and obtained victory over suffering."[63]

This means eternal life in incorruptibility for us (the burden of Athanasius's *On the Incarnation*), but it equally means we are no longer slaves to sin and death and can live an "eternal kind of life" now.[64] This is our deification (what Athanasius can call our "making-God" or "son-making"[65]), in which the impassible Son makes us impassible. In his *Life of Antony*, Athanasius considers Antony the monk an exemplar who images the holiness and impassibility of Christ: "For joy and a settled state of soul show the holiness of him who is present."[66] Leithart expounds on this: "This does not mean that deified humans lack feeling. It means that they are not subjected to and enslaved by their feelings. They are determined by their soul's fixed orientation to the unchangeable God, which directs the bodily actions toward God. . . . What does an impassible human look like? For Athanasius, he or she looks like a martyr."[67] A martyr is far from indifferent; such a person is consumed with zeal for the Lord's house (Ps. 69:9; John 2:17). We can think of one's impassibility as one's unswervability, a wholehearted devotion in which the person's passions have been settled, catechized, and charged with the grandeur of God.

Now that we have examined the first point, that the Word really did become flesh, we can move on to our second point. This next point—that the Word remains himself—can be clarified by the third, namely, that his becoming is entirely and only ever "on our behalf" and for our sake. The telos of the incarnation is our salvation. If he had *not* become flesh, he could not have died. If he had not died, he would not have risen. "And if Christ has not been raised, your faith is futile and you are still in your sins" (1 Cor. 15:17).[68] We must not speak of a promotion of the Word, but rather of the exaltation of humanity in

---

63. Gavrilyuk, *Suffering of the Impassible God*, 175.
64. This is Dallas Willard's language. He explores the concept at length, lamenting its neglect in favor of merely future-oriented accounts of God's eternal life, in *Divine Conspiracy*.
65. Leithart, *Athanasius*, 159.
66. Athanasius, *Life of Antony* 36.
67. Leithart, *Athanasius*, 163.
68. If the heart of Scripture for Irenaeus is Rom. 5 (or possibly Eph. 1), for Athanasius it is 1 Cor. 15, with its promise that we will bear the image of the heavenly man as the perishable puts on imperishability and death is swallowed up in victory. So, e.g., he will speak of the Word "transfer[ring] our origin into Himself" that we "may be carried to heaven by Him" (*Against the Arians* 3.33).

him.[69] He came "to sanctify the flesh" and "hallow all by the Spirit," which he did throughout the course of his life.[70] "The Spirit's descent on Him in Jordan was a descent upon us, because of His bearing our body. And it did not take place for promotion to the Word, but again for our sanctification, that we might share His anointing."[71] The one who gives the Spirit received him on our behalf. The one "from [whose] fullness we have all received, grace upon grace" (John 1:16), received grace on our behalf, too. "For when humanity alone receives, it is liable to lose again what it has received (and this is shown by Adam, for he received and he lost). But in order that the grace may not be liable to loss, and may be guarded securely for humanity, He himself appropriates the gift."[72]

While we looked earlier at the nature, shape, and implications of the incarnation, here we do well to consider that the incarnation is most properly something that happens *to* us, or at least *for* us. "For as he for our sake became man, so we for his sake are exalted." This understanding guides Athanasius's exegesis: "So 'he gave to him,' that is, 'to us for his sake'; 'and he highly exalted him,' that is, 'us in him.'"[73] The point in God's becoming is that it might provide for humanity's becoming. "For He did not, when He became man, cease to be God; nor, whereas He is God does He shrink from what is man's; perish the thought; but rather, being God, He has taken to Him the flesh, and being in the flesh deifies the flesh."[74] He did what he did for us precisely as he became one of us. The entire arc stretching from incarnation to crucifixion constitutes Christ's "vicarious humanity" in which the incarnate Son offers the one, faithful human response to his Father's love, culminating in his self-sacrifice for sins, by which "he has perfected for all time those who are being sanctified" (Heb. 10:14).[75]

## The Father Must Have a Son

For Athanasius, it is axiomatic that God is the Father and that the Father must have a Son. Unlike human fathers, though, God does not become a father

69. Athanasius, *Against the Arians* 1.40–41, 3.52.
70. Athanasius, *Against the Arians* 2.10, 2.14.
71. Athanasius, *Against the Arians* 1.47; also see later in 1.47 and in 1.48.
72. Athanasius, *Against the Arians* 3.38; cited in Anatolios, *Athanasius*, 160. Concludes Anatolios: "The unsurpassable gift of the incarnation is that we were given the very reception of the gift" (161).
73. Athanasius, *Against the Arians* 4.7.
74. Athanasius, *Against the Arians* 3.38.
75. James Torrance and T. F. Torrance consistently championed the "vicarious humanity of Christ" and a renewed attention to Christ's priestly office in the second half of the twentieth century. See especially J. Torrance, "Vicarious Humanity of Christ"; J. Torrance, *Worship, Community and the Triune God of Grace*, 127–47; T. Torrance, *Mediation of Christ*.

when he grows up and gets married. He is ever Father, which means that there was never a time when the Son was not.[76] "For, a son not being, one cannot say father."[77] The Arian impulse is to discern in the Son one who at least in some meaningful sense comes *after* the Father, "but God, in that he ever is, is ever Father of the Son."[78] Indeed, such is the coequality of Father and Son that "the same things are said of the Son, which are said of the Father, except his being said to be Father."[79] Elsewhere Athanasius writes, "But they are ignorant that neither is the Father, qua Father, separated from the Son,—for the name carries that relationship with it,—nor is the Son expatriated from the Father. For the title Father denotes the common bond. But in their hands is the Spirit, who cannot be parted either from Him that sent or from Him that conveyed Him."[80]

At the end of the day, Athanasius's fight with Arius revolved around the question of whether the Son was properly understood as God or as a creature. From its earliest days, the Christian faith radically simplified the metaphysical options, such that only two remained: either Creator or creature. If the Son were not *ever* Son and "proper" to the Father, he would *have* to be a creature, as that is the only remaining category. God and only God is eternal, so any noneternal being is *by definition* part of God's creation. This means that the Son is neither Son as a product of God's willing nor Son by grace or participation; instead, he is Son and Word of God by nature.[81] The Son cannot be a son by the grace of participation, because that is how *we* are sons, and our being sons is contingent upon the eternal Son taking humanity to himself. He cannot be a son by will, because that suggests there is something prior to the Father, but "it were madness to place will and consideration between them."[82] God does not exist as God and then at some point decide to become a Father.[83] Instead, "as the Father is always good by nature, so he is always generative by nature." Still, "though it came not 'from will,' yet it is not without his pleasure or against his purpose."[84] "For the Son is the Father's All."[85] He does not

76. "Thus it belongs to the Godhead alone, that the Father is properly father, and the Son properly son [as opposed to humanity, where fathers are *not* properly fathers, nor sons properly sons]" (*Against the Arians* 1.21).
77. Athanasius, *Against the Arians* 3.6.
78. Athanasius, *Defence of the Nicene Council* 3.12.
79. Athanasius, *Against the Arians* 3.4.
80. Athanasius, *Defence of Dionysius* 17.
81. Athanasius, *Against the Arians* 3.63; 3.67; 3.6.
82. Athanasius, *Against the Arians* 3.66.
83. Thus Widdicombe: "The attributes of fatherhood and sonship, contingently expressed in human nature, are essentially expressed in the divine nature" (*Fatherhood of God*, 177).
84. Athanasius, *Against the Arians* 3.66.
85. Athanasius, *Against the Arians* 3.67.

derive from the Father's will but is himself the will of the Father.[86] Athanasius leaves no doubt on which side of the metaphysical divide the Son belongs: "The Son is not foreign, but proper to the Father's Essence."[87]

How are we to describe the unity of Father and Son? Nicaea opted for a nonscriptural word, confessing that the Son is *homoousios* ("of one being" or "essence") with the Father. In so doing, the Nicene fathers opened themselves to the charge of being extrabiblical in their theological formulations—a charge that quickly slides into that of being *non-* or even *anti-*biblical. It might, for instance, strike one as intuitively illicit to formulate dogma on the basis of a theological judgment alien to Scripture.

But this is precisely where the charge loses its way. Its superficial appeal to a properly "biblical" theology suggests a hermeneutical naivete in which one fails to take into account the whole in discovering the part. The word *homoousios* may not be found in any verse in the Bible, but the whole of Scripture steers us toward the conclusion that the Son is "of one being" with the Father. The "extrabiblical" charge could suggest a vicious intent. The Arian heresy "affects to array herself in Scripture language."[88] The heretics "pretend like their 'father the devil' to study and to quote the language of Scripture, in order that they may appear by their words to have a right belief."[89] As Jesus's contest with the devil in the wilderness demonstrates, mere appeal to Scripture hardly establishes orthodoxy.[90]

The converse likewise holds. "Yet, though a man use terms not in Scripture, it makes no difference so that his meaning be religious."[91] Athanasius discerns a difference between merely using the words of the Bible and adhering to its meaning or sense: "Even if the expressions are not in so many words in the Scriptures, yet, as was said before, they contain the sense of the Scriptures."[92] One must grasp the "scope and character of Holy Scripture," which "contains a double account of the Saviour; that He was ever God, and is the Son, being

---

86. "The Son is identified with this essential will, as the intra-divine ground for what eventually comes to be as the external effects of God's will" (Anatolios, *Athanasius*, 122, discussing Athanasius, *Against the Arians* 2.2). The priority of the immanent Trinity "itself constitutes a positive subsequent relation with creation" in which "creation is second to begetting precisely as derivative of the divine begetting" (122–23). The burden of Anatolios's book is to establish the radical transcendence of God vis-à-vis creation, *by virtue of which* God stands in positive relation with the creation, which participates in him for its very existence.

87. Athanasius, *Against the Arians* 2.82.

88. Athanasius, *Against the Arians* 1.1; also see 1.8.

89. Athanasius, *Circular to Bishops of Egypt and Libya* 4.

90. See Matt. 4:1–11; Mark 1:12–13; Luke 4:1–13.

91. Athanasius, *On the Councils of Ariminum and Seleucia* 39.

92. Athanasius, *Defence of the Nicene Council* 5.21. As Gregory of Nazianzus puts it with reference to the Trinity, some things are "meant, though not mentioned" by Scripture (*Or.* 31.24).

the Father's Word and Radiance and Wisdom; and that afterwards for us He took flesh of a Virgin, Mary Bearer of God, and was made man."[93] How do we know this isn't a case of special pleading? How does Athanasius know *this* is what Scripture is about? Admittedly, there is something circular in Athanasius's hermeneutic. But we need not find this unsettling. As Athanasius moves from the part to the whole and back again, in long, patient exegetical work, it turns out that it makes good sense of Scripture, revealing a unified depth to the Bible that is at once a more sophisticated and a simpler account than that offered by the Arians.[94]

Back to the *homoousion*.[95] While Athanasius did not make much of the term early in his career—"during the years 326–50 the term *homoousios* is rarely if every mentioned" by anybody—as his fight with the Arians continued, he turned to it as an Archimedean point.[96] "For the precision of this phrase detects their pretence. . . . This phrase only, as detecting their heresy, do they dread; which the Fathers set down as a bulwark against their irreligious notions one and all."[97] Nestled in this little technical term are the key theological moves necessary to preserve the apostolic testimony, the biblical witness, the gospel itself. Therefore, "we must conceive of Son's and Father's oneness in the way of essence."[98] The Son is of the essence of the Father and, as Athanasius frequently puts it, "proper" to him.[99] And this is an identity, not a mere likeness, of essence.[100] To name the Father is to name the Son.[101]

93. Athanasius, *Against the Arians* 3.29.

94. See primarily Athanasius, *Against the Arians*, for extended discussions of Ps. 95:7–8; Prov. 8:22; 9:1; Matt. 11:27; 26:39; Mark 13:32; Luke 2:52; John 3:35; 10:30; 12:27; 14:10; 17:3; Phil. 2:9–10; Heb. 1:4; 3:2.

95. *Homoousion* is the noun form; *homoousios* is the adjective form.

96. Ayres, *Nicaea and Its Legacy*, 431.

97. Athanasius, *On the Councils of Ariminum and Seleucia* 45. For all his vigilance, Athanasius could take a mediating position with certain (former) opponents: "Those, however, who accept everything else that was defined at Nicaea, and doubt only about the Coessential, must not be treated as enemies; nor do we here attack them as Ariomaniacs, nor as opponents of the Fathers, but we discuss the matter with them as brothers with brothers, who mean what we mean, and dispute only about the word" (41).

98. Athanasius, *On the Councils of Ariminum and Seleucia* 48; also see 52: "For what is it to be thus connatural with the Father, but to be one in essence with Him? For God attached not to Him the Son from without, as needing a servant."

99. Athanasius, *Against the Arians* 1.16.

100. Athanasius, *On the Councils of Ariminum and Seleucia* 53. At the same time, the identity of essence does not flatten the distinctions between persons. "Athanasius argues that the primary sense of the term *homoousios* implies a relationship of derivation" and "an intrinsic asymmetry to" the relation of Father and Son and consequently never describes the Father as *homoousios* with the Son (Behr, *Nicene Faith*, 244).

101. Athanasius, *Against the Arians* 2.41.

One cannot downgrade, criticize, or jeopardize the Son without doing the same to the Father; an "assault upon the Son makes the blasphemy recoil upon the Father," so that "he who dishonours the Son, dishonours also the Father."[102] If the Arians claim that there was a time when the Son was not, then they must have the courage of their convictions and admit that there was a time when the *Father* was not. Far from protecting God by demoting the Son, the Arians, in demoting the Son, unravel God himself.

Athanasius grounds God's creating and revealing in the eternal unity of Father and Son, in that each person is proper to the other. The Son is "the Hand . . . through whom the Father made all things," so that "if God be without Son, then he is without Work; for the Son is his Offspring through whom he works."[103] "And if through Him He creates and makes, He is not Himself of things created and made; but rather He is the Word of the Creator God."[104] Apart from the Son, the Father would not be Creator. Apart from the Son, he would likewise not be revealed.

Two of Athanasius's favorite images for the relation of Father and Son are that of a light and a fountain: "For the Son is in the Father, as it is allowed us to know, because the whole Being of the Son is proper to the Father's essence, as radiance from light, and stream from fountain; so that whoso sees the Son, sees what is proper to the Father, and knows that the Son's Being, because from the Father, is therefore in the Father. . . . For whoso thus contemplates the Son, contemplates what is proper to the Father's Essence, and knows that the Father is in the Son."[105] To mix the metaphors, the radiance of the light meets us downstream from the fountain, but it really does communicate the source, without change or distortion. In meeting the radiance and the stream, we meet the light and the fountain. There are not two lights, but one light and its radiance, and this is "fitly expressed" by the term "Coessential."[106]

Notice the way in which the term *"homoousios"* carries epistemological as well as ontological implications. In a synodical letter to the African bishops,

102. Athanasius, *Against the Arians* 1.25; 1.18.
103. Athanasius, *Against the Arians* 4.26; 4.4.
104. Athanasius, *Against the Arians* 2.22. Also 2.21: "For none of things which are brought to be is an efficient cause, but all things were made through the Word: who would not have wrought all things, were He Himself in the number of the creatures."
105. Athanasius, *Against the Arians* 3.3. On the image of light and radiance, see Athanasius, *Defence of the Nicene Council* 5.23–24; *Defence of Dionysius* 8; *Circular to Bishops of Egypt and Libya* 13; *Against the Arians* 2.2; 2.31; 2.35; 2.41; 2.42; 3.3; 3.13; 3.15; *On the Councils of Ariminum and Seleucia* 41, 52; *Synodal Letter to the Bishops of Africa* 6.
106. Athanasius, *On the Councils of Ariminum and Seleucia* 52, 41. While drawn to the imagery of light and fountain, Gregory of Nazianzus suggests their insufficiency (*Or.* 31.31–33). On the other hand, Leithart argues that "one paradigm cleanses another" (Leithart, *Athanasius*, 46).

Athanasius pairs John 10:30 and John 14:9 in a Nicene light: "And the meaning 'Coessential' is known from the Son not being a Creature or thing made . . . and he that calls him 'coessential,' calls the Son of God genuinely and truly so; and he that calls him genuinely Son understands the texts, 'I and the Father are one,' and 'he that hath seen Me hath seen the Father.'"[107] The *homoousios* serves as a hermeneutical key for Scripture here. Athanasius might also have called on John 1:18: "No one has ever seen God; the only God, who is at the Father's side, he has made him known." Rowan Williams argues that central to Arius's concerns was an apophatically charged notion of divine transcendence (making Arius a heretical Denys the Areopagite, if you will), according to which God is utterly unknowable, whereas Athanasius found in God one who "transcends his transcendence."[108] Thus, the debate over Nicaea can be seen as one about the character of God's transcendence and the related question of whether the one who "dwells in unapproachable light, whom no one has ever seen or can see" (1 Tim. 6:16) can manifest himself and make himself known, and if so, how.[109] If no one has ever seen God, and if the Son is *not* of one being with the Father, then the Son cannot have made him known in a fully reliable way and his claim to be transparent to the Father (John 14:9) is a lie. The incarnate Word can be a true revelation *of* God only if he *is* God. And, "for Athanasius, *what* the Son reveals about God is exactly *that* God is his Father."[110]

### Questioning Eternal Generation

Needless to say, Athanasius held to the eternal generation of the Son. For "whoso considers the Son an offspring, rightly considers Him also as 'coessential.'"[111] Recently, however, this position has again been called into question, and not only by revisionists. Three questions arise.

First, is "eternal generation" a coherent concept? After all, generation as we know it is always a derivative reality. One is generated from another. A child is generated from previously existing parents. To speak of *eternal* generation is, one might think, simply incoherent. Generation occurs in time, and furthermore, it involves a change in the generator. Adam and Eve become the parents of Cain and Abel in generating children; they become something they

107. Athanasius, *Synodal Letter to the Bishops of Africa* 9.
108. See R. Williams, *Arius*, 235–45 (esp. 242–43); R. Williams, *Wound of Knowledge*, 60.
109. Note that it is *Christ* in this passage who dwells in unapproachable light!
110. R. Jenson, *Triune Identity*, 83.
111. Athanasius, *On the Councils of Ariminum and Seleucia* 42.

were not previously. Consider: Have *you* ever known an eternally enduring generation, one without beginning or end? To speak of generation is to speak of generation's end in the one generated. If the Son is eternally generated, does that mean he is never fully generated? Or that he is generated anew every moment?

Of course, *all* speech about God is analogical. When calling God "Father," one does not move flatly from human paternity to divine paternity.[112] So an objection amounting to "That's not how it works for people!" cannot disqualify the idea of eternal generation. Indeed, Athanasius calls it "a grievous error, to have material thoughts about what is immaterial," speaking of "the impassibility and indivisibility of such a generation from the Father."[113] And "in saying 'offspring,' we have no human thoughts. . . . We entertain no material ideas concerning Him . . . we think suitably of God, for He is not as man."[114] In our zeal for conceptual coherence, surely right in itself, we ought not to presume to associate God's nature too closely with our own, and thereby pluck out the mystery of the manner of God's being triune.

The second question posed to eternal generation, and one receiving renewed interest these days, is whether it is a *biblical* concept. To determine this, one would have to consider individual proof texts (as Athanasius does at length throughout his orations against the Arians) as well as the global witness of Scripture.[115] The questions regarding particular proof texts focus on the translation of terms (Does the frequent Johannine use of *monogenēs* mean "one of a kind" or "only begotten"?) and whether language of the Son's begottenness describes a point in time—at the first moment of creation, at Jesus's baptism, or perhaps at the resurrection.[116] Regardless of how one translates *monogenēs*, it is clear in the Johannine literature that Jesus's sonship is unique in kind, different from any other sonship precisely in that this Son enables others to be sons. Here the Johannine and Pauline witnesses harmonize in the declaration that only those who abide in Christ the Son and receive his Spirit are adopted as sons. Theologically, we can say that this one is "one of a kind" precisely as he is "only begotten," and only because he is can he become the "firstborn" of many brethren. "For the term 'Only-begotten' is used where

112. In fact, Eph. 3:15 suggests that we understand human paternity on the basis of divine paternity—though again, here the move is analogical rather than univocal.
113. Athanasius, *Against the Arians* 1.15; *On the Councils of Ariminum and Seleucia* 41.
114. Athanasius, *On the Councils of Ariminum and Seleucia* 42.
115. The importance of the return to an explicitly theological interpretation of Scripture here cannot be overstated. For an introduction, see Billings, *Word of God for the People of God*; Treier, *Introducing Theological Interpretation of Scripture*.
116. The Johannine uses of *monogenēs* occur in John 1:14, 18; 3:16, 18; and 1 John 4:9. For a helpful overview of exegetical and theological objections, see Letham, *Holy Trinity*, 383–89.

there are no brethren, but 'First-born' because of brethren."[117] A similar point can be made with reference to a purported beginning to Christ's generation. While particular passages might gesture to the declaration or vindication of his sonship at, say, the baptism or resurrection, only one who is eternally Son and therefore fully God can reconcile alienated humanity to the Father and grant them his Spirit of adoption.

Finally, we might reasonably ask whether eternal generation is a *necessary* concept. That is, could we affirm the same points without recourse to eternal generation, possibly avoiding the complications it introduces? Are there simpler, more exegetically sound bases from which to argue the Son's divinity in the context of a trinitarian reading of Scripture? Here we do well to keep in mind that the point of eternal generation is to foreground the Father-Son relationship in the doctrine of God and to insist that this relationship is none other than who God was, is, and will be (if you'll pardon the temporal categories). The mechanics of generation can be unduly distracting, when the point is that the Father eternally has a Son who is his perfect image and that they are related (at least) by personal derivation. But this wording immediately raises the question of whether generation implies subordination, and if so, whether this introduces a kind of hierarchy that compromises the coequality of Father and Son. It is better, though, and in keeping with patristic counsel to discretion, to chasten our judgments and simply say that however the second person of the Trinity is toward the first person, he is so as Son.

Athanasius drew the line clearly—either this one is a son by nature, and so never not a son, or a son by grace, and so not always, or at least not necessarily, so.[118] Or to change the idiom, either one is (eternally) begotten of the Father or one is made a son (in time). The Son's eternal begottenness names both *that* he is God (having been begotten of the Father's being, not made from nothing) and *how* he is God (as the Son of the Father). This understanding falls in step with the creedal exposition of Jesus Christ as "begotten, not made, of one being [*homoousios*] with the Father." And if he is not the coessential Son of the Father, we are still in our sins, none of us sons by adoption.

117. Athanasius, *Against the Arians* 2.62.
118. Charles Hodge puts it this way: "The Council [of Nicaea] decided that the word Son as applied to Christ, is not a term of office but of nature; that it expresses the relation which the Second Person in the Trinity from eternity bears to the First Person, and that the relation thus indicated is sameness of nature, so that sonship, in the case of Christ, includes equality with God. In other words, God was in such a sense his Father that He was equal with God" (*Systematic Theology*, 1:471).

## The Only Begotten Becomes the Firstborn[119]

The Word became flesh in order that the Father might have a quiver full of sons (see Ps. 127:3–5). But whereas a bumper crop of babies is a sign of God's blessing to a man, a houseful of adopted sons and daughters is a sign of God's prior blessedness. Utterly happy in the divine life, God can extend that life to his creation freely, easily, without thought of loss or reward. The end of the incarnation is the family of God, the church, but it is an end entirely unnecessary for God.[120]

Where the Arians, and really where all heretical attempts to guard the Godness of God, go astray is in reckoning that divinity is best protected by cordoning it off from contact with creation. On the contrary, in Athanasius's blunt maxim: "He, indeed, assumed humanity that we might become God."[121] God does more than come into contact with creation; he takes on humanity and enables humanity to even become God. Such deification is mediated through the Son, of course. Our deification is our becoming "conformed to the image of his Son, in order that he might be the firstborn among many brothers" (Rom. 8:29).

Saint Antony is the paradigmatic case of such a brother, "a new man recreated in Christ, the new Adam."[122] In his *Life of Antony*, Athanasius fleshes out his own theology even as he conceptualizes the spiritual lives of the desert fathers, with whom he spent six years during one of his exiles. In Antony, we see the fruits of the second Adam's defanging of death; "as the old Adam had founded, in a lush garden, a city of sin and death, so Antony now founded, in a barren desert, a new city of holiness and life."[123] Having learned from and imitated the virtue of the saints in his town, the monk eventually migrated to the desert, where he fought the devil and mortified the flesh. Antony recalls: "How often in the desert has [a demon] displayed what resembled gold, that I should only touch it and look on it. I sang psalms against him, and he vanished away. Often [demons] would beat me with stripes, and I repeated again and again, 'Nothing shall separate me from the love of Christ,' and at this they rather fell to beating one another."[124] Antony knew that Christ must be God himself for his love to

---

119. See Leithart, *Athanasius*, 151.

120. That divine faithfulness renders the incarnation "fitting" and even in some sense "necessary" ought not to obscure the nonnecessity of God's creating or, though in a different sense, of his redeeming.

121. Athanasius, *On the Incarnation* 54.

122. Weinandy, *Athanasius*, 131.

123. Weinandy, *Athanasius*, 131. Though the *Life* was written later in his episcopal career, early on "Athanasius already possessed a theology that embraced the values of asceticism, yet made room for ordinary Christians" (Brakke, *Athanasius and Asceticism*, 268).

124. Athanasius, *Life of Antony* 40.

bind Antony so strongly to himself, and so he hurried back to Alexandria at one point to denounce Arius and teach the true faith regarding Christ.[125]

The true faith begins with the utter uniqueness of the Son's generation. Indeed, to say "Son by nature" is to say "not a creature."[126] Such a distinction carries soteriological implications: "If the Son were a creature, man had remained mortal as before, not being joined to God; for a creature had not joined creatures to God . . . ; nor would a portion of the creation have been the creation's salvation, as needing salvation itself."[127] It is precisely by establishing the Son's utter uniqueness that Athanasius can establish our being sons (and daughters) by the grace of participating in the life of the Son.[128] Jesus is not a spoiled only child but the perfectly generous Son of a perfectly generous Father, eager to share all he is and has with an ever-increasing family. In the Son we are "joined to God." "We are not sons by nature, but the Son who is in us . . . God is not our Father by nature, but of that Word in us, in whom and because of whom we cry, 'Abba, Father.'"[129] So it is that "we are made sons through him by adoption and grace, as partaking of his Spirit," though Athanasius also writes that "we by imitation become virtuous and sons."[130] We "could not become sons, being by nature creatures, otherwise than by receiving the Spirit of the natural and true Son."[131] We are not dehumanized in this, for "we shall be such, not as the Father is by nature in the Son and the Son in the Father, but according to our own nature."[132]

125. Athanasius, *Life of Antony* 69. This crucial element in Athanasius's life of Antony gives the lie to impatient dismissals of quibbles over theological terms like "*homoousios*" as irrelevant to Christian spirituality and the life of the church.

126. Athanasius, *Defence of the Nicene Council* 3.13.

127. Athanasius, *Against the Arians* 2.69.

128. In applying the category of "sonship" to men *and women* adopted in Christ, I in no way intend to establish a gendered hierarchy; instead, "sonship" follows the Pauline logic of our inclusion in God's family by virtue of being united with the Son and receiving the Spirit of sonship. That is, it makes transparent our becoming by grace what the second person of the Trinity is by nature.

129. Athanasius, *Against the Arians* 2.59.

130. Athanasius, *Against the Arians* 3.19. Leithart offers a plausible harmony: "We become sons by grace, and our growth in sonship comes about through grace-empowered effort, through imitation (*mimesis*)." Athanasius emphasizes "the transition from an 'extrinsic' to an 'intrinsic' gift of grace" (Leithart, *Athanasius*, 165, 158).

131. Athanasius, *Against the Arians* 2.59. There is much more to be said about the Spirit here. "For what the Word has by nature, as I said, in the Father, that He wishes to be given to us through the Spirit irrevocably. . . . It is the Spirit then which is in God, and not we viewed in our own selves; and as we are sons and gods because of the Word in us, so we shall be in the Son and in the Father, and we shall be accounted to have become one in Son and in Father, because that Spirit is in us, which is in the Word which is in the Father" (3.25). Also see the *Letters to Serapion*.

132. Athanasius, *Against the Arians* 3.20.

Robert Jenson puts the point in a characteristically quirky, yet probing way: "God can indeed, if he chooses, accommodate other persons in his life without distorting that life. God, to state it as boldly as possible, is roomy. Indeed, if we were to list divine attributes, roominess would have to come next after jealousy. He can, if he chooses, distinguish himself from others not by excluding them but by including them."[133] In this case, the Father distinguishes himself from the Son precisely by being the Father of the Son, and the Triune God distinguishes himself from humanity by including us within the divine life. It takes a God to make gods, we might say. It takes one who is Son by nature to make sons by grace.

### "And in the Holy Spirit"

In its original formulation, the Nicene Creed said only five words about the third person of the Trinity: "And in the Holy Spirit." That was it. Waging a war on a different front, the Nicene fathers contented themselves with a brief reference to the Spirit in their formal encapsulation of Christian belief. They could be forgiven for their benign neglect, what amounted more to an assumption of the Spirit's coequal status with the Father and the Son than any questioning, much less downgrading, of his divinity. When the creed was expanded at the Council of Constantinople in 381, it acknowledged the Spirit as "Lord and giver of life, who proceeds from the Father, who with the Father and the Son together is worshiped and glorified." Anyone who is Lord is God. Anyone who is worshiped and glorified (and that with the Father and Son) is God. While the creed did not extend the *homoousion* to the Spirit directly, all the entailments of coessentiality were there.

In recognizing the incarnation of the eternal Son as Athanasius's leitmotif, we must not miss the elaboration of that theme in a trinitarian counterpoint. While this fugue is never out of earshot, we can hear it most prominently later in Athanasius's career, especially in the letters he wrote to Bishop Serapion. These letters display a robust theology of Word and Spirit. For example, "And we are justified, as the Spirit said, *in the name of our Lord Jesus Christ and in the Spirit of God* [1 Cor. 6.11]. For the Spirit is not divided from the Word."[134] Athanasius recognized that decisions made regarding the Spirit run parallel to those made regarding the Son. In both cases it is fundamental to discern the right side of the ontological divide—Son and Spirit, who are both "of one being with the Father," are God and do the works of God. That

---

133. R. Jenson, *Systematic Theology 1*, 226.
134. Athanasius, *Letters to Serapion* 1.31.3.

much Nicaea made clear. "For this Synod of Nicaea is in truth a proscription of every heresy. It also upsets those who blaspheme the Holy Spirit, and call Him a Creature."[135] In the letters to Serapion, Athanasius sets his sights on those he names the Tropikoi, "those who have been deceived about the Spirit through a certain 'mode of exegesis.'"[136] Their error corresponds to that of the Arians: "For just as Arians by denying the Son also deny the Father, so too these people by disparaging the Holy Spirit also disparage the Son."[137] As with his strategy in his orations against the Arians, in these letters Athanasius moves through detailed exegetical arguments in countering the Tropikoi.

It is one thing to align the Spirit with the Father and Son as Creator rather than creature. These three are one God. But it is another thing to ask *how* they are one God. We have explored at length the way in which the Father reveals himself and saves the world he made through the incarnation of his Son. What can we say of the Spirit in the economy of salvation? Recall here Athanasius's description of the Son as the radiance of the Father's light (drawn from Heb. 1:3). Athanasius extends the image: "Thus the Father is Light and his Radiance is the Son . . . and so we are also permitted to see in the Son the Spirit in whom we are enlightened. For it says: *may he give you the Spirit of Wisdom and of revelation in the knowledge of him, having the eyes of your hearts enlightened* [Eph. 1.17–18]."[138] When we look at the Father we see the Son, and the actuality of our seeing him—our enlightenment—is the work of the Spirit. The Spirit, we might say, is the successful arrival of the sun's radiance as we are given eyes to see God in the clear light of day. Athanasius similarly extends the image of the fountain: "And again, the Father is the Fountain and the Son is called the River, and so we are said to drink of the Spirit." And yet "when we drink of the Spirit, we drink of Christ."[139] The Spirit's work is to bring completion to divine action, to bring all of God's ways with the world to their proper term. The Spirit is the one "in whom the Father through the Word perfects and renews all things."[140]

Later in the same letter Athanasius repeats this move: "For wherever there is Light, there is also Radiance; and wherever there is Radiance, there is its activity and luminous grace."[141] He picks up Paul's benediction—"The grace of our Lord Jesus Christ and the love of God and the fellowship of the Holy

135. Athanasius, *Synodal Letter to the Bishops of Africa* 11.
136. Athanasius, *Letters to Serapion* 1.2.2.
137. Athanasius, *Letters to Serapion* 1.1.3.
138. Athanasius, *Letters to Serapion* 1.19.3.
139. Athanasius, *Letters to Serapion* 1.19.4.
140. Athanasius, *Letters to Serapion* 1.9.7. In Kevin Vanhoozer's words: "The Father initiates, the Son executes, and the Spirit perfects" (*Drama of Doctrine*, 43).
141. Athanasius, *Letters to Serapion* 1.30.5.

Spirit be with you all" (2 Cor. 13:14)—commenting that "this grace and gift given in the Trinity is given by the Father through the Son in the Holy Spirit."[142] The Spirit of fellowship includes us in the grace and love of Father and Son. Apart from him, we are "strange and distant from God, and by the participation of the Spirit we are knit into the Godhead; so that our being in the Father is not ours, but is the Spirit's which is in us and abides in us."[143] Similarly, "there is one holiness which comes from the Father through the Son in the Holy Spirit."[144] From—through—in: here is the trinitarian dynamic in the economy of salvation.[145] "For there is nothing which is not brought into being and actualized through the Word in the Spirit."[146] "The Father creates all things through the Word in the Spirit. For where the Word is, there also is the Spirit, and the things created through the Word have their strength to exist through the Spirit from the Word."[147]

We are made sons as the Father adopts us in Christ by the power of the Spirit. "Our salvation therefore consists in our being included within the embrace wherein the Father 'delights' in the Son."[148] In receiving the Spirit of adoption, we are joined to Christ, through whom we are brought to the Father's household. This is another variation on the basic grammar in which the Father accomplishes his work through the Son in the Spirit.

This trinitarian grammar does not describe three acts but the "one activity of the Trinity. The Apostle does not mean [in 2 Cor. 13:14] that the gifts given by each are different and distinct, but that whatever gift is given is given in the Trinity, and that all the gifts are from the one God."[149] Commenting on 1 Corinthians 12:4–6, Athanasius writes: "The gifts which the Spirit distributes to each are bestowed by the Father through the Word. For all that the Father has is the Son's. Thus what is given by the Son in the Spirit is a gift of the Father. And when the Spirit is in us, the Word who gives the Spirit is

---

142. Athanasius, *Letters to Serapion* 1.30.6.

143. Athanasius, *Against the Arians* 3.24.

144. Athanasius, *Letters to Serapion* 1.20.4.

145. While this represents the best summary of the trinitarian dynamic, it should be used to elucidate, not elide, Scripture's description of "the three persons of the Trinity as standing in a large number of relations to each other." Fred Sanders laments traditional trinitarian theology's neglect of "the immanent-trinitarian implications of many parts of the story of the economic Trinity," rarely moving beyond consideration of relations of origin, and calls for the development of "categories adequate to the multiplicity and many-sidedness of the economic relations among Father, Son, and Spirit" as well as "a consistent hermeneutic for the economic evidence" (Sanders, *Image of the Immanent Trinity*, 178, 179, 177, 182).

146. Athanasius, *Letters to Serapion* 1.31.2.

147. Athanasius, *Letters to Serapion* 2.14.1.

148. This is Anatolios's summary of Athanasius's view (*Athanasius*, 210).

149. Athanasius, *Letters to Serapion* 1.31.1.

in us, and the Father is in the Word. And so it is just as has been said: *I and the Father will come and make our home with him* [Jn 14.23]."[150] It is not that the Spirit is the one of the Trinity who is near us, while Father and Son remain far off. Rather, the one God comes to make his home in his people as the Word is made flesh and dwells among us and as the Spirit dwells in us as "the temple of the living God" (2 Cor. 6:16). To have the Spirit is to have the Son is to have the Father. Those who have the Spirit of adoption as sons cry with Jesus, "Abba, Father!" (Rom. 8:15; Gal. 4:6).[151] Without the ministry of the Holy Spirit, the incarnation of the Word avails nothing. The Spirit gives and glorifies the Son, who pours him out on believers, making them sons in the Son. The Spirit "is given from the Son to all people and all that he has is the Son's."[152] The Spirit anoints us with the aroma of Christ and seals us with his form, and so "it is perfectly clear that the Spirit cannot be a creature."[153] "Who will join you to God if you do not have the Spirit of God himself but the spirit of the created order?"[154] We see again the soteriological necessity of the *homoousion*, this time as applied to the Spirit.

It does not take long to recognize that God the Son forms the center of Athanasius's theological vision. By way of conclusion, let's look at how God the Son travels its circumference, thereby establishing its scope and overall shape. Consider Paul's words to the Colossians:

> He is the image of the invisible God, the firstborn of all creation. For by him all things were created, in heaven and on earth, visible and invisible, whether thrones or dominions or rulers or authorities—all things were created through him and for him. And he is before all things, and in him all things hold together. And he is the head of the body, the church. He is the beginning, the firstborn from the dead, that in everything he might be preeminent. For in him all the fullness of God was pleased to dwell, and through him to reconcile to himself all things, whether on earth or in heaven, making peace by the blood of his cross. (Col. 1:15–20)

While not as central to Athanasius's debates with the Arian parties, Paul's words here nicely gather up the polemics and Athanasius's larger constructive

---

150. Athanasius, *Letters to Serapion* 1.30.4–5.
151. Athanasius, *Letters to Serapion* 1.25.4.
152. Athanasius, *Letters to Serapion* 2.10.4. See also *Against the Arians* 3.24.
153. Athanasius, *Letters to Serapion* 2.12.3.
154. Athanasius, *Letters to Serapion* 1.29.2. "So then, in the Spirit the Word glorifies creatures, and after he has divinized them and made them sons of God, he leads them to the Father. But that which joins creatures to the Word cannot be a creature. And that which makes creatures sons cannot be foreign to the Son" (1.25.5).

concerns. At first glance, the passage lends itself to an Arian exposition. Christ is (merely) the "firstborn of all creation." This status may afford him pride of place and possibly an exalted, unique status within creation, but it has little need for him to be God. The same goes for him being "firstborn from the dead," with the resurrection marking Christ as, perhaps, a second Adam, whose history holds the key to human history but, again, not necessarily God. We might even squint at the reference to Jesus as the "image of the invisible God" and find in him a being who mediates between God and humanity by occupying a midpoint between them as some sort of ontological middle manager.[155]

Athanasius insists, however, that "it is proper to the Word to work the Father's works and not to be external to Him"; "nor is there a thing which God says or does, but He says and does it in the Word."[156] To argue that the Father needs a middleman is to suggest that he cannot do his own work. In becoming flesh, the Word mediated between Creator and creation not by providing a diplomatic buffer but by reconciling God and humanity in and through his own flesh. And precisely this *is* the Father's work, for "the Son can do nothing of his own accord, but only what he sees the Father doing. For whatever the Father does, that the Son does likewise" (John 5:19). The Son (and the Spirit) are the way in which the Father is present to his creation.

Already, then, we see the Arian bind: in seeking to preserve the transcendence of God and take seriously some passages of Scripture, they handcuff God, eliminating the possibility that the Father accomplishes his works with his own two hands and quarantining him from contact with creation. This limitation defames the Father as much as the Son by denying that the Father can directly create, reign, or redeem and by denying that the Son is any more than an exalted intermediary.[157] On the contrary, insists Paul, "all the fullness of God was pleased to dwell" in Christ. Note the repetitions—"all" and "fullness" (as if some of one's fullness could dwell in another)—and the sheer pleasure with which God dwells in Christ, reconciling the world to himself through him. In retrospect, Paul can confess that the one who struck him blind on the Damascus Road, the one in whom the fullness of God dwells, is the very image of God, is the one by, through, and for whom *all* things were created, who is *before* all things, who has *reconciled* all things, and who will

---

155. On the contrast between a middleman and one who mediates as God and man, see Gunton, *Father, Son and Holy Spirit*, 166–67.

156. Athanasius, *Against the Arians* 2.20; 3.8.

157. Athanasius adds that, if the Word were a creature as mediator, another would be needed, and another, and another, resulting in an infinite regress (*Defense of the Nicene Definition* 3.8; also see *Against the Arians* 2.26).

be found preeminent in all things.[158] Anyone who is what Paul says Jesus is, who does what Paul says Jesus does, must be begotten, not made, of one being with the Father, himself the Creator of creatures.[159]

158. "Athanasius grounds the creative ability of God within his own being, as dependent upon his generative nature, for it is by his Son that creation came to be" (Behr, *Nicene Faith*, 245).

159. Athanasius, *Circular to Bishops of Egypt and Libya* 14.

# 3

# "THE LOVELY THINGS KEPT ME FAR FROM YOU"

## The Wayward Loves of Augustine

As he begins his *Confessions*, Augustine declares, "To praise you is the desire of man, a little piece of your creation. You stir man to take pleasure in praising you, because you have made us for yourself, and our heart is restless until it rests in you."[1] Praise comes naturally for us, made as we are by and for the living God. What's more, praising God is pleasurable; it's what we want to do. In fact, praise is "*the* desire of man," his greatest desire, perhaps his only *real* desire. And so it is in praising that we find peace, our heart finding its home in God.

Given all this, what is striking about Augustine's confession (and what suggests its scrupulous honesty) is its itinerary—a series of fits and starts, in which Augustine resembles not a pilgrim so much as a kid at a county fair, dazzled by lights and sounds, running from booth to booth, gorging himself on cotton candy and deep-fried everything. He zigs and zags, with little sense of direction, following the siren's song of pleasure—now this way, now that. An older Augustine laments his restless wandering: "Late have I loved you, beauty so old and so new: late have I loved you. And see, you were within and I was in the external world and sought you there, and in my unlovely state I plunged into those lovely created things which you made. You were with me,

1. Augustine, *Confessions* 1.1.1.

63

and I was not with you. The lovely things kept me far from you, though if they did not have their existence in you, they had no existence at all."[2] The beautiful One was with Augustine, but the beautiful things kept Augustine far from beauty itself. Yet, as he immediately acknowledges, they exist only in this One, from whom they keep Augustine. Here is the puzzle of Augustine's life: How could it be that these lovely things, made—and made lovely—by God himself, keep Augustine away from the One by whom and in whom they exist? Could Augustine be right? Is this, perhaps, a smokescreen, hiding the real source of alienation, Augustine himself?

## Augustine's Life

Augustine of Hippo (354–430) was born in Thagaste (in modern Algeria), a small town (at least by modern standards) of maybe a couple thousand people. His parents were not rich, though his father did own a bit of land and Augustine received an education—though never taking much of a liking to Greek. His Catholic mother, Monica, was a close and frequent presence in Augustine's life, so much so that he snuck off without telling her when he left Africa for Rome. She was instrumental, too, in his conversion, long interceding in prayer (and otherwise) for her son. They shared a mystical vision just before her death, ascending "by reflection and dialogue . . . to the region of inexhaustible abundance where [God feeds] Israel eternally with truth for food."[3] His pagan father, Patrick, became a Christian only late in life, dying not long after Augustine moved to Carthage when he was still a teenager.[4]

In Carthage, Augustine began to teach rhetoric, attached himself as a hearer in the Manichaean religion, and entered a fifteen-year relationship with a woman he never names.[5] He seems to have loved her deeply, and they soon had a son, Adeodatus. (She was later dismissed in favor of a more socially advantageous marriage—to a girl not yet twelve years old—never to occur. Adeodatus died as a teenager.) Eventually, Augustine moved to Rome, flirted with skepticism for a spell, and after a few years moved to Milan to take a new job as a professor of rhetoric (a sort of propaganda minister).[6] There he encountered the great Bishop Ambrose, whose spiritual interpretation of Scripture, keen intellect, and catholic imagination attracted Augustine. In

2. Augustine, *Confessions* 10.27.38.
3. Augustine, *Confessions* 9.19.24.
4. Chadwick, *Augustine*, 6.
5. Brown, *Augustine of Hippo*, 27.
6. Brown, *Augustine of Hippo*, 58–59. This was in autumn of 384; Monica arrived a few months later, in late spring 385.

Milan, around the age of thirty-two, he finally converted to Christ, being baptized in the church the following Easter.

Moving back to Africa, Augustine and his friends pursued a monastic life for a time until Augustine was forcibly ordained in the church in Hippo (North Africa's second greatest port) in 391. Even as bishop, Augustine set up a strict monastic life in common. In effect, one could not be a priest in Hippo without also being a monk.[7] He lived through a number of controversies while bishop, chief among which were the Donatist and Pelagian controversies. Hippo was largely Donatist when Augustine arrived, though it had become Catholic by the time he died in August 430 in the midst of the Vandals' takeover of Hippo.[8]

Before moving on to consider the role of love in Augustine's thought, we will catch a series of glimpses of Augustine as a convert in tears in order better to frame his life. We can speak of three conversions in Augustine's life. The first conversion was to seeking wisdom.[9] At age eighteen Augustine read Cicero's *Hortensius*, about which he says, "[It] changed my feelings. It altered my prayers, Lord, to be towards you yourself. It gave me different values and priorities. Suddenly every vain hope became empty to me, and I longed for the immortality of wisdom with an incredible ardour in my heart. I began to rise up to return to you."[10] Notice here how one conversion (to seeking wisdom) was the beginning of another (to Christ), even if a long Manichaean detour intervened between the two.

Augustine's second conversion was to philosophy.[11] This was philosophy as a contemplative way of life, not a merely academic exercise.[12] Someone gave him Latin translations of some "books of the Platonists"—likely the works of the Neoplatonist Plotinus and his student Porphyry.[13] "By the Platonic books I was admonished to return into myself," he writes.[14] They taught him to "seek for immaterial truth."[15] At one point in his quest, "in the flash of a trembling glance [I] attained to that which is. At that moment I saw your 'invisible nature understood through the things which are made' (Rom. 1:20). But I did not possess the strength to keep my vision fixed. My

---

7. See Brown, *Augustine of Hippo*, 412.
8. The same Vandals went on to sack Rome in 455.
9. Brown, *Augustine of Hippo*, 28.
10. Augustine, *Confessions* 3.4.7.
11. Brown, *Augustine of Hippo*, 93.
12. See Hadot, *Philosophy as a Way of Life*.
13. Augustine, *Confessions* 7.9.13.
14. Augustine, *Confessions* 7.10.16.
15. Augustine, *Confessions* 7.20.26.

weakness reasserted itself."[16] Augustine was too proud: "To possess my God, the humble Jesus, I was not yet humble enough."[17] In showing him the superiority of the immaterial, the books of the Platonists had shown Augustine the homeland he sought throughout his life; but they had not shown him how to get there.[18]

Finally, Augustine turned to Christ. In so doing, on his own account, he did not jettison his first two conversions but built on and deepened them, even if moving beyond them.[19] Close to the church but not yet baptized, Augustine was at odds with himself.[20] "Vain trifles and the triviality of the empty-headed, my old loves, held me back."[21] In anguish under a fig tree in Milan, he heard a child's voice repeating the words, "*Tolle lege, tolle lege*" ("Pick up and read, pick up and read"). Recalling the conversion of Saint Antony at a reading of the gospel, Augustine grabbed the book of Paul's epistles from his friend Alypius and read: "'Not in riots and drunken parties, not in eroticism and indecencies, not in strife and rivalry, but put on the Lord Jesus Christ and make no provision for the flesh in its lusts' (Rom. 13:13–14)." "I neither wished nor needed to read further," he writes, having begun to be converted to Christ, as well as to chastity and a monastic life.[22]

Next, let's look at three snapshots of Augustine in tears. The first instance was brought on by poetry.[23] The death of Dido for love in Virgil's *Aeneid* moved Augustine, but in these early days his own spiritual decay left him unperturbed. "What is more pitiable than a wretch without pity for himself who weeps over the death of Dido dying for love of Aeneas, but not weeping over himself dying for his lack of love for you, my God, light of my heart, bread of the inner mouth of my soul." In confessing the tears he shed at Dido's death, Augustine lays bare his abandonment of God "to pursue the lowest things of [God's] creation."[24]

Augustine wept again at his ordination. He arrived in Hippo in the spring of 391. The Catholics in the city were a beleaguered minority marginalized by Donatists, whose bishop had even forbidden them to bake bread for Catho-

16. Augustine, *Confessions* 7.17.23.

17. Augustine, *Confessions* 7.18.24.

18. Augustine, *Confessions* 7.21.27.

19. So, for instance, "Ambrose had ensured that Augustine could again regard the Christian Scriptures as an authoritative source of Wisdom" (Brown, *Augustine of Hippo*, 97).

20. He speaks frequently in *Confessions* 8 of his "two wills."

21. Augustine, *Confessions* 8.11.26.

22. Augustine, *Confessions* 8.12.29. Note the indirect role Athanasius played in Augustine's conversion, which occurred in the wake of the latter having read the former's life of Antony.

23. See Werpehowski, "Weeping at the Death of Dido."

24. Augustine, *Confessions* 1.13.21.

lics.[25] Quickly pressed into service by the congregation against his desire, Augustine wept at the prospect of becoming a priest. He was then asked to preach and eventually (in 395) became coadjutor bishop with Bishop Valerius, taking over as sole bishop after Valerius's death soon after.[26] Though he founded a monastic community in Hippo, the busy clerical life (he spent much of his time arbitrating disputes) meant the final end to Augustine's dream of a contemplative life.

The third set of tears comes at his death. Here is how Possidius, who was part of the monastery at Hippo, tells it in his *Life of Augustine*:

> Indeed, this holy man . . . was always in the habit of telling us, when we talked as intimates, that even praiseworthy Christians and bishops, though baptized, should still not leave this life without having performed due and exacting penance. This is what he did in his own last illness: for he had ordered the four psalms of David that deal with penance to be copied out. From his sick-bed he could see these sheets of paper every day, hanging on his walls, and would read them, crying constantly and deeply. And, lest his attention be distracted from this in any way, almost ten days before his death, he asked us that none should come in to see him, except at those hours when the doctors would come to examine him or his meals were brought. This was duly observed: and so he had all that stretch of time to pray.[27]

Perhaps Augustine recalled the lateness of his love for God as he wept penitential tears in his last days. Before returning to the question of his love's tardiness, though, we first consider the central place of love in Augustine's anthropology.

## The Priority of Love

To be human is to be a lover. The most basic thing to say about humans, according to Augustine, is not that we are social animals (as in Aristotle), thinking things (as in Descartes), or language animals (as in Charles Taylor's recent proposal); the most basic thing is that we are lovers. Augustine divides all of humanity throughout history into two cities, whose origins, developments, and ends he treats at length in *City of God*. He writes: "We see then that the

---

25. Brown, *Augustine of Hippo*, 132.

26. Brown, *Augustine of Hippo*, 132–33. Both of these moves—to allow someone other than a bishop to preach and to appoint him coadjutor bishop—were unorthodox, ecclesiastically illegitimate moves by an elderly Greek bishop that did little to curry favor with the local African bishops.

27. Cited in Brown, *Augustine of Hippo*, 436.

two cities were created by two kinds of love: the earthly city was created by self-love reaching the point of contempt for God, the Heavenly City by the love of God carried as far as contempt of self. In fact, the earthly city glories in itself, the Heavenly City glories in the Lord. The former looks for glory from men, the latter finds its highest glory in God."[28] Despite the rhetorically charged polarities here, Augustine ascribes certain commonalities to the two cities. Both are characterized by love; both desire glory. What distinguishes them is their orientation in doing so. Striking, too, is Augustine's implicit suggestion that, in the end, only two orientations are possible—toward self or toward God. The various penultimate loves of a society can finally be brought under one of these two headings.

In any case, love is a given. The object of love is not. "Love as much as you like," Augustine writes, "but take care what you love. Love of God and love of your neighbor are called charity; but love of the world, this passing world, is called greed or lust. Lust must be reined in, charity spurred on."[29] Augustine "pictured a human self as plastic, composed and articulated by what it loves, stretches toward, and identifies with."[30] In his work on worship and cultural formation, James K. A. Smith makes Augustine's point vividly: "What distinguishes us (as individuals, but also as 'peoples') is not *whether* we love, but *what* we love. At the heart of our being is a kind of 'love pump' that can never be turned off—not even by sin or the Fall; rather, the effect of sin on our love pump is to knock it off kilter, misdirecting it and getting it aimed at the wrong things."[31] To describe someone as "such a loving person" is, strictly speaking, to fail to pick her out from the crowd. All people are loving. Presumably, what we mean in commending a woman as "loving" is that she loves particular people in particular ways, that she loves *well*. If all humans are lovers, we cannot solve the problem of the lovely things by simply damming the flow of love. The answer is not to cease loving, but to love differently.

When Augustine speaks of love, he is collapsing a number of factors into one small word. For him, "love" consists in, among other things, (1) a certain focused attention of the mind, will, and affections (2) in a specific direction

28. Augustine, *City of God* 14.28.
29. Augustine, *Expositions of the Psalms* 31[2].5.
30. Miles, "Happiness in Motion," 44. Miles continues: "To love the fragile fleeting objects and people in the world as if they could provide a total stimulus, a reason for being, then, is to make (quite literally) a deadening choice. When the objects vanish into thin air, so does the soul identified with, and defined by, them. It is, then, a matter of survival for the soul to attach itself with desire and delight to a totally trustworthy object, an object that cannot die" (44–45).
31. Smith, *Desiring the Kingdom*, 52. Smith proposes that we understand humans not along the reductionistic lines of "person-as-thinker" or "person-as-believer," but "according to a non-reductionistic understanding of human persons as embodied agents of desire or love" (46–47).

(3) on an object of desire, an attention that (4) intends the good of that object, (5) possibly over against the good of other objects. Love, then, is dynamic and relational, depending on an other for its very coherence. The difference between life in the heavenly and earthly cities, between true and false worship, between obedience and sin, can be articulated with reference to this complex of willing, attending, and loving in a context of particular relationships.[32]

Love is a principle of movement. We speak of "moving toward" the object of desire, and we are even willing to "chase" something we really want. Augustine writes that "the foot of the soul is properly understood as love . . . [which] moves a thing in the direction toward which it tends."[33] Love transports us, physically or mentally, toward the beloved, so much so that Augustine can write that, while our bodies occupy a certain physical space, "the mind's place is what it loves."[34] Paul understands this double perspective as he exhorts the Colossians, "Set your minds on things that are above, not on things that are on earth" (Col. 3:2).

### Whose Fault Was It *Really*?

Augustine writes, "The lovely things kept me far from you," but there is a certain ambiguity in this claim. One wonders whether Augustine isn't shifting the blame, suggesting that he could hardly help himself. How could he resist being distracted by such beauty? He clarifies his position on the matter elsewhere: "For when the will leaves the higher and turns to the lower, it becomes bad not because the thing to which it turns is bad, but because the turning is itself perverse. It follows that it is not the inferior thing which causes the evil choice; it is the will itself, because it is created, that desires the inferior thing in a perverted and inordinate manner."[35] The fault does not lie in the lovely things but in the wicked will. And the will is not itself wicked, but only capable of becoming so. For all the severity of his account of sin (e.g., Augustine insisted that unbaptized infants will not inherit eternal life, a view that few find palatable), Augustine is equally insistent on the universal goodness of God's creation. "All things that exist, seeing that the Creator of them all is supremely good, are themselves good. But because they are not, like their Creator, supremely and unchangeably good, their good may be

---

32. This paragraph is taken from M. Jenson, *Gravity of Sin*, 7. Used by kind permission of Bloomsbury T&T Clark.

33. Augustine, *Expositions of the Psalms* 9.15.

34. Augustine, *Expositions of the Psalms* 6.9.

35. Augustine, *City of God* 12.6.

diminished and increased."[36] A good God creates good creatures, and "evil has no existence except as a privation of good."[37] But whereas the eternal God is perfectly and thus unchangeably good, his creatures can change. To be created out of nothing is to be mutable, for better or worse. Had Adam and Eve persevered in obedience and humbly depended on God, they would have become "gods not in their own nature but by participation in the true God." In their proud—and fatal—attempt to be like God apart from God, they fell: "By aiming at more, a man is diminished, when he elects to be self-sufficient and defects from the one who is really sufficient for him."[38] Augustine means this diminishment quite literally—sinful humanity ontologically shrinks: "And so, to abandon God and to exist in oneself, that is to please oneself, is not immediately to lose all being; but it is to come nearer to nothingness."[39] This is the movement of sin, a turning away from the Creator to his creation, a creation in itself good but simply not capable of taking God's place. "My sin consisted in this," writes Augustine, "that I sought pleasure, sublimity, and truth not in God but in his creatures, in myself and other created beings. So it was that I plunged into miseries, confusions, and errors."[40]

## Looking for Love in All the Wrong Places

If turning from God to his creation, worshiping creature rather than Creator, is the paradigm of sin, its outworking in an individual life is diffuse. Where worship of the one true God gathers a person into a harmonious unity with God, self, and others, sin scatters a person. Augustine describes "those many people who are completely fragmented by their desire for temporal things."[41] They are fragmented because they come to be at odds with themselves, wanting now one thing, now another. Their desires become disordered, shifting, changing, clashing. Because temporal things, while good, cannot grant lasting, secure happiness, none of them satisfies, or at least not for long. God saves Augustine, like God saves Israel, by gathering the scattered pieces of himself: "You gathered me together from the state of disintegration in which I had been fruitlessly divided. I turned from unity in you to be lost in multiplicity."[42]

36. Augustine, *Enchiridion on Faith, Hope, and Love* 12.
37. Augustine, *Confessions* 3.7.12.
38. Augustine, *City of God* 14.13.
39. Augustine, *City of God* 14.13.
40. Augustine, *Confessions* 1.20.31.
41. Augustine, *Expositions of the Psalms* 4.9.
42. Augustine, *Confessions* 2.1.1.

Closely related to the disintegration of the self is Augustine's departure from himself. In running from God, he ran from himself: "[I was] living outside myself, seeing only with the eye of the flesh."[43] He lived in exile from himself and from God: "You were there before me, but I had departed from myself. I could not even find myself, much less you."[44] "I had become to myself a vast problem," he concludes.[45] "I had become to myself a place of unhappiness in which I could not bear to be; but I could not escape from myself."[46]

Augustine applies this account of self-exile to the parable of the prodigal son. Like the younger son in the parable, the sinful soul proudly demands what is his father's, leaving the father's house to find happiness elsewhere. Similarly, in their pride Adam and Eve abandoned God, seeking to exalt themselves and become like him without him.[47] Thus begins our spiritual rebellion, "as the soul wanders off into darkness and abuses its free will, and so other sins follow. Hence the soul squanders its substance with harlots and lives wastefully, until the one-time companion of angels is reduced to minding pigs."[48] The prodigal son comes to his senses when he realizes that he has traded in the bounty of his father's house for pig scraps. He has wasted his inheritance on evanescent pleasures, having "travelled away from [God] into a far country to dissipate [his] substance on meretricious lusts (Luke 15:13)."[49] The point is not that no pleasure is to be found in the far country—the lovely things really are lovely—but that the pleasures of the father's house are infinitely greater, lasting, and secure.

### Hamstrung

In *On Christian Teaching*, Augustine diagnoses the problem we are to ourselves. It is a case of being "hamstrung by our love of lower things."[50] We are crippled, having fallen lame and having failed to run with endurance the race that is set before us (Heb. 12:1), precisely insofar as we have loved "lower" things—good things, certainly, but not things worthy of our love, or at least not *that much* love. We love penultimate goods as if they were ultimate, transient goods as if they were eternal, loving them for their own sakes rather

---

43. Augustine, *Confessions* 3.6.11.
44. Augustine, *Confessions* 5.2.2. Cf. 6.1.1.
45. Augustine, *Confessions* 4.4.9.
46. Augustine, *Confessions* 4.7.12.
47. Augustine, *City of God* 14.
48. Augustine, *Expositions of the Psalms* 18[2].15.
49. Augustine, *Confessions* 4.16.30.
50. Augustine, *On Christian Teaching* 1.3.3.

than for the sake of another. Our loves have become disordered. By contrast, the holy person is one

> who has ordered his love, so that he does not love what it is wrong to love, or fail to love what should be loved, or love too much what should be loved less (or love too little what should be loved more), or love two things equally if one of them should be loved either less or more than the other, or love things either more or less if they should be loved equally. No sinner, *qua* sinner, should be loved; every human being, *qua* human being, should be loved on God's account; and God should be loved for himself. And if God is to be loved more than any human being, each person should love God more than he loves himself.[51]

To speak of the "order of love" (*ordo amoris*) is to evoke a network of "attachment and affection," of things loved more and less, for their own sake or for the sake of another.[52] God is to be loved above all and for his own sake, though we are also to love our neighbors and ourselves.[53] In some cases, we should love people in one sense and not in another, so that sinners are not loved but humans (all of whom, except Jesus, are sinners) are loved for God's sake.

Augustine frequently has recourse to a distinction between enjoyment and use. "To enjoy something is to hold fast to it in love for its own sake. To use something is to apply whatever it may be to the purpose of obtaining what you love."[54] He ties this thought to the universal human desire for happiness: "Those which are to be enjoyed make us happy; those which are to be used assist us and give us a boost, so to speak, as we press on towards our happiness, so that we may reach and hold fast to the things which make us happy." The problem comes when we "choose to enjoy things that are to be used" and "our advance is impeded and sometimes even diverted, and we are held back, or even put off, from attaining things which are to be enjoyed, because we are hamstrung by our love of lower things."[55] Augustine is convinced that only the Trinity can make us happy, and so only the Trinity ought to be enjoyed (though later in *City of God* and elsewhere in *On Christian Teaching* he will speak of enjoying one another in God or on account of God).[56] Everything

51. Augustine, *On Christian Teaching* 1.27.28.
52. Augustine, *City of God* 15.22.
53. For a sustained consideration of self-love, see O'Donovan, *Problem of Self-Love in St. Augustine*.
54. Augustine, *On Christian Teaching* 1.4.4. See the discussion in O'Donovan, "*Usus* and *Fruitio.*"
55. Augustine, *On Christian Teaching* 1.3.3.
56. Augustine, *On Christian Teaching* 1.5.5; *City of God* 19.17; 19.13; *On Christian Teaching* 3.10.16. Still, in *On Christian Teaching* Augustine qualifies this: "When you enjoy a human being in God, you are enjoying God rather than that human being" (1.33.37).

else is only to be used for the sake of enjoying the Trinity. Augustine loved God so late because he had first sought to enjoy the lovely things, when they were only meant to be used on the way to enjoying God.

It is difficult to avoid hearing this distinction in a postutilitarian context as the commodification of creation in which we crassly take and use others (things, people) for the sake of our own advancement to God. This is to mishear Augustine at this point, however; his concern is more to avoid the transmutation of God's good gifts into idols through misdirected and inordinate love.[57] Indeed, it is only as we recognize the penultimate character of created goods—including other people—that we can treat them with love. The tyranny of ultimacy demands impossible things from those we idolize, whereas Christian love sees them as they are, sinners loved by God and in need of mercy.

It becomes easier to understand (and stomach) Augustine's distinction if we set it against the backdrop of pilgrimage.[58] Some of the greatest poems of the ancient world dealt with the trials of homecoming. Odysseus took nearly a decade to return to Ithaca after the Trojan War, waylaid by threats, but also distracted by lust, curiosity, pride, and a desire for glory. Aeneas, charged with the founding of Rome, nearly faltered in his mission, losing himself in love for Dido in Carthage along the way.

> Suppose we were travellers who could live happily only in our homeland, and because our absence made us unhappy we wished to put an end to our misery and return there: we would need transport by land or sea which we could use to travel to our homeland, the object of our enjoyment. But if we were fascinated by the delights of the journey and the actual travelling, we would be perversely enjoying things that we should be using; and we would be reluctant to finish our journey quickly, being ensnared in the wrong kind of pleasure and estranged from the homeland whose pleasures could make us happy. So in this mortal life we are like travellers away from our Lord [2 Cor. 5:6]: if we wish to return to the homeland where we can be happy we must use this world [cf. 1 Cor. 7:31], not enjoy it, in order to discern "the invisible attributes of God, which are understood through what has been made" [Rom. 1:20] or, in other words, to derive eternal and spiritual value from corporeal and temporal things.[59]

57. "Suppose brethren, a man should make a ring for his betrothed, and she should love the ring more wholeheartedly than the betrothed who made it for her. . . . Certainly, let her love his gift: but, if she should say, 'The ring is enough. I do not want to see his face again' what would we say of her. . . . The pledge is given her by the betrothed just that, in his pledge, he himself may be loved. God, then, had given you all these things. Love Him who made them" (Augustine, *Homilies on the First Epistle of John* 2.11, cited in Brown, *Augustine of Hippo*, 325).

58. See Brown, *Augustine of Hippo*, 323–35; and, more recently, Stewart-Kroeker, *Pilgrimage as Moral and Aesthetic Formation*.

59. Augustine, *On Christian Teaching* 1.4.4.

Augustine knows the difficulty of the way home, and his austere insistence that the lovely things of the world are not to be enjoyed but only used on our heavenly pilgrimage reflects this hard-won knowledge.

The earthly city is at home in the world; the heavenly city is on its way home. The earthly city "longs for earthly joys or clings to them, as though they were the only joys," and "rests satisfied with its temporal peace and felicity."[60] Here is the key difference between the two cities: the earthly city is prematurely satisfied, spiritually sedentary, while the heavenly city longs for the joys to come and sings of them along the way of its pilgrimage. Augustine counsels his congregation to travel light: "Make use of the world, do not be taken in by the world. You entered the world, you are making a journey, you came intending to leave, not to stay; you are a wayfarer; this life is a wayside inn. Use money in the way a traveler at a wayside inn uses the table, the cups, the pitcher, the bed—intending to leave, not to stay."[61] Settling down is not an option. The believer always has one foot out the door. Notice the language of "use" again. "Use" describes a pilgrim's engagement with things on the road. "Enjoyment" is a category of arrival. In Augustine's technical sense, I can properly be said to "enjoy" something only when I have arrived at my final destination. Thus I enjoy it "for its own sake" rather than for the sake of something else. When he demurs at the prospect of "enjoying" things along the way, this response should not be read primarily as a sour dismissal of God's good creation, much less as a spiritual stoicism. Instead, it reflects a judgment that our hearts really are restless until they rest in the Triune God, enjoying the One who has life in himself—coupled with a suspicion that most of our attempts to stop and smell the roses will end up with us building an altar by the side of the road and worshiping an idol.

None of these possibilities, it should be noted, leads Augustine to counsel retreat from society. Peter Brown writes that "the *City of God*, far from being a book about flight from the world . . . is a book about being otherworldly in the world."[62] As the Lord commanded Israel, "Seek the welfare of the city where I have sent you into exile" (Jer. 29:7), so "the Heavenly City in her pilgrimage here on earth makes use of the earthly peace and defends and seeks the compromise between human wills in respect of the provisions relevant to the mortal nature of man, so far as may be permitted without detriment to true religion and piety."[63] Of course, even here Augustine underscores how believers can "use" Babylon's peace to finally enjoy Zion's.

---

60. Augustine, *City of God* 15.15; 15.17.
61. Augustine, *Homilies on the Gospel of John* 40.10.
62. See Brown, *Augustine of Hippo*, 324.
63. Augustine, *City of God* 19.17.

## What about the Pears?

A seemingly trivial episode in Augustine's teen years presents a problem: late one night, he and his friends stole some pears. The difficulty, in light of the centrality of love to Augustine's account of humanity, is that there was little to love about the pears. Augustine acknowledges, "[The fruit] was beautiful because it was your creation," but he adds, "[It] was not that which my miserable soul coveted."[64] What's more, he seems less to be reflecting on the aesthetic quality of the pears than making a theological statement: the fruit *must* have been beautiful *by* definition, in that it was created by the beautiful God—even though it wasn't much to look at. He goes out of his way to point out that the pears were "attractive in neither colour nor taste." The boys did not want the pears at all, which "were not for our feasts but merely to throw to the pigs. Even if we ate a few, nevertheless our pleasure lay in doing what was not allowed."[65] "My feasting was only on the wickedness which I took pleasure in enjoying. If any of those pears entered my mouth, my criminality was the piquant sauce."[66]

Augustine struggles to make sense of this. He has come to understand sin as disordered love, in which we love good things in the wrong way, at the wrong time, to the wrong extent. But what does this gang of boys love in their sin? Certainly not the pears. The only thing that made the pears taste good was their being forbidden. Perhaps, Augustine considers, his sin was, like other sins, a perverse imitation of God.[67] But to what end? What did he and his friends want? Nothing at all, he concludes, in a damning judgment: "I became evil for no reason," he writes. "I had no motive for my wickedness except wickedness itself. It was foul, and I loved it. I loved the self-destruction, I loved my fall, not the object for which I had fallen but my fall itself."[68] Even to say, "I loved the self-destruction," is to speak imprecisely, for one cannot love nothing; or rather, it speaks to the absurdity of sin. And it is this that makes the incident with the pears—which to many readers seems overly scrupulous, perhaps even a sign of Augustine's pathological neuroticism—so vital to his overall diagnosis of the human condition. If elsewhere Augustine will seek to make sense of sin in terms of loving good things in bad ways, here he places a caveat on that explanation by pointing to the finally irrational character

64. Augustine, *Confessions* 2.6.12.
65. Augustine, *Confessions* 2.4.9.
66. Augustine, *Confessions* 2.6.12.
67. Augustine, *Confessions* 2.6.13–14.
68. Augustine, *Confessions* 2.4.9. This is in line with Samuel Taylor Coleridge's description of Iago's hatred for Othello as "motiveless malignity."

of sin. The best he can say is that he probably would not have done it if he hadn't been with his friends: "But my pleasure was not in the pears; it was in the crime itself, done in association with a sinful group."[69] It is precisely the mundane character of petty theft (who would miss the pears, after all?), coupled with the lack of any motivation, that lays bare the illogic of sin. Sin makes no sense. It is absurd. It is chaos.

## The Sickness unto Death

Why did Augustine, in his own words, "become evil"? Despite ransacking his conscience, he can find no motive for his sin. A backward look suggests at least part of an explanation. The evil within is a consequence of what took place in Adam. "Human nature was in the beginning created blameless and without any defect," he writes. "But that human nature, in which each of us is born of Adam, now needs a physician, because it is not in good health."[70] All of humanity was caught up in Adam, existing in him in germinal form, and so what he did finds a home in us.

> For we were all in that one man, seeing that we all were that one man who fell into sin through the woman who was made from him before the first sin. We did not yet possess forms individually created and assigned to us for us to live in them as individuals; but there already existed the seminal nature from which we were to be begotten. And of course, when this was vitiated through sin, and bound with death's fetters in its just condemnation, man could not be born of man in any other condition.[71]

In Adam, humanity was "condemned as a whole lump at the beginning."[72] In his sin, Adam did not merely suggest a trajectory for humanity, serving as a negative role model. No, he carried all of humanity in himself, such that his fate became ours. We are in Adam by propagation, not imitation. After all, Augustine reasons, why else would we baptize infants if they were not already stained by original sin by virtue of being born of Adam? Baptism is for the forgiveness of sins, and it makes no sense to baptize those who are without sin.[73] But Christ "has come, not to call the righteous, but sinners to

---

69. Augustine, *Confessions* 2.8.16.
70. Augustine, *Nature and Grace* 3.3, in *Selected Writings on Grace and Pelagianism*.
71. Augustine, *City of God* 13.14.
72. Augustine, *City of God* 15.2.
73. Augustine, *The Punishment and Forgiveness of Sins and the Baptism of Little Ones* 1.9.9, in *Selected Writings on Grace and Pelagianism*.

repentance. And since they are not yet held guilty of any sins from their own lives, the illness stemming from their origin is healed in them by the grace of him who saves them through the bath of rebirth."[74] None is excused from the plight of sinful humanity.

Augustine's statement that human nature after Adam is "not in good health" is an understatement. Human nature is mutable, having been created out of nothing: "So heinous was their sin that man's nature suffered a change for the worse; bondage to sin and inevitable death was the legacy handed on to their posterity."[75] We are born in bondage to sin, so that even when I want to do good, I find I just can't. "It is like someone who, once having been pushed, easily continues to fall, even though he does not want to and hates what is happening."[76] But Augustine will not allow himself, or us, to pass the buck to Adam. Even if we are sinful *in Adam*, it is still *we* who are sinful in Adam. We may not want to do what we do, but we still do it, and so in another sense we *do* want to do it, in that we choose to do it. Augustine recognizes the anguished cry of sinful humanity in Romans 7: "I was neither wholly willing nor wholly unwilling. So I was in conflict with myself and was dissociated from myself. The dissociation came about against my will. Yet this was not a manifestation of the nature of an alien mind but the punishment suffered in my own mind. And so it was 'not I' that brought this about 'but sin which dwelt in me' (Rom. 7:17, 20), sin, resulting from the punishment of a more freely chosen sin, because I was a son of Adam."[77]

Such is the sickness. Now we will consider the cure.

## The Humble Doctor

In his wisdom, God delivered humanity from this body of death through the dead body of Jesus. In a great reversal, God provided the antidote for human pride in the humility of the incarnate Son. Christ the Mediator was necessary "in order that the pride of man might be exposed and cured through the humility of God; that man might be shown how far he had departed from God, when God became incarnate to bring him back."[78] Augustine suggests

---

74. Augustine, *Punishment and Forgiveness of Sins* 1.19.24.

75. Augustine, *City of God* 14.1.

76. Augustine, *Miscellany of Questions in Response to Simplician* 1.1.12, in *Selected Writings on Grace and Pelagianism*.

77. Augustine, *Confessions* 8.10.22.

78. Augustine, *Enchiridion on Faith, Hope, and Love* 108. See further Daley, "Humble Mediator."

that the severity of sin is best known in light of salvation and that to be cured, the wound of sin must be exposed.

Augustine speaks of salvation in healing terms, as the divine doctor brings the medicine of grace to restore us to life. "It was because of this vice, this great sin of pride, that the Lord came in humility. This great sin, this devastating disease in the souls of men and women, brought down from heaven the all-powerful doctor, humbled him to take the form of a servant, loaded him with insults and hung him on a cross, and all this so that through the healing properties of such powerful medicine our swelling might be cured."[79] One must be careful in describing salvation in terms of healing. The central biblical description is of salvation as *resurrection*, new life on the other side of death; any sanative metaphors need to reckon with the fact that sinners are healed not from, say, a common cold, but from death itself. We were dead in soul and body because of sin, but Jesus has entered a "harmony of salvation" with us, such that "the one death of our savior was our salvation from our two deaths, and his one resurrection bestowed two resurrections on us."[80] The "grace of God which comes to our help as medicine through the mediator" is no mere antibiotic, nor even a form of chemotherapy; it is the power of the resurrection.[81]

Even after we are given new life, the healing continues. A strict regimen of grace structures the rest of the believer's life, all of which is designed to strengthen us to be able to enjoy God in the heavenly city. "And yet the mind of man, the natural seat of his reason and understanding, is itself weakened by long-standing faults which darken it. It is too weak to cleave to that changeless light and to enjoy it; it is too weak even to endure that light. It must first be renewed and healed day after day so as to become capable of such felicity. And so the mind had to be trained and purified by faith."[82] Forgiven, we are not yet capable of joy. We must be gradually strengthened, renewed, and healed by faith, until we are able to live in the light of God. In the following section, we look more closely at how the Spirit trains us to do just that.

## How God Makes Us Lovers of Him

Augustine frankly admits that we would not love God "if he had not first loved us and made us lovers of him. For love comes from him."[83] The love of

---

79. Augustine, *Expositions of the Psalms* 18[2].15.
80. Augustine, *Trinity* 4.5; 4.6.
81. Augustine, *Nature and Grace* 67.80.
82. Augustine, *City of God* 11.2.
83. Augustine, *Gift of Perseverance* 21.56, in *Selected Writings on Grace and Pelagianism*.

God for us comes from him, certainly, but so does our love for God. "Man has no capacity to love God except from God," Augustine writes. "So it is God the Holy Spirit proceeding from God who fires man to the love of God and neighbor when he has been given to him, and he himself is love."[84] Romans 5:5 is programmatic for Augustine: "God's love has been poured into our hearts through the Holy Spirit who has been given to us." It is the Spirit in and by whom we are made lovers. How does he do this? For one thing, he troubles us and so weans us from a love for temporal things. "If by any chance painful trials arise from unexpected quarters . . . let us understand that this is arranged for us by the Lord as discipline, to rid us of any complacency about temporal things, and guide us toward his kingdom by our steady desire. The desire is fostered in us by the troubles that batter us on every side, to render us tuneful in the Lord's ears, like long trumpets."[85] "Complacency" is a splendid word. It suggests both dull apathy and pleasure, and it names the threat of temporal things. It is not, as Augustine regularly reminds us, that these things are bad—they are God's good creatures, after all!—but that we are too easily pleased, contenting ourselves with insipid fare. The Lord "arranges" troubles to shake us, to get us on the move again. We begin to seek first the kingdom of God, resonating harmoniously as the wind of the Spirit blows through us.

Second, the Spirit makes us lovers of God by teaching us to groan for our true home in God. Referring to Romans 8:26, Augustine writes of the Spirit: "He groans in us, because he makes us groan. Nor is it a small matter that the Holy Spirit teaches us to groan; for he is reminding us that we are on pilgrimage and teaching us to sigh for our home country, and, with that longing, we groan."[86] Our longing for God is the way in which we love him while we are in exile in a foreign land, and this longing leads us home. As the psalmist sings, "Blessed are those whose strength is in you, in whose heart are the highways to Zion" (Ps. 84:5). Similarly, Augustine exhorts his congregation: "Let us emigrate with charity, dwell up above with charity, that charity with which we love God. Let us reflect on nothing else in the wandering of this life but that we will not always be here, and that by living good lives we shall be preparing a place for ourselves up there, from which we shall never move on."[87] Though we live all our lives in a foreign country, we are to be like those exiles who live with constant hope for return, whose dreams are filled with their homeland. Even as Israel dreamed of a land flowing with milk and

---

84. Augustine, *Trinity* 15.31. For this reason, "even what we call our deserts or merits are gifts of his" (13.14).

85. Augustine, *Expositions of the Psalms* 32[3].10.

86. Augustine, *Homilies on the Gospel of John* 6.2.

87. Augustine, *Homilies on the Gospel of John* 32.9.

honey and the Babylonian exiles wept over Zion, we are to set our hearts on the heavenly city.

It would not be too much to describe Augustine's entire theology as one of yearning for home. Theology *requires* yearning, in fact. Faith seeks understanding, and "we shall understand if we extend our yearning as far as we can."[88] To grasp the truth of things, we must expand our desires, not contract or suppress them. "This is what the divine scriptures do for us, what the assembly of the people does for us, what the celebration of the sacraments, holy baptism, hymns in praise of God, and my own preaching do for us; all this yearning is not only sown and grows in us, but it also increases to such a capacity that it is ready to welcome *what eye has not seen, nor has ear heard, nor has it entered the heart of man.*"[89] All the means of grace—Scripture, gathering for worship, sacraments, congregational singing, and preaching—conspire to "extend our yearning" to the point where we welcome the unheralded gifts God has prepared for those who love him. Here, knowledge and love are intertwined; we can know these things God has prepared for us only as we grow in our desire for him. It is this yearning by which the Spirit enables us to understand these things.

Let's consider how the divine Scriptures do this work. We read Scripture, according to Augustine, for one reason: to grow in the knowledge and love of God and neighbor. In a lengthy passage Augustine sketches a hermeneutic of love:[90]

> The chief purpose of all that we have been saying in our discussion of things is to make it understood that the fulfilment and end of the law and all the divine scriptures is to love the thing which must be enjoyed and the thing which together with us can enjoy that thing (since there is no need for a commandment to love oneself ). . . . So anyone who thinks that he has understood the divine scriptures or any part of them, but cannot by his understanding build up this double love of God and neighbour, has not yet succeeded in understanding them. Anyone who derives from them an idea which is useful for supporting this love but fails to say what the writer demonstrably meant in the passage has not made a fatal error, and is certainly not a liar. . . . If . . . he is misled by an idea of the kind that builds up love, which is the end of the commandment, he is misled in the same way as a walker who leaves his path by mistake but reaches the destination to which the path leads by going through a field. But he must be put right and shown how it is more useful not to leave the path, in case the habit of deviating should force him to go astray or even adrift.[91]

88. Augustine, *Homilies on the Gospel of John* 40.10.
89. Augustine, *Homilies on the Gospel of John* 40.10.
90. See the discussion of three ways of reading—Cartesian alienation, Quixotic identification, and Christian love—in Jacobs, *Theology of Reading*.
91. Augustine, *On Christian Teaching* 1.35.39–40.

In one sense, this teaching is straightforward enough. Augustine is simply appealing to Jesus's own summary of the law in the twofold love commandment (Mark 12:28–34 par.). One could not be more squarely biblical than that! In another sense, though, in prioritizing the telos of love in our reading, Augustine recasts the practice of reading itself. To paraphrase: if you read a text and completely miss the author's point, but grow in love as a result, *you haven't missed the point*. Of course, Augustine quickly places a caveat on that claim, reasoning that it really is important to succeed in saying "what the writer demonstrably meant in the passage"; however, he does not thereby back away from his primary claim that good readers are good lovers, that reading comprehension is to a significant extent a function of our faithfulness to love God and neighbor in light of a text. And he is less interested in authorial intention than we tend to be; or at least, he is not bothered by interpretations that move beyond what would have been in the mind of the original human author. After all, all faithful interpretations are in the mind of the Spirit, the true author of Scripture.[92]

Augustine's biblical exegesis often seems arbitrary, a classic case of patristic excess, something closer to free association than disciplined attention to the literal sense of the text in its immediate context. Here, for example, is how he reads Psalm 19:1: "*The heavens proclaim God's glory.* The righteous evangelists, in whom God dwells as though in the heavens, tell out the glory of our Lord Jesus Christ, or the glory with which the Son glorified the Father on earth."[93] One would be hard-pressed to assert that the psalmist had in mind the righteous evangelists when he wrote of the heavens. Presumably, the psalmist meant to refer to the sky and all that is in it. There is clear evidence that this is the case in Psalm 8, where the psalmist proclaims:

> You have set your glory above the heavens. . . .
> When I look at your heavens, the work of your fingers,
>    the moon and the stars, which you have set in place,
> what is man that you are mindful of him,
>    and the son of man that you care for him? (vv. 1, 3–4)

Augustine would likely be happy to acknowledge that the most immediate referent of Psalm 19:1 would be the visible witness of the sky and all that is in it, but he is likewise happy to countenance a multitude of faithful interpretations of a passage.

92. See Augustine, *On Christian Teaching* 3.27.38.
93. Augustine, *Expositions of the Psalms* 18[1].2.

What suggests reading "righteous evangelists" for "heavens"? Is Augustine's move justified? It depends on what criterion we use. Recall that the goal of Scripture in God's economy is to build up love of God and neighbor. Augustine takes this as an argument for figural readings of the Bible, writing that "anything in the divine discourse that cannot be related either to good morals or to the true faith should be taken as figurative. Good morals have to do with our love of God and our neighbour, the true faith with our understanding of God and our neighbour."[94] Scripture teaches us who God and our neighbor are and how to love them as we journey to God. The apparent irrelevance of a passage to the building up of the knowledge and love of God and neighbor should, then, be read as an invitation to figural interpretation.[95] Augustine's figural interpretation of Psalm 19:1 takes him closer to the center of the biblical account of God's love for us by evoking the evangelists' proclamation of Christ, presumably because the verse in itself could not be clearly related to good morals or true faith in its literal sense. Note that, as unexpected as they might be, figural interpretations are not arbitrary. They arise from the already existing associations of Scripture, written under the guidance of the Spirit.[96] Figural interpretation draws its warrants from Scripture; it is not a postbiblical innovation. The New Testament writers read Scripture figurally.[97] We may read Scripture figurally because it is itself a figural text.

### What about the Lovely Things?

What, then, are we to make of the lovely things? Augustine never backs away from his confession that the God who created all that is, seen and unseen, created only good and beautiful things. Even those things we call evil are really good things that have taken a turn for the worse. They have been perverted and distorted, but insofar as they exist at all, they remain God's good creatures. He can confidently write that "the good which you love is from him.

---

94. Augustine, *On Christian Teaching* 3.10.14.

95. For a robust proposal arguing for figural interpretation, see Radner, *Time and the Word*. Radner argues that Christians have almost always read the Bible figurally. It is only under the conditions of modernity, in which attention was restricted to the original historical context and intention of the human author alone, that figural interpretation became suspect.

96. John Cavadini gathers the evidence from Augustine's preaching on the Psalms and concludes that "as unlikely as this may at first seem . . . Augustine's primary and consistent image for the preacher [is] a cloud," and his "character image for Scripture itself" is "the sky" ("Augustine's Homiletic Meteorology," 68, 71). Nor is this arbitrary but rather reflective of the intratextual web of association found in Scripture.

97. See, e.g., Rom. 5, where Adam is a type of Christ, and Gal. 4, where "these two women [Hagar and Sarah] are two covenants" (v. 24).

But," he continues, "it is only as it is related to him that it is good and sweet. Otherwise it will justly become bitter; for all that comes from him is unjustly loved if he has been abandoned."[98]

The question is: How are we to relate the good we love to him? Augustine worried about idolatry; he saw how quickly good things could be melted down and molded into gods. And he knew that these gods could not deliver the goods.

> Let these transient things be the ground on which my soul praises you (Ps. 145:2), "God creator of all." But let it not become stuck in them and glued to them with love through the physical senses. For these things pass along the path of things that move towards non-existence. They rend the soul with pestilential desires; for the soul loves to be in them and takes its repose among the objects of its love. But in these things there is no point at rest: they lack permanence. They flee away and cannot be followed with the bodily senses.[99]

The danger is distraction, that we might get stuck on things that pass away. But if the soul that loves them "takes its repose" among them, it is due a rude awakening when they are gone. Like the Preacher of Ecclesiastes, Augustine warns of the vanity of life: "Worldly delight is futile. With great expectation is it hoped for before it arrives; and when it does come, it cannot be held."[100] A festival has come to town, but for all its anticipation, it will be a memory tomorrow. Think of how kids wait for Christmas, only to tear through their gifts and be on to the next thing. How could such a day ever live up to its expectations?[101] "All things pass away, and all things fly away, and vanish like smoke; and woe to those who love such things!"[102] While he was no Stoic—reserving sharp criticism for the inhumane apathy prized by Stoicism—Augustine urged his congregation to "realize that our true happiness only comes when these things have passed away." This stark exhortation might not convince many in the affluent West these days, though it would ring true to the hardscrabble lives that are most of humanity's lot. "Right now, my brothers and sisters, our joy must be in hope. No one should rejoice as if in present reality, or he may get stuck to the road."[103]

Still, Augustine's warning against the misuse of God's good gifts is neither his last nor his most important word about them. They have a proper use.

---

98. Augustine, *Confessions* 4.12.18.
99. Augustine, *Confessions* 4.10.15.
100. Augustine, *Homilies on the Gospel of John* 7.1.
101. "The *City* [*of God*] is a book about expectations" (Kaufman, "Redeeming Politics," 81).
102. Augustine, *Homilies on the Gospel of John* 7.1.
103. Augustine, *Homilies on the Gospel of John* 10.13.

They are to be "the ground on which my soul praises you," serving as an invitation to love the Creator. Late in *City of God*, Augustine rhapsodizes about the beauties of creation. Creation's harmonies are breathtaking, and Augustine is particularly struck that some parts of creation "are there simply for aesthetic reasons, and for no practical purpose—for example, the nipples on a man's chest, and the beard on his face." He acknowledges that he can offer only a "compressed pile of blessings. If I decided to take them singly, to unwrap each one, as it were, and examine it, with all the detailed blessings contained within it, what a time it would take! And these are all the consolations of mankind under condemnation, not the rewards of the blessed. What then will those rewards be, if the consolations are so many and so wonderful?"[104] Time does not allow Augustine to detail the wonders of God's good creation. Even a world that groans and waits, where the side of the road is littered with idols, is nevertheless a world charged with the grandeur of God, chock-full of beauty and blessing.

And it will only get better. In the resurrection, while there will be no marrying or being given in marriage—and thus no sex—even the sexual organs will be beautifully transfigured. Since they will no longer be necessary for reproduction, their entire function will be to move us to praise, as we contemplate the beauty of new creation. The female organs, Augustine writes, "will be part of a new beauty, which will not excite the lust of the beholder . . . but will arouse the praises of God for his wisdom and compassion, in that he not only created out of nothing but freed from corruption that which he had created."[105]

In the end, Augustine's cautionary tale about the lovely things reflects his sense that there are even lovelier things than these. Augustine was acquainted with pleasure. He had tasted earthly delights. If he cautions austerity, it is only from his having feasted on Christ. He knew—and proclaimed—where lasting joy was to be found: "Let all our joy be in hope to come, all our desire on eternal life. With all our sighs let us be panting for Christ. May he, the one most beautiful, be the one we desire, he the one who loved the foul and ugly in order to make them beautiful; to him alone let us pant as we run."[106]

104. Augustine, *City of God* 22.24. Thanks to John Cavadini for pointing me to this passage and the next and for pressing me on the point of Augustine's delight in the beauty of creation.
105. Augustine, *City of God* 22.17.
106. Augustine, *Homilies on the Gospel of John* 10.13.

# 4

# "THAT MOST BIBLICAL
# OF THEOLOGIANS"

*Denys the Areopagite and
the Brilliant Darkness of God*

Denys the Areopagite is "that most biblical of theologians"—at least according to David Bentley Hart.[1] This description might strike one as a curious statement, to say the least, upon encountering Denys's writing. To take just one example, he narrates a spiritual ascent to God in which "one is supremely united to the completely unknown by an inactivity of all knowledge, and knows beyond the mind by knowing nothing."[2] Denys's prose echoes Neoplatonic thought as much as it does that of the "theologians" (as he consistently refers to the writers of Scripture) in its form as in its matter—to the point that Martin Luther could complain that "he is downright dangerous, for he is more of a Platonist than a Christian."[3] True, his writing is thoroughly doxological, at many points becoming explicitly hymnic. But so, for that matter, is much of Neoplatonic thought.[4] Why, then, does he exert such a strong influence on later thinkers—to the point that, to take one compelling

1. D. Hart, *Beauty of the Infinite*, 241.
2. Pseudo-Dionysius, *MT* 1 1001A, in *Complete Works*. All references to Denys's works are drawn from *Complete Works*.
3. Luther, *LW* 36:109.
4. A quick glance at Plotinus's *Enneads* is enough to establish this point.

example, Thomas Aquinas's *Summa theologiae* is structurally modeled on the movement of procession and return at the heart of the Dionysian (and Neoplatonic) project?[5]

Denys's influence can be explained with reference to the scope and coherence of his theological imagination. He covers nothing short of the cosmos, along with its "cause" in the One. Furthermore, he ingeniously and inextricably weaves heaven and earth together. His multitiered description of higher hierarchies that are reflected in lower hierarchies stitches the constituents of reality together in such a way that everything is kept, nothing is lost, and yet one is not confused for the other. Heaven and earth belong together in Denys's vision, and yet heaven and earth do not *become* one another. There is one, rather wonderful, exception to this in Jesus, though it is to be remembered that Jesus is himself *above, beyond,* or *other than* heaven. He transcends heaven, even as he transcends earth as the one in whom heaven and earth cohere. Walking away from Denys's works, one feels as if one has heard the story of the world. In this, he may remind you of J. R. R. Tolkien or C. S. Lewis, though whereas they make new worlds, the Areopagite describes our world in a new way.

At the same time, for all its scope, Denys's cosmic vision can grow brittle. There is a calcified quality to his account of the ordering of the universe, as if this great theological artist frequently faces the temptation to become a mere mathematician—and not the sort who considers the weightier questions of cosmic relations, but the journeyman sort who crunches numbers. All of this might lead us to question Denys's status as "most biblical of theologians." It is tempting to scribble a quick label—"Neoplatonist," say, or "panentheist"—and leave Denys in the pile of theological oddities, or to make accusations regarding his orthodoxy.

And yet there is a whole lot of the Bible in there.[6] One of my first impressions each time I sit down to read Denys is how chock-full of proof texts his writing is. Not that—and this is an important point—the mere stringing together of proof texts is sufficient to render one's thinking "biblical."[7] (Recall Irenaeus's complaint about the Gnostics ransacking of Scripture, taking the precious jewels that formed the image of a king and rearranging them to

---

5. According to Jaroslav Pelikan in his introduction to Denys's complete works, Thomas quotes Denys about 1,700 times ("The Odyssey of Dionysian Spirituality," in Pseudo-Dionysius, *Complete Works*, 11–24 [21]).

6. "His stupendous knowledge of Scripture may not be overlooked; he does not quote much, but when he does it is with exactness and with sovereign mastery" (von Balthasar, *Glory of the Lord*, vol. 2, *Clerical Styles*, 208).

7. Note D. A. Carson's clever comment: "A text without a context becomes a pretext for a proof text" (*Exegetical Fallacies*, 115).

form the image of a dog or fox.[8]) Still, *The Divine Names* and *The Celestial Hierarchy*, in particular, are sustained attempts to take the Bible seriously on the level even of individual words, words that most of us skip past. Denys seems to think that interpretation on even such a close level will bear fruit, that it is a practice through which the interpreter might be lifted up to God. Sounds pretty biblical to me.

All of which to say, maybe Hart's throwaway quip has more to it than we first might think. At the very least, it's worth inquiring into the biblical, which is simply to say, the properly Christian character of Denys's thought. In what follows, I'll give you a bit of background on Denys, then proceed to sketch his thought along a few prominent lines and keep at least in the background this question of whether Denys's theology is "biblical." Admittedly, the word "biblical" is famously slippery. Answering the question of whether Denys fits the adjectival bill involves me in any number of assumptions. For now, let "biblical" stand for something like "evidencing a faithfulness to the shape and subject of Scripture."

## Background

Denys the Areopagite is also known as "Dionysius" or "Pseudo-Dionysius." That "Pseudo-" is enough to alert one to the difficulty of placing Denys in time and space. It is universally acknowledged now that "Dionysius" or "Denys" is a pseudonym. There are two directions to go at this point. One is to throw a cloak of skepticism over the whole project in the suspicion that someone who doesn't have the guts or the honesty to write in his own name is likely to be as cowardly or duplicitous in less trivial matters. The other is to recognize that pseudonyms were stock literary devices in antiquity and into the medieval period and to read Denys in light of this. Anonymity also abounded, as Christians in particular regarded personal broadcasting as more a function of pride than of authenticity. It's worth considering pseudonymity in its kinship with anonymity, seeing it less as a case of deliberate deception than as one of evoking a set of associations in a reader's mind. In this sense, Denys can be making a claim to a certain kind of derivative apostolicity. He is handing on what he has been handed by Paul, who himself received God's revelation directly from Jesus.

I believe the wiser direction, then, is to take Denys at his word, considering him (in some sense) as who he claims to be—the man converted to the Christian faith by Paul on Mars Hill, the one we hear about in Acts 17:34. Might

8. Irenaeus, *AH* 1.8.1.

his very pseudonymity, then, point to the biblical orientation of his thought?[9] At the very least, a charitable hermeneutic suggests we follow the lead of the author who identifies himself *with* Paul's convert by identifying himself *as* the same. That is, we take seriously his claim to offer a body of work that is Pauline. To do so we need not jettison a critical awareness. To hear the text well, we need to both follow the author's lead and do the spadework of placing him historically. A historically critical inquiry reveals that the twin contexts of the first-century Athens of the apostle Paul and the late fifth-century Athens of the Neoplatonist philosopher Proclus suggest just what we find in the texts, a brilliant synthesis of biblical and Neoplatonic thought.

What, then, of the historical details?[10] It seems that Denys lived in the late fifth or early sixth century. He is likely to have been a monk of Syrian or Egyptian origin, one who "wrote to and for monks."[11] As far as we can tell, he attended the Academy in Athens, where he would have heard Proclus (ca. 410–85), the great late Neoplatonist, lecture. Proclus directed the Academy beginning in 476, and it attracted pagans, Christians, and Jews from around the world—though it should be noted that the Academy took a consistently negative stance toward Christians.[12] Before reading Plato, Denys would have had to make it through two years of Aristotle as a required prerequisite. Indeed, Neoplatonism can be seen as a sort of amalgam of Platonism and Aristotelianism.[13]

Like Augustine, Gregory of Nyssa, and others, Denys was influenced by Neoplatonism. It was the hottest thing on offer in the intellectual climate of the late fifth century, and the conceptual rigor of Greek thought played a significant role in the development of early Christian doctrine at the councils of Nicaea (325) and Chalcedon (451).[14] As it developed, Neoplatonism continued to think through the question of the relation of spirit and matter and had moved in the direction of "theurgy." This late, Procline Neoplatonism is Plotinus systematized but more sympathetic to pagan religion. For Plotinus,

9. Charles Stang argues that Denys is best read in light of Paul, and that pseudonymity is an ascetic aid to the apophasis of the self and the indwelling of God. See his *Apophasis and Pseudonymity*.
10. See Riordan, *Divine Light*, 21–34.
11. Golitzin, *Mystagogy*, xxxiv. The quick and lasting acceptance of Denys's writings by the Christian East suggests Denys's identity as an Eastern Christian monk, according to Golitzin. Some of the apparently odd emphases of Denys's thought (e.g., his consideration of the consecration of oil as a sacrament) can be traced to common features of Syrian Christianity (Golitzin, *Mystagogy*, 25, 363). On the similarity of Denys's account of monasticism to the Syrian tradition, see Louth, *Denys the Areopagite*, 70.
12. Riordan, *Divine Light*, 72, n. 2.
13. Riordan, *Divine Light*, 76, n. 9.
14. Riordan, *Divine Light*, 73–75.

one approaches the One via contemplation (*theōria*), but for Iamblichus and Proclus theurgy (*theourgia*), religious ritual using material elements, is more effective. Similarly, for Denys, a person approaches the One not merely through contemplation but through (if beyond) sensible symbols—that is, the sacraments.[15] Neoplatonism was, further, concerned to articulate the ineffability of the One and of creation as the overflow of the superabundance of the One. All of reality is engaged in a cyclical movement of procession and return. But whereas for Neoplatonism this movement is a *necessary, eternal* process from and to an *impersonal* Absolute, for Denys this movement is understood to begin in a *loving creation ex nihilo* by a *personal* God.[16] Whereas Neoplatonism envisages a solitary, self-powered "flight of the alone to the Alone,"[17] Denys is clear that the return to God is a cooperative project in which we are lifted up by God in his beautifully ordered hierarchical universe.[18]

The Dionysian corpus first shows up in history during the reign of Justinian (532–33). While there were immediate questions regarding its authenticity (why, after all, had no one heard of it before?), it was quickly recognized and embraced for its theological depth. During the Renaissance questions of authenticity reared their head again, though it wasn't until 1895 that "the pseudonymity was proven" once and for all.[19]

On, then, to some important strands of Denys's thought.

### The Transcendence of God and the Problem of Theology

The center of Denys's thought is God—more particularly, the God who is in, above, and beyond his creation, majestically transcending it. And indeed, despite some reservations we'll eventually have with Denys, his theological vision is gloriously theocentric. As an aside, my repeated reference to Denys's "vision" is an important one. His thought is deeply aesthetic; that is, it is informed by the category of beauty at every turn. For Denys, one of the most important things about God is that he is beautiful. Denys is a contemplative theologian, one who delights to "gaze upon the beauty of the Lord" (Ps. 27:4).

15. Louth, *Origins of the Christian Mystical Tradition*, 162–63.
16. See Riordan, *Divine Light*, 71–112. This involves a *mutual eros* between God and the soul, rather than the one-sided desire of the soul for the One, as in Plotinus (109).
17. Plotinus, *Enneads* 6.9.11. While acknowledging this common rendering, Armstrong translates this as an "escape in solitude to the solitary."
18. Riordan, *Divine Light*, 10.
19. Rorem, *Dionysian Mystical Theology*, 5. The background discussion here reflects Riordan's scholarship and that for which he accounts.

Who is the One upon whom Denys seeks to fix his gaze? God is nothing short of the one in whom "all things hold together" (Col. 1:17). As Romans 11:36 has it, "From him and through him and to him are all things." Or to come closer to Denys's context, as Paul says in proclaiming the gospel at the Areopagus, "In him we live and move and have our being" (Acts 17:28). God is, we might say, the context of our lives—and not just ours. He is the context of the cosmos. He is the "cause," "source," and "destiny" of all things.[20] "To put the matter briefly, all being drives from, exists in, and is returned toward the Beautiful and the Good. . . . All things look to it. All things are moved by it. All things are preserved by it. Every source exists for the sake of it, because of it, and in it."[21] This is not to be understood mechanistically, though, but erotically, in terms of desire. "The divine longing is Good seeking good for the sake of the Good," Denys writes.[22]

God, then, is the ground, motive force, and goal of all. But as such, he is beyond all. He is "brimming causality and radical transcendence."[23] Of "this supra-existent Being," Denys writes that "it is and it is as no other being is."[24] Strictly speaking, "it is not a thing since it transcends all things in a manner beyond being."[25] God is not one among a number of "things" with whom we can compare ourselves or some other part of the cosmos. Nor is he simply the negation of his creation (in-visible, im-material, un-changeable, im-mortal), which would be only a clever way of containing him in our language by making him whatever creation is not. No, "he is the boundary to all things and is the unbounded infinity about them in a fashion that rises above the contradiction between finite and infinite."[26] It is not surprising, then, that Denys writes in a letter to Gaius the monk: "To the extent that he remains inimitable and ungraspable he transcends all imitation and all grasping."[27] We cannot even seek to conform our lives to his, because he is so completely other.

At this point, though, it's worth putting a question to Denys: "How do you know?" After all, God seems to be in every sense above and beyond our

20. Pseudo-Dionysius, DN 1 596C.
21. Pseudo-Dionysius, DN 4 705D. Also see 5 825B.
22. Pseudo-Dionysius, DN 4 708B. Earlier Denys follows a long antique tradition, though with more cosmic orientation than Augustine's anthropocentric concern, in writing: "All things are returned to it [the Good] as their own goal. All things desire it: Everything with mind and reason seeks to know it, everything sentient yearns to perceive it, everything lacking perception has a living and instinctive longing for it, and everything lifeless and merely existent turns, in its own fashion, for a share of it" (4 700B).
23. Pseudo-Dionysius, DN 5 824AB; 12 972AB.
24. Pseudo-Dionysius, DN 1 588B.
25. Pseudo-Dionysius, DN 1 593C.
26. Pseudo-Dionysius, DN 5 825B.
27. Pseudo-Dionysius, Ep. 2 1069A.

knowing. He is ungraspable, even unthinkable. The "inscrutable One is out of the reach of every rational process." It is "gathered up by no discourse, by no intuition, by no name."[28] This is a classic case of a square peg with a round hole. One just won't go in the other. God will not fit in the constraints of our mental faculties. Denys's radical account of God's transcendence suggests that we cannot speak of God at all. And yet, as Christians, we must—and Denys does. Furthermore, we are commanded to proclaim his name among the nations. Here, we have a problem. In fact, this is *the* problem of theology, and it is because in this problem we encounter a *crisis* that Denys's theology consistently begins in the humility of prayer.[29] In other words: "God, help!"

What is Denys's solution? It's actually twofold—prayer and the Bible. So, *The Mystical Theology*, his brief, brilliant methodological piece, begins with a hymnic invocation of the Trinity. *The Divine Names* opens with an appeal to Scripture as a guide and limit, precisely because the power that the Spirit granted the writers of Scripture is the same one by which "we reach a union superior to anything available to us by way of our own ability or activities in the realm of discourse or of intellect."[30] In this humble submission, Denys signals that this universal Cause "alone could give an authoritative account of what it really is."[31] So, "we must not dare to apply words or conceptions to this hidden transcendent God. We can use only what scripture has disclosed."[32]

Denys lays out his method in *The Mystical Theology*. It is important to note, as it is easily overlooked, that Denys explicitly acknowledges the propriety of both cataphatic and apophatic theology, the ways of affirmation and of negation. These two ways of speaking follow the cosmic pattern of procession and return. Affirmations occur throughout the movement of procession from God, beginning with the oneness of God, the Trinity and incarnation (in *The Theological Representations*[33]), moving to the conceptual names for God (which are the concern of *The Divine Names*) and then to the perceptible names for God (covered in a text we don't have called *The Symbolic Theology*). What may be surprising is how lavishly Denys applies names to God. Scripture tells us that God "is all," which is why "the theologians praise [God] by every name."[34] Because of this, Denys can be boldly cataphatic. And yet, God "is no thing," since he transcends all things and so is also praised by the theologians

---

28. Pseudo-Dionysius, *DN* 1 588B.
29. Pseudo-Dionysius, *DN* 3 680D.
30. Pseudo-Dionysius, *DN* 1 585B–588A.
31. Pseudo-Dionysius, *DN* 1 588B.
32. Pseudo-Dionysius, *DN* 1 588C.
33. A text we don't have and one for which we rely on Denys's testimony (*MT* 3 1032D–1033A).
34. Pseudo-Dionysius, *DN* 1 596C; 1 596A.

"as the Nameless One."[35] Negations occupy the return to God, beginning
with *The Mystical Theology* and moving through the two treatises on the
hierarchies.[36] This anagogical, or uplifting, movement of return occurs as we
deny that certain things are true of God. It is encouraged by the language
of Scripture, in which God offers a "concession" by way of poetic imagery
"to uplift our mind in a manner suitable to our nature."[37] Though Scripture
speaks of God in ways that are both similar and dissimilar to him, the latter
are "much more appropriate," since "God is in no way like the things that
have being." In this sense, *dissimilar* descriptions of God and the angels pay
them more honor and wean us from "our inherent tendency toward the material and our willingness to be lazily satisfied by base images." When God
likens himself to dry rot in the house of Jacob (as he does in Hosea 5:12), we
run no risk of thinking God actually *is* dry rot. Denys concludes that "the
sheer crassness of the signs is a goad," prodding us to lift our minds to the
one who transcends these descriptions.[38]

Denys takes as his model Moses in his ascent to Sinai.[39] As the editors of
his corpus note, Denys situates ascent liturgically.[40] The ascent is not a private religious experience but one that takes place in the context of corporate
worship. At the same time, Moses serves as prototype for the hierarch in
particular (who leads in worship), *not* for the people as a whole. This smacks
of an elitism ill fitting with the book of Hebrews, which describes our great
high priest as a *forerunner* into the holy of holies—that is, one who goes there
before, but not finally instead of, us (see Heb. 6:20).

In the ascent of Sinai, Moses must first be purified and separate himself
from those who have not been purified.[41] Having done so, he contemplates
things seen, then things unseen, and finally "plunges into the truly mysterious

35. Pseudo-Dionysius, *DN* 1 596C; 1 596A.
36. See editor's note at Pseudo-Dionysius, *MT* 3 1033D, n. 17.
37. Pseudo-Dionysius, *CH* 2 137B.
38. Pseudo-Dionysius, *CH* 2 140D–141B. Scripture tell us "that God is dissimilar and that he
is not to be compared with anything, that he is different from everything." Nevertheless, "the very
same things are both similar and dissimilar to God." "But we cannot say that God is similar to
them, any more than we can say that man is similar to his own portrait" (*DN* 9 916A; 9 913C).
39. There is a precedent in Gregory of Nyssa's *Life of Moses*, as well as in Gregory of
Nazianzus's first theological oration, for finding in Moses a model of the one who seeks God.
See Gregory of Nazianzus, *Or.* 28.2–3. Also see Heb. 11:23–29 for the Mosaic model, with an
emphasis on the faith of Moses.
40. Pseudo-Dionysius, *MT* 1 1001A, n. 10. The liturgy, and the language and understanding
of Scripture found in it, is "the fundamental context for Denys" (Louth, *Denys the Areopagite*,
30).
41. In a parenetic section not speaking directly of Moses, the author of Hebrews refers to
"the holiness without which no one will see the Lord" (12:14).

darkness of unknowing." In this unknowing he is united to God (union being the end of the Christian life for Denys, demonstrating the convergence of knowledge and love) and knows beyond knowing.[42] And he is silent, having been united "with him who is indescribable."[43]

There is a long tradition of mystical ascent, from Diotima's ladder in *The Symposium*, through Augustine's visions in *Confessions*, and later, in Bonaventure's *The Soul's Journey into God*. Dante offers a majestic account in poetic form in his *Divine Comedy*. Two things are worth noting here. The first is that, while it is entirely right and good to speak of ascent, it can encourage bouts of Babel building very quickly. The first movement concerning us as Christians must always be God's descent to us in Christ. Furthermore, the first ascent that concerns us is *Christ's* ascent, not ours. We piggyback on him and find that, as Colossians puts it, our life is hidden with him in God.[44] Second, Denys is clear that such ascents always require divine uplifting. It's not simply a matter of spiritual endurance, and that last step in particular demands the outreach of the God who is beyond our knowing: "By an undivided and absolute abandonment of yourself and everything, shedding all and freed from all, you will be uplifted to the ray of the divine shadow which is above everything that is."[45]

As a reminder, while it is tempting to hear only the apophatic accent in Denys, we should remember that he holds the *via affirmativa* and *via negativa* in dialectical tension. This means, for one, that even in his revelation God remains hidden.[46] "Since it is the Cause of all beings, we should posit and ascribe to it all the affirmations we make in regard to beings, and, more appropriately, we should negate all these affirmations, since it surpasses all being. Now we should not conclude that the negations are simply the opposites of the affirmations, but rather that the cause of all is considerably prior to this, beyond privations, beyond every denial, beyond every assertion."[47] Denys is concerned to avoid any hint of God's being rendered manageable in our knowing of him. It is not as though, by dutifully denying all our theological

42. Pseudo-Dionysius, *MT* 1 1000CD–1001A (quote at 1001A). This Mosaic model is reflected in Denys's advice to Timothy at the opening of *The Mystical Theology*. See *MT* 1 997B–1000A.

43. Pseudo-Dionysius, *MT* 3 1033C.

44. It is for this reason that Gregory of Nyssa can write that "the ascent takes place by means of the standing" on the Rock which is Christ (*Life of Moses* 2.243).

45. Pseudo-Dionysius, *MT* 1 1000A.

46. Denys writes that "the transcendent has put aside its own hiddenness and has revealed itself to us by becoming a human being. But he is hidden even after this revelation, or, if I may speak in a more divine fashion, is hidden even amid the revelation" (*Ep.* 3 1069b).

47. Pseudo-Dionysius, *MT* 1 1000B.

affirmations, we could discern the contours of God, like locating a black hole. No, "His transcendent darkness remains hidden from all light and concealed from all knowledge. Someone beholding God and understanding what he saw has not actually seen God himself but rather something of his which has being and which is knowable. For he himself solidly transcends mind and being. He is completely unknown and nonexistent. He exists beyond being and he is known beyond the mind. And this quite positively complete unknowing is knowledge of him who is above everything that is known."[48] Here, then, is what William Riordan calls the "superlative way," which together with the ways of affirmation and negation characterizes Denys's writing.[49] Typically, Denys will say something like this:

God is x.

God is *not x*—or, more accurately, not *x*.[50]

God is beyond, transcends x.

For all the mysticism of his *via negativa*, Denys remains keenly aware of the subtle idolatry that can accompany an unchastened or abstract apophaticism. Ironically, then, the very thing meant to protect the majesty of God can turn into a Trojan horse. What a shame it would be were we to move from acknowledging God as transcending our mental faculties to confessing him finally unknowable, despite his own best attempts to make himself known! No, this won't do. There really is a "knowledge of him who is above everything that is known," even if it is a "quite positively complete unknowing."[51]

The genius of Denys on this point cannot be gainsaid. His dialectic of knowing and unknowing and "superlative way" say the unsayable without rendering it sayable. While he is the paragon of the apophatic theologian, he is so in a deeply Christian way that belies the superficial apophaticism of many forms of contemporary revisionist theology.[52] To clarify this point, consider the old story about the blind men and the elephant. Though each of the men can feel something of the elephant—tusks or feet or tail—none can know the whole of the elephant. Neither can any one of them speak in any

---

48. Pseudo-Dionysius, *Ep.* 1 1065AB. Further, the knowing of unknowing is also union with "him who is indescribable" (*MT* 3 1033C).

49. Riordan, *Divine Light*, 104.

50. That middle term ("God is not *x*") is crucial and protects Denys from pantheism.

51. All this talk of knowing and unknowing brings to mind, again, the context of Acts 17, where Paul (with quick improvisatory wit and utter confidence) proclaims the heretofore unknown God.

52. Whether in thoroughgoing pluralist fashion (as in John Hick's work), or in some still Christian, if attenuated, form of theological correlation (as in Sally McFague's).

meaningful sense about what this thing is. They can describe phenomena, but they cannot get at the elephant per se. So it is with God, a certain kind of apophatic revisionist would tell us. God is beyond our knowing, not least because the best any one of us can do is touch a part of him without seeing the whole. We are *all* blind. And let's give up hope that we will ever be able to say, as one man did many years ago, "One thing I do know, that though I was blind, now I see" (John 9:25). Such claims are arrogant, we are told. They project a confidence ill fitting to a God who transcends our small minds and experience.

But Denys shows that one can honor God's transcendence and still know him and speak truthfully of him. From Denys, we hear of a God who is so transcendent that he can be immanent, one who is Lord over the created order in such a way that he can give himself to be known within that order. In this, Denys escapes the diabolical polarity reflected in much contemporary theology according to which God's infinitude mirrors our finitude and ultimately renders him incapable of revealing himself. Furthermore, as Denys is at pains to underscore, this is an obedient knowledge, which follows God's own self-revelation in Scripture and tradition. Revisionist theology moves from an impoverished (but purportedly lofty) view of transcendence to the conclusion that, since we lack any adequate knowledge of God, our only recourse is to pragmatic proposals in keeping with the needs of the spirit of the age. Denys sticks to the narrow way of the words and symbols that God has appropriated to himself, trusting that they will lead (with all appropriate caveats) to the one true God. I would love for Denys to have given three cheers for the incarnation on this point, to make more explicit the life, death, and resurrection of Jesus as the definitive self-revelation of the God who is beyond our knowing. Still, his account of radical transcendence is spot on.

## Hierarchy

If even speaking of God is as difficult as Denys supposes, we will need a lot of help. Central to his vision of God's creation are the hierarchies that manifest and mediate God's revelation, lifting us up to participate in the divine life. Denys coined the word "hierarchy." It is admittedly a difficult word to deal with, as many of us carry an allergy to anything hierarchical. It smacks of the straitjacketing of institutionalism, of calcified structures designed to put—and *keep*—people in their place. Fine and good for those with a window seat, but not so good if you're stuck in the middle. To dismiss Denys on this point simply in allergic reaction would be, though, to confuse the word with its abuse. Surely there is nothing inherently wrong with a hierarchy. For Denys, in fact, the very hierarchical character of the cosmos reflects the Triune God, what he calls the "thearchy." Furthermore, this character is a function of God's good creation and providence according to which he beautifully orders the cosmos. Each hierarchy "has God as its leader of all understanding and action."[53] Rather than setting order and beauty in contrast (akin to, say, drawing a false and hapless dichotomy between truth and love), Denys invites us to understand beauty as the glorious harmony of a perfectly ordered cosmos composed of perfectly ordered individuals, all reflecting a perfectly ordered God.

But on to the nuts and bolts. Let's start with a definition. A "hierarchy" is "a sacred order, a state of understanding and an activity approximating as closely as possible to the divine. And it is uplifted to the imitation of God in proportion to the enlightenments divinely given to it."[54] It's important to note right off the bat that this is not *merely* an order. It is also understanding and activity. A hierarchy is no mere static structure; it is dynamic, an order that reveals and accomplishes something. "It is forever looking directly at the comeliness of God. A hierarchy bears in itself the mark of God. Hierarchy causes its members to be images of God in all respects, to be clear and spotless mirrors reflecting the glory of primordial light and indeed of God himself. It ensures that when its members have received this full and divine splendor they can then pass on this light generously and in accordance with God's will to beings further down the scale."[55] "Splendor" is the right word here, capturing the divine beauty and the divine light in one word. As the members of a hierarchy gaze on the divine splendor, they reflect that splendor to others. They are mirrors of the divine light, or perhaps prisms. As the divine light streams out from God, it shines not merely "*on* the created order, but rather *through* it," such that "the more the created order is assimilated to God, the more it reflects his glory, becomes a perfect manifestation of God, a *theophany*."[56]

In speaking of the divine light, Denys has not turned away from his emphasis on divine inscrutability and "the darkness of unknowing." For him, darkness and light are both ways of speaking of divine transcendence. Notice how he plays light and darkness off each other to avoid the conclusion that "light" entails comprehensive knowledge and "darkness" entails complete ignorance of God. The "mysteries of God's Word" are hidden in "brilliant darkness," and Denys prays that we might "come to this darkness so far

53. Pseudo-Dionysius, *CH* 3 165A.
54. Pseudo-Dionysius, *CH* 3 164D.
55. Pseudo-Dionysius, *CH* 3 165A.
56. Louth, *Denys the Areopagite*, 39, 67.

above light!"[57] Like Moses on Sinai, we can only know God (but we can know him!) in "the truly mysterious darkness of unknowing."[58] This whole line of thought can be read as a commentary on the confession that God "dwells in unapproachable light, whom no one has ever seen or can see" (1 Tim. 6:16). In fact, Denys writes that "the divine darkness *is* that 'unapproachable light' where God is said to live."[59]

A hierarchy gazes on the beauty of the God who dwells in unapproachable light, and its goal is "to enable beings to be as like as possible to God and to be at one with him."[60] As Denys says later, "The aim of every hierarchy is always to imitate God so as to take on his form," and its task is "to receive and to pass on" purification, illumination, and perfection, through which we receive "an understanding of the Godhead."[61] The order is vital here. Only those whose minds are purified are capable of receiving the light of God.[62] Purification prepares one for illumination, which is in turn the prerequisite to perfection. As Jesus said, "Blessed are the pure in heart, for they shall see God" (Matt. 5:8). Revelation is not the mere passing on of information, then, but the way in which God raises us to union with him.[63]

Denys writes treatises on the "celestial" (or angelic) hierarchy and the "ecclesiastical" hierarchy. In each hierarchy there are "first [perfecting/unifying], middle [illuminating], and last [purifying] powers."[64] Those higher in the hierarchy guide the lower into "the divine access, enlightenment, and communion."[65] There are three celestial triads (as there are nine names in the Bible for heavenly beings). In the first are thrones, cherubim, and seraphim. In the second are authorities, dominions, and powers. In the third are angels, archangels, and principalities. The first triad lifts the second, which lifts the third, which lifts the ecclesiastical hierarchy with an "interlocking agency."[66] Denys is clear that the higher and middle members of each hierarchy possess the powers of the lower, but the relationship is not reversible.[67] Thus, while the highest member participates in the purification and illumination belonging

---

57. Pseudo-Dionysius, *MT* 1 997A–B; 2 1025A.
58. Pseudo-Dionysius, *MT* 1 1001A.
59. Pseudo-Dionysius, *Ep.* 5 1073A (emphasis added).
60. Pseudo-Dionysius, *CH* 3 165B; 3 165A.
61. Pseudo-Dionysius, *CH* 7 208A, C.
62. Pseudo-Dionysius, *Ep.* 8 1097B.
63. Louth, *Denys the Areopagite*, 43.
64. Pseudo-Dionysius, *CH* 9 257C.
65. Pseudo-Dionysius, *CH* 4 181A.
66. Pseudo-Dionysius, *CH* 10 273A. The phrase is the editors', at n. 107. Also see *CH* 15 328B.
67. Though see the editors' qualification of this with reference to the three sacraments at Pseudo-Dionysius, *EH* 5 504C, n. 150.

to the lower two, the other two do not participate in the work of perfection.[68] The higher always lifts the lower.[69] While each member of the hierarchy plays a role in the ascent of the cosmos to God, the hierarch's role is unique and representative. Denys writes that "every hierarchy . . . has one and the same power throughout all its hierarchical endeavor, namely the hierarch himself, and . . . its being and proportion and order are in him divinely perfected and deified, and are then imparted to those below him according to their merit, whereas the sacred deification occurs in him directly from God."[70] So, in speaking of the ecclesiastical hierarchy (what he will often call "our hierarchy"), Denys can write that the hierarch is "a holy and inspired man, someone who understands all sacred knowledge, someone in whom an entire hierarchy is completely perfected and known."[71] The hierarch (or bishop) alone "can accomplish the sanctification of the clerical orders, the consecration of the ointment, and the rite of consecrating the holy altar."[72] Furthermore, a subordinate member of a hierarchy may *never* correct a superior: "Even if disorder and confusion should undermine the most divine ordinances and regulations, that still gives no right, even on God's behalf, to overturn the order which God himself has established. God is not divided against himself."[73] This seems to suggest a claustrophobic ecclesiastical structure, wherein the laity and subordinate clergy have little recourse in the face of clerical abuse. Not that we should lay a catalog of centuries of pastoral sin at Denys's feet, of course. But it may be that here we have encountered an insidious quality to his otherwise captivating vision. Might it not be that the very completeness of his vision evidences an overly realized eschatology in which the possibility of sin is sidestepped?[74] Or to put it bluntly: Might this not be a vision that evokes heaven but overestimates what is possible on earth?

68. Pseudo-Dionysius, *EH* 5 508C; *CH* 5 196BC.
69. Pseudo-Dionysius, *CH* 8 240C–D.
70. Pseudo-Dionysius, *EH* 1 372CD–373A.
71. Pseudo-Dionysius, *EH* 1 373C. Rorem writes: "The word [*hierarch*] consists of *hieros* (sacred) and *arche* (source). . . . By creating the abstract noun *hierarchy* from the cultic title *hierarch*, Dionysius invented a word for a structure or system for 'sourcing' or channeling the sacred, and linked it all inextricably to the single leader" (*Pseudo-Dionysius*, 21).
72. Pseudo-Dionysius, *EH* 5 505C.
73. Pseudo-Dionysius, *Ep.* 8 1088C. Also see *CH* 3 165AB. Even the sequencing of Denys's letters reflects the importance of ecclesiastical order, and suggests something of the literary sophistication of the Dionysian corpus. See Louth, *Denys the Areopagite*, 18.
74. Such is bound to be the case for ecclesiologies in which, as in this one, "our most pious hierarchy" is modeled on the heavenly one (Pseudo-Dionysius, *CH* 1 121C; also see 1 124A; 8 241C–D). For an account of the implications of this kind of idealist ecclesiology and the need to speak of sin in a competent ecclesiology, see Healy, *Church, World and the Christian Life*. Note that, while he thoughtfully accounts for evil (as privative and accidental), Denys tends to

Denys's thought also tends toward a spiritual elitism. Deification occurs as the higher hand on to the lower what they have seen and heard of God. Denys's frequent, strong caution against handing over the mysteries to the uninitiated[75] expresses the early Christian recognition that knowledge of God involves communion with him and his people.[76] However, the hierarchical mediation of revelation in Denys's vision establishes more than the (quite appropriate) boundaries between church and world. It stratifies the people of God and suggests an interpretation of the laity as second-class Christians whose participation in the church is decidedly secondary and marginal to that of the hierarch, priest, and deacon. For instance, with reference to communion, "the sacrament of sacraments," Denys writes: "And while the general crowd is satisfied to look at the divine symbols [the hierarch], on the other hand, is continuously uplifted by the divine Spirit toward the most holy source of the sacramental rite and he does so in blessed and conceptual contemplations, in that purity which marks his life as it conforms to God."[77] Does this wording suggest that the hierarch will always be holier than, for example, a godly old woman in his congregation, that he will always be purer and more conformed to God? At the very least, the *manner* in which these two become like God is different. The "being and proportion and order are in [the hierarch] divinely perfected and deified, and are then imparted to those below him according to their merit, whereas the sacred deification occurs in him directly from God."[78]

Yet, for all the rigidity of this hierarchy and the threat of elitism, Denys radiates a pastoral warmth that tempers any tendency toward ecclesial despotism. In a letter rebuking a monk named Demophilus for his violation of hierarchical order, Denys just as sharply, and more poignantly, criticizes Demophilus for his hasty, ungracious refusal to countenance the priest's embrace of a penitent sinner.[79] "We do not hit the blind. We lead them by the hand," Denys writes. "You, however, beat back that man who was beginning

---

view sin as weakness more than wickedness, which in turn weakens his soteriology (Pseudo-Dionysius, *DN* 4 716A–736B; 8 897AB).

75. Pseudo-Dionysius, *DN* 1 597C; *MT* 1 1000A; *EH* 1 372A.

76. Hence Denys's ecstatic (*ek-stasis*) account of divine and human personhood. See his description of Hierotheus at Pseudo-Dionysius, *DN* 3 681D–684A.

77. Pseudo-Dionysius, *EH* 3 424C; 3 428A.

78. Pseudo-Dionysius, *EH* 1 372D–373A. Even as sympathetic a reader as Golitzin admits that "what appears to be his identification of advancement into God as coterminous with priestly rank must, from a Christian perspective, be reckoned one of the gravest defects of his system. In his defense I must add that the appearance here is not quite equivalent to the substance" (*Mystagogy*, 181–82).

79. Pseudo-Dionysius, *Ep.* 8. On the former point, see 1088C. On the latter, see the moving account of the vision of Carpos, a holy man from Crete, at the end of the letter (1097B–1100D).

to raise his eyes toward the light."[80] There is beauty and love in his hierarchical vision, too.

Andrew Louth counsels us to "be very careful: very rarely does ascent mean
movement *up* the system of the hierarchies. . . . What ascent means—at least
in part—is a more perfect union with that divine energy (or will) which establishes one in the hierarchy. So one 'ascends' *into* the hierarchy rather than
up it."[81] Denys writes that "our greatest likeness to and union with God is
the goal of our hierarchy."[82] Ascent is not for the sake of achievement, then,
but for communion. Louth illustrates this point with reference to Piccarda, in
her puzzling reply to Dante's question about whether she wanted to trade her
place in the lunar sphere for a higher circle of paradise. The question evidences
the pilgrim's eschatological naivete. Piccarda sets him aright, though, explain-
ing that "in His will is our peace." "Then it was clear to me," recalls Dante,

> that everywhere
> in Heaven is Paradise, though the high Good
> does not rain down His grace on all souls there
> Equally.[83]

Denys offers an explanation for why his grace may not rain down on all
souls equally: "For light to work there have to be organs capable of receiving
it."[84] To ascend "into" the hierarchy, to draw near to God, is bound up with
one's capacity for reception. Denys writes: "Each rank around God conforms
more to him than the one farther away. Those closest to the true Light are
more capable of receiving light and of passing it on. Do not imagine that the
proximity here is physical. Rather, what I mean by nearness is the greatest
possible capacity to receive God."[85] And the work of the hierarchy in purify-
ing, illumining, and perfecting those to whom it ministers is to increase their
capacity to receive God.

It may have struck you as odd—it did me, at least—that Denys is so deeply
committed to both mysticism and hierarchy. The two seem, prima facie, to be
strange bedfellows. Mysticism evokes a personal, interior spirituality, often
highly individualized (if not individualistic) and marked by the freedom of the
Spirit and direct encounter with Jesus. Hierarchy brings to mind institutions,

---

80. Pseudo-Dionysius, *Ep.* 8 1096C.
81. Louth, *Origins of the Christian Mystical Tradition*, 171.
82. Pseudo-Dionysius, *EH* 2 392A.
83. Dante, *Paradise* 3.85, 89–91.
84. Pseudo-Dionysius, *EH* 3 433A. This issue of capability of reception is an important one
in Denys's thought, and certainly a controversial one for children of the Reformation.
85. Pseudo-Dionysius, *Ep.* 8 1092B.

social arrangements, the dry and dusty details of polity, due process, and the like. The former is curious, adventuresome, surprising. The latter is predictable, stodgy, implacable.

What unites the two in Denys is a common liturgical and doxological context.[86] Thus, his mysticism is less the private flights of devotion one frequently finds in the mystical tradition and more the yearning upward that culminates in eucharistic participation.[87] The divinization that is the goal of the Christian life for Denys occurs in the church, "our hierarchy." God is "the source of all divinization," which Denys defines as "being as much as possible like and in union with God."[88] And God "has bestowed hierarchy as a gift to ensure the salvation and divinization of every being endowed with reason and intelligence."[89] This happens as "our fragmented lives" are drawn together into one.[90] In baptism a person is born anew as "order descends upon disorder within him. Form takes over from formlessness. Light shines through all his life."[91] We are gathered together, too. Our union with God implies a communion with one another. In a discussion of the Eucharist, Denys writes that "it is not possible to be gathered together toward the One and to partake of peaceful union with the One while divided among ourselves. If, however, we are enlightened by the contemplation of and knowledge of the One we are enabled to be unified, to achieve a truly divine oneness and it will never happen that we succumb to that fragmentation of desire which is the source of corporeal and impassioned hostility between equals."[92] Clearly, hierarchy is no mere conservative institution designed to keep people in their place. Its very nature is to aid in the movement of procession and return, to uplift its members into the divine life by initiating them into the mysteries of God.[93]

86. Golitzin suggests that "Dionysius' basic concern [is] to maintain . . . a 'cultic ambience' in all his works." He concludes that the Dionysian corpus "succeeded in its primary aim, i.e., the wedding of the ecclesial and the mystical which has ever since served to protect the Eastern Church from those divisions between the charismatic and institutional aspects of Christian life that have continued to trouble, on occasion, the Church of the West" (*Mystagogy*, 301, 396).

87. Golitzin argues that Denys's "fundamental goal" is "the reconciliation of ascetics, especially of ascetic visionaries, to the liturgy and sacraments of the Church" (*Mystagogy*, 21).

88. Pseudo-Dionysius, *EH* 1 376B; 1 376A.

89. Pseudo-Dionysius, *EH* 1 376B.

90. Pseudo-Dionysius, *EH* 3 424C; also see *DN* 1 589C. On divinization on this side of death, and its relationship to leadership, see *EH* 3 445B. On the unifying character of *eros*, or yearning, see *DN* 4 713AB.

91. Pseudo-Dionysius, *EH* 2 404C.

92. Pseudo-Dionysius, *EH* 3 437A.

93. Andrew Louth might be a bit sanguine, though he seems broadly correct in writing that "the hierarchies (and cataphatic theology) are concerned with God's manifestation of Himself in and through and to the cosmos. It is concerned with God's movement *outwards*. Apophatic theology is concerned with the secret, hidden relationship between the soul and God:

I wonder, though, whether Denys doesn't attribute too much to the celestial and ecclesiastical hierarchies. Jesus is noticeably absent from Denys's
discussion.

## Where's Jesus?

It's difficult to find Jesus in Denys's writings. While Jesus is less often on
Denys's lips than one might expect for a Christian theologian, Denys clearly
sees him as the center of God's work in revelation and sanctification. "The
most evident idea in theology" is "the sacred incarnation of Jesus for our
sakes," Denys writes.[94] Denys opens *The Celestial Hierarchy* with an exhortation to "call upon Jesus, the Light of the Father, the 'true light enlightening
every man coming into the world,' 'through whom we have obtained access'
to the Father, the light which is the source of all light."[95] "[I] hope," he says,
"that my discourse will be guided by Christ, by my Christ."[96] In *The Ecclesiastical Hierarchy*, Denys makes the comprehensive statement that it is Jesus
"who is the source and the being underlying all hierarchy, all sanctification, all
the workings of God, who is the ultimate in divine power."[97] Jesus serves as
"trainer" for the hierarch as he enters "the sacred contests," and the hierarch
"offers Jesus Christ to our view."[98] Denys can speak of "Jesus himself, our
most divine altar," on which "is achieved the divine consecration of intelligent
beings."[99] Even as Jesus is the source of every hierarchy, so "every hierarchy
ends in Jesus."[100] The sign of the cross "points to a life given over to the imitation of God and unswervingly directed toward the divine life of the incarnate
Jesus," which suggests the orientation of the Christian life to Jesus.[101]

All this leads Alexander Golitzin to conclude that "it is supremely to Jesus
as the expression of divine love that one must refer when looking for the key
and ultimate sense of the Dionysian universe. All reality, reality in the last
and deepest sense, meets, is held in, and proceeds from the 'single, theandric'
activity of Christ."[102] And so any account of Denys's work "that neglects or

---

it is concerned with the soul's movement *inwards* to God" (*Origins of the Christian Mystical
Tradition*, 176–77).
94. Pseudo-Dionysius, *DN* 2 648A.
95. Pseudo-Dionysius, *CH* 1 121A.
96. Pseudo-Dionysius, *CH* 2 145B.
97. Pseudo-Dionysius, *EH* 1 372A.
98. Pseudo-Dionysius, *EH* 2 401D; 3 444C.
99. Pseudo-Dionysius, *EH* 4 484D.
100. Pseudo-Dionysius, *EH* 5 505B.
101. Pseudo-Dionysius, *EH* 5 512A.
102. Golitzin, *Mystagogy*, 174–75.

loses sight of Christ's true centrality will see the system at once collapse into incoherence."[103] Denys may be an apophatic theologian, but this does not mean that, for him, God is "a faceless entity."[104] He has a face, the face of Jesus Christ. All of which to say, according to Golitzin, "the Christological element that underlies" all of Denys's work "cannot be overlooked."[105]

Fair enough. And yet, I think Golitzin protests too much.[106] An "underlying" element is precisely what *can* be overlooked. Precisely because it lies under the surface of the work, one needs to draw attention to it if one's readers are not to miss it.[107] Consider the question of mediation in Denys. For many Protestants, mediation is a suspicious term. There is nothing to fear in it, however; indeed, it is a deeply Christian concept. Still, it is a thoroughly christological concept. Here I worry that Denys, despite his best intentions, has so diluted the mediation of Christ that Jesus is decentered and the Triune God is distanced. One comment in *The Ecclesiastical Hierarchy* offers a case in point: "For one of the divine judgments has laid down that the gifts of God should be duly given to those worthy to impart them. Someone could perhaps show a lack of respect for this divine arrangement and, out of wretched self-regard, could imagine himself capable of disdaining the mediation of the saints and of entering into direct relationship with the divinity."[108] Access to God is always mediated for Denys, and it comes as a shock to think that a Christian would seek arrogantly to speak to God face-to-face. Indeed, Denys can speak of "the inability of the objects of his providential care to communicate directly with him."[109]

---

103. Golitzin, *Mystagogy*, 373. Golitzin's polemic is aimed at readings of Denys's corpus that privilege *The Mystical Theology* over *The Ecclesiastical Hierarchy*: "For without that center the *MT* must inevitably dominate and dissolve the *EH*."

104. Golitzin, *Mystagogy*, 298.

105. Golitzin, *Mystagogy*, 203.

106. Golitzin argues that Christ's presence can be (in the best sense) taken for granted, because, throughout Denys's writings, "Christ, in the Church, is our divine milieu" (Golitzin, *Mystagogy*, 40). All of life takes place in the "cultic ambience" of the church, and so the centrality of Christ can be assumed as given—and indeed as present on the altar in the Eucharist (see Golitzin, *Mystagogy*, 301, 374). I find Golitzin's argument that Denys took Christ for granted, especially given his monastic and cultic context, persuasive.

107. Paul Rorem's conclusion seems to me a more straightforward reading of things: "For Dionysius, appropriate recognition of the transcendence of God (in affirmations and negations and silence) leads inexorably to union with God and not, according to his basic conceptual scheme, to or through the incarnate Christ." He contrasts Denys with Maximus the Confessor and Luther, for whom "recognition of God's ultimate transcendence leads the believer to God's self-revelation in the incarnation" (Rorem, *Dionysian Mystical Theology*, 115). This also might explain why love for the crucified Christ is "not central in the Dionysian corpus" (Rorem, *Pseudo-Dionysius*, 216).

108. Pseudo-Dionysius, *EH* 7 561BC. This is given more context in *DN* 1 588C.

109. Pseudo-Dionysius, *Ep.* 9 1113B.

Set this side by side with a familiar passage from Hebrews 10: "Therefore, brothers, since we have confidence to enter the holy places by the blood of Jesus, by the new and living way that he opened for us through the curtain, that is, through his flesh, and since we have a great priest over the house of God, let us draw near with a true heart in full assurance of faith, with our hearts sprinkled clean from an evil conscience and our bodies washed with pure water" (vv. 19–22). While the mediation of Christ need not be in competition with other, derivative forms of mediation, that those other forms are *derivative* and thus thoroughly *secondary* is of vital importance.[110] As secondary, these forms of mediation must ever be seen as servants of Christ. The abiding danger is that discussion of these secondary mediations will outstrip that of the mediation of Christ, leading to a de facto marginalization of Christ's mediation and, in the process, of the abiding significance of his humanity as our great high priest, ascended to the right hand of the Father.[111] In other words, we can be so busy talking about the church that we forget to do things like invoke the Spirit or pray, "Maranatha! Come, Lord Jesus!"[112]

What, then, of David Bentley Hart's quip that Denys is "that most biblical of theologians"? Hopefully by now you are alert to some of the deeply biblical concerns and ways of thinking in Denys's thought. He is an arctic blast forcing us to catch our breath as we speak, so often lazily, of God. The scope of his cosmic vision can, and should, be seen as a nuanced resource from which to consider the coherence of all things in Christ. The combination of joyful praise and humble reverence that creates the Dionysian ambience surely matches the mood of Scripture far more than most theological texts. Still, he says too much, which is an unhappy inconsistency, given his theological commitments. His speculative angelology is relatively innocuous, and it helpfully models an understanding of angels as revelatory messengers.[113] But his

110. Angelic mediation thus can serve to speak of God's way of being present, not push him farther away. This was the case in first-century Judaism (though it did not have the added complication of properly subordinating angelic to christological mediation): "Belief in the existence of angelic and other mediators says more about the attempt of some Jewish writers to speak meaningfully about their god's *involvement with*, not detachment from, his creation, than about a proto-Deist theology such as was held by some in the pagan world" (N. T. Wright, *New Testament and the People of God*, 250–51; also see 258–59).

111. See Paul Minear's remarks on the unique high priesthood of Jesus in Hebrews in his *Images of the Church*, 98–99.

112. See Douglas Farrow's brilliant apology for the doctrine of the ascension in his *Ascension and Ecclesia*. This paragraph is taken from Jenson and Wilhite, *Church*, 151–52. Used by kind permission of Bloomsbury T&T Clark.

113. Furthermore, *The Celestial Hierarchy* is not first and foremost a treatise on angelology. It is part of Denys's doctrine of revelation, concerned with how God reveals himself, how we come to know God.

ecclesiology suffers from overdefinition, and in the process (though this could also be suspected earlier and elsewhere) Denys neglects Christology.[114] That he is more than Proclus Christianized should be patent. That he nevertheless obscures the person and work of Christ is, to say the least, unfortunate.

114. If the editors are right that we are to read Denys's method of mystical ascent as the experience of the hierarch in *eucharistic* worship (*MT* 1 1001A, n. 10), we may assume an implied christological ascent (though perhaps one all too implied).

# 5

# FAITH SEEKING UNDERSTANDING—OR UNDERSTANDING SEEKING FAITH?

*Anselm of Canterbury and the Logic of God*

## The Problem of Faith and Reason

Anselm of Canterbury is famous for three things: a far-reaching account of the atonement (to which we will return later), a description of the theological task as "faith seeking understanding," and the first articulation of the ontological argument for God's existence. These latter two make a prima facie odd couple. If the former claim suggests a fideist position submissive to revelation, the latter calls to mind a rationalism confident in the deliverances of naked human reason. Whereas the former makes Anselm a friend of theologians, the latter makes him a friend of philosophers (and prompts theologians to worry that his may be a case of the tail wagging the dog). If the first suggests the insularity and introspection of the monastery, the second anticipates the confident intellectual castle-building of the scholastics.

Consider Anselm's first major work, the *Monologion*, written at the request of monks who insisted on a certain approach: "Nothing whatsoever to be argued on the basis of the authority of Scripture, but the constraints of reason concisely to prove, and the clarity of truth clearly to show, in the plain style, with everyday arguments, and down-to-earth dialectic, the conclusions of distinct investigations."[1] At the outset, Anselm proclaims that even those who know nothing of the faith "can, even if of average ability, convince themselves, to a large extent, of the truth of these beliefs, simply by reason alone."[2] And what he demonstrates is God himself! Beginning with our universal desire for the good, Anselm sets out toward the source of that good, stringing together a daisy chain of arguments on creation ex nihilo, divine simplicity, and omnipresence, moving on to the divine essence and trinitarian persons and to their mirror in the mind.[3] Yet, all this rational demonstration does not render faith redundant. At the end of his confident meditation, Anselm is adamant: "One must, therefore, have faith in Father, in Son and in their Spirit, equally in each individual and in all three together. . . . The supreme essence is the only thing that everyone ought to believe. This is because the supreme essence is the only goal at which everyone, in every thought and deed, ought to aim. Hence it is clear that there is no possibility of progress without belief, and no benefit from belief without progress."[4]

Or take his second major work, the *Proslogion*, in which Anselm advances the ontological argument. He tells us that he is searching for "one single argument that for its proof required no other save itself, and that by itself would suffice to prove that God really exists."[5] He takes the tack of introspection, entering into the "little chamber" of his soul, shutting out all but God and what will aid him in his quest for God. The seeking begins in prayer: "Teach me to seek You, and reveal Yourself to me as I seek, because I can neither seek You if You do not teach me how, nor find You unless You reveal Yourself." Furthermore, the image of God in Anselm "is so effaced and worn away by vice, so darkened by the smoke of sin," that it must be renewed and reformed if it is to do "what it was made to do." "For I do not seek to understand so that I may believe; but I believe so that I may understand."[6]

1. In the prologue to the *Monologion*, in *Anselm of Canterbury: The Major Works*. All references to Anselm's works are drawn from *The Major Works*.
2. Anselm, *Monologion* 1.
3. This broadly Platonic project parallels Augustine's *The Trinity* at many points, though Augustine's conclusions in the closing paragraphs of *The Trinity* are more significantly qualified than Anselm's.
4. Anselm, *Monologion* 77.
5. In the preface to the *Proslogion*. Still, he writes "from the point of view of one trying to raise his mind to contemplate God and seeking to understand what he believes" (preface).
6. Anselm, *Proslogion* 2. Anselm's inward turn recalls Augustine's move in *The Trinity* and anticipates Calvin's claim at the outset of the *Institutes* that knowledge of God and self are mutually implicating.

From here Anselm sets out to prove the incoherence of the fool's statement in his heart that "there is no God" (Ps. 14:1; 53:1).[7] God is that than which none greater can be conceived, and the fool who thinks the nonexistence of God is not thinking the nonexistence of *God* but the nonexistence of one who is less than that than which none greater can be conceived. Existence, after all, is greater than nonexistence. It is not possible, therefore, to conceive God's nonexistence. To think of God, which even the fool does, is to acknowledge his existence. Hence, God necessarily exists. None of this argument requires faith,[8] in Anselm's mind, though the very search for it began in prayer.

It is worth noting the contrast between Anselm and Descartes, who would later offer his version of the ontological argument. Both shut themselves up in isolation. But whereas Anselm begins in prayer on the assumption of God's ever-present help, Descartes begins his first meditation in demolition, committed to a project of tearing down his assumptions and reestablishing indubitable foundations. Here is Descartes: "I realized that it was necessary, once in the course of my life, to demolish everything completely and start again right from the foundations if I wanted to establish anything at all in the sciences that was stable and likely to last. . . . I am here quite alone, and at last I will devote myself sincerely and without reservation to the general demolition of my opinions."[9] Descartes's project is straightforwardly rational; he must begin by rebuilding the house of knowledge from the ground up. Where he grabs a sledgehammer, Anselm kneels in prayer.

Finally, consider *On the Incarnation of the Word*, an apologetic work written in response to Roscelin's suggestion that either there are three gods or all three persons of the Trinity became incarnate. Roscelin has made an intellectual error, and Anselm sets him (and the record, as Roscelin had suggested that Anselm shared his views) straight. He recalls the *Monologion* and *Proslogion*, in which he sought "to show that compelling arguments apart from the authority of Scripture can establish things that we by faith hold about

---

7. Anselm, *Proslogion* 2.
8. Visser and Williams make this observation:
   Thus, the fool cannot grasp the reason of faith in the same way as someone who has the "experience" that comes from belief; yet there is always something the believer can say to the fool that the fool can understand. And (although Anselm does not say this explicitly) the fool who is convinced by the demonstration has not attained understanding of the same kind, or in the same degree, as the believer who formulated the proof. The convinced fool, no longer a fool, has simply been brought to a state in which faithful inquiry is possible for him. He can now retrace not only the believer's reasoning but the spiritual discipline that made such reasoning possible by yielding an understanding born of experience. (*Anselm*, 24)
9. This comes from the beginning of the first meditation in Descartes, *Meditations on First Philosophy*, 12.

the divine nature and the divine persons besides the incarnation," likening them to a kind of defense of the faith.[10] And yet Anselm is quick to point out that any attempt at defending the faith ("as if the faith should need my defence"!) would be as if Anselm were to trip around Mount Olympus with ropes and stakes trying to stabilize it.[11] Indeed, one is left wondering whether Roscelin needs to be argued into the right beliefs or rebuked into submission. "If one can understand, one should thank God; if one cannot, one should bow one's head in veneration." Faith, obedience, and humility are the necessary prerequisites for understanding, which leaves us in the curious situation of wondering whether *On the Incarnation of the Word* is meant to sway its target Roscelin at all. For "those who have not believed will not understand. For those who have not believed will not find by experience, and those who have not found by experience will not know." He goes on: "And not only is the mind without faith and obedience to the commandments of God prevented from rising to understand higher things, but the mind's endowed understanding is also sometimes taken away, and faith itself subverted, when upright conscience is neglected."[12]

Might *On the Incarnation of the Word* be an apologetic work intent on laying bare the logic of faith over against Roscelin's cavils, yet one in which Anselm assumes that Roscelin will persist in error as he refuses to humbly submit to the faith of the church? After all, it is one thing to be able to think one's way through to understanding; it is another to offer a coherent account of God's existence that is persuasive to heretics and non-Christians (not that Anselm would have known many of the latter). There is an ex post facto character to Anselm's reasoning in these treatises—should we expect it to be persuasive to those who do not yet believe? How much can reason really do?

Anselm's writings display a combination of deference and daring. On the one hand, his reflection begins (and, we assume, continues) in invocation, as he recognizes his need for God to guide him. Anselm does not seek to ground things for himself but is largely content with "the irrefutable arguments of the holy Fathers and especially blessed Augustine, after the apostles and evangelists."[13] He seeks to further explore their logic and share with others "what God shall see fit to reveal to [him] about this subject."[14] Still, it must be said that Anselm stands out in his time for the clarity and individuality of his

---

10. Anselm, *On the Incarnation of the Word* 6.
11. Anselm, *On the Incarnation of the Word* 1.
12. Anselm, *On the Incarnation of the Word* 1.
13. Anselm, *On the Incarnation of the Word* 6. Also see the commendation of *Why God Became Man* to Pope Urban II and Anselm's remark at *Why God Became Man* 1.1.
14. Anselm, *Why God Became Man* 1.1.

voice. He is inventive and creative, in an age more suspicious than celebratory of such things. His work is not explicitly exegetical. Whereas it was common to litter one's writing with appeals to authority—indeed, the offering of florilegia (literally, bouquets of flowers) of patristic citations was much more the norm—Anselm leaves even his intellectual debts to so influential a master as Augustine largely tacit.[15] It is hard to know what to make of this omission. Some in Anselm's day found it unsettling: "Lanfranc hated the *Monologion*'s reliance on reason rather than authority, and said so; Anselm ignored him."[16] Southern judges that Anselm utterly and unquestionably assumed—that is, took on the mind of—Scripture and the church fathers (chiefly Augustine), even though he seldom cited them.[17] This is either deeply subversive or thoroughly submissive, and it seems most likely that Anselm so took for granted his indebtedness to Scripture and the teaching of the church that it scarcely seemed necessary to reassert them.

In any case, we are left with a Benedictine monk—and that is what he was, before being a theologian or an archbishop—who everywhere assumed the priority of faith and yet took daring steps in the confidence of reason.[18] In what follows, after sketching a bit of the life and world of Anselm, I'll seek to locate this question of faith and reason within the context of the notions of freedom, necessity, and fittingness in Anselm, looking in detail at the importance of harmonious order and turning to the atonement as a case study before offering some concluding thoughts on the reason of faith.

## Biography

Though known for his ecclesial geography (he was an archbishop in England), Anselm of Canterbury was born in 1033 in the Italian Alps, in Aosta, east of Lyons, north of Nice, and west of Milan. His mountainous surroundings left an impression on him, from the early dream in which he climbed the "mountains of Jupiter" next to Aosta, ascended to God's house, and was fed with

---

15. Southern, *Saint Anselm*, 72–73.

16. Thomas Williams, in personal correspondence with the author. See also T. Williams, "Anselm's Quiet Radicalism."

17. "He was not a collector or arranger of material; he simply absorbed the Bible in his thought and language, and allowed his meditations to grow, as a river gathers strength from the springs from which it flows" (Southern, *Saint Anselm*, 70). "If he removed authority from his arguments, it was not to replace it with his own views: quite the contrary, it was to install authority so deep in the foundations that it was out of sight and beyond dispute" (*Saint Anselm*, 443–44).

18. Anselm's uniqueness can be indirectly witnessed in Leclercq's refusal to consign him to either monastic or scholastic theology. See Leclercq, *Love of Learning and the Desire for God*, 277.

God's bread, to the bracing, alpine ambience of his theological reflection and singular obedience.[19] Despite an early aspiration to the monastery, Anselm turned to a wilder youth, before his mother died in his late teens. In his early twenties Anselm's relationship with his father fractured, with father growing hostile and son renouncing his patrimony, crossing the Alps with a servant to seek his way in a far country.[20] He traveled for three years in Burgundy and the Loire region, spent some time at Avranches near Mont-Saint-Michel, and eventually arrived at Bec, a monastery in central Normandy. There he studied under the prior Lanfranc, whose career Anselm would follow in the years ahead. Anselm became a monk at age twenty-seven, a decision that he left to Lanfranc to make.[21] Though he would rise in rank and stature, Anselm was *always* a monk, never less and—unless authority or circumstance demanded it—seldom more.[22] When Lanfranc left Bec, Anselm became prior in his place and focused on teaching the monks. For a decade we find Anselm engaged in his work as prior and in teaching, but writing nothing.[23]

In the 1070s, around age forty, Anselm began to write his *Prayers* and *Meditations*, for which he was most widely known in medieval times.[24] These were richly pious; with Anselm we see a shift in "the environment of prayer," from corporate liturgical prayers to private devotional ones.[25] A few years later Anselm wrote his first two major works: the *Monologion* (a meditation on the essence of God) and the *Proslogion*, in which Anselm sets forth what has come to be known as the ontological argument, according to which God's necessary existence follows from his being the being than which no greater can be conceived. He became abbot of Bec in 1078 and began occasionally traveling to England to check in on the properties belonging to the monastery and, we can assume, reconnecting with his old friend and teacher Lanfranc, who had become archbishop of Canterbury. Of note in this middle period is a debate with Roscelin, an aggressive freelancing teacher whose heretical consideration of the incarnation claimed the support of Anselm and Lanfranc. In response, Anselm wrote *On the Incarnation of the Word* to clarify

19. See the wonderful description in Southern, *Saint Anselm*, 6.

20. Evans, *Anselm*, 3.

21. Southern, *Saint Anselm*, 31.

22. Indeed, "much in his later life as archbishop becomes clearer if we remember that every practical question had for him a monastic orientation" (Southern, *Saint Anselm*, 172).

23. On the reasons for this, see Visser and Williams, *Anselm*, 5.

24. Southern, *Saint Anselm*, 91.

25. "The environment of prayer [with Anselm] has shifted decisively from the church to the chamber, and from communal effort to severe and lonely introspection: we have not only withdrawn from corporate worship into the privacy of the chamber; we have withdrawn into the secrecy of the soul" (Southern, *Saint Anselm*, 102). Also see Evans, *Anselm*, 28.

that, though there are three persons in God, there are not three gods—but yet neither do all three become incarnate. (The key point is to understand that "the Son assumed a human being into the unity of his person and not into the unity of his substance."[26])

In 1093 Anselm became archbishop of Canterbury—quite against his will—taking up an office Lanfranc had held until a few years prior. When Anselm was called upon to administer last rites to the king, the king named him to the vacant archbishopric.

> Chaos and consternation ensued: Anselm resisted with tears streaming down his face, his nose bleeding, protesting his incapacity and predicting disaster; the king and bishops and his own clerks all harrying him to accept. The king attempted to press the pastoral staff into his clenched hand, and when he failed, the bishops forced open his fist and closed his fingers round the shaft. Anselm was then carried into church with the crozier thus held in his hand in the midst of acclamations, *"Vivat episcopus"* [*Long live the bishop!*] and *"Te Deum"* [*To you, O Lord*], while he continued to cry out *"Nihil est quod facitis"* [*Nothing is being done*]. So the long day ended in tears and confusion, but with Anselm, however reluctantly and certainly uncanonically, still in possession of the archiepiscopal crozier.[27]

Anselm preferred a life of contemplation and was fairly incompetent as an administrator. Furthermore, there were the sticky politics of allegiance to Pope Urban II (an allegiance that was unquestionable to Anselm) and William Rufus, king of England; it didn't help that Anselm was "a man of God who stuck out like a sore thumb among the worldly."[28]

Anselm would find himself frequently caught in debates over jurisdiction of spiritual and temporal affairs. The investiture controversy, in which Pope Urban forbade the conferral of spiritual authority by kings, found Anselm in a particularly difficult situation—sworn to papal allegiance but himself the fruit of an elevation to the archbishopric whose legitimacy was questionable.[29] Even if Anselm never sought power, he did seek the good of those entrusted to him. Even though he spent seven of his sixteen years as archbishop in exile, mostly embroiled in the tug-of-war between popes and kings, Anselm sponsored the local piety and doggedly campaigned for the primacy of Canterbury over the British isles.[30]

26. Anselm, *On the Incarnation of the Word* 9.
27. Southern, *Saint Anselm*, 189–90.
28. Evans, *Anselm*, 19.
29. Evans, *Anselm*, 22–23.
30. Southern, *Saint Anselm*, 238.

"After two years of failing health, Anselm died at Canterbury on 21 April 1109."[31] We have Eadmer chiefly to thank for the details of Anselm's life. Eadmer worked for years on his *Vita Anselmi*, drafting sections of it before transcribing them onto parchment. When Anselm pressed him as to what he was doing, Eadmer finally showed him. Anselm made some corrections, and Eadmer was ecstatic to have received his support. A few days later, though, Anselm ordered him to destroy it, "judging himself unworthy of any such literary monument for posterity." But having spent so long on the work, Eadmer "obeyed him in the letter by destroying the quires on which the work was written, having first transcribed the contents on to other quires."[32]

## Freedom, Necessity, and Fittingness

One way to uncover the reasons driving Anselm's faith is to examine his notion of the sorts of things God "must" do. Anselm makes much of the language of freedom, necessity, and fittingness as he accounts for the nature of God and why he does what he does. God being God, it would seem that he is free to do whatever he wants. And so he is. Anselm is clear that "it is incorrect to say of God that he 'cannot do something' or that he 'does it of necessity.' For all necessity, and all impossibility, is subject to his will. Moreover, his will is not subject to any necessity or impossibility. For nothing is necessary or impossible for any reason other than that he himself so wills it."[33] God is the one than which no greater can be conceived, and as such he is "so free that he is subject to no law and no judgment, and is so benevolent that nothing can be conceived of more benevolent than he." Therefore, "there is nothing right or proper except what he wishes."[34]

Again, God is free to do whatever he wants. But for Anselm, much hangs on the "whatever." Might God want to create for wanton sport? Might he want to do an about-face and decide to reward viciousness instead of virtue? We quickly recoil at this possibility and suggest that there must be some limits to "whatever God wants"; this intuition is basic to a number of moves Anselm makes throughout his work.

For instance, could God tire of his creation, turn his back on it, and consign it to oblivion? Could he take this drastic step of changing his mind? Isn't he

---

31. Southern, *Saint Anselm*, 414.

32. Southern, *Saint Anselm*, 412, quoting Eadmer, *Vita Anselmi*. As a result of Anselm's command to destroy the *Vita* and his subsequent withdrawal from Eadmer, Eadmer's account shrinks after about 1100.

33. Anselm, *Why God Became Man* 2.17.

34. Anselm, *Why God Became Man* 1.12.

capable of this? Absolutely not, says Anselm. But, we might retort, does this not suggest an inappropriate limitation of God's freedom? No, comes the reply, it evinces linguistic sloppiness. To plan something and then change one's mind is to be reactive and inconstant; it is thus to make one's will beholden to another, to allow it to be a function of external circumstances. But God wills whatever he wants, and so even the diabolical defection of humanity cannot change his mind about gathering people to himself. Were God capable of changing his mind—or, Anselm adds, of deceiving or wishing to lie—this "would be incapability more than capability."[35]

At times, Anselm will talk of God's doing something "of necessity," but this is the necessity of self-consistency rather than the necessity of compulsion. God is never other than God, and so some things are "necessary." But there is nothing other than God that moves God to do what God does. He is in no way constrained, "in no way forced to do, or prohibited from doing, anything."[36] Even this divine consistency is no straitjacket but God's "own spontaneous unchangeability"—"spontaneous" because arising from within, so that his unchangeability is an expression of his being fully himself, fully free in all he does.[37] God does "put himself under an obligation to bring his good beginning [in creation] to fulfilment," which eventually requires the incarnation and crucifixion, but it is better to call this grace than necessity.[38]

God does whatever he wants, which is his freedom. When we do whatever he wants, that is our freedom. Anselm sets out a basic, far-reaching principle in his treatise On Free Will, defining "the liberty of will" as "the capacity of preserving rectitude of the will for the sake of rectitude itself."[39] Justice is preserved when this capacity is exercised.[40] Elsewhere, Anselm closely aligns truth and justice, defining them both as "rectitude."[41] This is counterintuitive in a late modernity reared on libertarian notions of freedom and a market economy. For Anselm, to be free is not to choose whatever I want; it is to have the capacity to want the right things, and thereby follow the grain of the universe.

All God does is, in a word, "fitting." That is, God being God, he does things well and in good order. The theological sense of necessity is "the utter

35. Anselm, *Why God Became Man* 2.17.

36. Anselm, *Why God Became Man* 2.5.

37. Anselm, *Why God Became Man* 2.16.

38. Anselm, *Why God Became Man* 2.5.

39. Anselm, *On Free Will* 3.

40. Justice is "rectitude of the will preserved for its own sake" (Anselm, *On the Virgin Conception and Original Sin* 3).

41. Anselm, *On Truth* 2, 11, 12.

fittingness with which divine freedom expresses the goodness of its nature in the generosity of its act."[42] There is an unalloyed rightness to what God does. All his works are just. This drives Anselm's soteriology: "If it is not fitting for God to do anything in an unjust and unregulated manner, it does not belong to his freedom or benevolence or will to release unpunished a sinner who has not repaid to God what he has taken away from him."[43]

But perhaps all this talk of regulation and order goose-steps across the page too stridently. We fidget around such stark language and worry that this kind of structure is inimical to love and more suggestive of a tyrant. I suspect this reaction is in large part because, in our limitations and sin, we cannot imagine that an immaculately ordered world might be enlarging and life giving. To most of us, that scenario sounds stifling. But to Anselm, such perfect order is at once true and beautiful.[44] Similarly, Augustine, the master of the medievals, spoke of the "harmony of salvation" that Christ performs.[45] Or recall Irenaeus's logic of recapitulation, in which Christ undoes Adam by redoing Adam the right way. There is a beauty to what he does. It is "fitting," "appropriate," that God would redeem us in this way; and Anselm speaks of "the indescribable beauty of the fact."[46]

There is nothing, though, more unfitting than sin.[47] The problem with sin is that the sinner "is disturbing, as far as he is able, the order and beauty of the universe." Without recompense or punishment for sin, which have a certain "regulatory beauty," "there would be in the universe, which God ought to be regulating, a certain ugliness, resulting from the violation of the beauty of order, and God would appear to be failing in his governance."[48] As we turn to consider *Why God Became Man*, then, we note Anselm's initial answer to why God became man—because something had to be done to restore the ordered beauty of the universe. He offers the analogy of a dirty pearl: "What if he were to allow this same pearl to be knocked out of his hand into the mud

---

42. D. Hart, *Beauty of the Infinite*, 128.
43. Anselm, *Why God Became Man* 1.12.
44. This is the burden of Hogg, *Anselm of Canterbury*: "The most pervasive constituent of Anselm's *weltbild* . . . is aesthetics" (7).
45. The phrase comes from Augustine, *Trinity* 4.1.5.
46. Anselm, *Why God Became Man* 1.3. Anselm marvels at the beautiful truth of redemption: "In conformity with the fact that it is about someone beautiful . . . it is itself correspondingly beautiful in its logic, beyond the reasoning of men" (1.1). And the monk Boso praises the fitting style of *Why God Became Man*, which is as beautiful as it is true: "These pictures of yours are extremely beautiful and in accordance with logic" (2.8).
47. See Anselm, *Why God Became Man* 1.13.
48. Anselm, *Why God Became Man* 1.15. This helps explain, too, the fixed number of the elect picked up from Augustine and the need for the fallen angels to be replaced by the saints, though "there are to be more elect humans than there are bad angels" (1.18).

by some malignant person, although it was in his power to prevent this, and afterwards, picking it up from the mud, dirty and unwashed, were to store it away in some clean and costly receptacle of his, intending to keep it there in that state."[49] No, this action would not be fitting. A beautifully ordered universe suggests a recompense for sin that is "in proportion to the magnitude of the sin."[50] Mercy must align with justice.[51]

## Why *Did* God Become Man?

Why did God become man? Well, "for us and for our salvation": so goes the Nicene Creed. And true enough. But this raises the question of why our plight required this kind of saving action. Here is how Anselm puts it: "The question is this. By what logic or necessity did God become man, and by his death, as we believe and profess, restore life to the world, when he could have done this through the agency of some other person, angelic or human, or simply by willing it?"[52]

After all, if "God so loved the world," could he not more easily have simply zapped it all better? Why, if God is omnipotent, would he choose such a grisly manner of deliverance, such that not a few have detected in Anselmian accounts of the atonement "divine child abuse"?[53] The first question is theoretical: Might there not have been another way in general (possibly a simpler one)? The second question is closer to an objection, and it is a moral one: Isn't there something basically repugnant in forcing someone to die on behalf of others?

So Anselm sets out to lay bare the logic of incarnation and atonement.[54] The treatise is in dialogue form, with the figure of Boso (a monk Anselm had instructed at the monastery in Bec) playing the role of an unbeliever.[55] It is worth noting at the outset that Anselm's concern for justice is deeply aesthetic

49. Anselm, *Why God Became Man* 1.19.
50. Anselm, *Why God Became Man* 1.21. John Owen writes movingly (though in the milieu of penal substitution, not satisfaction) of the recompense required in light of such grave sin in *Communion with the Triune God*, 169–70.
51. Anselm, *Why God Became Man* 1.24.
52. Anselm, *Why God Became Man* 1.1.
53. On this charge, see Joanne Carlson Brown and Rebecca Parker, "For God So Loved the World?," and Rita Nakashima Brock, "And a Little Child Will Lead Us: Christology and Child Abuse," in Brown and Bohn, *Christianity, Patriarchy, and Abuse*, 1–30, 42–61.
54. As the eternal Son became incarnate in order to die (something that the narrative flow of the Gospels makes plain), to ask about the logic of incarnation is always also to ask about the logic of atonement, and vice versa.
55. Anselm, *Why God Became Man* 1.3.

in orientation.[56] Justice is not an abstract canon to which God is subject, but it reflects his beautiful, harmonious ordering of the world.[57] Anselm celebrates "the indescribable beauty of the fact that our redemption was procured in this way."[58] Justice is beautiful precisely in its alignment with God's good creation. This is important to point out, in light of how easily (if flatly) Anselm can be read as simply parroting the concerns of his medieval feudal society in such a way that God is merely a cosmic lord to whom honor is owed in a crassly economic relationship of quid pro quo.

One other word by way of introduction concerns Anselm's method. While there is a certain apologetic thrust to *Why God Became Man*, it is clear that Anselm is working from faith. His proposed *remoto Christo* methodology seeks to (only theoretically) abstract from Christ with regard to the questions at hand. Like a picture in which one chunk has been erased, Anselm paints the scene and tries to prove that the missing figure must of necessity be Christ.

*Why God Became Man* is divided into two parts. Book 1 considers the various objections of unbelievers to what they consider the irrationality of the Christian faith, eventually arguing that it is impossible that any can be saved without Christ. The book begins with the unbeliever's objection that the incarnation is unseemly.[59] It also seems to call into question God's omnipotence,[60] as he is required to condemn a just man for the salvation of sinners. But, Anselm insists, Christ was not coerced into giving up his life; he did so "of his own volition" for our sake.[61] Still, as the rationality of the death of Christ is a stumbling block, Anselm backs up to consider again whether one can reach a state of happiness, which requires the removal of sin, without Christ.

Anselm writes that sin is "not to give God what is owed to him."[62] The debt we owe him in return for his creating us is, simply, everything we are—the complete subjection of our wills to God, giving him all honor. "It is he who made us, and we are his" (Ps. 100:3). If we fail to give him all we are,

56. See Hogg, *Anselm of Canterbury*.
57. Gustaf Aulén's classic study tends toward a too reductive construal of "law" and "rationality" in Anselm. See Aulén, *Christus Victor*, 90–91.
58. Anselm, *Why God Became Man* 1.3.
59. Anselm, *Why God Became Man* 1.3; 1.8.
60. Anselm, *Why God Became Man* 1.8.
61. Anselm, *Why God Became Man* 1.8. Also see 1.9: "God, therefore, did not force Christ to die, there being no sin in him. Rather, he underwent death of his own accord, not out of an obedience consisting in the abandonment of his life, but out of an obedience consisting in his upholding of righteousness so bravely and pertinaciously that as a result he incurred death."
62. Anselm, *Why God Became Man* 1.11.

we rob him of what is rightfully his. A sinner who has robbed God of his honor is obliged to give him the satisfaction of repaying him more than he took, "in proportion to the insult which he has inflicted."[63] If God were to merely forgive without punishment or payment, then anarchy would rule with regard to sin. This is unfitting, in that it would make sinner and nonsinner similar before God,[64] when in reality sin has violated the "universal order."[65] Were sin to go without recompense, as we saw above, "there would be in the universe, which God ought to be regulating, a certain ugliness, resulting from the violation of the beauty of order, and God would appear to be failing in his governance."[66] From here a long digression ensues on whether the number of fallen angels is to be made up by humanity.[67] This question, too, relates to the good order of God's creation. Part of the relevance of the discussion is that it would be unfitting to admit into fellowship with the angels sinners who have not paid recompense.[68] Recompense must be "proportional to the magnitude of the sin."[69]

But—and herein lies the problem—how can we recompense God for sin if we already owe him everything? Where would we find the resources to pay God back? Furthermore, in robbing God, humanity robs itself; we are impoverished by our sin. In our defeat, "the devil took what belonged to God, and God lost it"—namely, God's intention for humanity.[70] So, unless we return to God what we took, we cannot receive from him what he planned to give. We are, in short "rotten . . . in a ferment with sin."[71] Not that this sad state, this incapacity, renders us innocent.[72] At this point, Boso states the dilemma: "How, then, will man be saved, if he does not himself pay what he owes, and is bound not to be saved if he does not pay?"[73] Book 1 concludes that humanity owes a debt to God it is unable to pay, and it is a debt that must be paid for humanity to be saved. Christ is necessary, then, for our salvation and for God's intention in creation to be accomplished—that is, for God to be seen to be God.

---

63. Anselm, *Why God Became Man* 1.11. Though note that "no one can honour or dishonour God, so far as God himself is concerned" (1.15).
64. Anselm, *Why God Became Man* 1.12.
65. Anselm, *Why God Became Man* 1.13.
66. Anselm, *Why God Became Man* 1.15.
67. Anselm, *Why God Became Man* 1.16–18. They are, by the way (1.19).
68. Anselm, *Why God Became Man* 1.19.
69. Anselm, *Why God Became Man* 1.20; 1.21.
70. Anselm, *Why God Became Man* 1.23.
71. Anselm, *Why God Became Man* 1.23.
72. Anselm, *Why God Became Man* 1.24. Anselm evocatively speaks of how original sin "percolates through to the whole human race from our first ancestors" (2.17).
73. Anselm, *Why God Became Man* 1.25.

Book 2, in which Anselm will make "another beginning,"[74] argues that humanity was created to "enjoy blessed immortality" and that "this could only happen through the agency of a Man-God."[75] Humanity was created rational (thus able to "love and choose the good") and righteous that it might attain to happiness "by rejoicing in the highest good, that is, in God."[76] Had we never sinned, we would not have died.[77] Despite our sin and the entrance of death, it is "necessary" that God "should finish what he has begun" with regard to humanity. It would hardly be fitting for the Creator to abandon his creation; no, he will bring it to fulfillment. Nevertheless, this necessity is more aptly called grace, in that it is performed by God freely, not under compulsion. So to speak of necessity in this case is to evoke "the unchangeability of God's honour . . . although the whole of what he does is grace."[78] But again, this can't be done without recompense paid for sin.[79] The payment has to be so great because it is the honor of *God* that has been stolen, because the offended party is infinite. And yet, while we cannot pay it, we must. Hence the necessity of a God-man: "For God will not do it because it will not be his obligation to do it, and a man will not do it because he will not be able to. In order, therefore, that a God-Man should bring about what is necessary, it is essential that the same one person who will make the recompense should be perfect God and perfect man. For he cannot do this if he is not true God, and he has no obligation to do so if he is not a true man."[80] God must take an Adamic human nature rather than creating a new one, because the one giving recompense on behalf of the race should be of that race.[81]

Because the God-man is not a sinner, he is not bound to die.[82] Thus, he dies freely, as mortality is not "a property essential for the genuineness of human nature."[83] His death, then, is something above and beyond what he owes to God. It is the ultimate human self-giving and, insofar as it is painful,

74. Anselm, *Why God Became Man* 1.25.
75. Anselm, *Why God Became Man* 2.preface.
76. Anselm, *Why God Became Man* 2.1.
77. Anselm, *Why God Became Man* 2.2. Related is Anselm's doctrine of both a human and an angelic probation.
78. Anselm, *Why God Became Man* 2.5.
79. Anselm, *Why God Became Man* 2.4.
80. Anselm, *Why God Became Man* 2.7.
81. Anselm, *Why God Became Man* 2.8. Anselm has a very thoughtful point about the role of women here: "Moreover, women might lose hope that they have a part in the destiny of the blessed ones, in view of the fact that such great evil proceeded from a woman: in order to prevent this, it is right that an equivalent great good should proceed from a woman, so as to rebuild their hope" (2.8).
82. Anselm, *Why God Became Man* 2.10.
83. Anselm, *Why God Became Man* 2.11.

is a fitting counterpart to the pleasure of sin. Yet, for all this, the God-man is not unhappy, as he takes on discomfort willingly rather than out of necessity.[84] Jesus's death outweighs all sins.[85] His death can even destroy the sin of those who killed him, since they did so in ignorance.[86] Boso asks how God produced a sinless man from sinful matter. Anselm grounds his answer in Mary's sinlessness, though he is quick to note that "his mother's cleanness, whereby he is clean, would not have existed, if it had not come from him, and so he was clean on his own account and by his own agency."[87] The question of Jesus's death seems again to suggest an improper necessity—that is, one in which Jesus was compelled rather than free to give his life. Anselm revisits the question of necessity, insisting that no necessity or impossibility exists in God, but only his will. Anselm reminds Boso of Jesus's words in John 10:18: "No one takes [my life] from me, but I lay it down of my own accord. I have authority to lay it down, and I have authority to take it up again." In addition to being a debt paid, Anselm considers Jesus's obedience and death as an example to imitate,[88] though this is subordinate to Anselm's satisfaction model of atonement. In conclusion, Anselm notes that Christ's death is the only time someone has given God something that he would not have lost by necessity; furthermore, it was the only debt paid to God by humanity that the person giving it didn't owe.[89] It seems that the Father should give the Son compensation for his great gift. But the Son is God and needs nothing, so the Father should give his gift to another.[90] Hence, the restoration of humanity.

## On the Atonement, Briefly

A brief comment about descriptions of the atonement is in order before we ask a key question of Anselm. Ever since Gustaf Aulén's work *Christus Victor*, teachers and scholars have found it useful to speak of three major models of atonement. The *Christus Victor* model emphasizes God's victory in Christ over sin, death, and the devil. Anselm is the classic exponent of the *satisfaction model*, in which Christ satisfies the demands of divine justice. A

---

84. Anselm, *Why God Became Man* 2.12.
85. Anselm, *Why God Became Man* 2.14.
86. Anselm, *Why God Became Man* 2.15.
87. Anselm, *Why God Became Man* 2.16.
88. Anselm, *Why God Became Man* 2.18.
89. Anselm, *Why God Became Man* 2.18. As beautiful as this passage is, I wonder how convincing it is. After all, it seems that, had Jesus *not* given his life, he would have sinfully disobeyed the Father. Why not see him as perfect, rather than as this supererogatory man?
90. Anselm, *Why God Became Man* 2.19.

later, significant modification of the satisfaction model is *penal substitution*, which foregrounds Christ's being punished for our sin in our place. The *moral influence*, or *exemplarist*, *model* is a "subjective" account focusing on the transformative power of Christ's suffering as an example for us. It's wise to deflate the language of "models," though, and refer instead to "descriptions" of the atonement that use certain metaphors to communicate the saving work of Christ. "Models" too readily suggests that only one such description is viable (when Scripture uses many descriptions) and also that one is *enough* to explain the mystery of salvation. It is worth noting in passing that, despite tendencies to read the models of atonement as alternatives, strands of them are often found in the same writings. While Anselm usually thinks in terms of a satisfaction account, he speaks stirringly of Christ's faithful obedience as an example for imitation.[91]

In speaking of the atonement in terms of satisfaction, Anselm explicitly rejected the then-popular understanding of the atonement as a ransom paid to the devil. At the fall, according to the ransom account, Adam and Eve came under the jurisdiction of the devil, who thenceforth was their "lawful possessor."[92] In light of this, some just way needed to be found to return humanity to God's possession. By orchestrating the killing of an innocent man (and God) in Christ, the devil forfeited his rights to humanity. At times in the tradition, this transaction could be described in terms of divine trickery, with God winning back humanity by being hidden in the humanity of Christ, like a Trojan horse.[93]

Ever quick to appeal to the honor and majesty of God, Anselm would not countenance a description of the devil as some sort of rival with God. Such talk veers toward a dualism in which God and Satan are foes struggling over disputed turf.[94] On the contrary, "neither the devil nor man belongs to anyone but God," and "neither stands outside God's power."[95] "Certainly God did not owe the devil anything but punishment, nor did man owe him anything but retribution—to defeat in return him by whom he had been defeated. But, whatever was demanded from man, his debt was to God, not to the devil."[96] Anselm's discrediting of a significant theme in the ransom account need not be taken to the point of excising ransom language from our soteriology. After

91. Anselm, *Why God Became Man* 2.18–19; also see 2.11.

92. Anselm, *Why God Became Man* 1.7.

93. Most famously, Gregory of Nyssa writes, "God, in order to make himself easily accessible to him who sought the ransom for us, veiled himself in our nature. In that way, as it is with greedy fish, he might swallow the Godhead like a fishhook along with the flesh, which was the bait" (*Catechetical Oration* 24).

94. The dualism charge is outlined in Gunton, *Actuality of Atonement*, 88–89.

95. Anselm, *Why God Became Man* 1.7. Also see 1.6. Note that this is Boso speaking.

96. Anselm, *Why God Became Man* 2.19.

all, Jesus gave his life "as a ransom for many" (Matt. 20:28; Mark 10:45), and we were "ransomed from the futile ways inherited from [our] forefathers" (1 Pet. 1:18) by the blood of Jesus for God (Rev. 5:9). The question, as always, is not the term but its intended meaning: What exactly do we mean by ransom? What is its price? How and to whom is it paid?

### Divine Child Abuse?

Now to our question for Anselm. What of the charge I mentioned earlier, that such a violent account of divine payback amounts to no more than divine child abuse? To many, Christian accounts of the cross of Christ smack of the worst form of inhumane paganism. A grisly scene is conjured in which a bloodthirsty, vengeful god tortures his divine son, rather than the sad account of a righteous man whose prophetic and peaceful ways provoked an angry world to kill him. In addition to misreading the gospel accounts, so goes the objection, to ascribe this kind of violence to God and inscribe it *within* God is to underwrite abusive patterns—an angry dad who holds all the power, a son who is convinced it's all his fault and so bears all the responsibility.[97] Better to learn the ways of resistance, not fall into a mode of victimization in the name of righteous martyrdom. So goes the objection. Can it be sustained in Anselm's case?[98]

The first thing to note is Anselm's insistence on Jesus's willing obedience. Given Anselm's construal of human freedom as the capacity to maintain rectitude of will for its own sake, it would seem that Jesus was *free* in his death. As he tells his disciples, "No one takes [my life] from me, but I lay it down of my own accord" (John 10:18). Still, Boso retorts, even if Christ was willing, "since he consented to the will of the Father, it nevertheless seems that the Father did coerce him, through the instructions he gave him."[99] There is plenty of evidence of abuse victims playing along, even at times actively complying in their abuse, but they are hardly free, given the power dynamics at play. Anselm

97. The cleaving of power and responsibility characterizes environments of abuse; so Keshgegian, "Scandal of the Cross."
98. I'll leave largely implicit whether it can be sustained at all. Suffice it to say that, ironically, the divine child abuse objection seems destined to end in violence. It can in no way countenance the view that Christ might triumph and bring peace through suffering and can, at best, propose instead continual vigilance in the face of injustice. This is right and good as far as it goes, but it is only Christ himself who "is our peace, who has made us both one and has broken down in his flesh the dividing wall of hostility by abolishing the law of commandments expressed in ordinances, that he might create in himself one new man in place of the two, so making peace, and might reconcile us both to God in one body through the cross, thereby killing the hostility" (Eph. 2:14–16).
99. Anselm, *Why God Became Man* 1.8.

argues, though, that God required *obedience* of Jesus, not death, because Jesus's sinlessness would not have issued in death. "Rather, he underwent death of his own accord, not out of an obedience consisting in the abandonment of his life, but out of an obedience consisting in his upholding of righteousness so bravely and pertinaciously that as a result he incurred death." It is vital to distinguish between "what Christ did because of the demands of his obedience" and "the suffering, inflicted upon him because he maintained his obedience, which he underwent even though his obedience did not demand it."[100]

Anselm's repeated insistence on divine impassibility further suggests that claims of divine child abuse are misguided. True, Anselm appeals repeatedly to the honor of God, which evokes the feudal society of his day and the nearly absolute ecclesial obedience that he frequently enjoined upon himself and others. But honor and submission were hardly mere tools for the inflation of ego and the negotiation of power. Rather, power itself was a tool for negotiating a properly ordered—that is, beautiful—society. The impassible God is not, strictly speaking, "affronted or offended by transgression."[101] He secures his honor through judgment and, finally, the cross for the sake of the world. This is no raging father lashing out. Similarly, Jesus Christ is no cowering victim, but the eternal Son in the flesh. As the eternal Son, he remains "incapable of suffering," so that "in the incarnation of God it is understood that no humiliation of God came about: rather it is believed that human nature was exalted."[102]

Anselm's soteriology is best understood through the lens of satisfaction, not punishment. Jesus paid our debt, but he was not punished in our place. In fact, Anselm's account of the atonement is "explicitly anti-penal."[103] Colin Gunton insists that "they are not only different but *alternatives*. Satisfaction is therefore according to Anselm the way by which God is enabled *not* to exact a tribute of compensating penalty from the sinner. He is therefore not propounding a version of what came to be called penal substitution, in which Jesus is conceived to be punished by God in place of the sinner. There is a substitution, an exchange, but it is not primarily penal in character."[104]

---

100. Anselm, *Why God Became Man* 1.9. "It must not be overlooked that for Anselm it is not Christ's *suffering* as such that is redemptive (the suffering merely repeats sin's endlessly repeated and essential gesture), but rather his innocence; he recapitulates humanity by passing through all the violences of sin and death, rendering to God the obedience that is his due, and so transforms the event of his death into an occasion of infinite blessings for those to whom death is condign" (D. Hart, *Beauty of the Infinite*, 371).

101. Gunton, *Actuality of Atonement*, 90.

102. Anselm, *Why God Became Man* 1.8.

103. Thomas Williams, in personal correspondence with the author.

104. Gunton, *Actuality of Atonement*, 90–91. Gunton is responding to John McIntyre's distinction between punishment and satisfaction.

But what if it were penal (and here I am speaking for myself, not Anselm)? Ought we to object to the notion that the Father punishes the Son in our place at the cross? It seems to me necessary at least to acknowledge the cross as an indirect form of punishment. Jesus takes on the consequences of our sin in suffering unjustly at the hands of the Romans and Jews. Furthermore, death for sin is a concept deeply imbedded in the animal sacrifices so central to Israel's life with God; clearly, the purification and reconciliation of Israel with God required stark measures. And this was a purification and reconciliation necessitated by Israel's failure to keep the conditions of the covenant. Surely this must be seen as some form of punishment, even if a merciful and restorative one.

An underdeveloped trinitarian theology might lead us to see such punishment in starkly oppositional terms, with the Father meting out suffering to the Son, who stands in our place.[105] But beside the theologically inadmissible claim that the Father and Son might be at odds, consider: What loving father could possibly bear the pain of killing his own son? Isn't it the mercy of God that he reserves such a task for himself and does not even require it of his faithful servant Abraham? If one reads the crucifixion next to the binding of Isaac (Gen. 22), one can more easily comprehend the compassion of the Father in the death of his Son for the world they love.

And what of the whole idea of substitution? Well, that is as deeply woven into the fabric of Scripture as one could imagine. It overlaps significantly with representation, which suggests a participation in the work of our representative. But substitution implies something done in our place, and it underscores the uniqueness and completeness of Christ's work. Consider just one verse, Ephesians 5:2: "And walk in love, as Christ loved us and gave himself up for us, a fragrant offering and sacrifice to God." There is Christ, priest and victim, the one who freely, actively gave his life for us—an act of total self-sacrifice pleasing and, Anselm might add, beautiful to the Father. Christ is our sacrificial substitute at the cross, doing something that we could not and will not be called to do, that he might represent us as a faithful high priest before the Father and serve as a model for our daily dying and rising with him.


### A Few More Thoughts on Faith Seeking Understanding

What, then, of the relation between faith and reason that we began with? Having impressionistically sketched the issues in the *Monologion*, *Proslogion*,

---

105. Though see now, and decisively, McCall, *Forsaken*, 13–91.

and *On the Incarnation of the Word*, we looked more in depth at freedom, necessity, and fittingness in *Why God Became Man* on the assumption that the notion of the sorts of things God "must" do might help uncover the reasons driving Anselm's faith. We could not improve on, and so conclude with, the following judgment of Sandra Visser and Thomas Williams:

> Anselm does not assume any incompatibility, even a prima facie one, between faith and reason; nor does he assign a distinctive role to each.[106] So rather than saying that Anselm has a view about the relationship between faith and reason, it is perhaps better to say that he has a view about "the reason of faith": the *ratio fidei*. "The reason of faith" is perhaps not idiomatic English, but the best idiomatic translations of *ratio fidei* are misleading. "The rational basis of faith" suggests something external: arguments in support of doctrinal formulations that have an apologetic or protreptic purpose. "The logic of faith" suggests something internal: the rational coherence of the doctrines of faith, the way they "all hang together" logically. Anselm's *ratio fidei* means both these things at once; it refers to the intrinsically rational character of Christian doctrines in virtue of which they form a coherent and rationally defensible system. . . .
>
> Anselm holds that the doctrines of the Christian faith are intrinsically rational because they concern the nature and activity of God, who is himself supreme reason and exemplifies supreme wisdom in everything he does. And because human beings are rational by nature, we can grasp the reason of faith.[107]

This is a lovely sketch of Anselm's take on faith and reason; one wonders, though, whether its rosy conclusion—that by virtue of our rational constitution, "we can grasp the reason of faith"—belies the sheer intellectual difficulty of following Anselm's lead. Faith may make sense, but who among us is smart enough to follow that sense through to its logical conclusion? Might it not be that Anselm is just right, but nevertheless inimitable? Perhaps he is a Mozart—utterly, beautifully ordered in his work, but the kind of prodigy that invites admirers rather than imitators.[108]

One reason for this is Anselm's failure—and I regard it as something of a failure—to tether his reflection more explicitly to Scripture. The absence

---

106. For Anselm "theological knowledge was a single science; it operated by reason under the guidance of faith; but the arguments, insofar as they were based on cogent reasons, could be meaningful to those who lacked faith" (Dulles, *History of Apologetics*, 103).

107. Visser and Williams, *Anselm*, 13–14.

108. See, possibly, Southern, *Saint Anselm*, 440, 443; Visser and Williams, *Anselm*, 73. The worry about such virtuosity in biblical exegesis, coupled with the suggestion that the brilliance of such virtuosos cannot be distilled to a methodology capable of imitation, comes from Brevard Childs, "Toward Recovering Theological Exegesis," *Pro Ecclesia* 6 (1997): 19, cited in R. Wright, "Karl Barth's Academic Lectures on Ephesians," vii–viii.

of direct biblical engagement obscures the sources of Anselm's assumptions and therefore shrouds his work from view. We cannot think his thoughts after him when we do not know where his thoughts came from. Perhaps a shared horizon can be assumed for Anselm and those for whom he wrote, which would render his sources transparent to the reader, but this is not the case for us today, when so few are biblically literate—which only magnifies the need for guidance in moving from Scripture to philosophical and theological conclusions. Nor, though, is it enough to simply lay bare these moves by an anemic and naive appeal to biblical proof texts, which themselves often function as wax noses easily shaped to fit the needs of the moment. Engagement with Scripture requires careful interpretation, not casual enlistment. Theology needs must serve the interpretation of the Bible; the Bible need not, and may not, bend the knee to theology. Scripture is the rudder of theology's ship; it is not merely authoritative ballast.

"I do not think that anyone deserves to be rebuked," writes Anselm, "if, after becoming well-grounded in the faith, he has conceived a desire to exercise himself in the investigation of its logic." After all, "the understanding which we gain in this life stands midway between faith and revelation."[109] In this, Anselm's *meditatio* anticipates the heavenly beatific vision.[110] "*Intellectus* [or understanding]," writes Karl Barth, "is the limited, but fully attainable, first step towards that vision which is the eschatological counterpart of faith. Therefore *fides* is essentially—*quaerens intellectum.*"[111] And so, in *Why God Became Man*, Anselm resolves, "Insofar as the heavenly grace deigns to allow [him], to arise to contemplate the logic of our beliefs."[112] As he put it in a letter to Fulk, bishop of Beauvais, soon after getting wind of Roscelin's heresy: "For a Christian ought to progress through faith to understanding, not reach faith through understanding—or, if he cannot understand, leave faith behind. Now if he can achieve understanding, he rejoices; but if he cannot, he stands in awe of what he cannot grasp."[113]

If Anselm is virtuosic—even prodigious—in his ability to abstract and analyze the logic of faith, we may nevertheless follow his lead in finding in meditation the vehicle by which the Spirit moves us from faith to understanding. Let us consider meditation that posture of patient attention to Scripture in which the Spirit deepens our delight in the God of the gospel through sustained and expansive exposure to God's ways with the world. In one sense, it is not that

---

109. In the commendation of *Why God Became Man* to Pope Urban II.
110. See Southern, *Saint Anselm*, 114, 127.
111. Barth, *Anselm*, 21.
112. In the commendation of *Why God Became Man* to Pope Urban II.
113. Cited in Visser and Williams, *Anselm*, 19.

meditation—or, for that matter, the beatific vision itself—tells us something new about God. After all, God has spoken definitively in his Son, the Word who is the last word about God. In another sense, though, it is when faith becomes sight that we will declare, with Job,

> I had heard of you by the hearing of the ear,
>     but now my eye sees you;
> therefore I despise myself,
>     and repent in dust and ashes. (Job 42:5–6)

# 6

# "ST. THOMAS OF THE CREATOR"

*Aquinas and the Beginning and End*
*of All Things in God*

In his rollicking, insightful, and occasionally ridiculous book on Thomas Aquinas, G. K. Chesterton comments that "there is a general tone and temper of Aquinas, which it is as difficult to avoid as daylight in a great house of windows. It is that *positive* position of his mind, which is filled and soaked as with sunshine with the warmth of the wonder of created things."[1] One might consider all of Thomas's theology as a resonant "Yes!" to God's good creation.[2] He is so enthralled by the brilliance of beings, so distracted by their dizzying diversity, that Chesterton suggests an apt epithet. He should be known as "St. Thomas of the Creator."[3]

---

1. Chesterton, *St. Thomas Aquinas*, 139–40.

2. The German theologian and martyr Dietrich Bonhoeffer wrote to his fiancée, Maria von Wedemeyer: "Our marriage must be a 'yes' to God's earth" (Bonhoeffer and von Wedemeyer, *Love Letters from Cell 92*, 64). Compare Josef Pieper's description of "the qualities which made Thomas what he was: the all-inclusive, fearless strength of his affirmation, his generous acceptance of the whole of reality, the trustful magnanimity of his thought" (Pieper, *Silence of St. Thomas*, 103).

3. Chesterton, *St. Thomas Aquinas*, 140. Chesterton writes, "It was his special spiritual thesis that there really are Things, and not only the Thing; that the Many existed as well as the One" (159).

If you have read even a bit of Thomas's work, this may come as something of a surprise. He seldom seems exuberant; he never exclaims. He is patient, quiet, even plodding. There is an Alpine purity and clarity to his writing, an "untroubled and unhurried serenity" to be sure,[4] but its peaceable manner frequently renders it soporific. No wild-eyed wonderer shouting from the rooftops, the contemplative Thomas is more likely to put his readers to sleep. We may as well admit this from the start. Plenty of readers of Thomas glaze over and struggle to get past the slow and steady march of his mind. If we would like more personality—and I, for one, would—we ought not to assume that biographical color is always an asset in theology. Read Augustine, and you will seldom forget you are reading *Augustine*. This creates sympathy and eases our passage into the flow of Augustine's thoughts and feelings. It enhances the sense that theology is self-involving speech. But perhaps we meet Augustine so vividly at least in part because of his difficulty in moving past himself. Thomas seems, by contrast, entirely self-forgetful.[5] Caught up in contemplation, Thomas seems unaware of himself and only slightly aware of his audience; he is enraptured, however, by his God and all else as it relates to him.[6]

## The Life of Thomas

Though his placidity seldom suggests it, Thomas was embroiled in controversy from his youth, whether despite himself (his personality hardly lent itself to picking fights) or because of himself (his principles often landed him on the side of the underdog).[7] The son of a prominent nobleman close to the emperor, Thomas was born in Aquino, midway between Rome and Naples.[8] He spent his grade school years with the Benedictine monks at the abbey of Monte Cassino. When imperial troops took over Monte Cassino in 1239, Thomas

4. Pieper, *Silence of St. Thomas*, 3.
5. For this contrast of Augustine and Thomas, see Pieper, *Silence of St. Thomas*, 3–4.
6. This language of being "caught up" betrays the fact that, for Thomas, the philosophical rigor and focus of his writing complements, rather than competes with, a certain mysticism. Theology is contemplative; it is also the fruit of contemplation, a handing on of what one has contemplated to others (*contemplate aliis tradere*). Mysticism serves a pastoral end: "For even as it is better to enlighten than merely to shine, so is it better to give to others the fruits of one's contemplation than merely to contemplate" (*ST* II-II.188.6). Also see Bauerschmidt, *Thomas Aquinas*, 173–74.
7. See Cessario, *Short History of Thomism*, 40.
8. On Thomas's life, begin with Torrell, *Person and His Work*. Also see Bauerschmidt, *Thomas Aquinas*, 1–37; Chenu, *Aquinas and His Role*; Chesterton, *St. Thomas Aquinas*; O'Meara, *Thomas Aquinas Theologian*, 1–40; Pieper, *Silence of St. Thomas*, 3–41.

was sent home and soon thereafter moved to study the liberal arts at Naples, where he was likely first exposed to Aristotle. After a few years studying in Naples, Thomas became a Dominican, entering the Order of Preachers, a group of begging friars committed to study and teaching the gospel. His family had hoped he would join the Benedictines and one day become the abbot of Monte Cassino, a powerful position that would befit and forward their standing in the world. To us, nearly nine centuries later, any difference between the Benedictines and the Dominicans may seem trivial. But in Thomas's day, the newly founded mendicant orders were firebrands, upsetting the established economic, educational, and religious orders.[9] Their vow of poverty alone was enough to unsettle a monastic culture that, in the eyes of Francis and Dominic, had grown fat on the wealth of the church. Marie-Dominique Chenu maintains that "Thomas Aquinas's refusal of Monte Cassino is the exact parallel to Francis of Assisi's gesture of renunciation."[10] His mother was so scandalized that she provoked Thomas's brothers to kidnap him while he was on the way to Paris as a novice Dominican; only a year later did she relent and allow him to continue his journey.

In Paris, the heart of Christian intellectual life and a seedbed of controversy, Thomas met his famous teacher, Albertus Magnus, or Albert the Great. After three years of study there, Thomas followed Albert to Cologne. Thomas returned to teach in Paris, commenting on Peter Lombard's *Sentences* (the regnant theological textbook of the day). Then, in 1256, he became a master of theology, or a "master of the sacred page." He was responsible for "reading" (or commenting on) Scripture, disputing, and teaching. An eager and able disputant, Thomas adopted a method that, "far from excluding the thought of his opponent, examines it instead as a step in his quest for truth."[11] And Thomas had plenty of opponents, chief among whom were those opposed to the mendicant orders and their presence on the faculty of the University of Paris and, especially late in life, those suspicious of Thomas's affinity for Aristotle.

Returning to Italy for nearly a decade, Thomas completed his *Summa contra gentiles* and began the *Summa theologiae* while teaching in Orvieto and Rome. Following this remarkably fertile period, he returned for a final time to Paris, where he taught for four years amidst a series of incandescent

9. "To vow 'mendicancy' in the thirteenth century was to refuse the feudal system of the Church both institutionally and economically" (Chenu, *Aquinas and His Role*, 8).

10. Chenu, *Aquinas and His Role*, 7.

11. Chenu, *Aquinas and His Role*, 68. This is everywhere evident in the *Summa theologiae*, where the opening objections are the strongest arguments against Thomas's eventual position and contribute to the nuanced distinctions and conclusions that follow.

debates over the interpretation of Aristotle, in which Thomas would be held guilty by association.

It is worth pausing at this point to locate Aristotle in Thomas's thought.[12] Recall Luther's quip that Denys "is more of a Platonist than a Christian."[13] Similarly, if some praise Thomas for "baptizing" Aristotle, others wonder just who is baptizing whom. It doesn't take long in reading Thomas to discover that the *form* of his thought is recognizably Aristotelian. He conceives of the being and act of creatures in terms borrowed from Aristotelian physics: form and matter, potency and act, a fourfold set of causes. Josef Pieper suggests that Thomas admired and appropriated Aristotle as "nothing more nor less than a clear mirror of the natural reality of creation."[14] One could read for pages with little awareness that Thomas is writing a theological text; Thomas learned from "the Philosopher" (his deferential title for Aristotle) to praise and ponder the immanent logic of creation. The natural order needs nothing beyond itself to move Thomas to joyful contemplation.[15] "Canadian geese flying south are driven by their own biology, not by an angel or by an instinct leading them to form crosses in the sky en route. Their life and not an imposed religious symbolism glorifies their maker."[16] To speak anachronistically and somewhat reductively, we can say that it is from Aristotle that Thomas learned to be an empiricist.

If Thomas found Aristotle "nothing less . . . than a clear mirror of the natural reality of creation," he also found "nothing more." Aristotle taught Thomas to attend to and trust his senses, but he could not lead Thomas all the way to God. "Our natural knowledge begins from sense. Hence our natural knowledge can go as far as it can be led by sensible things. But our mind cannot be led by sense so far as to see the essence of God; because the sensible effects of God do not equal the power of God as their cause."[17] The end of the rational creature is the vision of God, a vision at once beautiful and beatifying. So, while Aristotle could point Thomas to the importance of attending to the end of things and directing rational creatures to the happiness that consists in virtuous action, he could not articulate the name above all names that belongs to the One in whose presence the virtuous attain to blessedness.

12. See the perceptive account in Decosimo, *Ethics as a Work of Charity*.
13. Luther, *LW* 36:109.
14. Pieper, *Silence of St. Thomas*, 32.
15. Though Pieper's thesis, that the hidden secret of all things is that they are created—that is, that they are not themselves by themselves—merits bearing in mind. See Pieper, *Silence of St. Thomas*, 47–50.
16. O'Meara, *Thomas Aquinas Theologian*, 104.
17. Thomas Aquinas, *ST* I.12.12.

An old trope describes philosophy as the "handmaiden" to theology, and it nicely suggests Aristotle's role in Thomas's thought. Never master, Aristotle was nevertheless chief among the pagan ministers Thomas employed in his work as a Dominican, preaching and teaching the gospel. Jean-Pierre Torrell explains that Thomas began commenting on Aristotle's writings as an "urgent apostolic task" enabling him to proceed in certain difficult patches of doctrinal terrain as he wrote the *Summa theologiae*. "He did not put aside composition of the *Summa*; rather, he was given the means to carry it out."[18] There is no need, then, to posit a conflict between Thomas's Aristotelianism and his Christianity; the former fashions tools with which to make sense of the latter. For this reason, "Aristotle is a different kind of 'source' for Aquinas than is the Bible or Augustine." Thomas is "a Christian theologian whose starting point is provided to him by the teachings of scripture and the tradition interpreting scripture."[19]

Following Thomas's third period in Paris, he returned for a final time to teach in Naples. After a couple years there, while he was celebrating Mass, something happened. "After that Mass, he never wrote further or even dictated anything, and he even got rid of his writing material." He said later to his companion Reginald, "I cannot do any more. Everything I have written seems to me as straw in comparison with what I have seen."[20] A couple months later, Thomas was called by the pope to a council at Lyons to advise on reconciliation with Eastern Christians. He grew ill along the way and died at the abbey of Fossanova on March 7, 1274.

In Thomas, we find someone set apart by the Spirit to give witness to the Triune Creator in the midst of a sea change in Europe and the Western church. Perhaps more than any other, Thomas articulates a doctrine of creation that is profoundly theocentric and patiently attendant on the variety, order, and integrity of creation. In this respect, he seeks to give creation its due precisely by ascribing it to the Triune God,[21] recognizing that creation is as much a

---

18. Torrell, *Person and His Work*, 174. In *Idea of a University*, John Henry Newman makes this point colorfully: "With the jawbone of an ass, with the skeleton philosophy of pagan Greece, did the Samson of the schools put to flight his thousand Philistines" (226). Newman approvingly picks up the suggestion of Thomas's nineteenth-century French editors that Thomas "made an alliance, not with Plato, but with Aristotle," because Aristotle stayed in his lane, "confin[ing] himself to human science, and therefore was secured from coming into collision with divine" (202).

19. Wawrykow, *God's Grace and Human Action*, 264.

20. This material comes from one of Thomas's first biographers, cited in Torrell, *Person and His Work*, 289.

21. "We might even say he was always defending the independence of dependent things" (Chesterton, *St. Thomas Aquinas*, 38).

part of Christian confession as salvation and, indeed, that "error concerning creatures . . . spills over into false opinion about God, and takes men's minds away from Him."[22] Thomas's approach finds its center in the One who "for us and for our salvation" became flesh and dwelt among us. The richness of Thomas's insight circles around a doctrine of grace that seeks to honor his doctrine of creation—and yet ensures that humanity is effectively brought to its end in God. But before considering humanity, or creation itself, we need to turn our attention to the God who creates.

## Who Is God? (Part 1): He Is Who He Is

Considering how much Thomas wrote about God, it might come as a surprise to hear him insist at the beginning of the *Summa theologiae* that "what He is not is clearer to us than what He is."[23] Nor is this a pious admission largely ignored over the course of the *Summa*. Having established that God exists, Thomas proceeds to inquire into the manner of his existence. "Now, because we cannot know what God is, but rather what He is not, we have no means for considering how God is, but rather how He is not." Only after considering "how He is not" will Thomas turn to "how He is known by us" and "how He is named." The ensuing discussion of divine simplicity, perfection, infinity, immutability, and unity functions to show "how God is not, by denying Him whatever is opposed to the idea of Him."[24] We need to keep this apophatic function of the classical divine attributes in mind, in light of the charge that Thomas imprisons God in a metaphysical straitjacket tailored by Aristotle and hardly a fitting sartorial choice for the dynamic God of the Bible. God is not "necessary being," as he was for Aristotle, but the "cause of being"; with this move, Aquinas erases "any hint of 'onto-theology,' since the cause of being cannot itself *be* in the manner of anything which it causes."[25]

Thomas intends to deny a handful of claims we might make about God as dead ends along the way to the knowledge and love of God. We can summarize Thomas's account of how God is not in three claims:

1. God has no potential.
2. God does not have a real relationship with his creation.
3. God is utterly devoid of passion.

22. Thomas Aquinas, *SCG* 2.3.6.
23. Thomas Aquinas, *ST* I.1.9 ad 3.
24. Thomas Aquinas, *ST* I.3. See *ST* I.3–11.
25. Burrell, "Analogy, Creation, and Theological Language," 82.

Despite this inauspicious set of claims, Thomas can claim that God is, as Scripture frequently repeats, the "living God."[26] In fact, his very liveliness ensures the three negative claims above.

Consider the first claim, that God has no potential. I might tell one of my students, "You've got a lot of potential!" This could be a backhanded compliment—a way of saying, "You've got a lot of work to do." But even so, it holds out the possibility that my student really could become something, that what is now only potential could become realized, that the student could fulfill that potential. While my student may have a lot of potential, Thomas is clear that God has no potential at all. If my student had no potential, that would suggest she was a lost cause, a hopeless case. But with God, things are different. He has no potential because he is already fully himself. "God is pure act, without any potentiality."[27] God is who he is, and he can be no other. Thomas first demonstrates the existence of God in making sense of God's self-identification in conversation with Moses:

> Then Moses said to God, "If I come to the people of Israel and say to them, 'The God of your fathers has sent me to you,' and they ask me, 'What is his name?' what shall I say to them?" God said to Moses, "I AM WHO I AM." And he said, "Say this to the people of Israel: 'I AM has sent me to you.'" God also said to Moses, "Say this to the people of Israel: 'The LORD, the God of your fathers, the God of Abraham, the God of Isaac, and the God of Jacob, has sent me to you.' This is my name forever, and thus I am to be remembered throughout all generations." (Exod. 3:13–15)[28]

In what is at once a self-revelation and a radical challenge to any attempts to delimit him, the God of Abraham, Isaac, and Jacob bluntly tells Moses that he determines himself. He is who he is.[29] As the One who is, primordially, this One is pure act, and so can never be acted upon by another. In an

26. See Deut. 5:26; Josh. 3:10; 1 Sam. 17:26, 36; 2 Kings 19:4, 16; Pss. 42:2; 84:2; Isa. 37:4, 17; Jer. 10:10; 23:36; Dan. 6:20, 26; Hosea 1:10; Matt. 16:16; 26:63; Acts 14:15; Rom. 9:26; 2 Cor. 3:3; 6:16; 1 Tim. 3:15; 4:10; Heb. 3:12; 9:14; 10:31; 12:22; Rev. 7:2.

27. Thomas Aquinas, *ST* I.3.2, which Thomas says "has been shown" at *ST* I.2.3.

28. Kendall Soulen argues persuasively that the Tetragrammaton (YHWH), signaled in Exod. 3:15 and throughout the Old Testament by the pious surrogate "the LORD," is the divine name and is not to be collapsed into the two "I AM" statements, which "are not themselves the divine name but clarifications of it" (*Divine Name(s) and the Holy Trinity*, 140).

29. The very fact that "the Tetragrammaton itself has no certain semantic meaning at all" suggests the way in which God identifies himself by retaining utter freedom to identify himself (Soulen, *Divine Name(s) and the Holy Trinity*, 13). His very name evinces his infinite transcendence—though, precisely by identifying himself as at once "LORD" and "God of your fathers," he suggests the covenantal deployment of divine freedom. He is free for Israel.

"argument from motion," Thomas arrives at God as "first mover, put in motion by no other."[30] In Thomas's Aristotelian terminology, only things that have potential can change, can be "reduced to act," can be "moved."[31] God is ever Mover, never moved. He is who he is, without qualification. He is the living God.[32]

As *actus purus*, God cannot develop, improve, or become further fulfilled; neither can he devolve, deteriorate, or become corrupted.[33] He cannot "become" at all.[34] He cannot change. He is who he is. But this description is far from the sketch of a static, lifeless God Thomas's critics dash off. God's inability to change follows from his dynamic perfection; indeed, this dynamism, God's lively actuality, just *is* his perfection. "For we say that a thing is perfect in so far as it is actual, and we call a thing perfect when it lacks nothing of its perfection."[35] Recall that actual stands opposed to potential. God's perfection, then, is his fullness, his completion. It speaks to his moral excellence, yes, but also to his divine self-sufficiency, his blessedness.

A perfect God is also a simple God. Continuing in an apophatic vein, Thomas construes simplicity as the denial of composition; God has no parts. Under the rubric of simplicity, Thomas denies that God is a body, denies that he is composed of matter and form, affirms that his essence (*what* he is) *is* his existence (*whether* he is), and denies that there are any accidents in God.[36] All this serves to safeguard the perfect actuality of God as "uncaused," because "nothing is prior to God."[37] In fact, "He has no genus nor difference, nor can there be any definition of Him; nor, save through His effects, a demonstration of Him."[38] Divine simplicity "requires that in God, He *who possesses* and

---

30. Thomas Aquinas, *ST* I.2.3.

31. "That which is in potentiality needs to be reduced to act by something actual; and to do this is to move" (Thomas Aquinas, *ST* I-II.9.1).

32. To live is to be self-moved, according to Thomas: "Properly speaking, those things are said to live whose movement or operation is from within themselves" (*ST* II-II.179.1). "Life is in the highest degree properly in God. In proof of which it must be considered that since a thing is said to live in so far as it operates of itself and not as moved by another, the more perfectly this power is found in anything, the more perfect is the life of that thing" (*ST* I.18.3; also see *ST* I.18.1).

33. For an elaboration of *actus purus* and divine immutability along these lines, see Weinandy, *Does God Suffer?*, 119–27.

34. Obviously, this raises a number of issues, the most significant of which is the mystery of the incarnation, in which the Word who "was God" also "became flesh" (John 1:1, 14). Thomas is fully aware of these issues and develops a Christology sufficient to the task in close dialogue with the ecumenical councils. See *ST* III.1–26.

35. Thomas Aquinas, *ST* I.4.1.

36. See Thomas Aquinas, *ST* I.3.

37. Thomas Aquinas, *ST* I.3.7; I.3.5 sed contra.

38. Thomas Aquinas, *ST* I.3.5.

*what is possessed* be the same."[39] Steve Holmes notes how the lack of composition in God intertwines with the lack of conflict in God: "The doctrine of divine simplicity is Thomas's answer to the question concerning the relationships of the divine perfections. God's life is one, single and coherent; he is not divided into differing parts or pulled in different directions. Thus, all of our words used to describe perfection refer to the same single divine reality."[40] Thomas accords simplicity axiomatic status, which means that he will not be content to pit, say, justice against mercy in God. We might experience God differently as we encounter him over the course of our lives, but we only ever experience the one, simple God.

Divine simplicity entails, furthermore, that the living God has no real relationship with creatures.[41] Thomas readily admits that "creatures are really related to God Himself; whereas in God there is no real relation to creatures, but a relation only in idea, inasmuch as creatures are referred to Him."[42] This analysis hardly seems to square with Thomas's bedrock commitment to the God who creates in order to communicate his goodness, or to the God who "so loved the world that he gave his only Son" (John 3:16). A clue to Thomas's meaning can be found in a much later discussion of the hypostatic union. Thomas there argues that, in assuming human nature, the eternal Son of God remains exactly who he is, while humanity undergoes a transformation. So "every relation which we consider between God and the creature is really in the creature, by whose change the relation is brought into being; whereas it is not really in God, but only in our way of thinking, since it does not arise from any change in God."[43] To be in relation, it seems, requires one to be amenable to change. Brian Davies draws a helpful analogy: "For Aquinas, the fact that there are creatures makes no difference to God—just as the fact that I know Australia makes no difference to Australia."[44] Australia is what it is, Davies or no Davies. And God is who God is, creation or no creation.

We neither notice nor care that we make no difference to Australia; however, we are less comfortable with such indifference from God. Nor are we reassured by Thomas's third claim—that God is devoid of passion. Here again, the key to Thomas's denial is the ingredient of mutability in passion. Passion implies suffering the action of another, being receptive to that one.

39. Thomas Aquinas, *ST* I.39.4.
40. Holmes, "Simple Salvation?," 38.
41. See the discussion in Davies, *Thought of Thomas Aquinas*, 75–79. Also see Bauerschmidt, *Thomas Aquinas*, 114–19.
42. Thomas Aquinas, *ST* I.13.7; also see I.28.4.
43. Thomas Aquinas, *ST* III.2.7.
44. Davies, *Thought of Thomas Aquinas*, 77.

"Passion is the effect of the agent on the patient."[45] But "in God there are no passions."[46] God is not moved by us, in any sense; he is ever Mover, never moved. When Scripture predicates a human passion of God, then, we do best to read it metaphorically, "because of a likeness in the effect."[47]

Take love as a case in point. Thomas asks the bizarre question whether love exists in God.[48] God's love is bandied about among Christians these days and is often reduced to sentimentality. Given the dominance of the myth of romantic love in American culture, we privilege the strong emotional content of love. We admire the man who is "overcome" with love for a woman. But this sort of passion is just the sort of thing Thomas denies of God. He writes: "It seems that love does not exist in God. For in God there are no passions. Now love is a passion. Therefore love is not in God."[49] However, "God is love."[50] Love *must* be in God—but "He loves without passion."[51] Insofar as God does not change and is not moved, his love must be without passion. In God, such love is noble; it stands starkly over against human ways of loving.

> God's will is the cause of all things. It must needs be, therefore, that a thing has existence, or any kind of good, only inasmuch as it is willed by God. To every existing thing, then, God wills some good. Hence, since to love anything is nothing else than to will good to that thing, it is manifest that God loves everything that exists. Yet not as we love. Because since our will is not the cause of the goodness of things, but is moved by it as by its object, our love, whereby we will good to anything, is not the cause of its goodness; but conversely its goodness, whether real or imaginary, calls forth our love . . . whereas the love of God infuses and creates goodness.[52]

Clearly, then, to deny real relation to creatures and passion in God is not to affirm in him a disregard for what he has made, much less a disdain for it. Thomas believes that the denial is the surest way to safeguard the love of God that flows from his fullness. The very magnanimity of God—infusing and creating, rather than merely responding to human goodness—is grounded in his impassible nature. Do we not admire the passionate lover precisely for his devotion to his beloved, a devotion in which he will seek her good at all

45. Thomas Aquinas, *ST* I-II.26.2.
46. Thomas Aquinas, *ST* I.20.1 obj 1.
47. Thomas Aquinas, *ST* I.19.11.
48. Thomas Aquinas, *ST* I.20.1.
49. Thomas Aquinas, *ST* I.20.1 obj 1.
50. Thomas Aquinas, *ST* I.20.1 sed contra (citing 1 John 4:16).
51. Thomas Aquinas, *ST* I.20.1 ad 1.
52. Thomas Aquinas, *ST* I.20.2.

costs? If so, the loving God who creates goodness, who does not wait to find goodness but makes it out of nothing in giving creatures being, far surpasses the most passionate of lovers in his provision for his creatures.

## On Naming God from Creatures

In his careful attention to the Creator, who perfectly transcends his creation, Thomas develops an account of theological language that shapes and rules his manner of speaking of God and everything in relation to God. He understands the necessity, fragility, and imperfection of our habits of speech, and he wisely differentiates among our ways of speaking. While he never abandons his claim that we cannot know what God is, but rather what he is not, Thomas "does not share Dionysius's absolute apophatic stance, and that negation does not eliminate the need for affirmation."[53] In part, this conclusion is due to his abiding conviction that, while we cannot see the essence of God *in this life*, "it must be absolutely granted that the blessed see the essence of God."[54] It is fitting, then, that God would lead us in our advance to him by granting us a modicum of knowledge, spurring us on to the beatific vision.

One of the main ways we can know God in this life is through witnessing his handiwork. Thomas writes: "Because therefore God is not known to us in His nature, but is made known to us from His operations or effects, we can name Him from these."[55] Thomas describes three ways we can name God from his operations: "In this life we cannot see the essence of God; but we know God from creatures as their principle, and also by way of excellence and remotion. In this way therefore He can be named by us from creatures, yet not so that the name which signifies Him expresses the divine essence in itself."[56] On our way toward the vision of God, we can use a pilgrim grammar to speak of him as the One who is *behind* creatures (as their cause), *above* them (by way of excellence), and *distinct from* them (by way of remotion).[57] These three manners of speaking correct one another. For example, if we find ourselves overusing the way of excellence and thinking of God as the greatest being, we can recall that he is the *cause* of beings and also utterly *distinct from* beings.

53. Torrell, *Spiritual Master*, 39.
54. Thomas Aquinas, *ST* I.12.1.
55. Thomas Aquinas, *ST* I.13.8. All creatures bear a "trace" of God as his effects, though only humanity bears the divine "image" (*ST* I.93.6).
56. Thomas Aquinas, *ST* I.13.1.
57. See Torrell, *Spiritual Master*, 40–45. Aquinas adopts this triple way of speaking of God from Denys.

A second way Thomas sponsors, yet chastens, our talk of God is in his insistence on analogical language. Analogy lies somewhere between univocation and equivocation. In univocation, a word is used in the same way with reference to both parties. In equivocation, a word is used in utterly different ways. The problem with univocation is that it reduces God to a creature and predicates, say, goodness of God in the same way as it does of creatures. The problem with equivocation is that it disallows that "we can name God only from creatures," that, as Paul asserts, "his invisible attributes . . . have been clearly perceived, ever since the creation of the world, in the things that have been made" (Rom. 1:20). Analogy steers clear of both these mistakes, allowing a term to be "used in a multiple sense [that] signifies various proportions to some one thing; thus *healthy* applied to urine signifies the sign of animal health, and applied to medicine signifies the cause of the same health."[58] Analogy ensures that creation really is, as Gerard Manley Hopkins puts it, "charged with the grandeur of God," while cautioning that God is grand in a way that remains inaccessible to us.[59]

Thus "He can be named by us from creatures, yet not so that the name which signifies Him expresses the divine essence in itself."[60] Thomas makes this point forcefully by noting the nonreversible status of the claim that creation looks like God: "Although it may be admitted that creatures are in some sort like God, it must nowise be admitted that God is like creatures. . . . For, we say that a statue is like a man, but not conversely; so also a creature can be spoken of as in some sort like God; but not that God is like a creature."[61] Because creatures look like God, we can name God from creatures; but we must never confuse the matter, assuming that therefore God is like creatures and admits of comprehension. In fact, given that creatures bear a prismatic likeness to the perfect God from whom they proceed, even creatures themselves are finally incomprehensible.[62]

In his humble account of theological language, Thomas performs a riff on a Dionysian theme. God exceeds and eludes our cognitive and speech capacities. Our thoughts and words cannot contain him; they can, however, *attain* to him. The most recent Catechism of the Catholic Church (1992) gets the accent right: "Admittedly, in speaking about God like this, our language is

---

58. Thomas Aquinas, *ST* I.13.5.

59. This phrase is from "God's Grandeur," available at https://www.poets.org/poetsorg /poem/gods-grandeur. "We know, therefore, that God possesses in an eminent way everything that is a good in our world, but the way in which he possesses it absolutely escapes us" (Torrell, *Spiritual Master*, 42).

60. Thomas Aquinas, *ST* I.13.1.

61. Thomas Aquinas, *ST* I.4.3 ad 4.

62. See Pieper, "The Negative Element in the Philosophy of St. Thomas Aquinas," in *Silence of St. Thomas*, 43–71.

using human modes of expression; nevertheless it really does attain to God himself, though unable to express him in his infinite simplicity. Likewise, we must recall that 'between Creator and creature no similitude can be expressed without implying an even greater dissimilitude'; and that 'concerning God, we cannot grasp what he is, but only what he is not, and how other beings stand in relation to him.'"[63]

Thomas's conclusion matches the catechism's: "Hence it does not follow that He cannot be known at all, but that He exceeds every kind of knowledge; which means that He is not comprehended."[64] In eternity, we will attain to the vision of God, "whereby God's Essence is seen." But even now there is another, imperfect sight, "whereby, though we see not what God is, yet we see what He is not; and whereby, the more perfectly do we know God in this life, the more we understand that He surpasses all that the mind comprehends." Such recognition of God as incomprehensible *is* a kind of sight, even if an imperfect one that sees by way of negation.[65] This is an appropriate manner of seeing for those Thomas calls "wayfarers," or pilgrims, those who are on the way with the One who is the Way.[66] And the way does have a destination in the beatifying vision of God.

## Who Is God? (Part 2): The One Who Creates in Wisdom

In the second question of the *Summa theologiae*, Thomas sketches his task: "Because the chief aim of sacred doctrine is to teach the knowledge of God, not only as He is in Himself, but also as He is the beginning of things and their last end, and especially of rational creatures . . . we shall treat: (1) Of God; (2) Of the rational creature's advance towards God; (3) Of Christ, Who as man, is our way to God."[67] The *Summa* describes a journey, a pilgrimage in which all of creation makes its way toward God. Like the Bible, Thomas tells the story of creation through the lens of its protagonists, God and humanity. In the first part, Thomas considers the God who creates. In the second part, Thomas details our "advance towards God" as those created in God's image.[68]

63. *Catechism of the Catholic Church*, sec. 43. The catechism cites the chastening rendering of analogy from the Fourth Lateran Council (1215) and, following that, a remark from Thomas at *SCG* 1.30.
64. Thomas Aquinas, *ST* I.12.1 ad 3.
65. Thomas Aquinas, *ST* II-II.8.7.
66. Thomas Aquinas, *ST* II-II.8.7.
67. Thomas Aquinas, *ST* I.2.
68. The need for advance underscores "the progressive and dynamic character of the image. It is a reality in the process of becoming, present in human nature like a divine call" (Torrell,

As this image implies "an intelligent being endowed with free will and self-movement," Thomas develops a moral psychology and theology through an extensive account of the habits, virtues, and gifts of the Spirit that enable humanity to advance to its happiness in God.[69] In the third part, Thomas doubles back and reconsiders humanity's advance to God christologically, through an account of Jesus as "our way to God." In light of our first parents' retreat from God in sin, the way to God is not a steady advance but a deliverance, a way of salvation. The journey to God is a journey of discipleship, in which we receive the grace of Christ, primarily in the sacraments—a grace that converts us to, conforms us to, and confirms us in Jesus.[70]

This journey of advance toward God has a particular shape; it is a homecoming in which all of creation eventually arrives at its end in its beginning, the Triune God. You might think of this as a boomerang movement in which all things proceed from (*exitus*) and return to (*reditus*) God.[71] The very shape of creation suggests a return home; to be a creature is to be given and upheld in one's existence by God and to be ordered toward God as one's end.[72] "He wills both Himself to be, and other things to be; but Himself as the end, and other things as ordained to that end; inasmuch as it befits the divine goodness that other things should be partakers therein."[73] God creates to share his goodness with others.

But God does not need to create. He does so freely, not "by a necessity of His nature," such that "determined effects proceed from His own infinite perfection

---

*Spiritual Master*, 88). The Son is the perfect image of the Father, while the image of God in humanity is yet imperfect (Thomas Aquinas, *ST* I.35.2 ad 3).

69. Thomas Aquinas, *ST* I-II.prologue. Thomas is quoting John of Damascus. Also see *ST* I-II.69.1.

70. "Thomas focuses on Christ as the way (*via*) of salvation while not ignoring the wayfarer (*viator*) who undertakes the journey." Christ accomplishes our salvation, but we must appropriate that salvation. "This appropriation, while a truly human act, is at the same time the work of the Holy Spirit" (Bauerschmidt, *Thomas Aquinas*, 229).

71. On this "circular plan" that runs "like a subterranean current" through the *Summa*, see Torrell, *Aquinas's Summa*, 27–28.

72. David Burrell captures the way Thomas's doctrine of creation transforms Aristotelian substance, still according integrity and independence to creatures, but an independence established and sustained by the Creator:

So the very existence (*esse*) of a creature is an *esse-ad*, an existing which is itself a relation to its source. . . . What for Aristotle 'exists in itself' (substance) is for Aquinas derived from an Other in its very in-itselfness, or substantiality. Yet since the Other is the cause of being, each thing which exists-to the creator also exists in itself. Derived existence is no less substantial when it is derived from the One-who-is, so it would appear that one could succeed in talking of existing things without explicitly referring them to their source. (Burrell, "Act of Creation," 39; also see Burrell, "Analogy, Creation, and Theological Language," 85–86)

73. Thomas Aquinas, *ST* I.19.2.

according to the determination of His will and intellect."[74] While undetermined in any way, the divine freedom is far from caprice; it is a freedom formed in perfect accord with the goodness of God.[75] If we look in vain for a prior cause for creation—God creates because he wants to—we can certainly inquire into the end for which God created the world. Thomas learned from Aristotle to take the measure of things from their *telos*, their "end," "completion," or "perfection." The wise man is he who considers "the end of the universe, which is also the origin of the universe."[76] While the end may be "last in the order of execution, yet it is first in the order of the agent's intention."[77] Thus, "the first of all causes is the final cause."[78] God creates with a certain end in mind—namely, the communication of his goodness to creatures and their full participation in it, which is their perfection. Here we see the unique agency of God, who is the only agent who does not act to acquire, but only to communicate.[79]

> For He brought things into being in order that His goodness might be communicated to creatures, and be represented by them; and because His goodness could not be adequately represented by one creature alone, He produced many and diverse creatures, that what was wanting to one in the representation of the divine goodness might be supplied by another. For goodness, which in God is simple and uniform, in creatures is manifold and divided and hence the whole universe together participates the divine goodness more perfectly, and represents it better than any single creature whatever.[80]

Creatures receive and display the bounty of God's goodness, but they can do so only as an ensemble. The simplicity of God's goodness is reflected in the diversity of creaturely goodness. Thus the universe would not be perfect were not "all grades of being found in things."[81] This "all" includes beings that are incorruptible and corruptible; "so the perfection of the universe requires that there should be some which can fail in goodness, and thence it follows that sometimes they do fail."[82] Thomas likens God to an artist who "intends to give to his work the best disposition; not absolutely the best, but

74. Thomas Aquinas, *ST* I.104.3; I.19.4.

75. In underscoring the freedom of creation, Aquinas follows the Greek fathers in draining emanation of both pantheism and determinism, while preserving the sense of creation as a generous gift that is perfectly "natural" to God (Chenu, *Aquinas and His Role*, 98).

76. Thomas Aquinas, *SCG* 1.1.1.

77. Thomas Aquinas, *ST* I-II.1.1 ad 1.

78. Thomas Aquinas, *ST* I-II.1.2.

79. Thomas Aquinas, *ST* I.44.4.

80. Thomas Aquinas, *ST* I.47.1; also see I.65.2; II-II.183.2.

81. Thomas Aquinas, *ST* I.22.4.

82. Thomas Aquinas, *ST* I.48.2. On the role this principle plays in Thomas's account of the origin of sin, see Velde, "Evil, Sin, and Death," 146–47.

the best as regards the proposed end; and even if this entails some defect, the artist cares not."[83] One must read the whole of the book of nature to see how it manifests the goodness of God; some pages may be difficult to read, but together they beautifully represent God.

Thomas follows the Augustinian principle that the external acts of the Trinity are undivided: the Triune God is the Creator and "the first exemplar cause of all things," the model on which things were made.[84] While undivided, though, trinitarian acts admit of an inner distinction. The Word the Father speaks from eternity "is expressive not only of the Father, but of all creatures."[85] Thus Thomas can write that "God by knowing Himself, knows every creature," as he knows himself in the mirror of the Word, who is the Wisdom of God, as well as "the intelligibility of things made by Him," the one in whom things find their distinction and the one in whom "all things hold together."[86] As a craftsman conceives a word in his mind and loves an object with his will, so the Father creates through his Son the Word and through his Love, the Spirit.[87] Thomas reminds us that this is only an analogy, however, and a broken one at that, as in this case the Word and Love are consubstantial actors with the Father. The second person of the Trinity is the blueprint of creation as well as, with the Father and the Spirit, the Creator himself.[88]

Creation's beginning and end are in the triune goodness communicated to creation, which calls forth an echo in creaturely perfection.[89] Thomas's teleological account of creation requires a robust doctrine of providence, what he will also call government. It would not be fitting for God to "produce things without giving them their perfection," and so the divine goodness "lead[s] them to their end," like a sailor steering his ship into port.[90] As

83. Thomas Aquinas, *ST* I.91.3.

84. Thomas Aquinas, *ST* I.44.3.

85. Thomas Aquinas, *ST* I.34.3. Thus, all creaturely forms, whether spiritual or corporeal, existed in the Word from eternity (I.56.2). So "the Word contains the essences of all things created by God," and "all creatures are nothing but a kind of real expression and representation of those things which are comprehended in the conception of the divine Word" (Thomas Aquinas, *SCG* 4.42.3).

86. Thomas Aquinas, *ST* I.34.3; *SCG* 4.13.7; *ST* I.47.1, 2; Col. 1:17. "The knowledge of God is the cause of things. For the knowledge of God is to all creatures what the knowledge of the artificer is to things made by his art" (I.14.8). "The Word is thus the reason of creatures from a double point of view, that of exemplar causality (the expression, the conception of creatures) and that of efficient causality (the accomplishment of results, the production of creatures in being)" (Emery, "Trinity and Creation," 65).

87. Paraphrasing Thomas Aquinas, *ST* I.45.6.

88. See Thomas Aquinas, *SCG* 4.13.9. Also see the trinitarian pattern of creation and formation at *ST* I.74.3 ad 3.

89. Thomas Aquinas, *ST* I.22.4; I.44.4.

90. Thomas Aquinas, *ST* I.103.1; II-II.102.2.

Thomas grounded creation in the processions of the Son and Spirit within the Trinity, so he grounds creation's perfection in the temporal missions of Son and Spirit. "Just as we have been created by the Son and the Holy Spirit, so are we united by them to our final end."[91]

God is the Alpha and Omega of creation, its beginning and end. Creation's story begins as God speaks his Word, making space for creatures: "Let there be . . ." (Gen. 1:3). The story finds its consummation as the new Jerusalem descends from heaven, "prepared as a bride adorned for her husband" (Rev. 21:2). This is the new creation, one in which God's creatures have reached their end in him and been so transformed by that end that they have become entirely new. A question remains, however: What role, if any, do creatures have as they are led to their end in the Triune God by the Triune God?

### The Dignity of Causality

What must we say of creation if we are to echo the divine judgment that it is "very good"? Specifically, how are we to confess at once the integrity and completeness of creation—signaled in God's Sabbath (Gen. 2:2)—and creation's ongoing reliance on his sustenance and direction? Do we find a more apt analogy for creation's relation to God in the clutching infant, or in the young adult who has moved out of the house and no longer needs parental support? Does God need to do everything for creatures, or can they do things for themselves? "Some have understood God to work in every agent in such a way that no created power has any effect in things, but that God alone is the ultimate cause of everything wrought; for instance, that it is not fire that gives heat, but God in the fire, and so forth."[92] At first blush, this seems an obviously pious intuition. We'll see in Jonathan Edwards a celebration of the divine goodwill that sustains creation in being at every moment, to such effect that, perhaps, creatures are only occasions of divine causality but not themselves causal. The immediate dependence of creation on God—the One in whom we live, move, and have our being—magnifies his strength and provision. The psalmist writes:

> Sing to the LORD with thanksgiving;
>     make melody to our God on the lyre!
> He covers the heavens with clouds;
>     he prepares rain for the earth;
>     he makes grass grow on the hills.

91. Thomas Aquinas, *Scriptum super libros Sententiarum I*, d. 14 q. 2 a. 2, cited in Torrell, *Spiritual Master*, 60.
92. Thomas Aquinas, *ST* I.105.5.

> He gives to the beasts their food,
> and to the young ravens that cry. (Ps. 147:7–9)

Still, Thomas questions the adequacy of attributing sole causality to God, such that "God alone is the immediate cause of everything wrought." He continues:

> But this is impossible. First, because the order of cause and effect would be taken away from created things: and this would imply lack of power in the Creator: for it is due to the power of the cause, that it bestows active power on its effect. Secondly, because the active powers which are seen to exist in things, would be bestowed on things to no purpose, if these wrought nothing through them. Indeed, all things created would seem, in a way, to be purposeless, if they lacked an operation proper to them; since the purpose of everything is its operation.[93]

There are two problems with the claim that God is the sole cause of creaturely change. The first is that it, ironically, denigrates the power of God. Divine omnipotence does not require creaturely impotence. Instead, it is God's very power that "bestows active power on its effect"—such that the effect itself becomes a cause, a moved mover of others.

This point is not lost on the psalmist, and his doxological foregrounding of divine action need not suggest an ignorance or denial of natural processes of change. It is the Lord who "covers the heavens with clouds," "prepares rain for the earth," and "makes grass grow on the hills," but that sequence follows the way in which the Lord works, through a natural process in which clouds give rain which grows grass. Thomas affirms that this is the Lord's work, but his burden is to lay bare the process by which the Lord works, one in which we rightly speak of creatures also working to accomplish an end. "We must therefore understand that God works in things in such a manner that things have their proper operation."[94]

The design of creation's government belongs to God, but he shares its execution with others.[95] "He governs things inferior by superior, not on account of any defect in His power, but by reason of the abundance of His goodness; so that the dignity of causality is imparted even to creatures."[96] It's worth lingering over that phrase—*the dignity of causality.* God is not miserly but generous—so much so that God adorns his creatures with what Thomas will

---

93. Thomas Aquinas, *ST* I.105.5.
94. Thomas Aquinas, *ST* I.105.5.
95. Thomas Aquinas, *ST* I.103.6.
96. Thomas Aquinas, *ST* I.22.3.

call "secondary causality."[97] While God is the cause of all, their beginning and end, he has ordained certain creatures to be causes along with him. "Now it is a greater perfection for a thing to be good in itself and also the cause of goodness in others, than only to be good in itself. Therefore God so governs things that He makes some of them to be causes of others in government; as a master, who not only imparts knowledge to his pupils, but gives also the faculty of teaching others."[98] Not only does such pedagogy dignify the student; it also exalts the teacher. Anyone can impart knowledge, but a teacher who can make teachers of his students demonstrates at once his mastery of the material and his magnanimity toward those he teaches. All of this is in keeping with the divine design to manifest God's goodness in manifold ways in creation.

The second problem Thomas identifies in the claim that God is the sole cause of creaturely change is that it renders the apparent ability of creatures to act and affect others redundant at best, deceptive at worst. But this arrangement would denigrate the wisdom of God, which "orders all things sweetly." Thomas frequently returns to this remark from Wisdom 8:1: "God's wisdom *orders all things sweetly* (Wis. viii. 1), inasmuch as His providence appoints to each one that which is befitting it according to its nature. For as Dionysius says (*Div. Nom.* iv), *it belongs to providence not to destroy, but to maintain, nature.*"[99]

Providence is God's wise ordering and orienting of creation toward its end in God. It suggests the preserving and perfecting, not the undoing, of creation. Thomas adopts this axiom and applies it to God's government of all of creation and to the administration of divine grace. A question arises at this point: In emphasizing providence as "maintenance," does Thomas suggest that God is bound to only do what "comes naturally" to creation? And if so, what sense can be made of Scripture's testimony to miracles, those events commonly described as supernatural?

Miracles have come under attack in modernity as a cheap *Deus ex machina*, yet another instance of the church's derogatory consideration of the natural order of things. In order to prop up their dying God, so goes the argument, Christians interpret seemingly anomalous phenomena as proof of divine

97. "God's immediate provision over everything does not exclude the action of secondary causes; which are the executors of His order" (Thomas Aquinas, *ST* I.22.3 ad 2).

98. Thomas Aquinas, *ST* I.103.6.

99. Thomas Aquinas, *ST* II-II.165.1. For other citations of Wis. 8:1, see *ST* II-II.23.2; II-II.165.1; III.46.9. Actions attributed to divine wisdom should be predicated of the Father working through the Son, as Christ is "the power of God and the wisdom of God" (1 Cor. 1:24). See Thomas Aquinas, *Commentary on the Gospel of John, Chapters 1–5*, 33 (commenting on John 1:3). Thomas develops a Wisdom Christology in which "the exemplar principle is appropriated to the Son by reason of wisdom" (*ST* I.46.3). The Son is at once the One through or in whom all things were made (John 1:3; Col. 1:16) and the One according to whom all things were made.

intervention. What they fail to realize is that, in their rush to offer an apologetic for the divine wonder-worker, they compromise the integrity of his creation. Thus, a creator who didn't get it quite right performs miracles in the same manner as a boatswain plugging holes in a sinking ship.

Brian Davies argues convincingly that Aquinas does not believe in an interventionist God. A miracle is not a divine intervention, because God "can never intervene in his creation." He is already present and active, and "things in the universe (including events) are always the effect of God's will." Thus, "the occurrence of a miracle is not to be thought of as a matter of God doing violence to the created order."[100] Thomas takes up the question of whether God can do anything outside the established order of nature:

> If therefore we consider the order of things depending on the first cause, God cannot do anything against this order; for, if He did so, He would act against His foreknowledge, or His will, or His goodness. But if we consider the order of things depending on any secondary cause, thus God can do something outside such order; for He is not subject to the order of secondary causes; but, on the contrary, this order is subject to Him. . . . Wherefore God can do something outside this order created by Him, when He chooses, for instance by producing the effects of secondary causes without them, or by producing certain effects to which secondary causes do not extend.[101]

While it is true that "the secondary agent does nothing without the principal agent in operating," the converse is not true.[102] Davies summarizes: "Miracles, for him, do not occur because of an extra added ingredient (i.e., God). They occur because something is *not* present (i.e., a secondary cause or a collection of secondary causes)."[103] God will never violate his beautiful ordering of the universe, but he may choose to execute that order in an unusual—though never ill-fitting or unnatural—manner. Perhaps that is the best way to describe a miracle—as an event that is "unusual" in that it falls outside the normal course of events, but one that is still perfectly "natural" in its orientation to and execution of God's loving will for creation. The divine decision to leapfrog secondary causes is hardly an affront to creation, but a wise manifestation of one form of the divine government, a particularly striking reminder of the sovereign freedom of the One from whom all come and to whom all return.[104]

100. Davies, *Thought of Thomas Aquinas*, 173.
101. Thomas Aquinas, *ST* I.105.6.
102. Thomas Aquinas, *ST* III.71.4.
103. Davies, *Thought of Thomas Aquinas*, 174.
104. "But since the power of God, which is His essence, is nothing else but His wisdom, it can indeed be fittingly said that there is nothing in the divine power which is not in the order of the divine wisdom" (Thomas Aquinas, *ST* I.25.5).

A case in point is the descent of the Spirit in the form of a dove at Jesus's baptism (Matt. 3:16; Mark 1:10; Luke 3:22; John 1:32). This was a real dove, one that could fly and coo, eat and sleep. But while real, it was not born from other doves; it was created immediately by God to serve as a fitting form in which the Spirit would rest on Christ in the Jordan. Thomas affirms Augustine's remark that "it was easy for Almighty God, who created all creatures out of nothing, to frame the body of a real dove without the help of other doves, just as it was easy for Him to form a true body in Mary's womb without the seed of a man."[105] While the Father saw fit to eliminate the secondary cause of Joseph in Jesus's conception, Jesus was not less a real man for being conceived by the Spirit.

## Son and Spirit

While we will come back to the specifically human role in the return of things to God, first we must make a digression—which really takes us to the heart of the movement of procession and return—by way of the work of the Son and Spirit. It is far from self-evident as one thumbs through the contents of the *Summa* that the Son and Spirit occupy such a central place. While a loose historical sense can be discerned in the movement from eternity to creation to the end of all in God, Thomas's organization signals only mild interest in the history of salvation, whose pivotal moments are the twinned advents of the Son in incarnation and the Spirit at Pentecost. Still, just like Irenaeus, Thomas believes that God never works apart from his two hands, and his account of divine action in the world maps neatly onto the Triune God as he gives himself to us in Christ and the Spirit.

Admittedly, the *Summa* can seem for long stretches at a time as more a handbook for morals than a work of theology proper. This makes sense, given the likelihood that it "was originally conceived as a work on moral theology (hence its lengthy second part) for the Dominican theological students in Rome preparing for the proper Dominican ministry of preaching and hearing confessions."[106] What is novel, then, is the larger context into which Thomas placed the conventional moral theological questions of the day. His readers would likely have been more struck by his attention to broader theological concerns than the amplitude of his moral theology in the massive second part.

105. Thomas Aquinas, *ST* III.39.7.
106. O'Meara, *Thomas Aquinas Theologian*, 51. Other scholars suggest the *Summa* was intended as a scholastic work, possibly meant to replace Peter Lombard's *Sentences* (Joseph Wawrykow, in private correspondence with the author).

Still, the question remains: How is the second part related to the third part? You'll recall how Thomas mapped the *Summa*'s three parts in terms of (1) God, (2) "the rational creature's advance towards God," and (3) Christ, "Who as man, is our way to God."[107] The second and third parts display a curious doubling. The second part details our advance toward God, an advance we accomplish only by being in Christ; the third part offers an account of Christ as the "way" of advance, understood both as the means of our advance and the pattern of our advance. As means, he is the one who has trodden the way ahead of us; in fact, it is the life of Christ that is itself the principle of grace. The complex dynamics of human action that the second part treats require as their pre- and co-requisite the grace that comes to us in and through Christ. Thomas O'Meara points out that, "while the Christocentric tonality of grace is important, Aquinas emphasized the human milieu of grace."[108] O'Meara would do better to invert the emphasis: while the human milieu of grace is important, Aquinas emphasized the Christocentric tonality of grace.

As well as being principle, Christ is the pattern, or exemplar, of grace; his entire life is instructive for us as we walk along his way toward the beatific vision.[109] If the third part can be summarized in terms of humanity's life in Christ, we might conceive of the second part as Christ's life in us.[110] To speak of Christ in us is to name the Spirit; "it is possible to understand the entire second part of the *Summa*, which deals with human action oriented toward the beatific vision under the impulse of grace, as an extended, albeit mostly oblique, treatise on the Spirit's work."[111] One mustn't lean too hard on this claim, as the pneumatology of the second part is "mostly oblique." O'Meara more straightforwardly describes the second part of the second part as "an applied theology of grace through the description of many virtues."[112] But before speaking of grace's application by the Spirit, we should consider its source in the Son.

In his commentary on John's Gospel, Thomas reads John 1:16 ("from his fullness we have all received, grace upon grace") to mean that "Christ is the origin, as a fountain, of every spiritual grace," and "grace is dispensed to us through him and from him." This is a "fullness of efficiency and overflow,

107. Thomas Aquinas, *ST* I.2.
108. O'Meara, *Thomas Aquinas Theologian*, 109, 112.
109. Notice the parallel here with Thomas's doctrine of creation. The Word is principle and pattern of creation, and the Word incarnate is principle and pattern of grace.
110. Paul rejoices in "the riches of the glory of his mystery, which is Christ in you, the hope of glory" (Col. 1:27).
111. Bauerschmidt, *Thomas Aquinas*, 229.
112. O'Meara, *Thomas Aquinas Theologian*, 120.

which belongs only to the man Christ as the author of grace."[113] Note that this fullness belongs to the *man* Christ, that he is the author of grace. Thomas adheres to the hypostatic union, according to which the man Christ is who he is only by virtue of the Word's having assumed humanity to himself. At the same time, it is as man that Christ authors grace—that is, as one who receives grace by virtue of his union with the eternal Word of God. At one and the same time, Jesus is "the Word incarnate [who] is the efficient cause of the perfection of human nature" and the human recipient of grace, albeit in a unique manner through the grace of union with the Word.[114] As Thomas says, "Men become receivers of this grace through God's Son made man, Whose humanity grace filled first, and thence flowed forth to us."[115] The Word fills the humanity he assumes to himself, such that Jesus becomes an ever-flowing "fountain" of grace.

It is proper for grace to flow from Christ to the church because Christ is the head of the church, which is his "mystic body," so that they together form "one mystical person."[116] What the head does can properly be attributed thereby to the members: "And hence it is that Christ's merit extends to others inasmuch as they are His members; even as in a man the action of the head reaches in a manner to all his members, since it perceives not merely for itself alone, but for all the members."[117] Because Christ is the church's head, he is the origin of its grace as its representative and the one who, perfected in grace, dispenses that grace to others. He is also the example of the graced life, and Thomas's detailed treatment of the life of Christ frequently returns to the theme of Christ as exemplar.[118] Christ "assumed our defects" not only for our satisfaction but also for our instruction in virtue.[119]

113. Thomas Aquinas, *Commentary on the Gospel of John, Chapters 1–5*, 82 (commenting on John 1:16).

114. Thomas Aquinas, *ST* III.1.6.

115. Thomas Aquinas, *ST* I-II.108.1.

116. Thomas Aquinas, *ST* III.49.1; III.19.4. Thomas considers Christ's perfection in grace (1) as an individual man and (2) as head of the church (III.7–8). The image of the church as the body of Christ, though significant in the New Testament, needs to be complemented by the full wealth of scriptural imagery—especially the images of the church as the people of God and the temple of the Spirit. See the developed account of these three images in Badcock, *House Where God Lives*. In *Images of the Church*, Minear likens the use of multiple images to a kaleidoscope (226–27), concluding that "some realities are of such a nature that their perception is enhanced by the presence of pluriform modes of perception" (227).

117. Thomas Aquinas, *ST* III.19.4. Also see III.48.1.

118. Thomas Aquinas, *ST* III.27–59.

119. Thomas Aquinas, *ST* III.15.1. Still, Thomas denies that Christ can be our example in two of the three theological virtues. Christ cannot possess either faith or hope (III.7.3–4), as both of these are provisional virtues destined to obsolescence once one attains to the beatific vision. Thomas believed that Christ was a *comprehensor* in his soul, enjoying the

The question remains: *How* does grace flow from Christ the fountain to us? Thomas offers a traditional answer, though one rigorously Christocentric: "And since we cannot of ourselves obtain grace, but through Christ alone, hence Christ of Himself instituted the sacraments whereby we obtain grace."[120] The sacraments thus *cause* grace—a conviction the Reformers will forcibly reject—though in a carefully circumscribed sense. The sacraments are real, though mere, instruments of God. Thomas explains:

> A sacrament in causing grace works after the manner of an instrument. Now an instrument is twofold; the one, separate, as a stick, for instance; the other, united, as a hand. Moreover, the separate instrument is moved by means of the united instrument, as a stick by the hand. Now the principal efficient cause of grace is God Himself, in comparison with Whom Christ's humanity is as a united instrument, whereas the sacrament is as a separate instrument. Consequently, the saving power must needs be derived by the sacraments from Christ's Godhead through His humanity.[121]

Thomas suggests a nonreversible order to sacramental efficacy. God employs the humanity of Christ, which by virtue of the hypostatic union is a "united instrument," and Christ employs the sacraments as a "separate instrument." Like a person using his hand to use his stick to get something done, the eternal Son works by virtue of his humanity through the sacraments to dispense his grace to the church. The eternal Son, with the Father and the Spirit, remains the "principal efficient cause of grace," and only as extrinsic instruments can the sacraments be said to "cause" grace. This is yet another instance of God's wise dispensing of grace in a fitting way, leading people to a deeper knowledge and love of him through sensory means.[122]

The sacraments are the regular means of grace, but Thomas makes it clear that, if need be, God can easily give grace without the sacraments. "God did not bind His power to the sacraments, so as to be unable to bestow the

---

beatific vision and with it all virtues and grace, from conception—even if he remained a *viator* (or wayfarer) in his body (yet without sin) until his resurrection (*ST* III.11.2; II.34.4; also see III.7.8; III.34.1). See the persuasive critique, that this denial of Christ's faith was neither necessary nor consistent with Thomas's thought as a whole, in Allen, *Christ's Faith*. Joseph Wawrykow has pointed out to me in private correspondence that, while Christ did not possess the virtues of faith and hope, he did possess the perfections associated with them: trust and obedience.

120. Thomas Aquinas, *ST* I-II.108.2.

121. Thomas Aquinas, *ST* III.62.5.

122. "Divine wisdom provides for each thing according to its mode. . . . Now it is part of man's nature to acquire knowledge of the intelligible from the sensible" (Thomas Aquinas, *ST* III.60.4).

sacramental effect without conferring the sacrament."[123] Even if the matter of the sacrament (bread, wine, water) were absent, Christ would still be the giver of the gracious sacramental effects, and he would still give through the "united" or intrinsic instrument, his flesh. Likewise "neither did He bind His power to the ministers of the Church so as to be unable to give angels power to administer the sacraments," though one wonders why Thomas does not appeal more directly to the ascended Christ presiding directly over the sacrament in this case, rather than to the possibility of angelic administration.[124] What is of central importance is the Spirit, for "in the sacraments of the New Law, which are derived from Christ, grace is instrumentally caused by the sacraments, and principally by the power of the Holy Ghost working in the sacraments."[125]

Thomas describes the way in which grace flows to the body of Christ through the sacraments in the third part of the *Summa*. In the second part, Thomas maps the terrain over which grace flows and, like a spiritual botanist, names and describes the fruits that sprout from that terrain. Thomas's elaborate anthropology, where the human-in-action is seen in a carefully ordered account of the theological and cardinal virtues, gifts of the Spirit, and beatitudes, is without parallel in the tradition. Grace is given to pilgrims on the way to the vision of God to heal, elevate, and perfect us.

Most impressive in Thomas's moral theology is the layered and variegated account he gives to human action, integrating it into his account of the perfecting work of God. Take the concept of habit, to which we will return below. Thomas notes, with Aristotle, that repeated actions carve ruts in us that lead us to act in certain ways; habits of virtue and vice can be acquired. But "there are some habits by which man is disposed to an end which exceeds the proportion of human nature, namely, the ultimate and perfect happiness of man."[126] We cannot acquire the theological virtues of faith, hope, and charity; they must be infused in us by God.[127] Only then can we believe in, hope in, and love God.

Or take Thomas's distinction between virtues and gifts. O'Meara sketches the contrast: "Virtues and gifts are two different modes of grace prompting someone to follow God's plan: the first is frequent, deliberate, thoughtful; the second is more intuitive, prompt, supra-deliberative. What is most characteristic of the gifts is that they are inspirational and instinctual. The Spirit's

123. Thomas Aquinas, *ST* III.64.7.
124. Thomas Aquinas, *ST* III.64.7.
125. Thomas Aquinas, *ST* I-II.112.1 ad 2.
126. Thomas Aquinas, *ST* I-II.51.4.
127. Thomas Aquinas, *ST* II-II.6.1.

gift is spontaneous, liberating, and energetic."[128] One (admittedly oversimplified) way to think about this difference is to note that Protestants tend to believe in the unpredictability of grace, while Roman Catholics adhere to its regularity.[129] Caricatures of Thomas assume that he thinks of the workings of grace as perfectly predictable, perhaps through a mechanistic account of the sacraments. But in fact, the Spirit who brings the grace of Christ to us disperses both virtues (those oh-so-regular graced dispositions) and gifts (those spontaneous, unanticipatable blessings).

Finally, Thomas continually calls to mind the transcendent horizon of his moral theology. The whole economy of grace is oriented to our perfect happiness in the vision of God. Thomas "places the beatitudes after his treatment of the virtues—beyond matters of precept—as the first taste of the beatific vision and of the fulfillment of love."[130] "All these rewards will be fully consummated in the life to come: but meanwhile they are, in a manner, begun, even in this life."[131]

Our advance to God, the end for which we were created, is thus first and foremost a function of the missions of the Son and Spirit, who pour out grace on us. But this returns us to the question of creaturely—now specifically a question of *human*—causality, as it extends to the doctrine of grace.

## Causality and Grace

God does not need secondary causes, as we have seen, though he employs them "for the sake of preserving the beauty of the order of things, and for the sake of conferring the dignity of causality even upon creatures." Thomas writes these lines in the midst of asking whether the prayers of the saints can further predestination; he wants to know whether praying for someone can lead to his or her salvation. "In this God is helped by us; inasmuch as we execute His orders," he writes, citing Paul's words to the Corinthians: "*We are God's coadjutors.*"[132] The context of Paul's comment perfectly captures the dignity of causality to which Thomas appeals, as well as its strictly instrumental character: "What then is Apollos? What is Paul? Servants through whom you believed, as the Lord assigned to each. I planted, Apollos watered, but God gave the growth. So neither he who plants nor he who waters is anything, but

128. O'Meara, *Thomas Aquinas Theologian*, 125.
129. For an extreme Protestant account, see Karl Barth's doctrine of grace.
130. Chenu, *Aquinas and His Role*, 44.
131. Thomas Aquinas, *ST* I-II.69.2 ad 3.
132. Thomas Aquinas, *ST* I.23.8 ad 2.

only God who gives the growth. . . . For we are God's fellow workers. You are God's field, God's building" (1 Cor. 3:5–9).

The Corinthians take their name from God rather than Paul or Apollos. The apostolic task is ministerial, not magisterial, the task of a servant, not a master. In fact, one more aptly describes the entire work in terms of divine causation ("but God gave the growth"), and the secondary human causation can blend into the background without losing its dignity. This is because God works *by* Paul and Apollos; they are his tools. "Secondary causes cannot escape the order of the first universal cause," Thomas insists. Their role is to "execute that order."[133]

Still, this application of secondary causality to human agency transposes the discussion into a new key. It is one thing to notice the way in which God creates and governs a natural world in which a spring thunderstorm causes flowers to bloom, but in what sense does God in his providence enlist human agents as causes? How do we account accurately for human freedom under the umbrella of God's providence?

Having considered God and what proceeds from him in the first part of the *Summa*, Thomas turns in the second part to consider God's image, "in so far as the image implies *an intelligent being endowed with free-will and self-movement*" who is "the principle of his actions."[134] Thomas champions human freedom: "Man has free-will: otherwise counsels, exhortations, commands, prohibitions, rewards, and punishments would be in vain."[135] To deny freedom, as a corollary of either divine sole causality or a reductive physicalism in which people are only a function of neurochemistry, violates Scripture's frequent moral injunctions; it also denies common sense and our intuitive sense that people are responsible for their actions. For humans to be free, they must have a rational will; this is precisely what marks them off from other animals: "Now man differs from irrational animals in this, that he is master of his actions. Wherefore those actions alone are properly called human, of which man is master. Now man is master of his actions through his reason and will; whence, too, the free-will is defined as *the faculty and will of reason*."[136]

To be master of his actions, a person needs both will and reason. Will alone is insufficient, because he will invariably be confronted with an array of options among which to choose. (Visit any cereal aisle at your local supermarket

133. Thomas Aquinas, *ST* I.23.8 ad 3.
134. Thomas Aquinas, *ST* I-II.prologue. The italics indicate Thomas's quoting of John of Damascus.
135. Thomas Aquinas, *ST* I.83.1.
136. Thomas Aquinas, *ST* I-II.1.1.

if you need proof of this.) Reason alone is likewise insufficient, as without a will, he will stop short of pursuing the good. He may be able to recognize the good, but he will fail to embrace it as good *for him*. Freedom consists in the will's embrace of that which reason approves.[137] Indeed, "acts are called human, inasmuch as they proceed from a deliberate will. Now the object of the will is the good and the end."[138] To be human is to deliberate, decide, and do.

If the deliberative will distinguishes us from lower animals, it also sets us apart from angels and God. Lower animals do not deliberate, because they do not think at all; higher intellects do not deliberate, because they know at once. "The human intellect must of necessity understand by composition and division. . . . But the angelic and the Divine intellect, like all incorruptible things, have their perfection at once from the beginning. . . . They know at once whatever we can know by composition, division, and reasoning."[139] Human knowing takes time. People know the truth "by a kind of movement and discursive intellectual operation; that is to say, as they advance from one known thing to another."[140] Though Thomas describes ours as a "lower" intellect, this adjective ought not to mislead us into disparaging the discursive. Consider how many of the joys and energies of human life fold into our unique discursive orientation to the world. Those who understand by composition, division, and reason are those who can wonder, discover, long, reconsider, and hope.

The deliberative will is "the first mover in moral acts."[141] Correspondingly, an act devoid of will cannot be considered a moral act; in fact, it cannot properly be considered human. Any action performed under duress, then, any product of coercion, does not admit of moral evaluation. I am responsible for that which I will, but any "necessity of coercion is altogether repugnant to the will. For we call that violent which is against the inclination of a thing."[142] Human acts are founded in freedom.

The trouble is that free human acts are often vicious. Again and again, we twist our freedom into an opportunity for sin, to the point that we become sin's slaves (see Rom. 6). We are all too willing to sin and frequently resist the loving advances of God. Can Thomas make sense of our need to

---

137. In locating the image of God in human reason, Thomas draws a parallel, too, between divine and human freedom (see *ST* II-II.66.1).

138. Thomas Aquinas, *ST* I-II.1.3.

139. Thomas Aquinas, *ST* I.85.5. Also see II-II.180.3.

140. Thomas Aquinas, *ST* I.58.3.

141. Thomas Aquinas, *ST* II-II.110.1. Elsewhere, Thomas will divide the principles of human action into the intellect and appetite, subdividing the appetite into the rational appetite, or will, and the sensitive appetite (I-II.78.1).

142. Thomas Aquinas, *ST* I.82.1.

be saved from sin and still maintain his commitment to human freedom? Can he still say that grace "perfects" or "fulfills" nature, or does it not make more sense, at least in conversion, to speak of a saving coercion in which grace "violates" nature?

The key step comes as Thomas expands his notion of how the will is moved. He writes that "anything that has a nature or a form or a virtue perfectly, can of itself work according to them: not, however, excluding the operation of God, Who works inwardly in every nature and in every will."[143] Only two can move the will inwardly—the will itself and God.[144] A creature's working "of itself" does not preclude God's working inwardly in it. Note that God's inward movement of the will is not coercive, as coercion involves the application of outward force upon a person.[145] It is no more foreign for God to work inwardly in me than it is for me to move myself. The only agents capable of making a bad will good are the will itself and God. But the will is bad; it is the problem. This leaves only God.

Thomas displays surprisingly little confidence in the sinful person's ability to muster the resources to change. This can be seen early in the *Summa* when Thomas discusses predestination.[146] He treats predestination in the context of the divine attributes. Having already discussed love, justice, and mercy, Thomas treats predestination under providence and roots it in divine love.[147] "Predestination presupposes election in the order of reason; and election presupposes love."[148] The love of God is the beginning of our salvation, and this love, even more than his freedom, characterizes his work of predestination.[149]

143. Thomas Aquinas, *ST* I-II.68.2. A few questions later, Thomas states emphatically that "none can move the will inwardly save God alone" (I-II.75.3; also see I-II.9.6).

144. Thomas Aquinas, *ST* I-II.80.1.

145. And so God can work sovereignly within us and yet "not destroy contingency in things" (Thomas Aquinas, *ST* I.23.6; also see I.22.4 ad 1).

146. Though some would argue that single predestination, in which God foreordains certain people to beatitude, is incoherent, Thomas resists the implication that God's predestination of the elect entails a corresponding predestination of the reprobate. Instead, reprobation involves a "will to permit" and a withholding of blessing from some (*ST* I.23.3). Still, his position remains unstable; two articles later he writes: "The reason for the predestination of some, and reprobation of others, must be sought for in the goodness of God. . . . Now it is necessary that God's goodness, which in itself is one and undivided, should be manifested in many ways in His creation . . . in respect to those whom He predestines, by means of his mercy, as sparing them; and in respect of others, whom he reprobates, by means of His justice, in punishing them. This is the reason why God elects some and rejects others" (*ST* I.23.5 ad 3).

147. Thomas Aquinas, *ST* I.20–25.

148. Thomas Aquinas, *ST* I.23.4.

149. To pit divine love against divine freedom is already to misstep theologically, and I make the point about Thomas's emphasis for heuristic purposes. Thomas's commitment to divine simplicity precludes any juxtaposition of divine attributes in this manner. Love and freedom are two ways of speaking of the one ineffably simple God.

As "to love a thing is to will it good," love is the beginning of predestination.[150] And since God's love creates rather than responds to goodness, predestination cannot be mere foreknowledge of a person's future goodness. "Predestination is not anything in the predestined; but only in the person who predestines."[151] As part of divine providence, predestination and its effects ensure the return of humanity to the God from whom it proceeds.[152]

Does free will, then, have no role to play in the salvation of women and men? Might we at least say that God chooses some, offers them salvific grace, and simply requires them to muster a "yes, thank you"? Might a woman, for example, put herself in the way of grace, humbling herself in such a way that she is ready to receive grace when it arrives? This understanding leaves only a slender role to the unaided deliberative will. A common medieval trope posited that God would not withhold grace from those who "do what lies within them" (*facere quod in se est*). This seems to have been Thomas's position early in his career in his commentary on Lombard's *Sentences*, when he explained the gift of grace in terms of a "divine response to the correct exercise of human freedom," an exercise lying "within the powers of the human person." This "autonomous, freely performed action" seems a commonsensical reading of "doing what lies within one."[153] Joseph Wawrykow summarizes: "To put it bluntly (and yet fairly, I believe), in the *Scriptum* [the commentary on Lombard's *Sentences*] grace and the supernatural reward of heaven are 'there for the taking' through the gracious will of God. People must simply do their best, and they shall receive the appropriate response from God."[154]

But by the time he wrote his later works, the *Summa contra gentiles* and the *Summa theologiae*, Thomas had flipped the *facere quod in se est* upside down. He is happy to retain it, so long as its meaning is transparent to divine action. Instead of a small, but decisive, concession to human autonomy, it bespeaks divine prevenience. "Man can do nothing unless moved by God, according to Jo. xv.5: *Without Me, you can do nothing.* Hence when a man is said to do what is in him to do, this is said to be in his power according as he is moved by God."[155] Thomas makes the point in a discussion of justifica-

150. Thomas Aquinas, *ST* I.20.3.
151. Thomas Aquinas, *ST* I.23.2.
152. God "extends His providence over the just in a certain more excellent way than over the wicked; inasmuch as He prevents anything happening which would impede their final salvation" (Thomas Aquinas, *ST* I.22.2 ad 4).
153. Wawrykow, *God's Grace and Human Action*, 144.
154. Wawrykow, *God's Grace and Human Action*, 100.
155. Thomas Aquinas, *ST* I-II.109.6 ad 2. And so "this very preparation for grace is the result of grace. . . . In the light, then, of his deeper readings in Augustine in the 1260s as well as of his more theoretical considerations of the need for God to reduce human potential to

tion: "God does not justify us without ourselves because whilst we are being justified we consent to God's justification (*justitiae*) by a movement of our free-will. Nevertheless this movement is not the cause of grace, but the effect; hence the whole operation pertains to grace."[156] We do what lies within us, yes, consenting to God's justifying work, but even that is wholly due to grace.

What about the Lord's frequent calls to turn to him? "Turn ye to Me, . . . and I will turn to you," the Lord says in Zechariah. This turning seems to be a preparatory step to grace; *if* we turn to God, he will graciously turn to us.[157] Thomas affirms this movement of turning, but he insists that it requires a logically prior movement of being turned by God: "And that they are *turned* to God can only spring from God's having *turned* them."[158] "Man's turning to God is by free-will; and thus man is bidden to turn himself to God. But free-will can only be turned to God, when God turns it."[159] It is vital to avoid two errors in interpretation at this point. The first error would read this "turning" to imply that God does part and we do part. No, our turning is initiated and empowered completely by God. And yet what God initiates and empowers is our real turning to him; this is not (and here is the second error to avoid) a rhetorical sleight of hand in which genuine human action is lost. We really do turn to God of our own free will. Recall that God is the only one other than ourselves who can move our wills inwardly—and because inwardly, this really is the free movement of our will toward God.

Thomas discerns a Trojan horse in attributing even our "yes" to the good news of Jesus to free will alone, countering that we are not sufficient to produce our own assent to the gospel.

> The Pelagians held that this [internal] cause was nothing else than man's free-will: and consequently they said that the beginning of faith is from ourselves, inasmuch as, to wit, it is in our power to be ready to assent to things which are of faith, but that the consummation of faith is from God, Who proposes to us the things we have to believe. But this is false, for, since man, by assenting to matters of faith, is raised above his nature, this must needs accrue to him from some supernatural principle moving him inwardly; and this is God. Therefore

---

action, Thomas has re-read the *facere quod in se est* in such a way that he can argue for the human responsibility to prepare for grace without endangering the basic insight into God's free decision to save the individual as the source and origin of that person's salvation" (Wawrykow, *God's Grace and Human Action*, 210–11).

156. Thomas Aquinas, *ST* I-II.111.2 ad 2; also see I-II.113.3.

157. Thomas Aquinas, *ST* I-II.109.6 obj 1 (Thomas cites Zech. 1:3).

158. Thomas Aquinas, *ST* I-II.109.6. Thomas continues: "Hence it is clear that man cannot prepare himself to receive the light of grace except by the gratuitous help of God moving him inwardly."

159. Thomas Aquinas, *ST* I-II.109.6 ad 1.

faith, as regards the assent which is the chief act of faith, is from God moving man inwardly by grace.[160]

For anyone familiar with quick dismissals of Roman Catholic soteriology as based in works righteousness, this will come as something of a shock. Thomas denies a libertarian account of the will's freedom, in which the will can choose to affirm or deny the "things which are of faith," tarring it with a Pelagian brush.

Thomas's account of the conversion of sinners—for that has been the heart of the matter in this discussion of our reception of the first grace—flows from an account of God as the Alpha and Omega, the One from whom we and all of creation proceed and the One to whom we are oriented as our end. Recall the basic teleological structure of creation: God creates that he might communicate his goodness and draw all of his creation to its good in God. On the way to God, we need God to give us the resources adequate to the journey, yet in a way that is in keeping with our nature as rational creatures. In his doctrine of grace, Thomas seeks to affirm both these points.

In his masterful treatise on grace,[161] Thomas describes grace as a gift from God that heals and elevates people and helps them toward the end of union with God.[162] He makes a series of distinctions designed to further articulate the relation between divine and human action in the ambience of grace on the way to the beatific vision. Two of them concern us here. The first distinction is between habitual grace and helping grace. Grace can be considered either as a habitual gift from God or as a help from God, "whereby God moves us to will and to act."[163] A habit "incline[s] a power to act"; it is, if you will, a power's leaning toward an action.[164] Every human being has the power to obey God, considered as a necessary condition for being human; habitual grace inclines us toward obedience, even as the infused theological virtues incline us to faith, hope, and charity.

However, the inclination of habitual grace is not enough; Thomas recognizes that wayfarers on the return home to God need additional help along

160. Thomas Aquinas, *ST* II-II.6.1. Thomas writes of the proud, "especially of the Pelagians," that, "although they were trying to maintain our free will, they really undermined it." See Thomas Aquinas, *Commentary on the Gospel of John, Chapters 13–21*, 101 (commenting on John 15:5).

161. Thomas Aquinas, *ST* I-II.109–14.

162. The Reformers will be skeptical about the extent to which grace heals nature this side of the eschaton. It is later in the third part of the *Summa* that Thomas writes that "the end of grace is the union of the rational creature with God" (*ST* III.7.12).

163. Thomas Aquinas, *ST* I-II.111.2; also see I-II.112.2.

164. Thomas Aquinas, *ST* II-II.24.11. "A habit is a kind of medium between mere power and mere act" (I.87.2).

the way. Specifically, they need supplemental gifts from God to move them to action. A habit is a "steady disposition to act" but not yet an act; the disposition becomes act "by *auxilium* [help], by God moving people to actions in accord with habitual grace."[165] Habitual grace is God's lifting us up; help is what we need to walk in the way of the righteous.[166] One way to think of the two is like this: not only does God give us a new heart when we are born from above and make us people inclined to love our neighbors but he also moves us to love *this* neighbor in *this* moment. Unlike Thomas's contemporaries, who "tended to construe grace as principally, even exclusively habitual," Thomas insists that we must be sustained by divine helps if we are to finish the course and "see him as he is" (1 John 3:2).[167] To persevere in the faith we need the Father, Son, and Spirit "guiding and guarding [us] against attacks of the passions."[168]

Habitual and helping grace can each be divided into operative and cooperative grace. In operative grace, God is the sole mover. In cooperative grace, God cooperates with the soul in its action. God's grace working internally, moving our will, is operative. When our will issues in action, God works with the will that he has already moved, such that grace is cooperative. Thomas quotes Augustine with approval: "He operates that we may will; and when we will, He co-operates that we may perfect."[169] Joseph Wawrykow summarizes operative and cooperative helps, or *auxilia*, this way: "There will be as many *auxilia* as there are good acts done in the state of grace that further the progress to God as end. As operative, these *auxilia* will provide good intention and so perseverance in the state of grace; as cooperative, they will work with the person in adopting appropriate means for realizing these ends, oriented to the ultimate end that is God, and in executing the exterior act."[170]

Goodwill is up to God; good action is up to God, too, insofar as he works with those whose wills he has already moved to perfect them in action. If a friend slanders me and I forgive that person, God has worked operatively in me to will to forgive and cooperatively in me to form the words and actions proper to forgiveness. There is not a single good action I can perform on my own. In fact, I will not do one good thing apart from God's unilateral movement of my will to that good.

165. Wawrykow, "Grace," 194.

166. See Thomas Aquinas, *ST* I-II.109.9.

167. Wawrykow, "Grace," 194. "The gift of habitual grace is not therefore given to us that we may no longer need the Divine help" (Thomas Aquinas, *ST* I-II.109.9. ad 1). Thomas ties this explicitly to Christian perseverance at *ST* II-II.137.4.

168. Thomas Aquinas, *ST* I-II.109.10. Also see I-II.109.9 ad 2.

169. Thomas Aquinas, *ST* I-II.111.2.

170. Wawrykow, *Westminster Handbook to Thomas Aquinas*, 66–67.

**Finally, Friends**

All of this is Thomas's way of describing the return of all things to God, in a way that honors God's communication of his goodness to creation and yet ensures the homecoming of humanity in Christ. Nature, grace, and glory are oriented to one another. "Nature is to beatitude as first to second; because beatitude is superadded to nature. But the first must ever be preserved in the second. Consequently nature must be preserved in beatitude."[171] On the way to beatitude, grace cannot violate or desolate nature. Our natural end is in God. We naturally desire our final perfection as rational creatures—how could someone not desire his or her own perfection?—and this perfection, "which is the end of the whole universe, is the perfect beatitude of the Saints at the consummation of the world."[172] Torrell puts it nicely: "God has thus left, at the deepest level of every being, a desire to return to him."[173] The God who created us with natural desires will not allow them to be frustrated, and so "a natural desire cannot be in vain."[174] And yet, "everlasting life is a good exceeding the proportion of created nature; since it exceeds its knowledge and desire."[175] Beatitude is beyond nature. In itself, nature is not capable of the vision of God. "Now the vision of God's Essence surpasses the nature not only of man, but also of every creature. . . . Consequently neither man, nor any creature, can attain final Happiness by his natural powers."[176]

So God has structurally oriented us toward him as our end, but we are utterly unable to reach him from our resources. We are fit for him, but not capable of him without him. To be human is to be insufficient. To be human is to be set toward a destination we cannot reach without the One who is our end. Our very nature requires the ongoing gift of Son and Spirit for and as its integrity; their very nature enables us to persevere, ensuring the salvation that they bring in their wake.[177] Better, the nature the Son and Spirit share with the Father, as one God, secures the beatitude that is theirs in eternity and becomes ours, as the God of all fashions us for friendship with him. The

171. Thomas Aquinas, *ST* I.62.7.
172. Thomas Aquinas, *ST* I.73.1. "By the name of beatitude is understood the ultimate perfection of rational or of intellectual nature; and hence it is that it is naturally desired, since everything naturally desires its ultimate perfection" (*ST* I.62.1).
173. Torrell, *Spiritual Master*, 343.
174. Thomas Aquinas, *ST* I.75.6.
175. Thomas Aquinas, *ST* I-II.114.2.
176. Thomas Aquinas, *ST* I-II.5.5.
177. "Thomas argues for an unmerited grace of perseverance" such that "perseverance is a free gift of God by which God applies a person to good action and keeps the person away from sin, all in accordance with God's predestining will for that person" (Wawrykow, *God's Grace and Human Action*, 269).

reason God makes us partakers in the divine nature (2 Pet. 1:4) is that we might be fit to be the friends of God.[178] As the Spirit conforms us to Christ, who is the image of the Father, through faith, hope, and charity, we enter into the fellowship of his friends.[179] Consider, in closing, Thomas's theology as an expansive commentary on Jesus's words to his disciples in the upper room:

> Greater love has no one than this, that someone lay down his life for his friends. You are my friends if you do what I command you. No longer do I call you servants, for the servant does not know what his master is doing; but I have called you friends, for all that I have heard from my Father I have made known to you. You did not choose me, but I chose you and appointed you that you should go and bear fruit and that your fruit should abide, so that whatever you ask the Father in my name, he may give it to you. (John 15:13–16)

178. "Now the gift of grace surpasses every capability of created nature, since it is nothing short of a partaking of the Divine Nature, which exceeds every other nature. And thus it is impossible that any creature should cause grace" (Thomas Aquinas, ST I-II.112.1). "Grace is nothing else than a participated likeness of the Divine Nature, according to 2 Pet. i. 4: 'He hath given us most great and precious promises; that we may be (Vulg.,—you may be made) partakers of the Divine Nature'" (III.62.1).

179. Indeed, charity is friendship with God and "is impossible without faith and hope" (Thomas Aquinas, ST I-II.65.5). On the Spirit as the one who makes us friends with God, see SCG 4.21–22; Torrell, Spiritual Master, 164–72.

# 7

# "ONE LITTLE WORD
# SHALL FELL HIM"

## The Word of God and the Faith of Martin Luther

He had never intended this. A critic, yes, even a reformer, but Martin Luther had not planned on being a revolutionary. Despite a sharp tongue and a proneness to hyperbole, he had no interest in dividing the Western church. If the pope was the antichrist and the church itself in spiritual exile, it was still Christ's church, and Luther loved it.

By the beginning of 1521, though, the die had been cast. Luther had been excommunicated (three times, he would point out), and the evangelical churches (those devoted to the newly rediscovered "evangel," or gospel) set about the work of pruning, planting, and cultivating.[1] The decade must have been a blur to Luther, as he preached thousands of sermons, translated the Bible into German, prepared catechisms, provided pastoral oversight, fought error on his right and on his left, guided liturgical reform, and advised princes. He even wrote hymns, none more famous than "A Mighty Fortress Is Our God" (1529).

---

This chapter is adapted from Matt Jenson, "Much Ado about Nothing: The Necessary Non-Sufficiency of Faith," in *Luther Refracted: The Reformer's Ecumenical Legacy*, ed. Piotr J. Małysz and Derek R. Nelson (Minneapolis: Fortress Press, 2015), 141–68. Used by kind permission of Fortress Press.

    1. On the three excommunications, see Luther, *LW* 54:30 (Table Talk).

> A mighty fortress is our God, a bulwark never failing;
> Our helper He, amid the flood of mortal ills prevailing:
> For still our ancient foe doth seek to work us woe;
> His craft and power are great, and, armed with cruel hate,
> On earth is not his equal.

The hymn sounds a note of utter confidence to begin with, then immediately descends into the strife of earthly life, in which "our ancient foe" works tirelessly to crush us. Luther never imagined the Christian life as one of placid contemplation; it was, it is, struggle, combat. And it is a struggle in which we are helplessly outmatched, feeble Davids facing a ferocious Goliath.

> Did we in our own strength confide, our striving would be losing;
> Were not the right Man on our side, the Man of God's own choosing:
> Dost ask who that may be? Christ Jesus, it is He;
> Lord Sabaoth, His name, from age to age the same,
> And He must win the battle.

If we are hardly fit to fight our foe, this Man, who is the Lord of hosts, the Captain of a great army, is more than capable. Christ, writes Luther, is "that mighty giant"—he, not Goliath!—who "has abolished the Law, condemned sin, and destroyed death and every evil."[2] He has done this in his death and resurrection, and the unchanging Christ will continue to "win the battle." His accomplished and assured victory rouses courage in his followers.

> And though this world, with devils filled, should threaten to undo us,
> We will not fear, for God hath willed His truth to triumph through us:
> The Prince of Darkness grim, we tremble not for him;
> His rage we can endure, for lo, his doom is sure,
> One little word shall fell him.

Here it is not "the right Man" so much as the truth of God that triumphs. All it takes to topple the Prince of Darkness himself is "one little word." Those two modifiers—"one" and "little"—underscore the irony in which a bit of speech can overcome the rage of humanity's great enemy.

With remarkable consistency and reach, Luther spent his life reading, meditating on, preaching, and praising the Word that silences the voice of the accuser. The Word of God, according to Luther, is the church's greatest weapon. It is God's chosen instrument to achieve and manifest his reign in

2. Luther, *LW* 26:378.

creation, and it is the way in which he is present. In a 1522 sermon, only a few years after his first public criticism of the current practice of penance, Luther could already rejoice in the triumph of the Word: "I opposed indulgences and all papists, but never with force. I simply taught, preached, and wrote God's Word: otherwise I did nothing. And while I slept [cf. Mark 4:26–29], or drank Wittenberg beer with my Philip and Amsdorf, the Word so greatly weakened the papacy that no prince or emperor ever inflicted such losses upon it. I did nothing: the Word did it all."[3] But this confidence in the Word of God was hard-won, as we will see.

## Luther's Life[4]

Trapped in a thunderstorm and afraid for his life, a twenty-one-year-old Luther cried out to Saint Anne, vowing to become a monk. Delivered, he promptly fulfilled his vow, entering the Augustinian cloister at Erfurt on July 17, 1505, just two weeks after the storm had passed. Remembering the event years later, Luther said, "I took the vow not for the sake of my belly but for the sake of my salvation, and I observed all our statutes very strictly."[5] "He was driven by his desire to find the merciful God," writes Heiko Oberman. "And that was precisely what the order demanded of the candidate for admission."[6] Luther had come to the right place.

Luther had no difficulty finding a *righteous* God. He knew that God was righteous and that such an exacting God demanded righteousness from his people—that was the problem. He would later recall his hatred of the biblical phrase "the righteousness [or justice] of God" (*iustitia Dei*). Its occurrence in Romans 1 was the "single word . . . that stood in [his] way."

> I hated that word "righteousness of God," which, according to the use and custom of all the teachers, I had been taught to understand philosophically regarding the formal or active righteousness, as they call it, with which God is righteous and punishes the unrighteous sinner.
>
> Though I lived as a monk without reproach, I felt that I was a sinner before God with an extremely disturbed conscience. I could not believe that he was placated by my satisfaction. I did not love, yes, I hated the righteous God

3. Luther, *LW* 51:77.
4. In this biographical sketch, I follow Bainton, *Here I Stand*; Oberman, *Luther*; Brecht, *Road to Reformation*; Brecht, *Shaping and Defining the Reformation*; Brecht, *Preservation of the Church*.
5. Luther, *LW* 54:338 (Table Talk).
6. Oberman, *Luther*, 127.

who punishes sinners, and secretly, if not blasphemously, certainly murmuring greatly, I was angry with God, and said, "As if, indeed, it is not enough, that miserable sinners, eternally lost through original sin, are crushed by every kind of calamity by the law of the decalogue, without having God add pain to pain by the gospel and also by the gospel threatening us with his righteousness and wrath!" Thus I raged with a fierce and troubled conscience.[7]

Chesterton once wrote: "The Christian ideal has not been tried and found wanting. It has been found difficult; and left untried."[8] Luther tried. His spiritual rigor was notable. For his sins he could turn to the sacrament of penance, which offered a process whereby the sinner could make amends. Penance requires contrition, confession, and satisfaction—that is, appropriate sorrow for sin, the spoken acknowledgment of that sin before a priest, and compensatory action. But tender consciences worried: How sorry do I have to be? And what if I forget a sin? Luther "confessed frequently, often daily, and for as long as six hours on a single occasion. Every sin in order to be absolved was to be confessed. Therefore the soul must be searched and the memory ransacked and the motives probed."[9] Luther was no outlier, either. In the late medieval period, such spiritual scruples were so common that pastoral care manuals were written instructing confessors how to respond.[10] Luther later recalled the anxiety that plagued him and many others of his time, concluding that "the more someone tries to bring peace to his conscience through his own righteousness, the more disquieted he makes it."[11]

The wildly popular indulgence bonanza hardly helped. Officially, indulgences were papal dispensations entitling the holder to a remission of the temporal punishment for sins. They took care of the satisfaction portion of penance, but penitent sinners still needed to be duly contrite and confess their sins to a priest. Too often, such subtlety was lost on the masses—or discreetly hidden from them—as the sale of indulgences became a way to minimize the negative effects of sin by avoiding the pains of purgatory. By venerating the more than 19,000 relics of the castle church at Wittenberg, a person could receive more than 1,900,000 days' indulgence, which would take off more than

---

7. Luther, *LW* 34:336–37, written in 1545 in the preface to the complete Latin edition of Luther's works. Compare with this Luther's account in a letter to Staupitz (*LW* 48:64–70), in which Luther tells the story in terms of a new understanding of *poenitentia* (Latin, "penance") as repentance, literally a changing of mind (Greek, *metanoia*).

8. Chesterton, *What's Wrong with the World*, in *Collected Works*, 4:61. Chesterton was not speaking of Luther, it should be said.

9. Bainton, *Here I Stand*, 54.

10. Oberman, *Luther*, 177.

11. Luther, *LW* 27:13.

5,000 years from time in purgatory.[12] What Roland Bainton calls "the bingo of the sixteenth century" financed the Crusades, built St. Peter's Basilica, and distracted Christians from the weightier matters of genuine repentance.[13] The penitential system, which lay at the heart of medieval Christendom, had been tried—and found wanting. It crushed the earnest, and it sedated the complacent. As for Luther, he had exhausted its resources, and "the great revolt against the medieval Church arose from a desperate attempt to follow the way by her prescribed."[14]

Even as he suffered under the weight of his sin and sought in vain for a merciful God, Luther continued his education. Having been trained in philosophy, he attained three theology degrees over five years. As chair of biblical theology at the University of Wittenberg (a small, unimpressive town), Luther began a series of exegetical lectures. From 1513 to 1520 he would lecture on Psalms, Romans, Galatians, Hebrews, Psalms again, and possibly Titus and Judges. Penance had presented a problem; exegesis provided the solution.[15] Recall his exasperation at Paul's reference to the revelation of the righteousness of God in Romans 1. He continues:

> Nevertheless, I beat importunately upon Paul at that place, most ardently desiring to know what St. Paul wanted.
>
> At last, by the mercy of God, meditating day and night, I gave heed to the context of the words, namely, "In it the righteousness of God is revealed, as it is written, 'He who through faith is righteous shall live.'" There I began to understand that the righteousness of God is that by which the righteous lives by a gift of God, namely by faith. And this is the meaning: the righteousness of God is revealed by the gospel, namely, the passive righteousness with which merciful God justifies us by faith, as it is written, "He who through faith is righteous shall live." Here I felt that I was altogether born again and had entered paradise itself through open gates. There a totally other face of the entire Scripture showed itself to me.[16]

Luther would quip: "The Spiritus Sanctus gave me this realization in the cloaca."[17] The reference is either to the toilet or to a study in the tower above it. Both fit the man and the moment. Luther could certainly be crass (one

---

12. Brecht, *Road to Reformation*, 117.
13. Bainton, *Here I Stand*, 74.
14. Bainton, *Here I Stand*, 35–36. Also see Brecht, *Road to Reformation*, 69.
15. "The advances in Luther's theology were almost always the fruit of intensive exegetical work" (Brecht, *Road to Reformation*, 223).
16. Luther, *LW* 34:336–37, written in 1545 in the preface to the complete Latin edition of Luther's works.
17. Cited in Oberman, *Luther*, 155.

strategy with the devil was to chase him off with a fart).[18] More to the point, though, his discovery of the good news about God's righteousness—that it describes his saving work, that precisely *as* righteous, this God is merciful—reached him in the filth of his sin and represented the fruit of his study.

This realization came in the spring of 1518.[19] Luther had already attacked the practice of indulgences and many other ecclesiastical abuses in the ninety-five theses that he wrote for debate and nailed to the door of the castle church in Wittenberg on October 31, 1517. He began proclaiming repentance as a reality both deeper and grander than the contemporary form of penance: "When our Lord and Master Jesus Christ said, 'Repent' [Matt. 4:17], he willed the entire life of believers to be one of repentance."[20] One never outgrows the need for repentance; yet, for all its gravity, repentance possesses an elegant simplicity in comparison to the elaborate apparatus in the medieval sacrament of penance. One need only repent to be forgiven: "Any truly repentant Christian has a right to full remission of penalty and guilt, even without indulgence letters."[21] Having met the righteous and merciful God, Luther discovered a matching vision of repentance—breathtakingly free, unfettered by notions of achievement, recompense, and reward. This "rent the very fabric of Christian ethics. Reward and merit, so long undisputed as the basic motivation for all human action, were robbed of their efficacy."[22]

This insight also threatened to rend the fabric of God's church. While the Luther affair appeared initially to be a local squabble, his pugnacity and popularity and the quiet yet firm support of Frederick the Wise (who had financed Luther's doctorate in theology) raised the profile of the German monk. Three times in less than three years he was brought to trial—before Cardinal Cajetan at Augsburg in October 1518, in debate with Johannes Eck at Leipzig in July 1519, and at the imperial diet of Worms in April 1521. Each time, Luther championed the authority of the Scriptures, in which he had found the good news of forgiveness. Along the way, he questioned and challenged the authority of canon law, the pope, and church councils. (In return, the pope excommunicated him at the beginning of 1521.) At times vilified and at others heroized, Luther declared his intention at Worms: "I have desired nothing in all this except a reformation according to holy Scripture."[23] The implications were clear: "Unless I am convicted by Scripture and plain

18. Luther, *LW* 54:16 (Table Talk).
19. Brecht, *Road to Reformation*, 226.
20. Luther, *LW* 31:25.
21. Luther, *LW* 31:28.
22. Oberman, *Luther*, 154.
23. Luther, *LW* 32:122.

reason—I do not accept the authority of popes and councils, for they have contradicted each other—my conscience is captive to the Word of God."[24]

Once the break with Rome was complete, much of Luther's career vacillated between skirmishes and the patient work of building up the evangelical churches. Luther rejoiced at the liberating good news of Christ, but he was dismayed to witness the rash, libertine manner in which his colleagues and followers responded. After the imperial diet at Worms, Luther went into hiding at the Wartburg, a castle in central Germany, where he managed to translate the New Testament into German in eleven weeks. Returning to Wittenberg, he witnessed a rude iconoclasm, a hasty abandonment of long-held liturgical forms and customs, and a cavalier independence of spirit. He had to step over a broken crucifix in one church to make his way into the pulpit—where he preached a sermon advocating the tolerance of images.[25] Later, he lashed out at the extreme measures of revolting peasants, Anabaptists, "Sacramentarians," and other "enthusiasts" who had followed the spirit of the age rather than listening to the Word of the Lord.

Luther contributed to the nurture of the evangelical churches in a remarkably comprehensive way. In the 1520s alone he published a German New Testament, a hymnbook, a German Mass (with more Scripture and more instruction than the one it replaced), and two catechisms.[26] He never stopped preaching and lecturing, preaching 121 times one year and spending the final decade of his life lecturing on Genesis.[27] He continued to translate the Bible into German, publishing the complete version in 1534. In the middle of all this activity, Luther took in nine nuns who had escaped from a convent, saw to their being married off, and then, to the surprise of his friends, married the last one, Katherine von Bora. They had six children and a large household, with sometimes up to twenty-five people living in his former Augustinian cloister, which had been given to the Luthers as their home.[28]

Bainton points out, gently but honestly, that "the conflicts and the labors of the dramatic years had impaired his health and made him prematurely an irascible old man, petulant, peevish, unrestrained, and at times positively coarse."[29] While not racially motivated—Luther always thought like a theologian—his vitriol toward Jews is a sorry mark on his career, certainly a sign that, as he

24. Cited in Bainton, *Here I Stand*, 185.

25. Brecht, *Shaping and Defining the Reformation*, 160.

26. The observation about the German mass is Bainton's in *Here I Stand*, 340.

27. In 1529, "he preached no fewer than 121 times, on forty days twice each day" (Brecht, *Defining and Shaping the Reformation*, 284).

28. Bainton, *Here I Stand*, 294.

29. Bainton, *Here I Stand*, 373.

put it, the Christian is *simul iustus et peccator*, at once entirely righteous in Christ and entirely sinful in himself.[30] As far as we can tell, the last words Luther wrote were "Wir sind bettler. Hoc est verum." ("We are beggars. This is true.")

## The Voice of the Law

Throughout the welter of Luther's life, he listened for the Word of God. But what Word did he hear? He heard Jesus's declaration that he came not to call the righteous, but sinners.[31] "God saves no one but sinners," Luther writes. "He instructs no one but the foolish and the stupid. He enriches none but paupers, and He makes alive only the dead; not those who merely imagine themselves to be such but those who really are this kind of people and admit it."[32] But this is the very thing we fail to do—admit it. The deceitfulness of sin has us thinking that we are doing quite well, thank you very much, or at least better than the next guy. We can always find someone whose moral failure dwarfs our own, allowing us to rest comfortably in the knowledge that, on balance, we're not all that bad. Sin hides us from ourselves.

We are curved inward, according to Luther.[33] At work and at play, in love and war and at prayer, we only ever seek ourselves. "For man cannot but seek his own advantages and love himself above all things. And this is the sum of all his iniquities. Hence even in good things and virtues men seek themselves, that is, they seek to please themselves and applaud themselves."[34] Like Narcissus, we are fascinated with ourselves and deaf to the voice of love.[35] We even use God himself for our own ends, employing him like a tool for our vain self-fashioning.[36] "This is spiritual fornication, iniquity, and a terrible curving in on itself."[37] And it has become something of a second nature to us. Luther puts it more sharply: "This crookedness . . . is our very nature itself, wounded and totally in ferment, so that without grace it becomes not only

30. Bainton describes Luther's position as "entirely religious and in no respect racial" (Bainton, *Here I Stand*, 379).

31. Matt. 9:13; Mark 2:17; Luke 5:32.

32. Luther, *LW* 25:418.

33. See M. Jenson, *Gravity of Sin*, 47–97.

34. Luther, *LW* 25:222.

35. In *Paradise Lost*, a newly created Eve gazes with delight at her own image, unwittingly risking the fate of Narcissus (though yet without sin), until a voice calls her out of herself into relationship with her husband. Milton offers a dramatization of the Word that comes to us in our self-fascination, awaking us to the love of God and neighbor. See *Paradise Lost* 4.460–91.

36. See Luther, *LW* 25:291.

37. Luther, *LW* 25:346.

incurable but also totally unrecognizable."[38] Against any attempts to find in nature something salvageable, a yet untarnished part of us that might provide God something to work with in remaking us, Luther insists that there is not a square inch in the whole domain of human existence over which I do not cry, "Mine!"[39] "Man is by nature unable to want God to be God. Indeed, he himself wants to be God, and does not want God to be God."[40] We can't help ourselves.

This message was utterly lost on those who preached that God would not withhold his grace from those who do what lies within them (*facere quod in se est*).[41] Luther disdains this principle, which he calls "the foremost principle of their faith," suggesting that "as a result of this the whole church has almost been overturned."[42] Paul and Augustine saw that when we do what lies within us, we only get worse.[43] To throw a person back on herself, even suggesting God might meet her halfway, is disastrous spiritual counsel. Luther urgently insists on human incapacity and intransigence in questions of salvation: "But no man can be thoroughly humbled until he knows that his salvation is utterly beyond his own powers, devices, endeavors, will, and works, and depends entirely on the choice, will, and work of another, namely, of God alone."[44]

But how can we know this? If sin involves us in ever-subtler forms of self-deception, how can we arrive at the kind of painful self-knowledge that causes us to despair of ourselves and look to God? We look into the mirror of the law.[45] In the life of the church, "the proper use and aim of the Law is to make guilty those who are smug and at peace, so that they may see that they are in danger of sin, wrath, and death, so that they may be terrified and despairing, blanching and quaking at the rustling of a leaf (Lev. 26:36)."[46] The law makes sinners; that is, it indicts the complacent, exposing and exacerbating their sin,

---

38. Luther, *LW* 25:351.
39. "Note how the voice of the flesh is always saying 'my,' 'my' . . ." (Luther, *LW* 25:376). Abraham Kuyper evoked the lordship of Christ in writing, "There is not a square inch in the whole domain of human existence over which Christ, who is Sovereign over all, does not cry, 'Mine!'" ("Sphere Sovereignty," 488).
40. Luther, *LW* 31:10. Philip Watson argues that Luther's theology is thoroughly theocentric in *Let God Be God!*
41. Luther railed against the *facere quod in se est* in Gabriel Biel's work in particular. On Biel, see Oberman, *Harvest of Medieval Theology*.
42. Luther, *LW* 36:214; 25:497.
43. Luther, *LW* 32:153–54.
44. Luther, *LW* 33:62. The humble person also does what lies within—that is, "ask," "seek," "knock," "cry out." "The sinner does what is in him when he cries out for a virtue which he does not have and which he is all too painfully conscious that he lacks" (Steinmetz, *Luther and Staupitz*, 88).
45. Luther, *Large Catechism*, I, 187.
46. Luther, *LW* 26:148.

demanding justice.[47] It "make[s] men not better but worse"; "it does nothing but reveal sin, work wrath, accuse, terrify, and reduce the minds of men to the point of despair. And that is as far as the Law goes."[48] "For the Law demands: 'Do this!'"[49] But we can't, and won't. Even when we attempt to comply, "the Law always terrifies and accuses, saying: 'But you have not done enough!'"[50]

Nor *can* we do enough. If the law can teach us to know ourselves as sinners, it can do nothing to deliver us.[51] The law can only "furnish knowledge" of sin; it cannot "reveal or confer any power." We wrongly suppose that an imperative (*Thou shalt . . .*) presupposes an indicative, "as if once a thing is commanded it must forthwith necessarily be done or be possible to do."[52] But when the Lord commands his people to have no other gods before him, he does not thereby imply an ability to obey him. In fact, "no man can achieve so much as to keep one of the Ten Commandments as it ought to be kept."[53]

This line of thought seems a ministry of despair—and it is. But the law is not the last word. It leads the sinner (and every Christian remains a sinner) to say, with Paul, "Wretched man that I am! Who will deliver me from this body of death?" (Rom. 7:24). By virtue of "this humiliation, this wounding and crushing by the hammer," the law serves as "a minister and a preparation for grace. For God is the God of the humble, the miserable, the afflicted, the oppressed, the desperate, and of those who have been brought down to nothing at all."[54] The law strips the sinner, who then longs to be clothed with Christ. The law starves the sinner, who then hungers for Christ.[55] "As the dry earth thirsts for rain, so the Law makes the troubled heart thirst for Christ. . . . He gladly soaks and irrigates this dry ground."[56]

### The Word of the Gospel

With its demands, the law brings us to the end of ourselves. Demands cease with the gospel, "which does not teach me what I should do—for that is the proper function of the law—but what someone else has done for me, namely,

47. Luther writes that "without the Law there would be no sin or old man, but through the Law he is aroused" (*LW* 25:58).
48. Luther, *LW* 26:327, 313.
49. Luther, *LW* 26:303.
50. Luther, *LW* 26:149.
51. Luther, *LW* 31:349.
52. Luther, *LW* 33:127.
53. Luther, *Large Catechism*, I, 316.
54. Luther, *LW* 26:314.
55. Luther, *LW* 26:345.
56. Luther, *LW* 26:329.

that Jesus Christ, the Son of God, has suffered and died to deliver me from sin and death."[57] If the law reveals sin, the gospel removes sin; it does so by changing the subject.[58]

Luther recalls the anxious scrupulosity of his monkish years, in which he curved in on himself in a sincere—and sinful—attempt to please God and assuage his conscience: "When I was a monk, I made a great effort to live according to the requirements of the monastic rule. I made a practice of confessing and reciting all my sins, but always with prior contrition; I went to confession frequently, and I performed the assigned penances faithfully. Nevertheless, my conscience could never achieve certainty but was always in doubt and said: 'You have not done this correctly. You were not contrite enough. You omitted this in your confession.'"[59] "The law says, 'do this,' and it is never done. Grace says, 'believe in this,' and everything is already done."[60] It is already done, because it is done for me by another. "Behold that one who alone fulfils the law for you, whom God has made to be your righteousness, sanctification, wisdom, and redemption, for all those who believe in him [1 Cor. 1:30]."[61] When Luther discovered the Pauline "not I, but Christ" (Gal. 2:20), he realized that the gospel "commands us to look, not at our own good deeds or perfection but at God Himself as He promises, and at Christ Himself, the Mediator."[62] The good news is that our faithful God keeps his promises and has fulfilled them in Christ. Thus our attention is turned from our impoverished selves to Christ and his riches. Faith is "a constant gaze that looks at nothing except Christ, the Victor over sin and death and the Dispenser of righteousness, salvation, and eternal life."[63] Like the Israelites in the wilderness, who had only to look at the bronze serpent to be healed, sinners need only fix their eyes on Christ to be delivered from sin, death, and the devil.[64] Faith's only proper object is Christ, and the one who "diverts his gaze from this object does not have true faith."[65]

---

57. Luther, *LW* 26:91. "For the Law demands: 'Do this!' The promise grants: 'Accept this!'" (*LW* 26:303).

58. Luther, *LW* 32:223, 226. Robert Kolb contrasts Luther's construal of the law-gospel distinction with earlier uses: "No longer a matter of salvation-history, the proper distinction of law and gospel became God's way of addressing the existential situation of fallen human beings" (*Martin Luther*, 51–52).

59. Luther, *LW* 27:13.

60. Luther, *LW* 31:41. All of Scripture can be summarized, for Luther, in the words of John the Baptist: "Repent [the proper response to the law] and believe [the proper response to the gospel]" (Mark 1:15).

61. Luther, *LW* 31:231.

62. Luther, *LW* 26:387.

63. Luther, *LW* 26:356.

64. Luther, *LW* 26:356–57.

65. Luther, *LW* 26:88.

Faith gazes at Christ; it also grasps Christ. Luther describes Christ as a jewel that a believer possesses by faith.[66] So closely united are Christ and the one who trusts in him that they become one flesh.

> By [faith] you are so cemented to Christ that He and you are as one person, which cannot be separated but remains attached to Him forever and declares: "I am as Christ." And Christ, in turn, says: "I am as that sinner who is attached to Me, and I to him. For by faith we are joined together into one flesh and one bone." Thus Eph. 5:30 says: "We are members of the body of Christ, of His flesh and of His bones," in such a way that this faith couples Christ and me more intimately than a husband is coupled to his wife.[67]

As a result, "what is ours becomes His and what is His becomes ours."[68] At the cross, this perfectly righteous One took on himself the sin of the world, becoming "the highest, the greatest, and the only sinner."[69] So fully has he appropriated our sin that Paul can teach that "there is no more sin, no more death, and no more curse in the world, but only in Christ."[70]

As Christ takes on my sin and death, through faith I receive his righteousness and life. "Therefore a man can with confidence boast in Christ and say: 'Mine are Christ's living, doing, and speaking, his suffering and dying, mine as much as if I had lived, done, spoken, suffered, and died as he did.'"[71] Luther offers a spiritual reading of Boaz covering Ruth with his cloak, an act of protection, love, and redemption, suggesting that "the soul lays itself down at Christ's humanity and is covered with his righteousness."[72] Similarly, Luther can speak of Christ sheltering believers under his wings like a mother hen.[73] "Faith is precisely that which makes you a chick, and Christ a hen, so that you have hope under his wings."[74] The language of covering captures Luther's emphasis on the imputation of Christ's righteousness and the corresponding nonimputation of our sin. "There is therefore now no condemnation," not for those who are now without sin—for sin remains—but "for those who are in Christ Jesus" (Rom. 8:1).[75]

The gospel testifies to Christ's righteousness and invites people to place their trust in him, such that "Christ is our principal, complete, and perfect

66. Luther, *LW* 26:89.
67. Luther, *LW* 26:168.
68. Luther, *LW* 26:292.
69. Luther, *LW* 26:281.
70. Luther, *LW* 26:285.
71. Luther, *LW* 31:297.
72. Luther, *LW* 25:265. Also see 31:189–90.
73. For Jesus's self-description in these terms, see Matt. 23:37; Luke 13:34.
74. Luther, *LW* 32:236. Also see Luther, *Complete Sermons*, 2.1:59–60.
75. Luther, *LW* 32:239; 32:255.

righteousness."[76] Luther means much the same thing in writing that "faith is our righteousness in this present life,"[77] because faith is nothing other than a confident repose in Christ the Righteous. Because Christian righteousness changes the subject, to speak of "my righteousness" is to speak of the One who is righteous for me. We "do not perform but receive" righteousness.[78] Here is the root of Luther's invective against Aristotle. "Virtually the entire *Ethics* of Aristotle is the worst enemy of grace," Luther writes, recognizing that this places him "in opposition to the scholastics."[79] Aristotle is "the destroyer of godly doctrine" and stands directly opposed to Scripture.[80] "We do not become righteous by doing righteous deeds [as Aristotle thought] but, having been made righteous, we do righteous deeds."[81] Our righteousness is an "alien righteousness, that is the righteousness of another, instilled from without. This is the righteousness of Christ by which he justifies through faith."[82]

According to the doctrine of justification, "we are pronounced righteous and are saved solely by faith in Christ, and without works."[83] Luther praises "that single solid rock which we call the doctrine of justification, namely, that we are redeemed from sin, death, and the devil and endowed with eternal life, not through ourselves and certainly not through our works, which are even less than we are ourselves, but through the help of Another, the only Son of God, Jesus Christ."[84] *Sola fide* means *solus Christus*, understood with reference to the human role in salvation.[85] What is our role? Faith alone. That is, we are to trust in "the help of Another" and never in ourselves. Faith is thus never alone, insofar as it grasps Christ; faith praises the believer's insufficiency and thereby glorifies the sufficiency of Christ. "There is only one article and one rule of theology," Luther concludes, "and this is true faith or trust in Christ. Whoever doesn't hold this article and this rule is no theologian. All other articles flow into and out of this one; without it the others are meaningless."[86]

76. Luther, LW 27:71.
77. Luther, LW 27:64.
78. Luther, LW 26:6.
79. Luther, LW 31:12. While characteristically boorish, Luther was not ignorant of Aristotle, having lectured on the *Ethics* at Wittenberg in 1508. Nor was he universally dismissive of Aristotle, who still could be useful in certain places.
80. Luther, LW 32:258.
81. Luther, LW 31:12. Also see 25:152, 242.
82. Luther, LW 31:297.
83. Luther, LW 26:223.
84. Luther, LW 27:145.
85. Luther can attribute our justification to "God alone" working "solely by His grace through Christ" (LW 26:99), to "faith in Christ" alone (26:223), and to "Christ alone" (27:17).
86. Luther, LW 54:157 (Table Talk).

## Faith Comes by Hearing

How does one come to have faith? "But if they hear His Word and believe, Christ becomes present to them, justifies and saves them."[87] Luther's answer is Paul's: "So faith comes from hearing, and hearing through the word of Christ" (Rom. 10:17). Significantly, according to Luther's translation of this verse, faith comes from *preaching*, a testament to the centrality of the public ministry of the Word in the gathered assembly. Even "a seven-year-old child knows what the church is: holy believers and 'little sheep who hear the voice of their shepherd.'"[88] If the church is marked by its readiness to hear its shepherd's voice, one "becomes a Christian, not by working but by listening."[89] "For the Word proceeds from the mouth of the apostle and reaches the heart of the hearer; there the Holy Spirit is present and impresses that Word on the heart, so that it is heard. In this way every preacher is a parent, who produces and forms the true shape of the Christian mind through the ministry of the Word."[90]

We are born again as we hear the good news preached to us, and so believers have preachers for parents and the Word for a womb. Luther expands on this image with reference to Paul's description of Christians as sons and heirs of God. An heir "obtains the inheritance in a purely passive, not in an active way; that is, just his being born, not his producing or working or worrying, makes him an heir. He does not do anything toward his being born but merely lets it happen. . . . Therefore just as in society a son becomes an heir merely by being born, so here faith alone makes men sons of God, born of the Word, which is the divine womb in which we are conceived, carried, born, reared, etc."[91] The Word is a womb we never leave, though, being "born, reared, etc." in it. "Thus everything happens through the ministry of the Word."[92] All Christians are priests, and so the ministry of the Word belongs to the whole church.[93] The church has only one task, which is to "preach the Gospel correctly and purely and thus give birth to children."[94] If a church does not preach the gospel—well, it simply is not a church.[95]

87. Luther, *LW* 26:240.
88. Luther, *Schmalkald Articles* III, 12, 2.
89. Luther, *LW* 26:214.
90. Luther, *LW* 26:430.
91. Luther, *LW* 26:392.
92. Luther, *LW* 26:442.
93. See Luther, *LW* 36:88, 113, 116, 138. Paul Althaus makes a necessary clarification: "The universal priesthood expresses not religious individualism but its exact opposite, the reality of the congregation as a community" (*Theology of Martin Luther*, 314).
94. Luther, *LW* 26:441.
95. Luther, *LW* 32:73.

Not all have ears to hear, however. While one need only "let it happen," need only listen to become a Christian, the Spirit must "impress that Word on the heart, *so that it is heard*." Such spiritual hearing is a gift and signals the divine presence surrounding faith. Luther stresses that faith is a divine gift mediated through the Word. Faith is not a human accomplishment, something to be mustered; it is given to us by God as he nourishes us on his Word throughout our lives.

> This is why we continually teach that the knowledge of Christ and of faith is not a human work but utterly a divine gift; as God creates faith, so he preserves us in it. And just as He initially gives us faith through the Word, so later on He exercises, increases, strengthens, and perfects it in us by that Word. Therefore the supreme worship of God that a man can offer, the Sabbath of Sabbaths, is to practice true godliness, to hear and read the Word. On the other hand, nothing is more dangerous than to become tired of the Word.[96]

Luther can imagine "no more terrible disaster with which the wrath of God can afflict men than a famine of the hearing of his Word" and also "no greater mercy than when he sends forth his Word."[97] God gives himself to us clothed in the Word, and we receive God's gift of himself by faith alone in the Word of God.[98] In fact, this is the only way in which we can encounter God, who "deals with us in no other way than by his holy word and sacraments, which are like signs or seals of his words."[99] (Hence the importance of translating the Bible and the Mass into German.) Note that Luther's celebration of the Word does not lead to a denigration of the sacraments but instead to an emphasis on their eloquence. Luther laments how few "know that the Mass is the promise of Christ."[100] The Lord's Supper says it all: "'Take and eat, this is my body.' This word is the whole gospel."[101] Word and sacrament form the foundation of a consistently extrinsic spirituality, in which the Spirit draws those curved inward out of themselves and into the life of Christ. Every error Luther discerned throughout his life could best be characterized as a vain attempt to deal with God apart from his Word. Such "enthusiasts . . . boast that they have the Spirit apart from and before contact with the word."[102]

96. Luther, *LW* 26:64.
97. Luther, *LW* 31:346.
98. Luther, *LW* 33:139; 31:346.
99. Luther, *LW* 32:15. Also see Luther, *Schmalkald Articles* III, 8, 9, 10; *LW* 36:42.
100. Luther, *LW* 36:41.
101. Luther, *LW* 36:288.
102. Luther, *Schmalkald Articles* III, 8, 3.

The Word stabilizes and strengthens believers by instructing them in and reminding them of the promises of God. It tethers faith to its object.[103] Despite common usage, "faith" cannot name a posture or attitude devoid of an object. One cannot have faith per se; one must have faith in someone or something. And everyone has faith, according to Luther. Each of us has a god, has someone or something "to which we look for all good and in which we find refuge in every time of need." He continues: "To have a god is nothing else than to trust and believe him with our whole heart. As I have often said, the trust and faith of the heart alone make both God and an idol. If your faith and trust are right, then your God is the true God. . . . That to which your heart clings and entrusts itself is, I say, really your God."[104] In the womb of the Word, faith clings to God as it is nourished by the Spirit.

Of course, "so far as the words are concerned, this doctrine of faith is very easy, and everyone can easily understand the distinction between the Law and grace; but so far as practice, life, and application are concerned, it is the most difficult thing there is."[105] Faith trusts in the Word of God, which publishes the good news about Christ and is received as the Spirit enables a person to hear it as good news *for her*.[106] "Rather ought Christ to be preached to the end that faith in him may be established that he may not only be Christ, but be Christ for you and me, and that what is said of him and is denoted in his name may be effectual in us."[107] It is precisely this "for you and me" that we find so difficult. Of the opening words of the Lord's Prayer—"Our Father who art in heaven"—Luther writes that "this one word 'your' or 'our' is the most difficult of all in the whole Scripture."[108]

How does Christ become Christ "for you and me"? How do we learn to pray "Our Father"? We have to learn this by experience, as it is "experience alone [that] makes the theologian."[109] Oswald Bayer is quick to point out that it is "not experience as such, but the experience of scripture" that does so.[110] Luther finds in Psalm 119, David's paean to the divine Word, three "rules" for theologians—*oratio, meditatio*, and *tentatio* (prayer, meditation, and spiritual attack)—which together describe how experience of Scripture makes

---

103. "Where there is no promise, there is no faith; and where there is no faith, the promise is nothing" (Luther, *LW* 36:169).
104. Luther, *Large Catechism* I, 2–3.
105. Luther, *LW* 26:144.
106. The Spirit thus "bridges that 'loathsome ditch' between past and present" and makes the Christian contemporaneous with Christ (Lohse, *Martin Luther's Theology*, 236).
107. Luther, *LW* 31:357.
108. Luther, *LW* 54:9 (Table Talk).
109. Luther, *LW* 54:7 (Table Talk).
110. Bayer, *Theology the Lutheran Way*, 63.

a theologian.[111] Because Scripture is God's Word, the Spirit of God must illumine our hearts and minds to understand it; so we pray, that we might "lay hold of the real teacher of the Scriptures himself" rather than become our own teachers.[112] This "laying hold" is all the more necessary given our sin and stupidity, which lead us to resist the Word that "comes contrary to our thinking and our will"[113] and ushers in "a state of tumult" as it comes "to change and renew the world."[114]

Second, like David, we ought to "talk, meditate, speak, sing, hear, read, by day and night and always about nothing except God's Word and commandments."[115] Hearing the Word, for Luther, is an ongoing activity in which, as we meditate on Scripture, the Christ clothed in the Word becomes Christ "for you and for me." We must remain vigilant, for biblical meditation incites the ire of the evil one. "See only that you pay heed to God's Word and remain in it, like a child in the cradle. If you let go of it for a moment, then you fall out of it. This is the devil's sole aim, to tear people out of it and to cause them to measure God's will and work by human reason."[116] Faith is so very vulnerable in itself. It suffers the slings and arrows of sin, the flesh, and the devil; and "cross and conflict follow immediately upon the knowledge of Christ."[117] This response is fitting; servants of a crucified Lord can hardly expect anything else. "The cross alone is our theology," Luther proclaims.[118]

The corresponding third rule for theologians considers spiritual attack. Whereas Anselm envisioned the theological project as "faith seeking understanding," Luther finds it to be "attack seeking certainty (*tentatus quarens certitudinem*)."[119] "This is the touchstone that teaches you not only to know and understand, but also to experience how right, how true, how sweet, how lovely, how mighty, how comforting God's Word is, wisdom beyond all wisdom. . . . For as soon as God's Word takes root and grows in you, the devil will harry you, and make a real doctor of you, and by his assaults will teach you to seek and love God's Word."[120]

111. Luther, *LW* 34:285–88. See the discussion in Bayer, *Theology the Lutheran Way*, 33–66, which has informed my account.

112. Luther, *LW* 34:286.

113. Luther, *LW* 25:415.

114. Luther, *LW* 33:52.

115. Luther, *LW* 34:286, cited in Bayer, *Theology the Lutheran Way*, 51.

116. Luther, *LW* 36:345.

117. Luther, *LW* 27:25. Also see Luther, *Large Catechism* III, 65.

118. Luther, *Weimarer Ausgabe* 5.176.32–33, cited in McGrath, *Luther's Theology of the Cross*, 152.

119. Bayer, *Theology the Lutheran Way*, 212. "Thus the doctrine of 'Anfechtung' is the clue to Luther's conception of Faith," writes Gordon Rupp (*Righteousness of God*, 114).

120. Luther, *LW* 34:286–87.

Luther acknowledges his debt to those he calls "my papists," writing that they "have made a fairly good theologian of me, which I would not have become otherwise."[121] "Almost every night when I wake up the devil is there and wants to dispute with me," he once said.[122] He complained of the devil's accusations and attacks throughout his life, but he also retained a sense of their strategic service in nurturing faith. Despite himself, the devil is a *Doktorvater*, whose students become doctors of the church. Unwittingly, he teaches saints the sweetness and loveliness of God's Word. Like Jesus in the wilderness, believers quickly learn that their only recourse is to Scripture, the truth of which gives the lie to Satan's condemnation. Satan teaches them to use the sword of the Spirit, which is the Word of God, only to find himself on the receiving end of the blade, "sharper than any two-edged sword" (Heb. 4:12; see also Eph. 6:17). "Nothing is so effectual against the devil, the world, the flesh, and all evil thoughts as to occupy oneself with the Word of God, talk about it, and meditate on it. . . . This, indeed, is the true holy water, the sign which routs the devil and puts him to flight."[123]

Faith is also attacked from within, in the conspiracy of reason and the flesh. These two "simply want to work together. . . . Conscience is always murmuring and thinking that when righteousness, the Holy Spirit, and eternal salvation are promised solely on the basis of hearing with faith, this is too easy a way."[124] Reason knows that the way of the world is quid pro quo, and the flesh seeks and glories in its own achievement. Neither is content with the simple receptivity of faith, and so they seek to destabilize it by troubling the conscience. Ever embattled, ever victorious, "faith always has a 'nevertheless' character about it."[125]

### The Ground of Assurance

"But are you *sure*?" Or in the words of the serpent, "Did God *really* say . . . ?" Even—especially—for those who have heard the Word, questions remain. "The interior life is often stupid," writes Annie Dillard.[126] A pastoral genius, Luther knew that scrupulous consciences could turn even the liberating proclamation of salvation by faith alone on its head. Faith can become fascinated with itself, curving inward. Indeed, faith can easily become the last refuge of

121. Luther, *LW* 34:287.
122. Luther, *LW* 54:78 (Table Talk).
123. Luther's preface to the *Large Catechism*.
124. Luther, *LW* 26:215.
125. Althaus, *Theology of Martin Luther*, 172.
126. Dillard, *American Childhood*, 20.

works righteousness, the one work I *can* do to justify myself in the sight of God. Faith, however, can also worry about itself. It can turn the joyful call to trust in Christ into a legal demand for action. In these moments, faith grows introspective, and this reflexivity throws it into despair: Have I believed enough? Did I really mean it? Luther recognizes the blind alley here: "But if Christ is put aside and I look only at myself, then I am done for. . . . By paying attention to myself and considering what my condition is or should be, and what I am supposed to be doing, I lose sight of Christ, who alone is my Righteousness and Life."[127]

In light of his diagnosis of sinners as curved in on themselves, Luther consistently calls believers to find their lives outside of themselves in Christ, and thus to meet the law's insidious questions about the adequacy of their faith with the gospel's insistence on the adequacy of Christ's faithfulness.[128] For Luther, the logic of faith requires it to attend to its object, the promise of the gospel, and to disregard itself. He will exhort his congregation to faith, but he will not invite them to examine their faith. Phil Cary explains: "Luther makes Christian faith profoundly unreflective. . . . Christian faith puts no faith in faith, precisely because it is faith in God's word alone. . . . So for Luther the doctrine of justification by faith alone means that Christians do *not* rely on faith. Faith does not rely on itself but only on the promise of Christ."[129]

This hardly depersonalizes faith. Recall Luther's insistence that mere belief is not faith, but that true faith "believes without wavering that Christ is the Saviour not only to Peter and to the saints but also to you," for "he died and rose, not for himself but for me."[130] Cary writes: "To believe this word is to learn about myself from another, rather than to trust my own personal experience or feeling. Thus the Lutheran *pro me* does not make Luther's faith reflective, but precisely explains why it is unreflective: to believe Christ's word is to be uninterested in the fact that I believe but captivated by what Christ has to say to me. Even apart from its character as word of address, the gospel is good news *for me* because it is Christ's story, not mine."[131] In contrast, a "reflective faith has itself for object in addition to God's word. As a result, in most forms of Protestantism there is a tendency for the experience of faith to become part of the content of faith."[132] We seek assurance of our salvation,

127. Luther, *LW* 26:166.
128. Even Luther on occasion fell into locating assurance in the believing subject, albeit derivatively. See *LW* 26:379.
129. Cary, "Why Luther Is Not Quite Protestant," 452.
130. Luther, *Complete Sermons*, 1.1:21; 2.1:59–60.
131. Cary, "Why Luther Is Not Quite Protestant," 452–53.
132. Cary, "Why Luther Is Not Quite Protestant," 455.

all too often, in moments of strong religious emotion rather than the good news of Christ. But Luther sees the trap, recognizing how unreliable and inconstant experience can be; he concludes that "feeling is opposed to faith and faith is opposed to feeling."[133]

Luther did not mince words: "May every single sermon be forever damned which persuades a person to find security and trust in or through anything whatever except the pure mercy of God, which is Christ."[134] This is the shortest route back to Egypt, to the enslaving terrors of the conscience. It is an anxious way in which we abandon the path of peace. "You cannot walk in a security which has been produced of you and by yourself, but rather in one which has been sought and looked for from His mercy."[135] A Cartesian quest for certainty questions the subject of faith, looking for weaknesses, questions, quiet doubts. The Lutheran alternative looks to the object of faith in the Word of promise. Whereas the former is subject to all the horrors of the funhouse of the human psyche, the latter trusts in "the help of Another."

It is both foolish and faithless to seek assurance of my salvation through a diagnosis of my faith, rather than simply redirecting my attention to the object of faith, Jesus. Our interest should be in the One believed, not the one who believes. Luther picks up on an image from Israel's wilderness wandering that Christ applied to himself to make his point:

> The Jews, who were being bitten by the fiery serpents, were commanded by Moses to do nothing but look at that bronze serpent with a fixed gaze. Those who did so were healed merely by their fixed gaze at the serpent. But the others, who did not listen to Moses, looked at their wounds rather than at the serpent and died. Thus if I am to gain comfort in a struggle of conscience or in the agony of death, I must take hold of nothing except Christ alone by faith, and I must say: "I believe in Jesus Christ, the Son of God, who suffered, was crucified, and died for me. In His wounds and death I see my sin; and in His resurrection I see victory over sin, death, and the devil, and my righteousness and life. I neither hear nor see anything but Him." . . . Therefore in Him we live and move and have our being (Acts 17:28).[136]

When I fix my gaze on the crucified and risen Christ, I am oblivious to my own contrition and faith.[137] I see only the One who gave himself for me and prom-

---

133. Luther, *Complete Sermons*, 1.2:244.
134. Luther, *LW* 31:209.
135. Luther, *LW* 25:495.
136. Luther, *LW* 26:357.
137. Luther praises Johannes von Staupitz, vicar general of the Augustinian Observant Order and Luther's spiritual counselor, for urging Christians to fix their gaze on Christ. "Staupitz is

ises to pardon my sin. "Your heart may deceive you," Luther admits, "but he will not deceive you."[138] The promise clothed in the sacrament is particularly useful here. Luther points out that preaching addresses the congregation as a whole, while the sacrament "is directed to definite individuals."[139] Bread and wine feed faith, as the words of Christ are spoken to each believer: "This is my body, broken for *you*." And "God's promise in the sacrament is sure," even if "our contrition is never sure."[140]

## Faith or Love

Luther saw more clearly than anyone in the Christian tradition that moral self-fashioning is the enemy of Christianity. Attempts to establish ourselves as righteous before God founder and fall afoul of the gospel, in which I hear the good news of what Christ has done for me and the consequent irrelevance of even my best efforts. Luther insists therefore that "faith is not a work."[141]

And yet, two millennia of violence in the name of Jesus demand that questions be put to faith. What difference does it make? Does the simple fact that one professes a belief in a series of claims about Christ entail a life lived in his light? What about the hypocrisy? What about the compromises that even the well intentioned make, quiet treacheries against the One they name as Lord? In a society in which baptism made the citizen, how could one tell the sheep from the goats? Questions like these, already voiced in the Epistle of James (see 2:14–17), prompted a scholastic distinction between unformed and formed faith. The latter faith was "formed by love," and it was this that justified.

Despite the respectable tone of the distinction, Luther detects in it the bankruptcy of faith and a collapse back into justification by works. "Just as our opponents refuse to concede to us the freedom that faith in Christ alone justifies, so we refuse to concede to them, in turn, that faith formed by love justifies."[142] For his opponents, "faith is the body, the shell, or the color; but love is the life, the kernel, or the form."[143] It is the form that makes a thing what it is, and so the scholastics implicitly deny that faith is anything apart from love. If this superficially resembles James's claim that faith without

---

the one who started the teaching [of the gospel in our time]" (*LW* 54:97 [Table Talk]). On their relationship, see Steinmetz, *Luther and Staupitz*.

138. Luther, *LW* 31:195.
139. Luther, *LW* 36:348.
140. Luther, *LW* 32:54.
141. Luther, *LW* 36:47.
142. Luther, *LW* 26:90.
143. Luther, *LW* 26:129.

works is dead (James 2:26), it conceals a subterranean assault on the proper sufficiency of the faith in Christ that alone justifies sinners.

This is Aristotle's error again, the belief that the unrighteous can become righteous through doing righteous works. In contrast, Luther appeals to Jesus's analogy of a tree and its fruits; no matter the effort, diseased trees cannot bear good fruit.[144] A person must be changed before his or her works will change. Thankfully, "God does not accept a person because of his works but the works because of the person, therefore the person before the works."[145] God's love is utterly unlike ours. Our love is responsive; we love those we find lovable, those who please us. "The love of God does not find, but creates, that which is pleasing to it."[146]

In contrast to the scholastic claim, Luther insists that, rather than love, it is *Christ* who forms faith. Indeed, Luther can even claim that "Christ is my 'form,' which adorns my faith as color or light adorns a wall."[147] As my form, Christ makes me who I am in faith, an adopted son of God. Here again, we see Luther's defense of *sola fide* as a way to underscore *solus Christus*. Faith needs no adornment by love but is sufficient to itself precisely because it is adorned by Christ, who is present in faith.[148] "Christian faith is not an idle quality or an empty husk in the heart, which may exist in a state of mortal sin until love comes along to make it alive. But if it is true faith, it is a sure trust and firm acceptance in the heart. It takes hold of Christ in such a way that Christ is the object of faith, or rather not the object but, so to speak, the One who is present in the faith itself."[149] Christ, not love, makes faith what it is, this "sure trust and firm acceptance in the heart" that grasps Christ and brings him near. Here Luther approaches Paul's gnomic statement in Galatians 2:20: "It is no longer I who live, but Christ lives in me." As the object of faith, Christ becomes the reigning subject of the Christian's life.

Perhaps it is Christ's presence to and in faith that gives Paul—and Luther—such confidence in speaking of it. An example is Paul's hypostasizing of faith "working through love" in Galatians 5:6, which Luther picks up on in

144. Luther, *LW* 31:361, commenting on Matt. 7:18.
145. Luther, *LW* 25:256. Luther finds Romans to be structured in terms of person (Rom. 1–11) and works (Rom. 12–16). "For being comes before doing, and suffering comes before being. Therefore the order is: becoming, being, and then working" (*LW* 25:104).
146. Luther, *LW* 31:41.
147. Luther, *LW* 26:167.
148. While an overcorrection, Tuomo Mannermaa's rethinking of the Lutheran doctrine of justification foregrounds Christ's presence in faith and its implications for Christian holiness. See Mannermaa, *Christ Present in Faith*. For an antithetical account, see Forde, *Where God Meets Man*.
149. Luther, *LW* 26:129.

describing a robust faith whose instrument is love. "Paul does not make faith unformed here, as though it were a shapeless chaos without the power to be or to do anything; but he attributes the working itself to faith rather than to love. . . . He makes love the tool through which faith works. Now who does not know that a tool has its power, movement, and action, not from itself but from the artisan who works with it or uses it?"[150] Thus, while Luther reminds us that "faith is not a work," he goes on to call it "the lord and life of all works."[151]

## Faith and Love

Faith is not formed by love; love is formed by faith.[152] In Luther's mind, this never implies love's denigration; rather, it puts love in its place and frees it from the burden of the law. Luther does not reject the law per se, but rather its trespassing into the territory of the gospel. As a salve for conscience, the law has no place, but that does not mean it has no place at all. Similarly, if Luther appears at times to dismiss works, closer examination reveals that his vitriol is reserved for works considered as a basis for justification. "Our faith in Christ does not free us from works but from false opinions concerning works, that is, from the foolish presumption that justification is acquired by works."[153] Our works are good for nothing, soteriologically speaking, but they sure do help our neighbor. "A good work is good for the reason that it is useful and benefits and helps the one for whom it is done; why else should it be called good!"[154]

   Luther remains adamant that faith alone, apart from works, justifies us before God: "and yet it does not remain alone, that is, idle. Not that it does not remain alone on its own level and in its own function, for it always justifies alone. But it is incarnate and becomes man; that is, it neither is nor remains idle or without love."[155] The allusion is deliberate.[156] Just as Christ, "though he was in the form of God, did not count equality with God a thing to be grasped, but emptied himself, by taking the form of a servant, being born in the likeness of men" (Phil. 2:6–7), so faith, which has ascended to

---

150. Luther, *LW* 27:29.
151. Luther, *LW* 36:47.
152. See Luther, *LW* 26:161.
153. Luther, *LW* 31:372–73.
154. Luther, *Complete Sermons*, 1.1:35.
155. Luther, *LW* 26:272.
156. Faith should be "diffused" throughout love in the same way that Christ's divinity was diffused through his humanity (Luther, *LW* 26:266).

the heights with Christ, descends in humble love to its neighbor.[157] Christ the gift is also Christ the example, and "every act of Christ is instruction for us."[158] Having been united to Christ by faith, I have all I could ever want or need. Embarrassed with the riches of Christ, I am free of concern, free of the demands of quid pro quo and the miserly tendency to give "in the manner of a mercenary."[159] I can give freely to my neighbor, with a "joyful, willing, and free mind that serves [my] neighbor willingly and takes no account of gratitude or ingratitude, of praise or blame, of gain or loss."[160] Rich in Christ, I can become poor with him. "Faith brings and gives Christ to you with all his possessions. Love gives you to your neighbor with all your possessions. These two things constitute a true and complete Christian life."[161]

No longer curved in on himself, the Christian finds his life in Christ and his neighbor. "Otherwise he is not a Christian. He lives in Christ through faith, in his neighbor through love. By faith he is caught up beyond himself into God. By love he descends beneath himself into his neighbor. Yet he always remains in God and in his love."[162] In fact, faith and love are linked so closely that the lack of the latter throws the former into question: "If you do not find yourself among the needy and the poor, where the Gospel shows us Christ, then you may know that your faith is not right, and that you have not yet tasted of Christ's benevolence and work for you."[163] Works of love are entirely necessary, just not necessary for justification. We love not in order that we might be loved, but "because he first loved us" (1 John 4:19). Love thus follows faith "as a kind of gratitude."[164] "Truly good works . . . flow from this faith and joy conceived in the heart because we have the forgiveness of sins freely through Christ."[165] The Holy Spirit, who indwells us by faith as we are united to Christ, agitates us to love. "He does not permit a man to be idle but drives him to all the exercises of devotion, to the love of God, to patience in affliction, to prayer, to thanksgiving, and to the practice of love toward all men."[166] And yet, the Spirit never constrains.

---

157. This christological analogy frames Luther's sermons titled *Two Kinds of Righteousness* (*LW* 31:297–306) and *The Freedom of a Christian* (*LW* 31:333–77).

158. Luther, *LW* 25:120.

159. Luther, *LW* 25:455.

160. Luther, *LW* 31:367.

161. Luther, *Complete Sermons*, 1.1:34.

162. Luther, *LW* 31:373.

163. Luther, *Complete Sermons*, 1.1:111–12.

164. Luther, *LW* 26:138.

165. Luther, *LW* 26:133. And "what is the whole gospel but the good tidings of the forgiveness of sins?" (36:56).

166. Luther, *LW* 26:155.

Those who by faith are born of the Spirit "desire, will, do, and are exactly what the law of Moses expressly commands and requires."[167] They walk by the Spirit and do the works of the law "not because they have to but because they want to."[168] Just as works are good in their place, so is the law. The law is God's creation, his gift to his people. It is "the best thing that the world has on earth . . . which, like a sun, is added to feeble reason, the earthly light or human flame, to illumine and direct it" and is, "except for faith . . . the best, the greatest, and the loveliest among the physical blessings of the world."[169] "The Law is good (1 Tim. 1:8), holy, and useful; but it does not justify."[170]

The "whole of the Christian life" is faith and love or works.[171] "Both topics, faith and works, must be carefully taught and emphasized, but in such a way that they both remain within their limits."[172] Luther even shares his opponents' disdain for faith without works, a faith that is "worthless and useless," "a fantastic idea and mere vanity and a dream of the heart"—and therefore no faith at all.[173] Thus the champion of *sola fide* can write that "if faith alone is taught, unspiritual men will immediately suppose that works are not necessary."[174] Luther did not banish good works, then; he transposed them. If they inevitably led one astray in the search for a merciful God, they nevertheless paved the way to the neighbor in need.[175]

### The God Who Bears

In one of the funniest passages of the Bible, Isaiah lampoons the gods of Babylon:

> Bel bows down; Nebo stoops;
>     their idols are on beasts and livestock;
> these things you carry are borne
>     as burdens on weary beasts.

---

167. Luther, *LW* 36:200.
168. Luther, *LW* 25:474.
169. Luther, *LW* 26:184, 251.
170. Luther, *LW* 26:180. See the clarifying discussion of two senses of the law, as relational (mediating between God and sinners) and as instructive, in Wilson, "Law of God."
171. Luther, *LW* 27:30.
172. Luther, *LW* 27:63.
173. Luther, *LW* 26:155.
174. Luther, *LW* 27:63.
175. As Oberman writes, "Luther horizontalized Christian ethics: he transferred its goal from Heaven to earth" (Oberman, *Luther*, 80; also see 192).

> They stoop; they bow down together;
>     they cannot save the burden,
> but themselves go into captivity. (Isa. 46:1–2)

The gods of Babylon are lifeless, inert. They cannot even walk but must be carried by donkeys and oxen. These ones whom the Babylonians worship certainly cannot save their people. Contrast Bel and Nebo with the God of Israel, who speaks to his people in the following verses:

> Listen to me, O house of Jacob,
>     all the remnant of the house of Israel,
> who have been borne by me from before your birth,
>     carried from the womb;
> even to your old age I am he,
>     and to gray hairs I will carry you.
> I have made, and I will bear;
>     I will carry and will save. (Isa. 46:3–4)

Bel and Nebo are carried. The Lord carries. Bel and Nebo are deaf and dumb; they cannot move, hear no cries for help, and cannot save those who trust them from their troubles (v. 7). But the Lord, who has borne Israel throughout its life, "will bear," "will carry," and "will save."

The contrast is evident:

> To whom will you liken me and make me equal,
>     and compare me, that we may be alike? . . .
> I am God, and there is no other;
>     I am God, and there is none like me. (Isa. 46:5, 9)

Only God bears his people, and God alone is glorious—his glory he gives to no other (42:8). But nevertheless he will share his glory with his servant, who "shall be high and lifted up, / and shall be exalted" (52:13). And this servant will, like the Lord, bear God's people.

> Surely he has borne our griefs
>     and carried our sorrows;
> yet we esteemed him stricken,
>     smitten by God, and afflicted.
> But he was pierced for our transgressions;
>     he was crushed for our iniquities;
> upon him was the chastisement that brought us peace,
>     and with his wounds we are healed.

> All we like sheep have gone astray;
>    we have turned—every one—to his own way;
> and the LORD has laid on him
>    the iniquity of us all. (Isa. 53:4–6)

This is the Word that Martin Luther heard in Paul's proclamation of the righteousness of God—that God would carry his people, would bear their burdens for them, and would do so by taking the form of a servant, taking our sins and sorrows on his shoulders and becoming obedient to the point of death, even death on a cross.[176]

---

176. Amid a torrent of controversy and condemnation, Luther sketches a picture of Christ's righteousness as a wagon bearing the faithful to heaven. See the *Fourteen Consolations for Those Who Labor and Are Heavy-Laden*, of August/September 1519, in Luther, *LW* 42:121–66, referenced in Brecht, *Road to Reformation*, 354.

# 8

# "WHAT DO YOU HAVE THAT YOU DID NOT RECEIVE?"

*John Calvin on Having God as Father*

"What do you have that you did not receive?" Paul asks the Corinthians (1 Cor. 4:7). The rhetorical question admits of only one answer—*Nothing!* Everything the Corinthians have they've received. Everything they have finds its source not in themselves but in another. Everything they have, that is, has been given to them. Gifts invite gratitude, but the Corinthians seem to have been preening themselves on their splendid achievements. Paul scratches his head in mock confusion: "If then you received it, why do you boast as if you did not receive it?"

This conviction—that we have nothing that we have not received—drives John Calvin's life and work from first to last. "Every good gift and every perfect gift is from above," James writes, "coming down from the Father of lights with whom there is no variation or shadow due to change" (James 1:17). God is the all-sufficient one, the giver of every good and perfect gift. Since we have received everything from the Father, Calvin can conclude that "our salvation consists in having God as our Father"—a Father who, "having once embraced us with paternal love . . . cannot deny himself" and so continues to pour "innumerable benefits upon us, in constant succession."[1]

1. Calvin, *Comm. Romans* 8:17; *Comm. Genesis* 18:18.

All of this is a far cry from caricatures of Calvin as stentorian spokesman for an arbitrary and vengeful God concerned only with himself. In reality, as we will see, Calvin's God is the loving Father who gave his Son and sent his Spirit, a God whose gifts at times appear stark against the backdrop of sin and death but ultimately serve to lead the prodigal children of God home.

## A Reluctant, Relentless Reformer[2]

Calvin was born on July 10, 1509, to Gérard Cauvin and his wife, Jeanne, in Noyon, France, sixty miles north of Paris. His mother died when Calvin was very young, leaving six children—two of whom would eventually join the reformer in Geneva. When Calvin was fourteen, Gérard sent him to Paris for further studies, intending him to be a priest. After a brief stint at the Collège de la Marche, Calvin entered the Collège de Montaigu, where he studied five years. Calvin later moved to Orléans to study law (his father being convinced that this was the more lucrative option), where he eventually received a law degree.[3] Along the way he became an aspiring humanist, publishing an early commentary on Seneca's *De clementia* in a bid to impress.

At some point in these early years of literary promise, Calvin found himself set on a new course of study. In one of the few autobiographical reflections in his extant writings, he recalls how "God by a sudden conversion subdued and brought my mind to a teachable frame, which was more hardened in such matters than might have been expected from one at my early period of life. Having thus received some taste and knowledge of true godliness, I was immediately inflamed with so intense a desire to make progress therein, that although I did not altogether leave off other studies, I yet pursued them with less ardour."[4]

Characteristically, Calvin describes this conversion in terms of his being made teachable. He frequently refers in his writings to God the Teacher and insists that "teachers would shout to no effect if Christ himself, inner Schoolmaster, did not by his Spirit draw to himself those given to him by the Father."[5] Having become teachable, Calvin could turn with profit to a new course of study, one that promised to induct him into "true godliness." Calvin did not turn his back on his previous learning, though, and what François Wendel aptly calls Calvin's "conversion to the Reform" did not overwrite his humanism.[6] He

2. In this biographical sketch, I follow Gordon, *Calvin*; Wendel, *Calvin*, 15–107.
3. Calvin, author's preface to *Comm. Psalms* (xl).
4. Calvin, author's preface to *Comm. Psalms* (xl).
5. Calvin, *Inst.* 3.1.4.
6. See Wendel, *Calvin*, 33.

retained humanism's "concern for external forms" and "refinement of taste," along with a suspicion of tradition related to the "humanist contempt for scholasticism." But with Calvin's conversion, sin entered the scene and played a leading role. In the place of humanism's paeans to the dignity of humanity, Calvin recognized a deep depravity.[7]

Late in 1534 it became dangerous for Calvin, who had become outspoken in support of reform, to remain in France. He left for Basel in early 1535, never again to make his home in France. "Exile was his defining experience," Bruce Gordon writes, and it taught him to find his home in God.[8] Calvin's stay in Basel was short-lived. He traveled to Italy. He also traveled back to France, stopping over in Geneva (a city of around twelve thousand at the time) on the return trip.[9] There Guillaume Farel cornered Calvin, hoping to enlist him in his efforts to draw Geneva into the cause of reform. "And after having learned that my heart was set upon devoting myself to private studies," Calvin recalls, "he proceeded to utter an imprecation that God would curse my retirement, and the tranquillity of the studies which I sought, if I should withdraw and refuse to give assistance, when the necessity was so urgent."[10] Terrified, Calvin relented. Farel had passion, but "what the party of the Reform needed was a leader capable of organizing the Church and setting it upon firm foundations. . . . It was Calvin's fortune to be able to build upon new ground which no traditions had as yet overgrown."[11] Willing or no, Calvin set to work with Farel, completing *Articles concerning the Organization of the Church*, a confession of faith, and a catechism. A motley group of antagonists resisted Farel and Calvin's attempts at reform, though, and circumstances conspired to find them banished from Geneva. Calvin was "mentally and physically shattered, disorientated and without emotional articulation."[12] He had never wanted such a busy, public role in any case, and he resolved to retire to study in Basel.

This time it was Martin Bucer's turn to rebuke Calvin. Calvin was a latter-day Jonah, so Bucer charged, fleeing the call of the Lord to speak his prophetic word that people might repent. "Alarmed by the example" of Jonah, Calvin joined Bucer in Strasbourg and stayed three years, again taking up the work of teaching and pastoring.[13] The time in Strasbourg was a boon. Bucer became a spiritual father to Calvin, a "model churchman, and the greatest influence

7. Wendel, *Calvin*, 44.
8. Gordon, *Calvin*, viii.
9. Gordon, *Calvin*, 68.
10. Calvin, author's preface to *Comm. Psalms* (xlii–xliii).
11. Wendel, *Calvin*, 49.
12. Gordon, *Calvin*, 85.
13. Calvin, author's preface to *Comm. Psalms* (xliii).

on his formation as a minister and teacher."[14] Calvin regained his confidence as he oversaw the ministry to refugees, implemented discipline, held a chair of exegesis, and began traveling on behalf of church unity.[15] He expanded his *Institutes*—whose first, 1536 edition had been catechetical—into a full-blown system of doctrine, organized around Pauline commonplaces and including extended disputations on controversial topics.[16] Calvin also married in Strasbourg, in 1540, wedding a widow named Idelette de Bure, who proved to be a wonderful companion until her death in 1549.

Remarkably, Calvin returned to Geneva at age thirty-two. He set about realizing his vision of Geneva as a "saintly city," a sort of urban monastery marked by "a dispositional deflection from the world while remaining ensconced within it." The next two decades found him in nearly constant turmoil as he struggled with Genevans who resented his comprehensive plan for the sanctification of the city and as he engaged city officials in a protracted turf war with the church.[17] The former didn't want Calvin telling them what to do, and the latter didn't want church leaders encroaching on their civic authority.[18] But rules for holiness require discipline to enforce them, and Calvin repeatedly emphasized the importance of discipline in the life of a holy church, a discipline that inevitably brought pastors into competition with magistrates.[19] Added to this mix was a flood of immigrants, many of them religious exiles from France, who "turned a tense situation in which political factionalism was rife into a powder keg."[20] In the late 1540s two groups faced off—"the native Geneva families, who saw themselves as defenders of the city's traditional liberties, and the French, made up of the ministers and their wealthy, often aristocratic, patrons who had come to Geneva. . . . To be sworn or spat at in the street was not an uncommon experience for Calvin and his colleagues."[21]

14. Gordon, *Calvin*, 54. On Bucer as a father figure, see Gordon, *Calvin*, 89.

15. See Wendel, *Calvin*, 59.

16. The *Institutes* are "systematic" in the broad sense that Calvin attends to the "right order of teaching" and the interrelations of the various commonplaces he covers. On the changes to the *Institutes* from the first edition in 1536 to the 1539 edition, see Muller, *Unaccommodated Calvin*, 130.

17. Wendel, *Calvin*, 85; Boulton, *Life in God*, 26. Boulton adds that Calvin's vision for a saintly city expressed, "not a hatred of the world, but rather a particular kind of detachment from it that is nonetheless thankful for it as an incomparable blessing" (206).

18. Certainly, Calvin's exactitude seemed to infringe the freedoms of Geneva, and "the first effect of setting up this system of ecclesiastical police was to exasperate a great part of the population" (Wendel, *Calvin*, 85).

19. However, Calvin "refused to make discipline a mark of the Church" (Gordon, *Calvin*, 295). Even if Calvin insisted on the importance of discipline for the life of the church, he refused to take the step of denying that a church that does not practice discipline is itself a church.

20. Gordon, *Calvin*, 198.

21. Gordon, *Calvin*, 202.

Many who know nothing else about Calvin know him for his role in the death of Michael Servetus. Servetus was clearly a heretic; even more, he seems to have been a recalcitrant and pugnacious one, egging Calvin on. When Servetus cavalierly arrived in Geneva, Calvin called for his arrest. Servetus was eventually burned alive for heresy, though Calvin and other pastors pled for a more humane mode of execution. This hardly excuses Calvin, though Wendel's grim conclusion seems reasonable: "Calvin was convinced, and all the reformers shared this conviction, that it was the duty of a Christian magistrate to put to death blasphemers who kill the soul, just as they punished murderers who kill the body."[22]

Despite the fraught nature of much of Calvin's tenure in Geneva, Wendel can judge that "the Church of Geneva as he left it at his death was in fact his personal work. . . . Rarely has it been given to one man to exercise so wide and so enduring an influence as Calvin's has been in this domain."[23] The very question of what constitutes his greatest legacy suggests something of his achievement: Is it his matchless doctrinal synthesis in the *Institutes*? His eminently wise, instructive biblical commentaries? His sponsorship of an academy for the training of pastors? His development of a consistory to rule and shepherd the lives of believers?[24] For all his initial reluctance, Calvin's dream of a holy city was remarkably realized in Geneva, sin notwithstanding.

In what follows, we will consider the biblical teaching that grounded all of Calvin's work. Indeed, the holiness of God's people is nothing less than its loving attendance and obedience to the Word of God. In all of his writing, preaching, teaching, and organizing, Calvin aimed to expound the Scriptures with clarity, convinced as he was that in them God has made himself known.

## Lost in the Labyrinth

Calvin begins the *Institutes* with an extended meditation on Romans 1, where Paul describes the obviousness of God in the world he has made. "For what can be known about God is plain to them, because God has shown it to them. For his invisible attributes, namely, his eternal power and divine nature, have been clearly perceived, ever since the creation of the world, in the things that

22. Wendel, *Calvin*, 97. "Tolerance, in the sixteenth century," he continues, "was not, and could not be, anything but a sign of religious opposition or apathy" (98). Gordon also covers the episode. See Gordon, *Calvin*, 217–32.
23. Wendel, *Calvin*, 69.
24. Compare Wendell, *Calvin*, 105, and Gordon, *Calvin*, 328.

have been made" (vv. 19–20). The universe "was founded as a spectacle of God's glory."[25] In each of God's works, but especially in all of them taken together, "God's powers are actually represented as in a painting."[26] More dynamically, Calvin speaks of the "magnificent theater of heaven and earth, crammed with innumerable miracles," in which God's glory is enacted.[27] We are the audience, and like any good audience, we should enjoy the show. We ought to "take pious delight in the works of God open and manifest in this most beautiful theater."[28] In fact, we have "been placed in this most glorious theater to be a spectator" of God's works.[29]

In another metaphor (one of his favorites), Calvin praises "this skillful ordering of the universe" as "a sort of mirror in which we can contemplate God, who is otherwise invisible."[30] On a smaller scale, Calvin finds God visible in humanity itself, also "a clear mirror of God's works."[31] There is a "sense of deity inscribed in the hearts" and a corresponding "seed of religion" sown in the minds of every man and woman.[32] We know him, and in some sense we are wired to worship him.

The marvelous manifestation of God in creation serves only to incriminate, however. We are the worst kind of audience in this theater—inattentive, ungrateful, self-serving. Paul draws the conclusion: "So they are without excuse. For although they knew God, they did not honor him as God or give thanks to him, but they became futile in their thinking, and their foolish hearts were darkened. Claiming to be wise, they became fools, and exchanged the glory of the immortal God for images resembling mortal man and birds and animals and creeping things" (Rom. 1:20–23). Had God been hidden from view, perhaps we could claim ignorance, even blame him for our lack of knowledge, and thus our lack of praise and gratitude. But we saw him; we knew him— and we failed to honor the one whose glories we saw or to thank him for his gifts. We confused Creator and creation, forgetting the one and praising the other. Living a lie, we became "stone-blind, not because the manifestation is furnished obscurely, but because we are *alienated in mind*, (Col. i. 21) and for this matter we lack not merely inclination, but ability."[33] Calvin insists that God's self-manifestation in creation "is, with regard to the light itself,

25. Calvin, *Inst*. 1.5.5.
26. Calvin, *Inst*. 1.5.10.
27. Calvin, *Inst*. 2.6.1.
28. Calvin, *Inst*. 1.14.20.
29. Calvin, *Inst*. 1.6.2.
30. Calvin, *Inst*. 1.5.1.
31. Calvin, *Inst*. 1.5.3.
32. Calvin, *Inst*. 1.3.1; 1.4.1.
33. Calvin, *Comm. 1 Corinthians* 1:21.

sufficiently clear; but that on account of our blindness, it is not found to be sufficient."[34]

Being blind, we quickly become lost. We find ourselves not in a theater of divine glory but in a labyrinth of idolatry and ignorance, "in which [we] will neither discover the entrance, nor the means of extricating [ourselves]."[35] Having once sought to know more than God allowed, in a way he would not allow it, we continue to be marked by Adam and Eve's mixture of pride and curiosity.

> For the blindness under which they labor is almost always mixed with proud vanity and obstinacy. Indeed, vanity joined with pride can be detected in the fact that, in seeking God, miserable men do not rise above themselves as they should, but measure him by the yardstick of their own carnal stupidity, and neglect sound investigation; thus out of curiosity they fly off into empty speculations. They do not therefore apprehend God as he offers himself, but imagine him as they have fashioned him in their own presumption.[36]

These "miserable men" continue to seek God; they are not atheists. But the seed of religion sown in them by God "is so corrupted that by itself it produces only the worst fruits."[37] They make themselves the measure of God, rather than measuring him by himself. Instead of receiving him "as he offers himself," they presume to make an image of him—an image that can only ever be an idol. Human nature, hell-bent on worshiping something, is "a perpetual factory of idols."[38]

Calvin's suspicion of the idolatrous imagination leads him to take a hard line on the prohibition of images at Mount Sinai. "You shall not make for yourself a carved image," the LORD said (Exod. 20:4), and Calvin takes this command to imply that, despite the widespread practice and conciliar acclamation of the use of images in worship, "all who seek visible forms of God depart from him."[39] The holy one "dwells in unapproachable light, [and] no one has ever seen or can see [him]" (1 Tim. 6:16). Any attempt to picture him amounts to a raid on the holy place, a profane violation of God that betrays an ignorance of him. Human-made images of God are only ever idols, never icons; they do not lead a worshiper to the God they present but shove God out of the way and set themselves up in his place. Calvin would apply Hosea's

34. Calvin, *Comm. Romans* 1:20.
35. Calvin, *Comm. John* 15:9.
36. Calvin, *Inst.* 1.4.1.
37. Calvin, *Inst.* 1.4.4.
38. Calvin, *Inst.* 1.11.8.
39. Calvin, *Inst.* 1.11.2.

denunciation of the calf of Samaria to all such images: "A craftsman made it; it is not God" (8:6). Thus any knowledge of God "sought from images is fallacious and counterfeit."[40]

Calvin's distrust of images arises from his conviction that we are blind to the splendor of God manifest in the world and that we have lost our way. "We stray off as wanderers and vagrants even though everything points out the right way."[41] Our minds themselves are labyrinths, in which we lose ourselves in a maze of idolatrous ignorance. Instead of studiously attending to God's revelation of himself in creation, we "indulge [our] curiosity" and "fly off into empty speculations" about God.[42] Curiosity, of course, can be a very good thing. In common parlance, curious people are hungry for knowledge, eager to learn about new things, open to others and the world. But for Calvin, curious people are fundamentally disobedient. They are less like the sympathetic young girl who stops to smell the flowers than the brash young man who ignores all warning signs and sets off into the wilderness without supplies or a map. We quickly lose the thread of truth in our labyrinthine minds, "so that it is no wonder that individual nations were drawn aside into various falsehoods. . . . Surely, just as waters boil up from a vast, full spring, so does an immense crowd of gods flow forth from the human mind."[43]

## The Thread of the Word

Lost in the maze of our own making, we have no hope but to be found. "The commencement of salvation consists in our being drawn out of the labyrinth of sin and death," Calvin writes.[44] To know God, we need "another and better help," one that will restore sight to our blind eyes.[45]

> Just as old or bleary-eyed men and those with weak vision, if you thrust before them a most beautiful volume, even if they recognize it to be some sort of writing, yet can scarcely construe two words, but with the aid of spectacles will begin to read distinctly; so Scripture, gathering up the otherwise confused knowledge of God in our minds, having dispersed our dullness, clearly shows us the true

40. Calvin, *Inst*. 1.11.5.
41. Calvin, *Inst*. 1.5.15.
42. Calvin, *Inst*. 1.13.21; 1.4.1. For a contemporary meditation on the virtue of *studiositas* and the vice of *curiositas*, see Griffiths, *Intellectual Appetite*.
43. Calvin, *Inst*. 1.5.12.
44. Calvin, *Comm. 1 Corinthians* 1:30.
45. Calvin, *Inst*. 1.6.1.

God. This, therefore, is a special gift, where God, to instruct the church, not merely uses mute teachers but also opens his own most hallowed lips.[46]

Scripture gives us eyes to see God. The image of God we see in Scripture is utterly reliable, because God himself speaks in Scripture. Calvin will repeatedly insist that "God himself is the sole and proper witness of himself."[47] God witnesses to himself by Word and Spirit. After the perilous confusion to which we had descended in sin, what a relief to learn that "by his Word, God rendered faith unambiguous forever."[48] Indeed, "the human mind because of its feebleness can in no way attain to God unless it be aided and assisted by his Sacred Word."[49] The Word does not need to be propped up by anything else. Calvin argues that Scripture's authority does not rest on arguments or the approbation of the church; it is self-authenticating.[50] But the Word can do nothing without the Spirit. God "sent down the same Spirit by whose power he had dispensed the Word, to complete his work by the efficacious confirmation of the Word."[51] To call the Word "self-authenticating," then, speaks to the sufficiency of the Spirit's confirmation of the Word and the irrelevance of external human confirmation of it. The same Spirit who inspired the writers of Scripture inwardly teaches God's people to "rest upon Scripture," sealing it on our hearts.[52] The "splendor of the divine countenance" is itself "for us like an inexplicable labyrinth unless we are conducted into it by the thread of the Word."[53] The Spirit is our Ariadne, giving us the thread by which we may find our way into the presence of God.

Who is the God revealed by the Spirit in the Word? He is the one we meet in Christ. Christ is himself the subject matter of Scripture, so that "just in proportion, therefore, as any man knows Christ, is the proficiency which he has made in the word of God."[54] Christ is the thread of the Word, such that anyone aspiring to know God apart from Christ is condemned to "wander . . . in a labyrinth."[55] God has never revealed himself "out of Christ," and the name of God cannot be spoken apart from Christ.[56] Such a comprehensive

46. Calvin, Inst. 1.6.1.
47. Calvin, Inst. 1.11.1.
48. Calvin, Inst. 1.6.2.
49. Calvin, Inst. 1.6.4.
50. Calvin, Inst. 1.7.1, 5.
51. Calvin, Inst. 1.9.3.
52. Calvin, Inst. 1.7.4–5.
53. Calvin, Inst. 1.6.3.
54. Calvin, Comm. John 5:38.
55. Calvin, Comm. John 8:19; also see Comm. John 14:6.
56. Calvin, Comm. John 5:23.

claim suggests that even in revealing himself to Israel in the wilderness, the Lord was somehow revealing himself "in Christ." Needless to say, Christ is not a rival to, or even a surrogate for, God, but the one in whom God is made manifest, and "there is no other way in which God is *known* but in the face of *Jesus Christ,* who is the bright and lively image of Him."[57] What we failed to see in creation, blind as we were, the Spirit enables us to see in the Word, as he opens our eyes to see "the glory of God in the face of Jesus Christ" (2 Cor. 4:6).[58]

Again, though, who is the God we meet in Christ? Granted that Christ is the image of the invisible God, what do we see when we look at his life? In this Son we see the Father who sent his Son, the Son who said, "Whoever has seen me has seen the Father" (John 14:9). Scripture tells us of Christ, who tells us of his Father. Calvin describes Christ as "the pledge of the mercy of God, and of his fatherly love towards us."[59] That is, we see not only *who* God is but *how* he is toward us. In Christ we find a loving Father, and never more so than when looking at the cross, where, "as in a magnificent theatre, the inestimable goodness of God is displayed before the whole world."[60]

The night before he died, Jesus prayed to his Father. "This is eternal life," he said, "that they know you, the only true God, and Jesus Christ whom you have sent" (John 17:3). But pieties aside, how could mere knowledge yield eternal life? Could simply *knowing* God be such an infinite good that Jesus would equate it with the happiest of lives, with the life of God himself? Much depends here on what we understand the knowledge of God to be. According to Calvin, the knowledge of God is "that by which we not only conceive that there is a God but also grasp what befits us and is proper to his glory, in fine, what is to our advantage to know of him. Indeed, we shall not say that, properly speaking, God is known where there is no religion or piety."[61] Of course, to know God, one must know there *is* a God, but that is not Calvin's point. "What help is it . . . to know a God with whom we have nothing to

<hr>

57. Calvin, *Comm. John* 17:3; also see *Comm. John* 5:22. Thus, Calvin does not outlaw all images, only those "dead images" made by humans. God's images, by contrast—Christ himself and the sacraments, among others—are "living." On the contrast between dead and living images, see Zachman, *Image and Word,* 7–9. Zachman goes so far as to argue that "manifestation is as essential to Calvin as proclamation" (7).

58. Calvin turns out to believe "that the invisible God does become somewhat visible . . . while nonetheless remaining invisible." He seeks to "maintain the dialectical relationship between the visibility and invisibility of God, and the presence and absence of God, which he thinks is maintained by images of divine creation but not by images of human devising" (Zachman, *Image and Word,* 2, 440).

59. Calvin, "The Argument to the Gospel of John," in *Comm. John.*

60. Calvin, *Comm. John* 13:31.

61. Calvin, *Inst.* 1.2.1.

do? Rather, our knowledge should serve first to teach us fear and reverence; secondly with it as our guide and teacher, we should learn to seek every good from him, and, having received it, to credit it to his account."[62]

What matters is that we know God in a way that suits him, that is "proper to his glory," and in a way that helps us. That kind of knowledge of God cannot exist apart from what Calvin calls religion, or piety, which is "that reverence joined with love of God which the knowledge of his benefits induces."[63] Only when we grasp all that God is and does for us will we love him with a holy love, and only then can we properly be said to know him. Calvin continues: "For until men recognize that they owe everything to God, that they are nourished by his fatherly care, that he is the Author of their every good, that they should seek nothing beyond him—they will never yield him willing service. Nay, unless they establish their complete happiness in him, they will never give themselves truly and sincerely to him."[64] Conversely, *when* women and men recognize that all they have has been given to them by God and that God tenderly cares for them as a loving Father, *then* they will indeed happily and gratefully serve him. So important is this recognition that Calvin can write that our salvation consists in "knowing his fatherly favor in our behalf."[65]

## Adoption through Propitiation

But there's a problem. God's fatherly favor is precisely what we in our sin do *not* know. We do not know the love of the Father because we are "children of wrath," "alienated and hostile in mind," "having no hope and without God in the world" (Eph. 2:3; Col. 1:21; Eph. 2:12). We are totally depraved, flooded by sin "from head to foot, so that no part is immune from sin and all that proceeds from [us] is to be imputed to sin."[66] We do not become sinful by imitation, at some point falling into sin like our first parents. We are sinful from birth, Adam having "in himself corrupted, vitiated, depraved, and

62. Calvin, *Inst.* 1.2.2.
63. "Calvin's ultimate, governing purpose in the *Institutio* is Christian formation to true *pietas*: the embodied knowledge, filial love, willing service, and immersive intimacy with God for which human beings are made" (Boulton, *Life in God*, 53). Boulton's own sustained argument for a Reformed Christian formation is as compelling as it is elegant.
64. Calvin, *Inst.* 1.2.1.
65. Calvin, *Inst.* 2.2.18.
66. Calvin, *Inst.* 2.1.9. It is a common mistake to understand the Calvinist "total depravity" in terms of our being the worst we could possibly be, such that each act is one of unalloyed sin, when more typically for Calvin it describes the reach of sin, which affects every part of the person.

ruined our nature."[67] Thus, while we are good insofar as we are created by God, we are "corrupted through natural vitiation," even if it is "a vitiation that did not flow from nature."[68] And yet, we cannot punt to Adam, casting aspersions on him in the hope of finding some place to stand securely before God. We really are sinners and have "no reason to complain except against ourselves."[69]

It gets worse. Sin has consequences—and *all* sin has consequences. Rejecting the scholastic distinction between mortal and venial sins, Calvin bluntly concludes that "all sin is mortal. For it is rebellion against the will of God, which of necessity provokes God's wrath, and it is a violation of the law, upon which God's judgment is pronounced without exception."[70] Calvin will have no truck with distinctions that provide loopholes for sinners subject to the wrath of God; "the wrath of God rests upon all so long as they continue to be sinners."[71] It is tempting to credit this conclusion to Calvin's temperament, considering it a function of a morose, pessimistic, and exacting character. However, it is more to the point to explain the reality and severity of divine wrath in Calvin's theology in light of his work as a biblical theologian. Calvin read, preached, lectured on, and wrote about the Old Testament, with its promises of blessings and its threats of wrath. Furthermore, Calvin placed Romans, with its withering exposé of sin, at the center of his theology. Following Philipp Melanchthon, Calvin loosely organized the *Institutes* according to the topics and structure of Romans, convinced that "when any one understands this Epistle, he has a passage opened to him to the understanding of the whole Scripture."[72]

The whole of Scripture, encapsulated in Romans, testifies to the wrath of God against sinners, and even our consciences agree, showing us "in our sin just cause for [God's] disowning us and not regarding or recognizing us as his sons."[73] "God, without having regard to Christ," writes Calvin, "is always angry with us."[74] As we are helpless and exposed to the wrath of God, "it is necessary that Christ should come to our aid," which he does in his role as "propitiator," the one who pleases God and restores us to his favor.[75]

---

67. See Calvin, *Comm. Romans* 5:12.
68. Calvin, *Inst.* 2.1.11.
69. Calvin, *Inst.* 2.1.10.
70. Calvin, *Inst.* 2.8.59.
71. Calvin, *Inst.* 3.11.21.
72. Calvin, "Dedicatory Epistle," in *Comm. Romans*, xxiv. On the importance and nature of Calvin's adoption of the topics and structure of Romans in the 1539 *Institutes*, see Muller, *Unaccommodated Calvin*, 128, 130, 188.
73. Calvin, *Inst.* 2.6.1.
74. Calvin, *Comm. Romans* 3:25.
75. Calvin, *Comm. Romans* 3:22; *Inst.* 2.6.1.

But what is it about Christ that pleases God and, in turn, moves God to be pleased with us?

Calvin focuses his treatment of Christ on Christ's mediation between God and humanity. The eternal Son "came down from heaven . . . and was made man" because we could not ascend to God.[76] He *can* mediate between God and humanity insofar as he is a "comrade and partner in the same nature with us."[77] Calvin speaks of Christ's mediation in terms of a threefold office; he is prophet, priest, and king. While all three together describe Christ's person and work, Calvin privileges Christ's priestly work in atoning for sins. "The principal office of Christ is briefly but clearly stated; that he takes away the sins of the world by the sacrifice of his death, and reconciles men to God. There are other favours, indeed, which Christ bestows upon us, but this is the chief favour, and the rest depend on it; that, by appeasing the wrath of God, he makes us to be reckoned holy and righteous. For from this source flow all the streams of blessings, that, by not imputing our sins, he receives us into favour."[78]

To atone for sins and restore us to God's favor, Christ had to qualify as a high priest: "Therefore he had to be made like his brothers in every respect, so that he might become a merciful and faithful high priest in the service of God, to make propitiation for the sins of the people" (Heb. 2:17). Following Hebrews, Calvin speaks of the priest's commonality with those he represents to God. To be one of us, the priest must be fully human. He must possess whatever all humans possess—a body, a soul, and also, Calvin emphasizes, "feelings or affections."[79] Christ's was not a cosmetic humanity; rather, it involved him in a full complement of emotions and other internal states. In that he was sinless, all of Christ's feelings were voluntary; he always exhibited self-control in obedience to the Father. But his feelings are the more remarkable for having been freely chosen. Whereas we find ourselves seized by fear, Christ feared "not through constraint, but because he had, of his own accord, subjected himself to fear."[80] Thankfully, "we do not have a high priest who is unable to sympathize with our weaknesses, but one who in every respect has been tempted as we are, yet without sin" (Heb. 4:15). Christ "learned obedience through what he suffered" (Heb. 5:8). He learned the difficulty of

---

76. See Calvin, *Inst.* 2.12.1. On the theme of descent and ascent in Calvin, see Canlis, *Calvin's Ladder.* Canlis argues that "Calvin dislodges ascent from anthropology and relocates it to christology." "Crucifixion is at the nexus of descent and ascent," with Christ's descent as our substitute paving the way for our participatory ascent with him (92–93).

77. Calvin, *Inst.* 2.13.2.

78. Calvin, *Comm. Romans* 1:29.

79. Calvin, *Comm. Hebrews* 4:15.

80. Calvin, *Comm. John* 12:27.

faithfulness from within, and just so was able to faithfully represent before the Father those in whose temptations he shared.

Calvin writes that "Christ alone is the fully qualified priest," in that he meets the requirements of being "just, harmless, and pure from every spot."[81] He is like us in every way, but without sin. Whereas Adam turned away from God in rebellion, Christ walked in the way of the righteous. In assuming humanity to himself, the Son "took the person and the name of Adam in order to take Adam's place in obeying the Father, to present our flesh as the price of satisfaction of God's righteous judgment, and, in the same flesh, to pay the penalty that we had deserved."[82] His obedience qualified him to serve as a priest, and it qualified him to serve as a sacrifice, without spot or blemish.

The work of Christ did not begin on the cross. The "whole course of his obedience," from his birth, was one long reconciliation of us to God, as Christ lived a life of faithful obedience in our place and absorbed the consequences of our sin, including suffering the just judgment of God on the cross.[83] If the work of Christ did not begin on the cross, it did end there. Jesus appeases the wrath of God and restores us to the Father's favor by offering himself as a perfect sacrifice for sins. The Lamb of God who was slain is "the sole offering for sins, the sole expiation, the sole satisfaction."[84] Christ's death satisfies the just judgment of God, cleanses us, removes our guilt, and liberates us from death's tyranny.[85] Nor was this only a painful physical death—miserable as that was. Christ died in our place in the fullest sense, undergoing our bodily death, yes, but also "the severity of God's vengeance, to appease his wrath and satisfy his just judgment."[86] "And surely no more terrible abyss can be conceived than to feel yourself forsaken and estranged from God; and when you call upon him, not to be heard. It is as if God himself had plotted your ruin."[87] Calvin speaks daringly and at length about the agonies Christ suffered in our place on the cross. Had Christ not suffered so acutely, he would have failed to completely redeem those he came to save. "Unless his soul shared

81. Calvin, *Comm. Hebrews* 7:26.
82. Calvin, *Inst.* 2.12.3.
83. Calvin, *Inst.* 2.16.5. By his obedience, Christ "truly acquired and merited grace for us with his Father" (2.17.3). Calvin rails against our seeking a merit of our own not least because he is convinced that Christ has acquired all the merit we can ever have or need by virtue of his obedience (see 2.10.4; 3.15.2; 3.15.6; 3.16.2; 4.1.21). For a careful analysis of this, along with a surprisingly compelling account of how Calvin "approximates in significant respects the notion of condign merit by his teaching on regeneration," see Wawrykow, "John Calvin and Condign Merit," 89.
84. Calvin, *Inst.* 3.4.26.
85. Calvin, *Inst.* 2.16.6; *Comm. Romans* 3:24.
86. Calvin, *Inst.* 2.16.10.
87. Calvin, *Inst.* 2.16.11.

in the punishment, he would have been the Redeemer of bodies alone."[88] And so "if we desire to return to God our Author and Maker, from whom we have been estranged, in order that he may again begin to be our Father," we ought humbly to embrace the preaching of the cross, in which we hear the good news of the death of Christ, in which "he has restored us to favour with the Father."[89]

J. I. Packer offers a three-word summary of the message of the New Testament: "adoption through propitiation."[90] This is certainly an apt summary of Calvin's soteriology. We can have God as our Father only if we have Christ his Son as our brother. Right at the outset of the *Institutes*, in his prefatory address to King Francis, Calvin asks, "What is better and closer to faith than to feel assured that God will be a propitious Father where Christ is recognized as brother and propitiator?"[91] People will feel assured that the Father is favorable to them where—or insofar as—they know Christ as their brother. Christ becomes our brother through adoption. By virtue of the "shining innocence" of this one in whom the Father is well pleased, we are forgiven, cleansed, and clothed in righteousness, welcomed into the Father's house.[92] "He is the Son of God by nature, while we are the sons of God only by adoption; but the grace which we obtain through him is so firmly established, that it cannot be shaken by any efforts of the devil, so as to hinder us from always calling him our Father, who hath adopted us through his Only-begotten Son."[93]

Still, we are left with a nagging question: Did Jesus change the Father's mind about sinful humanity? Calvin calls Christ "the only mediator, by whose intercession the Father is for us rendered gracious and easily entreated."[94] If Christ must "render" the Father gracious, does this imply that, left to himself, the Father would be anything but? Consider that "God cannot without the Mediator be propitious toward the human race."[95] In what way should we take that "cannot"? Are the Father's hands tied—or worse, is he simply hateful toward us—until Christ intervenes? Popular piety often celebrates the way in which Christ "interposes his precious blood," hiding us behind the cross from the withering stare of a vengeful God. And Calvin himself says that "God, without having regard to Christ, is always angry with us." He continues: "God does not indeed hate in us his own workmanship, that is, as we are formed

88. Calvin, *Inst.* 2.16.12.
89. Calvin, *Inst.* 2.6.1; *Comm. Ephesians* 1:7.
90. Packer, *Knowing God*, 214.
91. Calvin, "Prefatory Address to King Francis," in *Inst.*, p. 13.
92. Calvin, *Inst.* 2.16.5.
93. Calvin, *Comm. John* 20:17.
94. Calvin, *Inst.* 3.20.19.
95. Calvin, *Inst.* 2.6.2.

men; but he hates our uncleanness, which has extinguished the light of his image. When the washing of Christ cleanses this away, he then loves and embraces us as his own pure workmanship."[96] We might say that God is at odds with himself, that our sin has placed him in a dilemma—loving us insofar as we are his creation, but hating our uncleanness, which renders us unfit to dwell in his presence. Christ resolves the dilemma by dying for us, cleansing us from our sin and reconciling us to God, who embraces us as his own.

But that's too oppositional. It is not that Christ solves the Father's dilemma but that Christ is himself the Father's own resolution to the dilemma, into whose life we are brought by the Spirit. Following Paul's declaration that "he who did not spare his own Son but gave him up for us all" will surely with him "graciously give us all things," Calvin regularly returns to the Father's love for humanity as the origin of our salvation (Rom. 8:32). Calvin employs the fourfold Aristotelian causes to account for salvation as a gift of the Trinity: "The efficient cause of our salvation consists in God the Father's love; the material cause in God the Son's obedience; the instrumental cause in the Spirit's illumination, that is, faith; the final cause, in the glory of God's great generosity."[97] And so the Son certainly did not need to persuade the Father to love those whom he would not have otherwise loved. Jesus himself confessed that "God so loved the world, that he gave his only Son, that whoever believes in him should not perish but have eternal life" (John 3:16). Instead, in speaking of the Father's seeming inability to love sinful humanity apart from and outside the Son, Calvin means to take seriously the wrath of God against sin in order to stir us up to hope in the mediation of Christ in his life, death, and resurrection as the ultimate demonstration of the Father's love.[98]

In a moving passage near the end of book 2 of the *Institutes*, Calvin evokes the fullness of salvation in Christ:

> We see that our whole salvation and all its parts are comprehended in Christ.
> We should therefore take care not to derive the least portion of it from anywhere

96. Calvin, *Comm. Romans* 3:25.
97. Calvin, *Inst.* 3.14.21. Also see 4.15.6.
98. "Expressions of this sort [where Scripture describes God as our enemy] have been accommodated to our capacity that we may better understand how miserable and ruinous our condition is apart from Christ. For if it had not been clearly stated that the wrath and vengeance of God and eternal death rested upon us, we should scarcely have recognized how miserable we would have been without God's mercy, and we would have underestimated the benefit of liberation" (Calvin, *Inst.* 2.16.2). "The word *wrath*, according to the usage of Scripture, speaking after the manner of men, means the vengeance of God; for God, in punishing, has, according to our notion, the appearance of one in wrath. It imports, therefore, no such emotion in God, but only has a reference to the perception and feeling of the sinner who is punished" (*Comm. Romans* 1:18).

else. If we seek salvation, we are taught by the very name of Jesus that it is "of him." If we seek any other gifts of the Spirit, they will be found in his anointing. If we seek strength, it lies in his dominion; if purity, in his conception; if gentleness, it appears in his birth. For by his birth he was made like us in all respects that he might learn to feel our pain. If we seek redemption, it lies in his passion; if acquittal, in his condemnation; if remission of the curse, in his cross; if satisfaction, in his sacrifice; if purification, in his blood; if reconciliation, in his descent into hell; if mortification of the flesh, in his tomb; if newness of life, in his resurrection; if immortality, in the same; if inheritance of the Heavenly Kingdom, in his entrance into heaven; if protection, if security, if abundant supply of all blessings, in his Kingdom; if untroubled expectation of judgment, in the power given him to judge.[99]

If our salvation consists in knowing God as Father, as Calvin says it does, it consists no less in knowing Christ his Son, the "bright and lively image" of the living God.[100]

## "He Had to Become Ours"

Christ has "in his flesh accomplished the whole of our salvation," Calvin writes.[101] But "we must understand that as long as Christ remains outside of us, and we are separated from him, all that he has suffered and done for the salvation of the human race remains useless and of no value for us. Therefore, to share with us what he has received from the Father, he had to become ours and to dwell with us."[102] Christ has done absolutely everything; nothing needs to be added to complete his saving work. And yet, though he has worked salvation, not all are saved. Calvin's genius was to take the accomplishment of salvation in Christ and the necessity of its application to sinful humanity by the Spirit with equal seriousness. He suspected late medieval theology and practice of compromising the former point by suggesting that something was lacking in the suffering and death of Christ, which needed to be completed in the sacrifice of the Mass, the doing of penance, and the purification of purgatory. By contrast, he insisted that "the hope of all the godly has ever reposed in Christ alone."[103] And yet, apart from the participation in the Spirit (2 Cor.

99. Calvin, *Inst.* 2.16.19.
100. Calvin, *Comm. John* 17:3.
101. Calvin, *Inst.* 2.9.2.
102. Calvin, *Inst.* 3.1.1.
103. Calvin, *Inst.* 2.6.3. This "ever" is meant quite literally, stretching back before the time of Christ to the covenant God made with Israel. Calvin writes that "the covenant made with all the patriarchs is so much like ours in substance and reality that the two are actually one and

13:14), "no one can taste either the fatherly favor of God or the beneficence of Christ."[104] "The peculiar office of Christ was, to appease the wrath of God by atoning for the sins of the world, to redeem men from death, to procure righteousness and life; and the peculiar office of the Spirit is, to make us partakers not only of Christ himself, but of all his blessings."[105]

The Spirit makes us partakers of Christ and his blessings by uniting us to Christ through faith.[106] Faith is the "principal" and "peculiar" work of the Spirit, the way in which he brings Christ to us and us to Christ.[107] Through faith we "possess Christ, and thus become the sons of God."[108] In fact, only by being united to Christ, by being "engrafted into the body of the only-begotten Son," can we be considered sons and daughters of God.[109]

Critical of the notion of implicit faith, which surrenders to the church "the task of inquiring and knowing," Calvin insists that faith is a form of knowledge, specifically "a knowledge of God's will toward us, perceived from his Word."[110] This knowledge "consists in assurance rather than in comprehension."[111] Faith is more than mere knowledge *that* something is the case and less than perfect knowledge of the object of faith, which is God himself. It is the settled assurance of those who know the love of the Father in the face of Jesus Christ, "a firm and certain knowledge of God's benevolence toward us, founded upon the truth of the freely given promise in Christ, both revealed to our minds and sealed upon our hearts through the Holy Spirit."[112] It is fitting, then, that faith "brings to mind that sweetest name of Father" and "opens our mouth freely to cry, 'Abba, Father.'"[113]

Calvin summarizes the benefits of partaking of Christ in terms of a "double grace: namely, that being reconciled to God through Christ's blamelessness, we may have in heaven instead of a Judge a gracious Father; and secondly, that sanctified by Christ's spirit we may cultivate blamelessness and purity of life."[114]

---

the same. Yet they differ in the mode of dispensation" (2.10.2; also see 4.16.16). The Old Testament no less than the New "was established upon the free mercy of God, and was confirmed by Christ's intercession" (2.10.4).

104. Calvin, *Inst.* 3.1.2.
105. Calvin, *Comm. John* 14:16.
106. See Calvin, *Inst.* 3.11.5. Calvin can also speak of Christ as the agent of our union with him: "But he unites himself to us by the Spirit alone" (3.1.3).
107. Calvin, *Inst.* 3.1.4; 3.2.39.
108. Calvin, *Comm. John* 6:29.
109. Calvin, *Inst.* 2.6.1. Also see *Comm. John* 6:35.
110. Calvin, *Inst.* 3.2.2; 3.2.6.
111. Calvin, *Inst.* 3.2.14.
112. Calvin, *Inst.* 3.2.7.
113. Calvin, *Inst.* 3.13.5.
114. Calvin, *Inst.* 3.11.1.

These are the graces of justification and regeneration. Calvin calls justification by faith "the sum of all piety," in which a sinner "grasps the righteousness of Christ through faith, and clothed in it, appears in God's sight not as a sinner but as a righteous man."[115] Justification "consists in the remission of sins and the imputation of Christ's righteousness."[116] Calvin clarifies that, strictly speaking, it is Christ, not faith, who justifies; or rather, that faith justifies only insofar as it unites us to Christ. "Faith, even though of itself it is of no worth or price, can justify us by bringing Christ, just as a pot crammed with money makes a man rich."[117] If justification is completed when we are united to Christ, regeneration "is always imperfect in this flesh" and continues throughout our lives.[118] While Calvin clearly and consistently distinguishes the two, he clarifies that "the grace of regeneration is never disjoined from the imputation of righteousness."[119] Justification may be "the sum of all piety," but regeneration is the point of it all. We are reconciled to God that we may walk in holiness, as the Spirit "renews us to a holy life."[120]

"What do you have that you did not receive?" Paul asks (1 Cor. 4:7). Calvin might ask the same question. With Paul, he might proclaim that "our sufficiency is from God" (2 Cor. 3:5).[121] Our salvation consists in having this all-sufficient God as Father, which we do when the Spirit unites us to Christ his Son and we are welcomed into his household. Calvin was convinced, though, that this salvation reaches back into eternity and stretches over the course of the Christian life.

### "Every Part of Our Salvation Depends on Election"

The doctrine of election makes people anxious. To many, it seems to suggest a mysterious, even arbitrary God, who saves and damns whomever he will,

115. Calvin, *Inst.* 3.15.17; 3.11.2.
116. Calvin, *Inst.* 3.11.2.
117. Calvin, *Inst.* 3.11.7.
118. Calvin, *Inst.* 3.13.5.
119. Calvin, *Comm. Romans* 8:2.
120. Calvin, *Comm. Romans* 6:2.
121. Todd Billings and Philip Butin argue that the all-sufficiency of God does not eclipse human agency, but rather encloses it in the trinitarian dynamics of grace. The Spirit, who unites believers to Christ by faith, "authenticat[es] in turn their humanity" as they participate in Christ and empowers "an authentically human and genuinely free response to God." See Billings, *Calvin, Participation, and the Gift*; Butin, *Revelation, Redemption, and Response* (with citations from Butin, 93, 85). Calvin himself puts the point nicely: "Nothing now prevents us from saying that we ourselves are fitly doing what God's Spirit is doing in us, even if our will contributes nothing of itself distinct from his grace" (*Inst.* 2.5.15).

just because he will. It is a vertiginous doctrine, a perplexing maze that can leave one feeling lost. But Calvin, election's greatest patron, finds the doctrine to be eminently comforting, an antidote to the poison of anxiety.[122]

It is easy to forget, amid the affluence and ease of the modern West, the vulnerability of human life. In a harrowing catalog of danger, Calvin writes: "Wherever you turn, all things around you not only are hardly to be trusted but almost openly menace, and seem to threaten immediate death."[123] At sea or on land, in the street or at home, any number of contingencies could kill us on any given day. In such a world, Calvin writes, "ignorance of providence is the ultimate of all miseries; the highest blessedness lies in the knowledge of it."[124] Fully aware of the calamities of life, Calvin concludes that, "though all things fail us, yet God will never forsake us, who cannot disappoint the expectation and patience of his people. He alone will be for us in place of all things."[125] He seems to realize, however, that such a confession, while true, will be difficult to sustain under the onslaught of the slings and arrows of outrageous fortune. "We shall never be clearly persuaded, as we ought to be, that our salvation flows from the wellspring of God's free mercy until we come to know his eternal election, which illumines God's grace by this contrast: that he does not indiscriminately adopt all into the hope of salvation but gives to some what he denies to others."[126] At the heart of Calvin's treatment of election is its rhetorical force. He believes that Scripture teaches election, but even more he believes election will convince us that God really is merciful. Throughout the *Institutes*, Calvin expounds doctrine for both instruction and comfort,[127] and for people to be comforted by the mercy of God they must be instructed about its origin in eternity. How, then, does election comfort? By making our salvation sure. For Calvin, salvation does not merely begin in election; it is a *function* of election. God elects some to salvation, and their being saved in time is an outflow of that election.

Furthermore, *all* of salvation is a function of election. "Every part of our salvation depends on election," Calvin writes, from our being called by God all the way to the end.[128] Election is "the mother of faith."[129] It is the mother,

---

122. "The anxiety of the sinner for Calvin makes Christianity at once plausible and necessary" (Bouwsma, *John Calvin*, 40). Though he overpsychologizes, Bouwsma's consideration of "Calvin's anxiety" provides a helpful angle on his thought (see 32–48).
123. Calvin, *Inst.* 1.17.10.
124. Calvin, *Inst.* 1.17.11.
125. Calvin, *Inst.* 3.20.52.
126. Calvin, *Inst.* 3.21.1.
127. Calvin, *Inst.* 1.17.12.
128. Calvin, *Comm. John* 13:18.
129. Calvin, *Inst.* 3.22.10.

too, of the perseverance of the saints. "This very circumstance—that they will persevere—he ascribes to their election; for the virtue of men, being frail, would tremble at every breeze, and would be laid down by the feeblest stroke, if the Lord did not uphold it by his hand. But as he governs those whom he has elected, all the engines which Satan can employ will not prevent them from persevering to the end with unshaken firmness. And not only does he ascribe to election their perseverance, but likewise the commencement of their piety."[130] If any part of our salvation—its beginning, continuance, or completion—were seated in ourselves, we could only ever be anxious and, finally, despite our best efforts, lost.[131]

The doctrine of election grounds a person's salvation in God unequivocally. "For by grace you have been saved through faith," Paul writes. "And this is not your own doing; it is the gift of God, not a result of works, so that no one may boast" (Eph. 2:8–9). Salvation is God's gift to us, not something that follows our action. We ought to praise him for saving us, not boast as if salvation were somehow in our hands. This is just what Paul does at the beginning of Ephesians, blessing the God who "chose us in [Christ] before the foundation of the world" and "predestined us for adoption to himself as sons through Jesus Christ, according to the purpose of his will" (1:4–5).

If we ask *why* God chose us—and why he chose *us* and passed over others—we can find "no cause higher than his own will."[132] For grace to be grace, it must in no way be conditioned by human action. Calvin rejects any sense that God elects people in light of his foreknowledge of them, as this would subtly convert salvation from gift to reward; so "we must seek the cause of election outside of men."[133] "God loves us: and what is the cause of his love, except his own goodness alone?"[134] God's mercy, "being gratuitous, is under no restraint, but turns wherever it please."[135] The doctrine of election, we might say, is the way in which the God of Israel remains true to himself. The one who identified himself by saying, "I AM WHO I AM," turns to sinful humanity and says, "I will have mercy on whom I have mercy" (Exod. 3:14; Rom. 9:15, quoting Exod. 33:19).[136]

---

130. Calvin, *Comm. John* 13:18. Also see *Comm. Romans* 11:22.

131. Calvin quotes Bernard of Clairvaux's gloss on Ps. 103:17 ("The mercy of God is from everlasting to everlasting upon those who fear him") with approval: "From everlasting because of predestination, to everlasting because of beatification—the one knowing no beginning, the other, no end" (*Inst.* 3.22.10).

132. Calvin, *Comm. Romans* 9:15. Also see *Inst.* 3.22.5.

133. See Calvin, *Comm. Romans* 11:6; *Inst.* 2.3.8.

134. Calvin, *Comm. Romans* 1:7.

135. Calvin, *Comm. Romans* 9:15. Also see *Inst.* 3.22.6.

136. Thanks to Andy Perry for a witty comment that inspired this thought.

Though he does not place Christ at the center of his account of election in the way that Karl Barth will, Calvin is clear that one cannot make sense of election apart from Christ. Christ is the subject or "author" of eternal election, along with the Father.[137] Election, like all of salvation, is in Christ, so that "those whom God has adopted as his sons are said to have been chosen not in themselves but in his Christ."[138] For this reason, we can be assured of our election only by contemplating Christ, "the mirror wherein we must, and without self-deception may, contemplate our own election."[139] Were all those anxious about their election to follow Calvin's counsel at this point, and look not to themselves but to Christ to discern the Father's love for them, I imagine they would find election far more comforting than threatening.

Calvin insists that election implies reprobation, that there is a clear, if stark, symmetry between the two—and that this dichotomy is not only logically necessary but biblically warranted. "Election itself could not stand except as set over against reprobation," he writes. "Therefore, those whom God passes over, he condemns; and this he does for no other reason than that he wills to exclude them from the inheritance which he predestines for his own children."[140] Calvin's almost *aesthetic* judgment that election "illumines God's grace by this contrast" is troubling.[141] When he writes that "the infinite mercy of God towards the elect must appear increasingly worthy of praise, when we see how miserable are all they who escape not his wrath," he evinces an almost Manichaean sense of the mutual necessity of mercy and wrath, light and darkness.[142] Like the painter Caravaggio, whose method of chiaroscuro traded on the dramatic contrasts of light and darkness, Calvin seems at times driven by the conviction that grace makes sense only when it is set over against judgment. In one sense, this conclusion is only the logical extension of Calvin's conviction that "nothing can befall except he determine it."[143] Perhaps it is the shadow side of his hearty affirmation that "our sufficiency is from God." But it strikes me as a surprisingly speculative conclusion, a rare case of Calvin saying more, or at least saying it with more confidence, than Scripture warrants.

Still, Calvin is quick to exhort believers to "pray for the salvation of all whom we know to have been created after the image of God" and insists that

137. Calvin, *Comm. John* 13:18; *Inst.* 3.22.7.
138. Calvin, *Inst.* 3.24.5.
139. Calvin, *Inst.* 3.24.5.
140. Calvin, *Inst.* 3.23.1.
141. Calvin, *Inst.* 3.21.1.
142. Calvin, *Comm. Romans* 9:23.
143. Calvin, *Inst.* 1.7.11.

we "leave to the judgment of God those whom he knows to be reprobate."[144] Particularly when it comes to reprobation in the ponderous chapters of Romans 9–11, Calvin shuttles back and forth between an emphasis on mystery, a defense of divine prerogative, and a reminder of the justice of punishing sin. Predestination, too, is a "labyrinth" through which we must be conducted by the Word of God.[145] "We should not investigate what the Lord has left hidden in secret," but we also "should not neglect what he has brought into the open, so that we may not be convicted of excessive curiosity on the one hand, or of excessive ingratitude on the other."[146] Calvin emphasizes the inscrutability of the divine wisdom as well as the justice of what God has made manifest: "As far as God's predestination manifests itself, it appears perfectly just."[147] And yet, "the cause of eternal reprobation is so hidden from us, that nothing remains for us but to wonder at the incomprehensible purpose of God."[148] In the end, election is for Calvin the most comforting of doctrines, designed to assure us of the indefatigable love of God for his children.

## The Pedagogy of Prayer

In the final two sections, we will explore prayer and the Lord's Supper, two means by which the Father provides for his children as the Spirit brings us the blessings of Christ. By prayer, we "reach those riches which are laid up for us with the Heavenly Father" and "dig up . . . the treasures that were pointed out by the Lord's gospel, and which our faith has gazed upon."[149] In prayer we come to know the blessings of being children of God (see Eph. 1:3–14). Calvin points out the folly of refusing to take advantage of the opportunity to pray to the source of every good and perfect gift (James 1:17): "To know God as the master and bestower of all good things, who invites us to request them of him, and still not go to him and not ask of him—this would be of as little profit as for a man to neglect a treasure, buried and hidden in the earth, after it had been pointed out to him."[150]

144. Calvin, *Comm. John* 17:9. Calvin finds fault with the "foolish and presumptuous who calculate the number of the elect according to the extent of their own perception" (*Comm. Romans* 11:2).

145. Calvin, *Inst.* 3.21.1.

146. Calvin, *Inst.* 3.21.4.

147. Calvin, *Comm. Romans* 9:22.

148. Calvin, *Comm. Romans* 11:7.

149. Calvin, *Inst.* 3.20.2.

150. Calvin, *Inst.* 3.20.1.

At the same time, one might have reason to hesitate on the threshold of the throne room of God. Considered in itself, prayer is audacious, even dangerous. It involves drawing near to the living God, who is a consuming fire (Heb. 12:29), something only God's children can do with confidence. Calvin lays down a principle, "that we do not rightly pray to God, unless we are surely persuaded in our hearts, that he is our Father." This persuasion is the work of the Spirit, who "testifies to us, that we are the children of God" and "at the same time pours into our hearts such confidence, that we venture to call God our Father."[151] From the Spirit we receive "the testimony . . . by which we know that God is our Father, and on which relying, we dare to call on him as our Father."[152] The elect are set apart from those with only a "transitory faith" by their confidence to "loudly proclaim Abba, Father."[153]

Fittingly, Jesus teaches us to address our prayer to "our Father," and in that prayer "he warns us and urges us to seek him in our every need, as children are wont to take refuge in the protection of the parents whenever they are troubled with any anxiety."[154] To seek help in time of need from the Father is an act of faith, for the one who prays "acts like the son, who commits himself into the bosom of the best and the most loving of fathers, that he may be protected by his care, cherished by his kindness and love, relieved by his bounty, and supported by his power."[155] Calvin insists that, because God is a loving Father, "nothing is more to his nature than to assent to the prayers of suppliants."[156]

Prayer is a school of filial devotion. When life is easy, we often forget our radical dependence on God. Without realizing it, we live under the assumption that we have our lives under control and that we are competent to run our lives and acquire the resources necessary to do so. We forget that every good and perfect gift comes from the Father. God wants us to trust him as a loving Father, and he will deprive us for a time in order to prod us to seek his help. Calvin explains the pedagogical purpose at work: "On account of these things, our most merciful Father, although he never either sleeps or idles, still very often gives the impression of one sleeping or idling in order that he may thus train us, otherwise idle and lazy, to seek, ask, and entreat him to our great good."[157] Suffering prompts us to pray, which is "to our great good." Think about how instinctually, often, and earnestly people pray when

---

151. Calvin, *Comm. Romans* 8:16. See also *Inst.* 3.1.3.
152. Calvin, *Comm. Romans* 8:26.
153. Calvin, *Inst.* 3.2.11.
154. Calvin, *Inst.* 3.20.34.
155. Calvin, *Comm. Romans* 10:14. Also see *Comm. John* 11:3.
156. Calvin, *Inst.* 3.20.13.
157. Calvin, *Inst.* 3.20.3.

life is difficult. "The Lord often suffers us to hunger, in order to train us to earnestness in prayer."[158] We are to ask for *daily* bread so that we might see, know, and trust in God's regular, paternal provision.[159] The daily repetition of this request exposes our poverty, which all too often is hidden underneath a vain presumption of self-sufficiency.

### The Father Feeds His Children by the Hand of His Son

In adopting those he has chosen, the Father takes on the responsibility of caring for them throughout their lives. That's just what a father does. He protects his children, provides for them, preserves them in the faith, and sees to their ongoing nourishment. The two sacraments are central to the Father's household management. God adopts us in baptism, and the Lord's Supper is "a sort of continual food on which Christ spiritually feeds the household of his believers."[160] Calvin explains:

> God has received us, once for all, into his family, to hold us not only as servants but as sons. Thereafter, to fulfill the duties of a most excellent Father concerned for his offspring, he undertakes also to nourish us throughout the course of our life. And not content with this alone, he has willed, by giving his pledge, to assure us of this continuing liberality. To this end, therefore, he has, through the hand of his only-begotten Son, given to his church another sacrament, that is, a spiritual banquet, where Christ attests himself to be the life-giving bread, upon which our souls feed unto true and blessed immortality.[161]

In seeing to our ongoing nourishment, the Father leads us deeper into the life of Christ. We feast on bread and wine, which nourish the body and gladden the heart and lead us "by a sort of analogy to spiritual things."[162] "Just as" we feed physically on bread and wine, so we are fed spiritually by Christ.[163] Bread and wine, then, are not empty representations of what they signify but symbols, "by which the reality is presented to us." In giving us these symbols, Christ "gives us at the same time his own body," which leads Calvin to conclude that Christ's body is "*truly* given to us in the Supper, to be wholesome

---

158. Calvin, *Comm. John* 15:7.
159. See Calvin, *Inst.* 1.16.7.
160. Calvin, *Inst.* 4.18.19. In the Lord's Supper he "discharges the function of a provident householder in continually supplying to us the food to sustain and preserve us in that life into which he has begotten us by his Word" (4.17.1).
161. Calvin, *Inst.* 4.17.1.
162. Calvin, *Inst.* 4.17.3.
163. Calvin, *Inst.* 4.17.1.

food for our souls."[164] He is not "received only by understanding and imagination," but we "enjoy true participation in him."[165]

There is a problem, however. Calvin, as we have seen, takes the humanity of Christ with utmost seriousness. Standard accounts (both Roman Catholic and Lutheran) of how Christ and his people commune with one another in the Lord's Supper require things of Christ that no human being can do. They require him to be simultaneously physically present in heaven, at the right hand of the Father, and in thousands of churches around the world. But no body can do that, and "Christ's body is limited by the general characteristics common to all human bodies, and is contained in heaven."[166] Calvin's solution is to turn the problem on its head. We do not need to find a way to bring Christ down to earth, but for us to ascend to him in heaven.[167] The Supper "does not require a local presence, nor the descent of Christ," but "Christ, while remaining in heaven, is received by us."[168] This is in keeping with God's broader plan, which is "to lift us up to himself, by appropriate means."[169] Lest one be tempted to indulge in science fiction fantasies at this point, Calvin emphasizes that we spiritually ascend to Christ by the power of the Spirit, who "can not merely bring together, but join in one, things that are separated by distance of place, and far remote."[170] Calvin laughs at the contortions required to make Christ physically present in the Lord's Supper: "But greatly mistaken are those who conceive no presence of flesh in the Supper unless it lies in the bread. For thus they leave nothing to the secret working of the Spirit, which unites Christ himself to us. To them Christ does not seem present unless he comes down to us. As though, if he should lift us to himself, we should not just as much enjoy his presence!"[171] The flesh of Christ, which we truly feast on by faith, is present in the Lord's Supper in heaven, to which we are lifted by the Spirit. This feasting is spiritual, in that the Spirit effects it by faith, but it is a real feasting on Christ nonetheless. For "just as" we eat the bread and drink the cup, "so" we feed on the body and blood of our risen and ascended Lord.

---

164. Calvin, *Comm. 1 Corinthians* 11:24.

165. Calvin, *Inst.* 4.17.11.

166. Calvin, *Inst.* 4.17.12.

167. Canlis suggests that "Christ's ascent functions as the interpretive grid for the ongoing Christian life" in Calvin (*Calvin's Ladder*, 118).

168. Calvin, *Comm. 1 Corinthians* 11:24.

169. Calvin, *Inst.* 4.17.15.

170. Calvin, *Comm. 1 Corinthians* 11:24, though see Billings's caution that "spatial distance is simply the wrong category" here, since heaven's distance "is not literally one of space, but one of transcendence" (*Calvin, Participation, and the Gift*, 138).

171. Calvin, *Inst.* 4.17.31.

In the Lord's Supper, the Father feeds us by the hand of Christ and also assures us of his "continuing liberality." The Supper is the sacrament of spiritual sustenance and an aid to faith. Calvin recommends that people feast at the Lord's table at least weekly, as this is one of the primary ways in which the Triune God nourishes his people in the course of their life together.[172] He polemicizes against the Roman Catholic notion of the Eucharist as a "sacrifice" for turning such a grace into a work: "There is as much difference between this sacrifice [of the Mass] and the sacrament of the Supper as there is between giving and receiving."[173] And what do we have that we did not receive from the Father by the hand of his Son in the power of the Spirit?

"Then what becomes of our boasting?" Paul asks. "It is excluded" (Rom. 3:27). God has given us all things, and above all himself, in that the Father has given us his Son and Spirit. To boast is to descend into ingratitude, spitefully disdaining the gifts of God in a foolhardy attempt to secure our very vulnerable selves. It is to refuse to honor the divine descent, the condescension in which Jesus made himself nothing, taking on the form of a servant and becoming obedient unto death. The Father gave his Son to us, and the Son in turns gives us back to the Father. Christ "stretch[es] out his hand to us that he may lead us to heaven," with his cross serving as "a chariot, by which he shall raise all men, along with himself, to his Father."[174]

---

172. Calvin, *Inst.* 4.17.43. Calvin consistently underscored the primary divine agency in the sacraments: "The only question here is whether God acts by his own intrinsic power (as they say) or resigns his office to outward symbols. But we contend that, whatever instruments he uses, these detract nothing from his original activity" (4.14.17).

173. Calvin, *Inst.* 4.18.7.

174. Calvin, *Comm. Hebrews* 7:15; *Comm. John* 12:32.

# 9

# THE BEAUTY OF HOLINESS

*Jonathan Edwards's Religion of the Heart*

### Preaching to the Choir

Imagine a place where to be a citizen was to be a Christian, where church and school and market and hearth flowed into one another seamlessly, each taken for granted as just the way things are. Now imagine entering the pulpit each Sunday as that town's pastor, keen to tell your congregation the good news about Jesus and invite them to die to the ways of the world and find new life in him.

The people might understandably wonder which "world" you had in mind. Did you mean *their* world, this place where steeple and town hall locked arms in friendship? Why would they need to die to *this* world? Surely this would jar the ears of people for whom Christianity just came naturally.

In some ways, it was an unnatural message for Jonathan Edwards to preach.

Edwards was born on October 5, 1703, in East Windsor, Connecticut, into a regional dynasty, with a pastor father and a maternal grandfather nicknamed the "Pope of the Connecticut River Valley." He might have settled into a privileged place in ministry with little reason to ruffle pious feathers.[1] His Puritan heritage, however, inclined Edwards from an early age to an earnest interest

1. In this brief biographical sketch, I follow Marsden, *Jonathan Edwards*; McClymond and McDermott, *Theology of Jonathan Edwards*; Sweeney, *Edwards and the Ministry of the Word*.

in divine things. As a child, he encouraged his friends in the serious business of religion. After graduating from Yale in 1720, Edwards was converted. He served brief pastoral stints in New York City and Bolton, Connecticut, and then, at the ripe old age of twenty, returned to Yale as tutor and de facto president, where at one point he collapsed from overwork. (His asceticism, work habits, and bouts of depression would conspire to render him susceptible to illness throughout his life.)

With Solomon Stoddard, Edwards's papal grandfather, getting old, the town of Northampton, Massachusetts, voted in a meeting to call Edwards as assistant pastor. He was ordained early in 1727, at the age of twenty-three, and later that summer married Sarah Pierpont, "his Beatrice."[2] She gave birth to their first child, also Sarah, when Edwards was twenty-four. (They would eventually have eleven children.) Jonathan deeply loved Sarah, speaking at his death of their "uncommon union" and finding in her a model of Christian piety. He also depended on her utterly, often spending a dozen hours or more a day in his study, reading and writing and attending to pastoral business (he rarely made house calls), while Sarah ran the household and the farm.

When Stoddard died in 1729, he left Edwards in charge of a church of around thirteen hundred people. Despite being such a public figure, Edwards could give the impression of a man lost in the clouds: on solitary walks he had the habit of pinning slips of paper to his clothes to associate with an idea he wanted to remember, suggesting his mind's "characteristic fugal development of every variation on a theme."[3] But he did love his family and his church, and above all his God, devoting himself to the building up of "one holy and happy society."[4] Moreover, people looked to him as a moral and spiritual authority after the death of his grandfather. The young people of the town had grown lax, and following the death of one of their number, Edwards challenged them to consider the far deeper pleasures of heaven. Evenings that had been devoted to partying were replaced by small groups gathering for "social religion."[5] A great revival broke out in the region in 1734–35. A request came for an account of the events in Northampton, and Edwards wrote A Faithful Narrative of the Surprising Work of God.

Even as he entered the spotlight, he faced a sad decline at home. Even more quickly than it began, the revival fire was smothered. A rash of suicides and suicidal tendencies, beginning with Edwards's always unstable uncle,

2. Marsden, *Jonathan Edwards*, 94.
3. Marsden, *Jonathan Edwards*, 153–54.
4. Edwards, *WJE* 5:146.
5. Marsden, *Jonathan Edwards*, 155. "Nothing was more distinctive about Puritanism than its encouragement of lay spirituality" (156).

quenched the pious fervor and threw the community into confusion. Edwards's deepening reflection on the nature of true piety grew in large part as he watched many apparently converted Northamptonites fall back into worldly ways.[6] (Later, when a young dynamo named George Whitefield came to New England in 1739–40, an even greater revival lasting two years swept through the region.[7])

Despite—or perhaps because of—his focused attention on the wandering ways of the human heart, Edwards remained convinced that the sovereign Spirit could only be followed, never led. This held true in large-scale revival, even as it did in individual conversion. William McLoughlin describes Edwards's "almost incredulous wonderment" at the "surprising work of God" in Northampton. Edwards contrasts sharply with Charles Finney a century later, for whom a revival "is not a miracle, or dependent on a miracle in any sense. It is a purely philosophical result of the right use of the constituted means." The difference between Edwards and Finney is essentially the difference between the medieval and the modern temper. One saw God as the center of the universe; the other saw man. One believed that revivals were "prayed down," and the other that they were "worked up."[8]

Still, once the Spirit had led, Edwards was keen to see his church follow. Having learned from the previous revival, Edwards led Northampton in the drafting of a church covenant in March 1742, in which he attempted "to institutionalize the spirit of the revival."[9] Edwards always respected the function of various means of grace, both in calling people to Christ and in sustaining them in him. The means alone cannot guarantee that people will walk in Christ, though, and the church covenant was one of a number of grasping attempts by Edwards to harness the town's piety. Two specific incidents alienated much of the town. In what became known as "the bad book case," Edwards rightly lambasted young men for harassing young women with explicit midwifery books (the pornography of the day), but he did so in a clumsy, impolitic way

6. The language of "falling back" rather than "backsliding" reflects Edwards's Calvinist belief that the elect persevere, despite seasons of sin, and that the reprobate will eventually return to their sin, despite seasons of apparent repentance.

7. On the extraordinary influence of Whitefield, his partnership with Edwards, and his friendship with Benjamin Franklin, see Marsden, *Short Life of Jonathan Edwards*, 52–55, 60–65.

8. McLoughlin, *Modern Revivalism*, 11.

9. Marsden, *Jonathan Edwards*, 262. Of the first awakening, Marsden insightfully comments: "This seemingly almost universal awakening also temporarily relieved one of the deepest tensions within the Puritan and Protestant heritage. Was the church to be a separated communion, called out from the world and made up of believers only? Or was it to be a state church to which all respectable citizens belonged? Edwards' ideal for the church and ultimately for the town was that everyone should follow a virtually monastic standard for all of life" (160).

(including publicly naming names without distinguishing who was party to the offenses and who simply had information about the case). And then, in a controversy over communion, Edwards overturned Solomon Stoddard's method of administering the Lord's Supper. In what could be viewed as a hopeful or a pragmatic move, Stoddard considered the Supper a "converting ordinance." Most New England churches had adopted the "half-way covenant," whereby the children of baptized but not converted members could be baptized. Stoddard went further in the latitude with which he treated church membership, admitting to communion those who "professed Christian belief and whose lives were free from scandal."[10] Claiming to have long been uncomfortable with his grandfather's policy, Edwards insisted on "a 'credible profession'—which he would judge—of a *heartfelt* faith and dedication to serve God."[11] That was enough. Eventually, Edwards was voted out as pastor by a landslide.

After an awkward year of pulpit supply for the church that fired him, Edwards moved to Stockbridge, on the Housatonic River, in the Berkshire Mountains of western Massachusetts. It was a strange move in many ways, out to a frontier post and away from positions of influence. Yet the mission to Native Americans had been an embarrassing afterthought for many Puritans, and Edwards joined in the apocalyptic hope that their conversion would portend the long-awaited millennium. (He had joined efforts to organize international concerts of prayer for revival and the coming of the kingdom.) Stockbridge brought new headaches, with the ever-present threat of violence in the ongoing strife among the French, Native Americans, and British colonists; even worse was a rather cancerous family of settlers. Edwards was a man acquainted with grief—if not more so than the typical New Englander, still very much so. Perhaps this difficult setting explains in part why he so prized the witness of David Brainerd, a witness to absolute surrender in the midst of profound suffering rather than conventional success in missionary work.[12] In the midst of this, Edwards preached regularly, served as a (fairly patriarchal) representative of the Mahican Indians, and wrote most of his significant major writings.

In 1758, somewhat against his wishes but in obedience to a council of pastors that he consulted, Edwards became the third president of the College of New Jersey (now Princeton University). He was fifty-four. Edwards had been reluctant, citing his temperamental body and mind and his preoccupation with

10. Marsden, *Jonathan Edwards*, 30.
11. Marsden, *Jonathan Edwards*, 347; see discussion of the affair at 345–56.
12. Marsden, *Jonathan Edwards*, 332. Edwards's *Life of Brainerd* is "*Religious Affections* in the form of a spiritual biography" (331).

two major works—*A History of the Work of Redemption*, which would be "a body of divinity in an entire new method, being thrown into the form of an history," and *The Harmony of the Old and New Testament.*[13] Quickly thereafter, after a smallpox inoculation gone bad (he had been trying to set an example for others fearful of vaccination), Edwards died, feverish and unable to swallow.

## Conversion as Beatific Vision

As Edwards reflected on "the surprising work of God" in Northampton, he considered the nature of the conversion of hundreds of souls in the town. What had happened? In brief: they had seen the Lord. They had tasted and seen that he is good (Ps. 34:8). What mandatory church attendance and steady adherence to the means of grace failed to bring about on their own, the surprising Spirit accomplished in giving the stony-hearted citizens of Northampton a taste for divine things.

It might strike one as strange that a congregation weekly exposed to lengthy expositions of Scripture and a Puritan spirituality of relentless introspection would remain cold to the gospel. While Edwards trusted this to the vagaries of providence, he located piety's missing piece in a spiritual and divine light in the soul, "a true sense of the divine excellency of the things revealed in the Word of God, and a conviction of the truth and reality of them, thence arising."[14] It is this *sense*—what Edwards will elsewhere call a "taste" or "relish"—of God's excellency that Northampton lacked. They knew the Westminster Catechism, to be sure, but they didn't relish the one of whom it spoke. Edwards writes:

> Thus there is a difference between having an opinion that God is holy and gracious, and having a sense of the loveliness and beauty of that holiness and grace. There is a difference between having a rational judgment that honey is sweet, and having a sense of its sweetness. A man may have the former, that knows not how honey tastes; but a man can't have the latter, unless he has an idea of the taste of honey in his mind. So there is a difference between believing that a person is beautiful, and having a sense of his beauty. The former may be obtained by hearsay, but the latter only by seeing the countenance. There is a wide difference between mere speculative, rational judging anything to be excellent, and having a sense of its sweetness, and beauty. The former rests only in the head, speculation only is concerned in it; but the heart is concerned in

13. Edwards, *WJE* 16:727.
14. Edwards, *WJE* 17:413.

the latter. When the heart is sensible of the beauty and amiableness of a thing, it necessarily feels pleasure in the apprehension.[15]

Notice a few things in this passage. First, the importance of what Søren Kierkegaard calls "autopsy."[16] Writing in a similar established-church context, Kierkegaard insisted on seeing for oneself and responding personally to Jesus's call to discipleship. Where Kierkegaard sought to disqualify implicit faith, a trusting in the church to tell one what to believe, Edwards sought to commend the richness of seeing for oneself rather than merely hearing about something secondhand. In fact, autopsy is just what good secondhand reports encourage. If I were to tell you how good this honey tastes, how sweet it is and how richly it coats the throat, you would quickly grow impatient for a spoonful. Of course, holiness and grace are infinitely sweeter than honey. Looked at this way, satisfaction with "mere speculative, rational judging" earns derision.

A second point to note is the aesthetic and affectional character of the "sense of the loveliness and beauty of that holiness and grace." What matters is the sense of the heart, not the speculation of the head. We ought not to miss Edwards's point: he hardly intends to banish knowledge to make room for emotion. Nor did he disdain reason. Nevertheless, "it is out of reason's province to perceive the beauty or loveliness of anything: such a perception don't belong to that faculty. Reason's work is to perceive truth, and not excellency."[17] Instead, by the divine light, we see and savor the divine excellency. And the sight of beauty leads to the conviction of truth.[18] "A true faith is what arises from a spiritual sight of Christ."[19] While Edwards would insist, with the Reformed tradition, that "faith comes from hearing" (Rom. 10:17), he would also assert that it does not come by hearing alone. While this view initially seems like a departure from a Protestant emphasis on the sole efficacy of the Word preached and promised in the sacrament, Edwards can hardly be accused of neglecting or selling short the Word of God.[20] Rather, his state church context required a robust theology of Word and Spirit, in which the Word's efficacy is matched by the Spirit's illumining, renewing work. The Spirit sheds light on the Word's excellency and causes its hearers to delight in what they see. "The mind can't see the excellency of any doctrine, unless that doctrine be first in the mind; but the seeing the excellency of the doctrine may be immediately

15. Edwards, *WJE* 17:414.
16. Kierkegaard, *Philosophical Fragments*, 70, 102.
17. Edwards, *WJE* 17:422.
18. See Edwards, *WJE* 17:413–14.
19. Edwards, *WJE* 17:418.
20. Witness Sweeney, *Edwards and the Ministry of the Word*.

from the Spirit of God; though the conveying of the doctrine or proposition itself may be by the Word."[21] Sure, the mind needs to know the doctrine in question. But such knowledge is incomplete, even inconsequential, if pursued no further. Strangely, it is a *blind* knowledge, until the doctrine's beauty is seen. Such a beautiful excellence moves the heart to embrace the doctrine. Edwards is quite clear: "This sense of divine beauty is the first thing in the actual change made in the soul, in true conversion, and is the foundation of everything else belonging to that change."[22]

This had been Edwards's own experience. Though he came from a family of high-profile pastors and was himself a little revivalist as a child, Edwards nevertheless dated his conversion to his late teen years. He remembers the moment in his *Personal Narrative*:

> The first that I remember that ever I found anything of that sort of inward, sweet delight in God and divine things, that I have lived much in since, was on reading those words, 1 Timothy 1:17, "Now unto the King eternal, immortal, invisible, the only wise God, be honor and glory forever and ever, Amen." As I read the words, there came into my soul, and was as it were diffused through it, a sense of the glory of the Divine Being; a new sense, quite different from anything I ever experienced before. Never any words of Scripture seemed to me as these words did. I thought with myself, how excellent a Being that was; and how happy I should be, if I might enjoy that God, and be wrapt up to God in heaven, and be as it were swallowed up in him. I kept saying, and as it were singing over these words of Scripture to myself; and went to prayer, to pray to God that I might enjoy him; and prayed in a manner quite different from what I used to do; with a new sort of affection. But it never came into my thought, that there was anything spiritual, or of a saving nature in this.
>
> I had an inward, sweet sense of these things, that at times came into my heart; and my soul was led away in pleasant views and contemplations of them. And my mind was greatly engaged, to spend my time in reading and meditating on Christ; and the beauty and excellency of his person, and the lovely way of salvation, by free grace in him.[23]

Far from an isolated account of one man's conversion, Edwards understood a joyful sense of God's excellency and glory as the beginning and end (humanly speaking) of Christian religion. He concludes that "there arises from

---

21. Edwards, *WJE* 17:416–17.
22. Edwards, *WJE* 25:636, cited in McClymond and McDermott, *Theology of Jonathan Edwards*, 71. McClymond and McDermott are right to highlight the priority of beauty in Edwards's thought, but they too often fail to draw attention to the *moral* character of divine beauty.
23. Edwards, *WJE* 16:792–93.

this sense of spiritual beauty, all true experimental knowledge of religion. . . . He that sees not the beauty of holiness, knows not what one of the graces of God's Spirit is."[24]

But what is holiness, and why is it said to be beautiful? Sure, the Scriptures use that language, but few would think of the holiness of God as something pleasant to behold. Holiness frightens and threatens; surely it doesn't delight. To follow Edwards, consider his (fairly standard) distinction between natural and moral perfections. Natural perfections, like knowledge and power, are not beautiful in themselves; intelligence and strength can tear down as easily as build up. But when they are joined with moral perfections, these natural perfections are lovely.

> The true beauty and loveliness of all intelligent beings does primarily and most essentially consist in their moral excellency or holiness . . . : 'tis this that gives beauty to, or rather is the beauty of their natural perfections and qualifications. . . . Holiness is in a peculiar manner the beauty of the divine nature. . . . This renders all his other attributes glorious and lovely. 'Tis the glory of God's wisdom, that 'tis a holy wisdom, and not a wicked subtlety and craftiness. This makes his majesty lovely, and not merely dreadful and horrible, that it is a holy majesty. 'Tis the glory of God's immutability, that it is a holy immutability, and not an inflexible obstinacy in wickedness.
>
> A true love to God must begin with a delight in his holiness, and not with a delight in any other attribute; for no other attribute is truly lovely without this.[25]

God's holiness is that perfection whereby his greatness is wedded to his goodness. He is the only one not absolutely corrupted by absolute power, because the almighty one is holy (see Rev. 4:8). In beholding the luminously beautiful God—that is, the only righteous one, the faithful keeper of the covenant—we are made new.

Faith, we might say, follows sight. "The Scripture is ignorant of any such faith in Christ . . . that is not founded in a spiritual sight of Christ. That believing on Christ, which accompanies a title to everlasting life, is a seeing the Son, and believing on him, John 6:40."[26] When the Reformers spoke of salvation by faith alone, they meant to draw attention to the object of faith rather than faith as such. The slogan's "rhetoric of indication" signals that it is Christ alone who saves by grace alone and that, rather than do *anything*, our "part" consists simply in clinging to the One who is sufficient for our

---

24. Edwards, *WJE* 2:275.
25. Edwards, *WJE* 2:257.
26. Edwards, *WJE* 2:175. And "they can exercise faith only just in such proportion as they have spiritual light" (176).

salvation.[27] Since God's grace is utterly efficacious, we need contribute *nothing*.[28] Inveterate in our attempts at self-justification, we can turn such a small thing as faith into a Trojan horse, the one final work that we must do to earn the right to stand before God. One salutary effect of the priority of vision is to ground conversion in the God who reveals himself in Christ and the Spirit who gives us eyes to see his beauty.

## The Marks of Conversion

The Puritans had developed a rather sophisticated morphology of conversion, an ordered account of the necessary steps along which one becomes a Christian, and people were instructed to measure the state of their souls against that pattern. Aware of what Amy Plantinga Pauw names "the dangers of preparationism," Edwards downplays the form and order of events leading up to conversion, not least because of the idiosyncrasies of his own conversion.[29] The Spirit blows where it will (John 3:8) and cannot be so neatly time-tabled. "Experience plainly shows, that God's Spirit is unsearchable and untraceable, in some of the best of Christians, in the method of his operations, in their conversion. Nor does the Spirit of God proceed discernibly in the steps of a particular established scheme, one half so often as is imagined." Indeed, "the Spirit is so exceeding various in the manner of his operating, that in many cases it is impossible to trace him, or find out his way." One could measure the entrenched status of the morphology of conversion, however, in that, when it comes to people telling their stories, "what they have experienced is insensibly strained to bring all to an exact conformity to the scheme that is established."[30] Every story started to sound the same.

Of course, *some* pattern could be discerned. Alan Jacobs describes the genre of Christian testimony as some variation on the story that in its simplest

27. The phrase is John Webster's, *Word and Church*, 124, in his description of the church. Parallel to this is his description of testimony as a form of "astonished indication" (*Confessing God*, 185).

28. Edwards eschewed the Calvinist description of grace as "irresistible," because it suggested that people "do not participate in their own decisions." "In grace God moves our will, but it is *our* will" (McClymond and McDermott, *Theology of Jonathan Edwards*, 363; also see Edwards, *WJE*, vol. 1).

29. Pauw, *Supreme Harmony of All*, 97; also see Sweeney, *Edwards and the Ministry of the Word*, 118–20. "But the thing that I speak of as unscriptural, is the insisting on a particular account of the distinct method and steps, wherein the Spirit of God did sensibly proceed, in first bringing the soul into a state of salvation, as a thing requisite in order to receiving a professor into full charity as a real Christian" (Edwards, *WJE* 2:418).

30. Edwards, *WJE* 2:162.

form runs, "I once was lost, but now am found."[31] And Edwards, like all Puritans, stressed the importance of recognizing that one is lost before one can be found.[32] It all sounds so clear. But anxious Puritans, due no doubt in part to the very specificity of their diagnostics of conversion, worried scrupulously and incessantly about whether they *had* been found. Trained to look for signs in the world of God's presence and action, they looked for signs in their souls that they were among the elect. Edwards knew the need for such discernment, acutely so after the heartbreaking slump that followed Northampton's awakening, precipitated by the suicide of Edwards's uncle.[33] Many apparently pious citizens returned to their old ways, and the need to find signs of true religion and sort the wheat from the chaff was urgent.

Perhaps due in part to his own disillusionment, coupled with a sense of the ambivalence of religious experience during the awakening, Edwards wrote, "We are often in Scripture expressly directed to try ourselves by the *nature* of the fruits of the Spirit; but nowhere by the Spirit's *method* of producing them."[34] What, then, is the nature of the Spirit's gracious work in believers?[35] While Edwards countenances a broad range of the Spirit's work within and outside the church, in the *Religious Affections* he focuses on the gracious marks of the Spirit (saving that term for his work in the regenerate). At the outset, Edwards states his argument: "True religion, in great part, consists in holy affections."[36] It is common to equate "affections" with "emotions" and to distinguish "emotions" from "thoughts."[37] But this is mistaken.

The soul possesses two faculties: understanding and will. The understanding is "that by which it is capable of perception and speculation, or by which it discerns and views and judges of things." The will is that by which the soul "is some way inclined [or disinclined] with respect to the things it views or considers," and so it is "sometimes called the *inclination*: and, as it has respect to the actions that are determined and governed by it, is called the

31. Jacobs, *Looking Before and After*, 22.

32. "And that it is God's manner of dealing with men, to lead them into a wilderness, before he speaks comfortably to them, and so to order it, that they shall be brought into distress, and made to see their own helplessness, and absolute dependence on his power and grace, before he appears to work any great deliverance for them, is abundantly manifest by the Scripture" (Edwards, *WJE* 2:152).

33. On spiritual discernment in pastoral care, see Spohn, "Finding God in All Things."

34. Edwards, *WJE* 2:162.

35. Edwards "identified the traditional fruits of the Spirit with affections" (Edwards, *WJE* 2:8).

36. Edwards, *WJE* 2:95.

37. This would not do justice to the nature of the affections (as we will see) *or* the emotions. As Robert Roberts has argued, emotions are "concern-based construals," thus a function of both head ("construal") and heart ("concern") (*Spiritual Emotions*, 153).

*will*: and the *mind*, with regard to the exercises of this faculty, is often called the *heart*."[38] The affections are "the more vigorous and sensible exercises of the inclination and will of the soul." They are stronger, more long-term inclinations or disinclinations of the soul. They differ from passions, though, in that they are less violent, more constant, and more subject to the mind.[39] "Holy affections are not heat without light; but evermore arise from some information of the understanding, some spiritual instruction that the mind receives, some light or actual knowledge. The child of God is graciously affected, because he sees and understands something more of divine things than he did before, more of God or Christ and of the glorious things exhibited in the gospel. . . . Knowledge is the key that first opens the hard heart and enlarges the affections."[40] Religious affections are not merely warm feelings. We cannot have religious affections without light, without seeing and knowing the beauty of God in Christ. At the same time, we cannot have religious affections if our hearts are not "strangely warmed."[41]

> As there is no true religion, where there is nothing else but affection; so there is no true religion where there is no religious affection. As on the one hand, there must be light in the understanding, as well as an affected fervent heart, where there is heat without light, there can be nothing divine or heavenly in that heart; so on the other hand, where there is a kind of light without heat, a head stored with notions and speculations, with a cold and unaffected heart, there can be nothing divine in that light, that knowledge is no true spiritual knowledge of divine things. If the great things of religion are rightly understood, they will affect the heart.[42]

As abiding inclinations, the affections are the "spring" of human action.[43] They motivate us in particular directions, as our hearts are stirred in response to our minds being enlightened. A stirred heart is basic to piety; it is no mere affectation or ornamentation. "Nothing is more manifest in fact, than that the things of religion take hold of men's souls, no further than they affect them."[44]

Though he was something of a mystic, Edwards did not think of the affections primarily in terms of mystical experience but as the regular fruits of the Spirit. They represented the heart's abiding response to the loveliness of Jesus.

38. Edwards, *WJE* 2:96.
39. Edwards, *WJE* 2:97–98.
40. Edwards, *WJE* 2:266.
41. This is how John Wesley describes the effect of hearing the preface to Luther's commentary on Romans read in Aldersgate, a pivotal moment in his life.
42. Edwards, *WJE* 2:120.
43. Edwards, *WJE* 2:110, 393.
44. Edwards, *WJE* 2:101.

In the end, Edwards attended less to initial experiences or episodic displays of emotion than he did to an ongoing relish for divine things as displayed in love of God and neighbor.[45] Most striking in the *Religious Affections*—other than its dignified restraint and nuance in the chaotic aftermath of the Great Awakening—is Edwards's conclusion that true religious affections can be seen most certainly not in dramatic displays of emotions but in a holy life: "Christian practice or a holy life is a great and distinguishing sign of true and saving grace. But I may go further, and assert, that it is the chief of all the signs of grace, both as an evidence of the sincerity of professors unto others, and also to their own consciences."[46] For those wondering whether they are numbered among the elect, Edwards counsels holy obedience. "Assurance is not to be obtained so much by self-examination, as by action."[47] Conversely, right action and true virtue take their bearings from, are empowered by, and aim toward God. By insisting that goodness and God could not be separated, Edwards "was laying gunpowder at the foundations of the entire project of all the celebrated moral philosophers of the day."[48]

Faith is formed by the affections, the first of which is love.[49] That is, the vision of "the glory of God in the face of Jesus Christ" (2 Cor. 4:6) moves us to bet our all on him—that is, to trust him—and thus we cling to him in love. "The soul shall be as it were all eye to behold and yet all act to love."[50] In an early treatise titled "The Mind," Edwards wrote: "A speculative faith consists only in assent; but in a saving faith are assent and consent together. . . . Now the true spiritual consent of the heart cannot be distinguished from the love of the heart."[51] It is not just that faith works through love, but that faith, as a clinging to the Savior, *is* love, a "Yes-ing" consent of the heart to the gospel that issues in self-giving love to others. In this "Yes," we receive and rejoice in—that is, we affirm—the promises of God fulfilled in Christ. And as we do, we turn toward our neighbor in love.

## Loving Consent

Recall Edwards's words that "in a saving faith are assent and consent together." In consent we find the first signs of religious affection. This category of "con-

45. McClymond and McDermott, *Theology of Jonathan Edwards*, 65.
46. Edwards, *WJE* 2:406.
47. Edwards, *WJE* 2:195.
48. Marsden, *Jonathan Edwards*, 467.
49. McClymond and McDermott, *Theology of Jonathan Edwards*, 19.
50. Edwards, *WJE* 2:195, n. 2.
51. Edwards, *WJE* 8:139.

sent" is central to Edwards's ontology. It encapsulates his understanding of the Trinity, creation, beauty, and love. Edwards defines excellency as the "consent of being to being, or being's consent to entity. The more the consent is, and the more extensive, the greater is the excellency."[52] Precisely as *con*-sent, excellency requires relationship. "One alone, without any reference to any more, cannot be excellent; for in such a case there can be no manner of relation no way, and therefore, no such thing as consent. Indeed, what we call 'one' may be excellent, because of a consent of parts, or some consent of those in that being that are distinguished into a plurality some way or other. But in a being that is absolutely without any plurality there cannot be excellency, for there can be no such thing as consent or agreement."[53] A nontrinitarian god could not be excellent.[54] Or if such a god were excellent, he would require a created counterpart to make him so. Indeed, this is precisely the path process theology has traveled. On this read of things, since God is relational, he needs an Absolute Other in relation to whom he can become himself. That other is creation. History is a tandem bike on which God and the world ride into the future, where they will become themselves. For Edwards (as for Athanasius), the Father is himself as he is Father of the Son. These two love each other perfectly in the love that is the Spirit. Edwards can also speak of God's love for himself, though this must be read in light of (while itself also pressuring our read of) his principle of consent.

To return to the passage above, we see that excellence requires the consent of two parties in relationship. Fittingly, then, "one of the highest excellencies is love. . . . The highest excellency, therefore, must be the consent of spirits one to another."[55] The Triune God, who is love (1 John 4:8), is the most excellent Being, as the Father and Son are "united in infinitely dear and incomprehensible mutual love" by "the spirit of divine love."[56] The infinite perfection of the triune consent demonstrates the excellence of this God.

Conversion, as we have seen, happens when people see this God in his lovely glory for themselves. Following on this first beatific vision, they are

---

52. Edwards, *WJE* 6:336.
53. Edwards, *WJE* 6:337.
54. Amy Plantinga Pauw argues that Edwards is uncomfortable with the divine simplicity tradition in light of this (*Supreme Harmony of All*, 57–90). I suspect she dismisses the simplicity tradition a bit quickly, however, despite recognizing how talk of "relations" in God must steer clear of tritheism. Some form of divine simplicity, tailored to the triunely one God, but eliminating the possibility of dualism or composition in God, still seems necessary. For a defense of Edwards on this front and a critique of Pauw, see Crisp, *Jonathan Edwards on God and Creation*, 94–116; Strobel, *Jonathan Edwards's Theology*, 39.
55. Edwards, *WJE* 6:337.
56. Edwards, *WJE* 8:369, 370.

united to him in a consent that Edwards describes as being "sweetly united in a benevolent agreement of heart," or "a *cordial* agreement that consists in concord and union of mind and heart."[57] This loving consent to God—and, through him, to all "spiritual" (that is, intelligent) beings—constitutes virtue. "True virtue most essentially consists in benevolence to Being in general. Or perhaps to speak more accurately, it is that consent, propensity and union of heart to Being in general, that is immediately exercised in a general good will."[58] Virtue is the beauty of human action. It is that "which renders any habit, disposition, or exercise of the heart truly *beautiful*"; "so 'tis primarily *on this account* they are beautiful, viz. that they imply *consent* and *union* with Being *in general.*"[59] In a rapturous sermon titled "Heaven Is a World of Love," Edwards describes the beauty of the *communio sanctorum* in heaven: "Every saint is as a flower in the garden of God, and holy love is the fragrancy and sweet odor which they all send forth, and with which they fill that paradise. Every saint there is as a note in a concert of music which sweetly harmonizes with every other note, and all together employed wholly in praising God and the Lamb."[60] Notice how the saints' common object of praise—their consent to God and the Lamb—forms their harmony—their consent to one another.[61]

Consent even obtains in the nonspiritual (i.e., merely material) creation. As it is with the Creator, so it is with the creation: "The beauty of the world consists wholly of sweet mutual consents, either within itself, or with the Supreme Being." The planets display an image of "trust, dependence and acknowledgment" in orbiting the sun, and the earth is filled with harmony and proportion.[62] Edwards marvels at a "remarkable analogy" and "consentaneity" in God's works as he orders "one thing to be in an agreeableness and harmony with another. And if so, why should not we suppose that he makes the inferior in imitation of the superior, the material of the spiritual, on purpose to have a resemblance and shadow of them?"[63] Edwards takes creation's consents and the typological readings of events, people, and objects in Scripture as warrant for reading the book of nature—as well as history—typologically. The principle of consent suggests just such an elaborate order

57. Edwards, *WJE* 8:565.
58. Edwards, *WJE* 8:540.
59. Edwards, *WJE* 8:539, 548. If virtue is loving consent, we might best characterize sin as dissent. It is that lonely, solipsistic, divisive posture in which we spurn all that is beautiful and good.
60. Edwards, *WJE* 8:386.
61. Edwards can speak of the divine light that moves the soul to "symphonize with" the gospel (*WJE* 17:424).
62. Edwards, *WJE* 6:305.
63. Edwards, *WJE* 11:53.

and harmony and encourages the associations Edwards draws as he scans the scene and history of God's redemption. Even non-Christian religions fit into this legible cosmos, as an extension of Edwards's conviction that "all being is communicative," coupled with a speculative reading of primordial history (in which, e.g., Noah was China's first king and passed down true religion).[64] As Michael McClymond and Gerald McDermott write, "Typology was less a method than a worldview for Edwards."[65]


## Why the World?

Having begun in medias res, we should stop and take stock. Many know Edwards for his unabashed glee in the glory of God, in God's infinite self-sufficiency, his supreme happiness in himself. But the picture developing here is one in which this happiness spills over into creation. Still, why create at all? What initially seems a hopelessly speculative question can reveal much about the nature of God and the world.

Typically, the question is answered from the beginning. We might ask what drove God to create a world. But that's a dead end. God—precisely as God—is driven by nothing. He is perfectly happy in his life as Father, Son, and Spirit, needs nothing from creation, and so is in no way constrained to create.

> That no notion of God's last end in the creation of the world is agreeable to reason which would truly imply or infer any indigence, insufficiency and mutability in God; or any dependence of the Creator on the creature, for any part of his perfection or happiness. Because it is evident, by both Scripture and reason, that God is infinitely, eternally, unchangeably, and independently glorious and happy: that he stands in no need of, cannot be profited by, or receive anything from the creature; or be truly hurt, or be the subject of any sufferings or impair of his glory and felicity from any other being.[66]

> The notion of God's creating the world in order to receive anything properly from the creature is not only contrary to the nature of God, but inconsistent with the notion of creation; which implies a being's receiving its existence, and

---

64. McDermott, *Jonathan Edwards Confronts the Gods*, 112, 213. See the discussion of typology and the religions (110–29).

65. McClymond and McDermott, *Theology of Jonathan Edwards*, 17. See the helpful investigation in McDermott, "Is a Typological View of Reality Legitimate?" Edwards believed that "all the world is typical . . . . Scripture overflows with a surplus of meaning. It points from Old Testament to New Testament realities and is the guidebook to a world full of divine signs" (154).

66. Edwards, *WJE* 8:420.

all that belongs to its being, out of nothing. And this implies the most perfect, absolute and universal derivation and dependence.[67]

The doctrine of *creatio ex nihilo* establishes the radical claim that God creates with no materials for no reason. Creation is utterly contingent; it did not have to be.[68] All this is a corollary of God's gloriously perfect happiness in himself. Thus God "can't create the world to the end that he may have existence; or may have such attributes and perfections, and such an essence."[69]

But neither does he create the world for its own sake. God has a "disposition to diffuse himself, or to cause an emanation of his glory and fullness, which is prior to the existence of any other being, and is to be considered as the inciting cause of creation," Edwards writes. "This disposition or desire in God must be prior to the existence of the creature, even in intention and foresight."[70] God creates in order that his glory and fullness might be expressed outside himself. He has a "communicative disposition," a "perfection of his nature" inclining him to "flow out and diffuse" or "emanate" his fullness. In emanation, there is "as it were an increase, repetition or multiplication of it,"[71] which is what "moved him to create the world."[72] After all, reasons Edwards, it is "fitting" that the "glorious attributes of God" would be put to work and made manifest. "If the world had not been created, these attributes never would have had any exercise."[73] In

67. Edwards, *WJE* 8:420.

68. This is in contrast to Crisp, *Jonathan Edwards on God and Creation*, 146. Crisp argues that, for Edwards, God is essentially creative, such that creation *does* have to be—indeed, that God has to create the best possible world (though noting that this necessity flows from who God is rather than being an external constraint). I agree with Kyle Strobel, who argues that it is "God's *willing* that causes God to 'flow-out' of himself. This willing is caused by the *fit* and *suitable* desire to put his perfections into exercise." Strobel cites Edwards's statement "that it [eternal generation] is not an arbitrary production but a necessary emanation. Creation is an arbitrary production. They are the effects of the mere will and good pleasure of God" (Strobel, *Jonathan Edwards's Theology*, 85).

69. Edwards, *WJE* 8:469. Note again the contrast with later process theology.

70. Edwards, *WJE* 8:438. Recent debates about the character of Edwards's ontology swirl around the concept of disposition. Sang Hyun Lee proffers Edwards's "dispositional ontology" in "Jonathan Edwards's Dispositional Conception of the Trinity"; Lee, *Philosophical Theology of Jonathan Edwards*; Lee, "God's Relation to the World." Critiques come from Crisp, "Jonathan Edwards's Ontology"; Crisp, *Jonathan Edwards on God and Creation*; Holmes, "Does Jonathan Edwards Use a Dispositional Ontology?"; Strobel, *Jonathan Edwards's Theology*. McClymond wonders whether the debate isn't a "proxy war" between two powers (the defenders and critics of classical theism) in a third territory (Edwards's thought) (McClymond, "Hearing the Symphony," 76).

71. Edwards, *WJE* 8:433.

72. Edwards, *WJE* 8:434–35, 438.

73. Edwards, *WJE* 8:429. "So we find manifestation or making known God's *perfections*, his *greatness* and *excellency*, is spoke of very much in the same manner as God's glory" (*WJE* 8:496). While Edwards can speak of God's manifesting his perfections and describe hell as "a

fact, God's self-communication "belong[s] to the fullness and completeness of himself, as though he were not in his most complete and glorious state without it."[74] Edwards seems to want to claim both the divine sufficiency and an intrinsic divine disposition to communication. On the one hand, "God's joy is dependent on nothing besides his own act, which he exerts with an absolute and independent power." On the other hand, "God would be less happy, if he was less good, or if he had not that perfection of nature which consists in a propensity of nature to diffuse of his own fullness."[75]

The specter of Georg Hegel lurks here. Does God need creation to be himself after all? If the communication of his fullness belongs to his fullness, is he incomplete without creation? Here Edwards applies good common sense: "Surely, 'tis no argument of indigence in God that he is inclined to communicate of his infinite fullness. 'Tis no argument of the emptiness or deficiency of a fountain that it is inclined to overflow."[76] Such perfect generosity can hardly be labeled poverty. Admittedly, the image of a fountain founders precisely in that a fountain can't but overflow. It can't help itself. But God is nothing for Edwards if he is not a willing agent. Even his beauty is a function of the intratrinitarian consent, in which the Father and Son love one another in the Spirit. God's "inclination" to communicate himself, while perfectly "natural," is thoroughly *personal*, and therefore never an external constraint.[77]

If Edwards avoids Hegel (begging your pardon for the anachronism), he runs into deists who disdain a giant divine Ego who only ever does things for himself.[78] Edwards claims that "God's glory is the end of the creation."[79] One might object that it seems rather indulgent for God, already perfectly happy in the society of Father, Son, and Spirit, to create for his own glory. In reply, Edwards argues that God's seeking his glory and his seeking his creatures'

---

world prepared on purpose for the expression of God's wrath" (*WJE* 8:390), he discerns a certain divine hesitancy to do so. "God is often spoken of as exercising goodness and showing mercy, with delight, in a manner quite different, and opposite to that of his executing wrath. For the latter is spoken of as what God proceeds to do with backwardness and reluctance" (*WJE* 8:503, discussing Ezek. 18:32).

74. Edwards, *WJE* 8:439.

75. Edwards, *WJE* 8:447.

76. Edwards, *WJE* 8:448.

77. A crucial question is whether "communication" governs the meaning of emanation, "flowing forth," and the images of fountain and light that Edwards uses, or whether emanation governs the meaning of communication and those images. "If the first, one's reading of *End of Creation* will be more biblical, communication expressing an action, disposition, or will in God. If the second, one's reading will be more Neoplatonic, emanation meaning some sort of procession of or from God" (*WJE* 8:433, n. 5).

78. Edwards, *WJE* 8:450, 453.

79. Edwards, *WJE* 8:477. It is also the end of redemption (see 485, 488).

good are one and the same, "because the emanation of his glory . . . implies the communicated excellency and happiness of his creatures."[80] "Here God's acting for himself, or making himself his last end, and his acting for their sake, are not to be set in opposition; or to be considered as the opposite parts of a disjunction: they are rather to be considered as coinciding one with the other, and implied one in the other."[81] It is good for us that God seeks his own glory in creating. Why? Because the happiness of the creature consists in union with God through knowing, loving, and rejoicing in his excellency. And as the union increases, so will the creature's happiness—eternally.[82]

The internal glory of the Trinity (in God knowing, loving, and rejoicing in himself) is repeated externally as his people participate in this knowledge, love, and joy.[83] Here, "the glory of God is both exhibited and acknowledged; his fullness is received and returned. Here is both an *emanation* and *remanation*." The light of God shines on creation and is reflected back. "So that the whole is *of* God, and *in* God, and *to* God; and God is the beginning, middle and end in this affair."[84] The Triune God transcends egoism, in that the "delight which God has in his creature's happiness" is not something he "receives from the creature" but "only the effect of his own work," just as "the sun receives nothing from the jewel that receives its light, and shines only by a participation of its brightness."[85]

### Deism, Providence, and the Planned Obsolescence of God

With the rise of Newtonian physics and its supply of orderly laws of nature, the continuing involvement of God with the world began to look a bit clumsy, perhaps clutchingly despotic or simply unnecessary.[86] To a deism keen on regularity and rationality, the laws of nature, which worked like clockwork, were testimony to a wise deity who made a creation that worked well on its own, thank you very much. Negatively, deism sought to discredit miracles,

80. Edwards, *WJE* 8:459.
81. Edwards, *WJE* 8:440. While these two ends imply one another and are ever finally one end, the happiness of creation is ordered to the glory of God (8:447). Thus it is proper to say that God makes himself his end, rather than the creation.
82. Edwards, *WJE* 8:533. See the discussion of the dynamic eschatology involved in this claim in the appendix, "Heaven Is a Progressive State" (8:706–38).
83. Edwards, *WJE* 8:527–29. Just so are we re-created in the spiritual image of God (8:529, n. 4).
84. Edwards, *WJE* 8:531. God is both "first efficient" and "last final cause" (8:467).
85. Edwards, *WJE* 8:446.
86. McClymond and McDermott, *Theology of Jonathan Edwards*, 108, 153; Marsden, *Jonathan Edwards*, 71.

revelation, particularity (the election of Israel, incarnation of Jesus, and pre-destination of the saints), and history. Positively, one could read deism as a grand appeal on behalf of creation, an attempt to honor the integrity of the cosmos as it stands—and perhaps, thereby, to honor its Creator. Perhaps God is such a magnanimous Creator that we have a case of "planned obsolescence," God having created so well that he has worked himself out of a job.

How did Edwards respond? By claiming that what makes creation creation is its non-self-sufficiency.[87] If it is true that "in him we live and move and have our being" (Acts 17:28), then creation abides in radical dependence on God.

Even saying that creation "abides" might be saying too much, though. Edwards suggests that all creaturely continuity, including personal identity, is "arbitrary"—meaning that it is radically dependent on God's will, not that it is fickle.[88]

> God's upholding created substance, or causing its existence in each successive moment, is altogether equivalent to an *immediate production out of nothing*, at each moment, because its existence at this moment is not merely in part from God, but wholly from him; and not in any part, or degree, from its antecedent existence. . . . Therefore the antecedent existence is nothing, as to any proper influence or assistance in the affair: and consequently God produces the effect as much from *nothing*, as if there had been nothing *before*. So that this effect differs not at all from the first creation, but only *circumstantially*.[89]

According to Edwards, God continuously creates the universe anew moment by moment.[90] Oliver Crisp likens it to a movie, in which "the world is like the photographic exposures run together on a reel of film and projected onto a cinematic screen."[91] This idea could be no further from a deist conception of a closed causal nexus in which, once having set the scene, God never intervenes.

---

87. Kathryn Tanner makes a roughly parallel move in anthropology in the opening chapters of her *Christ the Key*.

88. Were Edwards to have had the benefit of modern biology, he could have appealed to research that shows that all the cells in our bodies "replace" themselves at least every few years.

89. Edwards, *WJE* 3:402.

90. "God's *preserving* created things in being is perfectly equivalent to a *continued creation*, or to his creating those things out of nothing at *each moment* of their existence. If the continued existence of created things be wholly dependent on God's preservation, then those things would drop into nothing, upon the ceasing of the present moment, without a new exertion of the divine power to cause them to exist in the following moment" (Edwards, *WJE* 3:401–2).

91. Crisp, *Jonathan Edwards on God and Creation*, 162. A film isn't really a "moving picture," of course, but only "a reel of photographic stills run together at speed to give the illusion of motion and action across time" (25). Just so, one wonders if Edwards's world is in any meaningful sense historical.

And yet, it seems to render causality itself problematic. In a strange way, Edwards shared an intuition with David Hume (1711–76). In *A Treatise of Human Nature* (1739), Hume severed the nerve between cause and effect. Just because one thing happens after another in a similar way time and again cannot guarantee that the one *caused* the other. For Edwards, this problem was avoided by an appeal to God's loving will.[92]

Still, at what cost? If "each successive moment" amounts to "an *immediate production out of nothing* . . . not in any part, or degree, from its antecedent existence," what place does this leave to creation? It seems clear from this that Edwards is an occasionalist, believing "not only that God is the only true cause but also that the decisions and actions of creatures are only occasions for God's activity."[93] Rather than, with Aquinas, celebrating the "dignity of causality," Edwards stoutly concludes that "the antecedent existence is nothing, as to any proper influence or assistance in the affair." Leaving aside the question of whether this view might lead to skepticism (it sure *looks* like secondary causality holds), doesn't this underwrite a doctrine of creation unworthy of the God of love whose disposition is to communicate himself?[94]

We can see Edwards struggling to affirm this kind of divine freedom vis-à-vis creation and a strong account of the will of God, while also accounting for the Newtonian laws of nature in the following miscellany: "Indeed, in natural things, means of effects, in metaphysical strictness, are not proper causes of the effects, but only occasions. God produces all effects; but yet he ties natural events to the operation of such means, or causes them to be consequent on such means according to fixed, determinate and unchangeable rules, which are called the laws of nature. And thus it is that natural means are the causes of the exercises of natural principles."[95] To paraphrase: God is the sole efficient cause, and yet he wills that things work according to regular laws of nature. This is a particularly difficult passage, even bordering on incoherence. Can it be true both that God "produces all effects" and that "natural means are the causes of the exercises of natural principles"? From his other statements, it seems that Edwards denies that there are secondary causes.[96] We discern laws of nature, but not because one thing affects another;

92. Marsden, *Jonathan Edwards*, 456.
93. Daniel, "Edwards' Occasionalism," 3.
94. Downstream of this question is a theodicy question: if secondary causality is dismissed, moral responsibility seems to go out the door with it (Crisp, "Jonathan Edwards's Ontology," 11, cited in Daniel, "Edwards' Occasionalism," 3).
95. Edwards, *WJEO*, 18:157 (Misc. 629).
96. This is counter to the conclusion of McClymond and McDermott, *Theology of Jonathan Edwards*, 109–10.

instead, these laws reflect God's orderly continuous creation of the world.[97] "'Tis the glory of God that he is an arbitrary being," Edwards writes, "that originally he, in all things, acts as being limited and directed in nothing but his own wisdom, tied to no other rules and laws but the directions of his own infinite understanding."[98]

In this whole discussion, Edwards seems to want to draw our attention to the sheer gratuity of things. It is not so much that the world is on autopilot (to use the kind of mechanistic metaphor that would soon dominate the intellectual landscape). There is nothing automatic about it! The beautiful God, the "first Being, the eternal and infinite Being," the one who "is in effect, *Being in general*," upholds all, moves all, orchestrates all.[99]

Really, it is in catching something of Edwards's *mood* that we can best get his point. And his mood is doxological, a mood of wonder. In this respect, he bears a striking resemblance to G. K. Chesterton, who laughs off Hume's objection with the same ease as Edwards. Here is Chesterton:

> When we are asked why eggs turn to birds or fruits fall in autumn, we must answer exactly as the fairy godmother would answer if Cinderella asked her why mice turned to horses or her clothes fell from her at twelve o'clock. We must answer that it is magic. It is not a "law," for we do not understand its general formula. . . . All the terms used in the science books, "law," "necessity," "order," "tendency," and so on, are really unintellectual, because they assume an inner synthesis, which we do not possess. The only words that ever satisfied me as describing Nature are the terms used in the fairy books, "charm," "spell," "enchantment." They express the arbitrariness [!] of the fact and its mystery. A tree grows fruit because it is a magic tree. Water runs downhill because it is bewitched. The sun shines because it is bewitched.[100]

Salvation is magical, too. We are just as dependent on God in our conversion as we are in our creation and preservation. In fact, we are more so. Natural means may work according to the laws of nature, but "the actings of the Spirit of God in the heart are more arbitrary and are not tied to such and

97. Oliver Crisp writes, "Laws, such as they exist, are merely the operations of divine will" (in private correspondence with the author).

98. Edwards, *WJEO* 23:202–3.

99. Edwards, *WJE* 8:461.

100. Chesterton, *Orthodoxy*, in *Collected Works*, 1:255–56. Thanks to Melissa Schubert for drawing this connection to *Orthodoxy* for me in conversation. Also see Annie Dillard, who reflects on the passé character of Newtonian laws of nature in a world where Heisenberg's principle of indeterminacy posits our inability to know both a particle's velocity and position— the result being that "some physicists now are a bunch of wild-eyed, raving mystics" (*Pilgrim at Tinker Creek*, 205).

such means by such laws or rules."[101] Only those who have been given a taste for divine things by the sovereign Spirit will be saved. Deists and "Arminians" object against the injustice of a God who saves who he will and damns sinners who couldn't help themselves.[102] Edwards responds in his influential *Freedom of the Will* by distinguishing between natural and moral necessity, firmly asserting that people can do anything they want (thus no natural necessity) but that sinners want only to sin (hence a moral necessity to do so).[103]

## A Theology of the Third Article?[104]

Reflecting on a lifelong struggle with Friedrich Schleiermacher, Karl Barth supposed that one could write faithful theology from the third article of the Nicene Creed, one that would be "a theology predominantly and decisively of the Holy Spirit."[105] Barth did not follow this course, deeming it necessary in postwar Europe to attend to the second article and the one Word God has spoken in Christ.[106] Gerhard Sauter puts it nicely: "The major points within Barth's theology . . . rise out of [a] partnership of the First Commandment with the Second Article."[107]

One could say the same of Edwards, with a proper transposition—that his theology arose out of a partnership of the first commandment with the *third* article of the Nicene Creed. And this is just where the first commandment is most needed, in a day of languishing pluralism, when Spirit collapses into spirit. Edwards insists that we have no other gods before the Lord who is the Spirit. "Spirit" did not signal a broader category than "Christ" for Edwards, as it does for many contemporary theologies keen to uncover common ground among religions. To speak of the Spirit is to name God's work with and in his creation. Thus a Spirit-oriented theology would not be less trinitarian, nor would it shunt Christology offstage in an effort to bring the Spirit into the

101. Edwards, *WJEO* 18:157 (Misc. 629).
102. "Arminian" is the broad term applying to lapsed Calvinists with less severe doctrines of sin and salvation who would soon become Unitarians.
103. Edwards, *WJE*, 1:156–62.
104. Parts of this final section appeared initially in Matt Jenson, "'Where the Spirit of the Lord Is, There Is Freedom': Barth on Ecclesial Agency," *Pro Ecclesia* 24 (2015): 517–37. Used by kind permission of *Pro Ecclesia*.
105. Barth, *Theology of Schleiermacher*, 278.
106. Critics continue to squabble over the character of Barth's pneumatology. The majority report finds him wanting, though see Ben Rhodes, "Spirit of Fellowship." On the one Word of God over against all other words, see the Barmen Declaration, largely written by Barth (accessible in Busch, *Barmen Theses Then and Now*).
107. Sauter, *Eschatological Rationality*, 131.

limelight. While the Spirit has his "own" work in the economy of salvation, his chief task is to communicate the gifts and graces Jesus has purchased in his life, death, and resurrection. These graces can never be severed from the presence of the Spirit of Jesus. Edwards goes even further:

> The Holy Spirit *is* the great purchase of Christ. God the Father is the person of whom the purchase is made; God the Son is the person who makes the purchase, and the Holy Spirit is the gift purchased. The sum of all those good things in this life, and the life to come, which are purchased for the church, is the Holy Spirit. And as this is the great purchase, so it is the great promise of God and Christ.[108]

> The nature of the Holy Spirit is love; and it is by communicating himself, or his own nature, that the hearts of the saints are filled with love or charity. Hence the saints are said to be "partakers of the divine nature" [II Pet. 1:4].[109]

Kathryn Tanner riffs on the Augustinian description of the Spirit as the love of the Father and Son, referring to the Spirit as the "exuberant, ecstatic carrier" of their love to us.[110] Her concern is to personalize their love and so establish the distinct personhood of the Spirit. Similarly, Edwards shuttles back and forth between a description of the gifts and graces of God and the Spirit who bears but also just *is* those gifts and graces. "All graces are only the different ways of acting of the same divine nature, as there may be different reflections of the light of the sun. . . . Grace in the soul is the Holy Ghost acting in the soul, and there communicating his own holy nature. As it is in the fountain, it is all one and the same holy nature; and only diversified by the variety of streams sent forth."[111]

For all Edwards's attention to individual piety, his aim in the *Religious Affections* is to identify the saving work of the Spirit, not religious experience per se. Yes, Edwards is an experimental theologian, one whose empirical mind hankered after phenomena to sort and analyze. But he is far from a psychologist of religion—or, if he is that, he is so only in the interests of a doctrine of the Holy Spirit that accounts properly for his work in the conversion of sinners. "Religious experience" as such is of no interest to him. He is after (to borrow the title of another of Edwards's works) the *distinguishing* marks of the Spirit, those pious evidences that God himself is at work in the regeneration of those chosen in Christ before the foundation of the world.

---

108. Edwards, *WJE* 8:353–54 (emphasis added).
109. Edwards, *WJE* 8:132.
110. Tanner, *Jesus, Humanity and the Trinity*, 14.
111. Edwards, *WJE* 8:332.

But how to characterize that work? In his collection of sermons on 1 Co-rinthians titled "Charity and Its Fruits," Edwards makes two key distinctions within the "gifts and operations of the Spirit." Such gifts may be common or saving, and they may be ordinary or extraordinary.[112] Extraordinary gifts (like the more miraculous apostolic gifts) are "great privileges," but they do not inhere in a person. "They are something adventitious . . . precious jewels, which a man carries about him. But true grace in the heart is, as it were, the preciousness of the heart . . . by which the very soul itself becomes a precious jewel." The ordinary, saving grace, which is the Spirit, is far better.[113]

Though the extraordinary gifts draw a crowd, their glory fades. Saving grace abides, however, because the Spirit makes himself at home in the believer. "The Spirit of God is given to the true saints to dwell in them, as his proper lasting abode; and to influence their hearts, as a principle of new nature, or as a divine supernatural spring of life and action. . . . And he is represented as being there so united to the faculties of the soul, that he becomes there a principle or spring of new nature and life."[114] When the Spirit makes his home in the saints, he brings them life.

This is a fitting answer to the calamity of the fall, where death entered in when Adam and Eve turned from God, and "the Holy Spirit, that divine in-habitant, forsook the house."[115] At creation, God had implanted two kinds of principles in humanity, an inferior, natural kind oriented to self-love and made up of "natural appetites and passions" and a superior, spiritual kind oriented to the love of God, "wherein consisted the spiritual image of God, and man's righteousness and true holiness." The former "are like fire in an house; which, we say, is a good servant, but a bad master; very useful while kept in its place, but if left to take possession of the whole house, soon brings all to destruction."[116] At the fall, our passions swept through the house. And all hell broke loose. As in Ezekiel's vision, where the glory of the Lord departs from the temple and Israel languishes in exile, a sinful humanity suffers the absence of the Spirit and banishment from Eden. In conversion, however, the Holy Spirit returns to the temple, precisely as believers are placed in Jesus the temple.[117]

Man in his first estate had the Holy Spirit, but he lost it; [it was thrown] away. But a way is found out that it may be restored, and now it is given a second

112. Edwards, *WJE* 8:152–53.
113. Edwards, *WJE* 8:157–58.
114. Edwards, *WJE* 8:200.
115. Edwards, *WJE* 3:382.
116. Edwards, *WJE* 3:381–83.
117. See Perrin, *Jesus the Temple*.

time, never again to depart. The Spirit of God is so given to the saints as to become theirs. . . . They [i.e., "our first parents"] had no proper right or sure title to the Spirit. It was not finally given and made over to our first parents as it is to believers in Christ. . . . Christ is become theirs [i.e., the regenerate's], and therefore his fullness is theirs, his Spirit is theirs, the Spirit of Christ is their purchased and promised possession.[118]

[Christ's] Spirit [is] united to them, as a principle of life in them; they don't only drink living water, but this living water becomes a well or fountain of water, in the soul, springing up into spiritual and everlasting life (John 4:14), and thus becomes a principle of life in them.[119]

The Spirit is so fully given that he becomes a fountain of life within us, and we become partakers of his nature.[120] He is so fully given as to be our "possession." Barth would have recoiled at such language. For him the Spirit is the promise of future possession, whereas for Edwards the Spirit is in addition the present possession of the promised Spirit. Both Barth and Edwards insisted that the Spirit remains Lord, but Barth's nervousness about human tendencies to manipulate the Spirit, to reduce him to a possession by appropriating his gifts for people's own ends (thereby violating the first commandment), led him to emphasize the outstanding character of the promise. The Spirit as *arrabōn* ("guarantee," "down payment"; see 2 Cor. 1:22, 5:5; Eph. 1:14) seems to operate in Barth more as a promissory note than a down payment.

Edwards's daring language suggests none of the theological hand-wringing that characterized Barth's discussions of piety. For him, we can—indeed *must*—say that the Spirit "belongs" to believers. That is precisely what distinguishes them from the unregenerate. The Spirit is a new divine principle within them and has somehow become native to them. Furthermore, this gift, unlike the original presence of the Spirit, is inalienable; the saints will persevere. Whereas Barth wants to protect the Spirit's lordship by refusing

118. Edwards, *WJE* 8:354.
119. Edwards, *WJE* 8:200.
120. Edwards, *WJE* 8:158:
> The Spirit of God communicates itself much more in bestowing saving grace than in bestowing those extraordinary gifts. . . . The Spirit of God may produce effects on many things to which it does not communicate itself. So the Spirit of God moved on the face of the waters, but not so as to impart himself to the waters. But when the Spirit by his ordinary influences bestows saving grace, he therein imparts himself to the soul in his own holy nature; that nature on account of which he is so often called in Scripture the Holy Ghost, or the Holy Spirit. By his producing this effect the Spirit becomes an indwelling vital principle in the soul, and the subject becomes a spiritual being, denominated so from the Spirit of God which dwells in him and of whose nature he is a partaker [II Pet. 1:4]. Yea, grace is as it were the holy nature of the Spirit of God imparted to the soul.

to speak of our possessing the Spirit, Edwards wants to magnify his saving grace, signaling the depth of his work. What could be more complete than for "his Spirit" to be "theirs"? Possession might be likened to marriage, in which there is potential for abuse and manipulation, but where the accent falls on mutual self-giving. Having become one flesh, writes Martin Luther, the soul and Christ share all things in common. "Accordingly the believing soul can boast of and glory in whatever Christ has as though it were its own, and whatever the soul has Christ claims as his own."[121] The Spirit of Jesus brings with him wedding gifts too, a luxurious concatenation of graces in conversion.[122] In "Heaven Is a World of Love," Edwards describes such mutuality in terms of possession: "All shall have *propriety* one in another. Love seeks to have the beloved its own, and divine love rejoices in saying, 'My beloved is mine, and I am his,' as Cant. 2:16."[123]

In asking whether we might refer to Edwards's theology of the third article, I mean to draw attention to the particular pneumatological urgency of his writing.[124] With all eyes on the awakenings of the Connecticut River Valley, Edwards consistently and carefully insisted that the indwelling presence of the Holy Spirit made all the difference. He diametrically opposed the deist conviction that revealed religion added nothing of substance to natural religion and would have balked at Schleiermacher's later claim that "piety is an essential component of human nature."[125] Only the Spirit can give one eyes to see the glory of God in the face of Christ.[126] Only the Spirit can create and cultivate a relish for divine things. As it is in conversion, so will it be at the end: "They shall have this Beatific Vision of God because they will be full of God, filled with the Holy Spirit of God."[127] To possess the Spirit is to be blessed.[128] Blessed are those whose hearts the Spirit has purified, for they have seen God.

121. Luther, *LW* 31:351.
122. See Edwards, *WJE* 8:327–34.
123. Edwards, *WJE* 8:380.
124. "In all of Edwards' major works, the Holy Spirit is seen to play a leading role within the lives of people flourishing in the world. . . . This pneumatological theme might well be called the defining feature of his ministry" (Sweeney, *Edwards and the Ministry of the Word*, 164). In his state church context, the conversion that only the Spirit can accomplish is essential.
125. Schleiermacher, *Christian Faith* §46.1. For an apologetic construal of the same claim, see his *On Religion*.
126. This is certainly a theology of Word and Spirit, but Edwards emphasizes the sight of the beauty and excellence of the Word, which is a gift of the Spirit.
127. Edwards, *WJE* 8:725.
128. "The Apostle's blessing, wherein he wishes 'the grace of the Lord Jesus Christ, the love of God the Father, and communion of the Holy Ghost' [2 *Corinthians* 13:14], contains not different things but is simple: 'tis the same blessing, even the Spirit of God, which is the comprehension of all happiness" (Edwards, *WJEO* 13:346 [Misc. 223]).

# 10

# A PIETIST
# OF A HIGHER ORDER

*Schleiermacher, Jesus, and the Heart of Religion*

On May 4, 1980, I sat by the fireplace in our living room as my parents explained the message of salvation to me. They told me that Jesus died for my sins and that if I received him, I would have eternal life. I prayed sincerely that Jesus would forgive my sins, and I asked him to come into my heart. And so, at four years old, I was born again. We celebrated my spiritual birthday with a cupcake and a candle. I drew a rainbow—the sign of God's promise—and my mom placed the drawing and the candle, with a note of the date, in a small wooden frame.[1]

That's my testimony, or at least the moment of decision. It's a familiar pattern to many Christians who have learned to tell the story of their lives in terms of how they have come to know Jesus as Savior and Lord. And it confirms Friedrich Schleiermacher's insight that "each person who can thus specify the birthday of his spiritual life and relate a wonderful tale of the origin of his religion, which appears as an immediate influence of the deity and as a movement of its spirit, can be unique, through whom something special is supposed to be said."[2]

1. At least, that's how I remember it. I'm certain we sat by the hearth. We framed the candle and drawing of a rainbow, with the date written by my mom. But was there a cupcake? Maybe it was a cake? All I know for sure is there was a birthday candle. Memories are so fragile.
2. Schleiermacher, *On Religion*, 107.

Schleiermacher could tell a similar story. He was fourteen when his family visited the town of Gnadenfrei. His father had experienced a profound spiritual awakening when he met a community of Moravian Brethren there five years earlier. Now he brought his family for a few months in the spring of 1783, and young Friedrich came alive spiritually. He came to think of this time as the birthday of his "higher life."[3]

But within four years, while still a teenager, Schleiermacher wrote an anguished letter to his father, in which he confessed: "I cannot believe that He, who called Himself the Son of Man, was the true, eternal God: I cannot believe that His death was a vicarious atonement, because He never expressly said so Himself; and I cannot believe it to have been necessary, because God, who evidently did not create men for perfection, but for the pursuit of it, cannot possibly intend to punish them eternally, because they have not attained it."[4] Schleiermacher had lost his faith. He pled with his father to pray that God would give him faith again, if his father did believe that, "without this faith, no one can attain to salvation in the next world, nor to tranquillity in this."

His father replied two weeks later, stern and impassioned in his concern. "Who has deluded thee, that thou no longer obeyest the truth, thou, before whose eyes Christ was pictured, and who now crucifiest him? . . . Strong and powerful are the conceit and pride of your heart, but not so your arguments, which a child could refute."[5] It pained Schleiermacher to write his initial letter and to break his father's heart, but he needed to face his doubts head-on. Whereas his father saw pride at the source of his doubts, Fritz (as his family called him) pointed to weak proofs of doctrine, the suppression of dissent at his Brethren school, the "absence of every opportunity for investigating these subjects [himself]," and his "natural predilection for whatever is evidently suppressed."[6] His were real doubts, and they required real answers. "How could I believe on mere assertion, that all the objections raised by our modern theologians, and supported by critical, exegetical, and philosophical reasons, were nought? How could I avoid reflecting on these matters, and, alas! how can I help that the result of my reflections has turned out so unhappily for myself!"[7] Schleiermacher knew he no longer belonged among the Brethren. He lamented, "A dissenter like myself cannot be tolerated here; they fear that I may impart to others the dangerous poison, and wherever I may be I

3. See Redeker, *Schleiermacher*, 8–9.
4. Schleiermacher, *Life of Schleiermacher*, 1:46–47.
5. Schleiermacher, *Life of Schleiermacher*, 1:50.
6. Schleiermacher, *Life of Schleiermacher*, 1:54.
7. Schleiermacher, *Life of Schleiermacher*, 1:55.

can no longer be considered as a member of the Brotherhood."[8] He would leave the Brethren school and move to the more freethinking University of Halle. "I should not be able to get rid of my doubts did I remain here," he wrote to his father, "whereas, while studying theology at Halle, this may very probably occur."[9]

Fifteen years later, Schleiermacher returned to Gnadenfrei, the site of his conversion. He wrote to a friend: "Here my awareness of our relation to a higher world began. . . . Here first developed that basic mystical tendency that saved me and supported me during all the storms of doubt. Then it only germinated, now it is full grown and I have again become a Moravian, only of a higher order."[10]

What had happened in the meantime? How could Schleiermacher claim continuity with the Pietism of his youth—the Pietism so dear to his father—after his abandonment of belief in the deity of Christ and his sacrifice for sin? Even in reminiscence, one feels the force of that rift; it was a "storm" that laid waste to his life. His letter, though nostalgic, does not suggest a mere return to an earlier form. His "basic mystical tendency" was only a seed back then, but it has grown into a mature tree.

In what follows, we seek to make sense of this claim that Schleiermacher had "again become a Moravian [or Pietist, to use a roughly equivalent term], only of a higher order." The Moravian Brethren represented one stream of Pietism, a renewal movement that arose in a context of established religion. Only one hundred years after Martin Luther and John Calvin, the embers of religion had grown cold. In response, these serious Christians began to gather in small groups (often illegally) to study the Bible intensively and encourage one another in the love of God and neighbor. Their piety centered on a warm, personal relationship with Jesus, the sanctifying work of the Spirit in which faith leads to love, and the ministry of the common priesthood.

We can best understand Schleiermacher as a liberal offshoot of Pietism, carrying on its Jesus-piety and its *Herzreligion* ("heart religion"). Like Edwards, he was primarily concerned with the religious affections. Indeed, no one has sought more comprehensively and consistently to theologize from religious experience than Schleiermacher, and no one has sought to do so with more attention to the twin contexts of Christianity and modernity. As will become clear, I believe he made some disastrous mistakes along the way. But he also saw things that those with more traditional doctrinal commitments missed,

---

8. Schleiermacher, *Life of Schleiermacher*, 1:54.
9. Schleiermacher, *Life of Schleiermacher*, 1:54.
10. Cited in Redeker, *Schleiermacher*, 9.

and his work is meticulous and worthy of careful consideration. Furthermore, his very consistency is instructive for others who draw—knowingly or not—from Pietism and the priority it places on religious experience.

## His Life[11]

Friedrich Daniel Ernst Schleiermacher was born on November 21, 1768, in Breslau in the Silesia region of Germany (now Wrocław in Poland). He came from a family of Reformed pastors, but perhaps the most significant early religious influence came in the spiritual awakening his father, Gottlieb, experienced when Fritz was nine years old. From that point, "Christ's expiatory sacrifice on the cross became the basis of [Gottlieb's] certainty of salvation and fountain of a new life. He now lived with his Savior in intimate communion and converted his wife and children to the Brethren's faithfulness in Christ."[12] Fritz came to share his father's faith when he, too, encountered the Moravian Brethren; and he spent nearly four years in Brethren schools at Niesky and Barby. Moravian Pietism was less penitential in orientation than other forms of Pietism, characterized instead by "joy in the assurance of salvation and the vividly experienced communion with the Savior." One of Pietism's chief concerns was that people not simply assent to right doctrines but also "taste and see that the LORD is good" (Ps. 34:8), and the Brethren "not only wanted the students to learn about the Christian teaching of sin and grace but to experience these for themselves."[13]

Schleiermacher lost his mother while he was away at school, just before his fifteenth birthday. Over the course of his schooling, he also lost his faith—or at least that is how he put it at first. We know that he departed from some of the central beliefs shared by his father and the Brethren; his father and the Brethren made it clear that, in their judgment, he had left the faith. Of necessity, and in order to think through his doubts, Schleiermacher left the Moravians for the University of Halle, where he pored over Immanuel Kant's writings.[14] From there, he moved in with his uncle Samuel, a pastor, in the town of Drossen. Though this was a depressing time, Schleiermacher engaged in independent philosophical study and started writing. He then took a position as private tutor in the household of Count Dohna in Schlobitten in East Prussia, where "a strong intellectual and spiritual recovery took place" over the next couple

11. For a more detailed account, see Redeker, *Schleiermacher*; Tice, *Schleiermacher*.
12. Redeker, *Schleiermacher*, 9.
13. Redeker, *Schleiermacher*, 10.
14. Redeker, *Schleiermacher*, 15.

years. Martin Redeker writes of how Schleiermacher was "taken by the cordial
and open atmosphere of the Dohna family" and afterward "became a virtuoso
in friendship and in the deeper sharing of human fellowship."[15]

From this point, Schleiermacher's life became a flurry of activity. He pas-
tored—at Landsberg (1794–96), as a chaplain at the Charité Hospital in Berlin (1796–1801), at Stolpe (1802–4), and, finally, at Trinity Church in Berlin
(1808–34). Trinity, where Schleiermacher was copastor, was the first church
in Prussia to unite Lutheran and Reformed congregations, which it did on
March 31, 1822.[16] Schleiermacher preached weekly for over forty years, and
"a great many of his friends regarded Schleiermacher's preaching as his best
work."[17] His published sermons make up a third of his collected works.[18] He
published a hymnal, too, the *Berliner Gesangbuch*.

Schleiermacher also taught—first at the University of Halle (1804–6), where
he was the lone Reformed professor on an all-Lutheran faculty and also served
as University Preacher. In a harbinger of things to come, he was called every
name under the sun, "an atheist, a Spinozist, a Herrnhuter [i.e., a Moravian],
a Reformed heretic, and a crypto-catholic."[19] In a time of tremendous up-
heaval, he collaborated with Wilhelm von Humboldt in the founding of the
University of Berlin, establishing the modern university as a place of critical,
scientific inquiry in a moment when education threatened to devolve into
technical training. Schleiermacher wrote the influential *Occasional Thoughts
on Universities* (from which Humboldt adopted many of his key principles),
served as secretary of the organizing committee, and organized the theology
faculty.[20] At Berlin, he taught nearly everything in theology, and quite a bit
in philosophy. Half of his courses were in New Testament exegesis, but he
never lectured on the Old Testament.[21]

He could do it all. We consider Schleiermacher a theologian, but he was
also one of the great Plato scholars of the age, translating almost all of Plato's
dialogues and writing hundreds of pages of introduction to this work. (Perhaps this is why one student remarked that he "taught theology as Socrates
would have taught it had he been a Christian."[22]) His hermeneutical writings
justly merit him being called the "father of modern hermeneutics." Something
of a bon vivant, Schleiermacher lived at the center of Berlin's cultural life,

15. Redeker, *Schleiermacher*, 18.
16. Tice, *Schleiermacher*, 15.
17. Redeker, *Schleiermacher*, 200.
18. Redeker, *Schleiermacher*, 199–200.
19. Tice, *Schleiermacher*, 11.
20. See Redeker, *Schleiermacher*, 95–97; Tice, *Schleiermacher*, 15.
21. Tice, *Schleiermacher*, 15.
22. Redeker, *Schleiermacher*, 79.

frequenting the salons in the home of Henriette Herz. He could write a series of apologetic speeches to religion's "cultured despisers" because he spoke a common language with them, the Romantic language of feeling and intuition.[23] He was a good friend. The warm domesticity and childlike wonder that he imagines in his dialogue *Christmas Eve Celebration* captures his conviviality and eagerness to affirm all that is good in humanity.[24]

For years, Schleiermacher cultivated an attachment to Eleonore Grunow, who was unhappily married to a Berlin clergyman. Though they considered themselves "secretly betrothed," Grunow stayed with her husband.[25] Schleiermacher eventually married the widow of a friend, Henriette von Mühlenfels. He was forty; she was twenty-one and "respected Schleiermacher like a father."[26] They were very different, but "each was very devoted to the other in his or her own distinct way."[27] Henriette brought two children into the marriage, and the couple had four children of their own, including one, Nathanael, who died young of diphtheria. "It was a warm, busy household," Terrence Tice writes, "the marriage was loving and sound, and he was much engaged with this large family."[28] Schleiermacher died of pneumonia on February 12, 1834. Conservative reports estimate that between twenty thousand and thirty thousand Berliners, including the king, mourned his passing.

**Feel for Yourself!**

In 1784 Immanuel Kant entered an essay competition in a Berlin magazine, answering the question, "What is enlightenment?" In the essay, Kant issued a call to freedom: "Enlightenment is the human being's emergence from his self-incurred minority. Minority is inability to make use of one's own understanding without direction from another. This minority is *self-incurred* when its cause lies not in lack of understanding but in lack of resolution and courage to use it without direction from another. *Sapere aude!* Have courage to make use of your *own* understanding! is thus the motto of enlightenment."[29]

This is easier said than done. "It is so comfortable to be a minor!" We are lazy and cowardly and would much prefer someone else to do our thinking for us. "If I have a book that understands for me, a spiritual advisor who

---

23. See Schleiermacher, *On Religion*.
24. See Schleiermacher, *Christmas Eve Celebration*.
25. Redeker, *Schleiermacher*, 69–70.
26. Redeker, *Schleiermacher*, 210.
27. Redeker, *Schleiermacher*, 211.
28. Tice, *Schleiermacher*, 13.
29. Kant, "What Is Enlightenment?," 17.

has a conscience for me, a doctor who decides upon a regimen for me, and so forth, I need not trouble myself at all. I need not think, if only I can pay; others will undertake the irksome business for me."[30] But this behavior is childish. It may be right for children to do what their parents say, but at some point wise parents ease their children into making decisions and discerning a life path—in short, to thinking for themselves. This is good parenting; the chances are that children who are never given a chance to think on their own will depart radically from what they had been forced to believe. It seems reasonable to conclude that, if we think for ourselves, we will be more likely to arrive at well-reasoned and firmly held conclusions. For Kant, the mature person, the enlightened adult, has put away traditional authorities and begun to navigate the world according to the inner light of reason.

In 1799 Schleiermacher published a series of speeches on religion, addressed to its "cultured despisers."[31] The speeches are an "intellectual seduction" in which Schleiermacher seeks to persuade the antireligious cultural elite that the thing they hate is not the thing itself.[32] The thing on which they heap their scorn is a phantom, or at most the outer shell containing the kernel of religion. True religion is not metaphysics or morals, belief or behavior. "Religion's essence is neither thinking nor acting, but intuition and feeling. It wishes to intuit the universe, wishes devoutly to overhear the universe's own manifestations and actions, longs to be grasped and filled by the universe's immediate influences in childlike passivity."[33] As such, religion is a "sensibility and taste for the infinite."[34] One doesn't *arrive* at religion, as if it could be deduced at the end of a train of thought or achieved through moral endeavor. Religion is an immediate experience, native to humanity, an intuition, taste, and feeling that precedes any reflection on it or expression of it in word or deed. Religion is not catechesis or Bible study. It cannot be taught, only evoked or aroused in another. Religion is the silent awe we experience from the top of a mountain, the wonder of motherhood, the warm joy of Christian fellowship. Words fail, being "only shadows of our intuitions and feelings," but there is "a music among the saints that becomes speech without words, the most definite, most understandable expression of what is innermost."[35] Eduard, a character in *Christmas Eve Celebration*, echoes these sentiments when he says that "every fine feeling comes completely to the fore only when we have found the right

30. Kant, "What Is Enlightenment?," 17.
31. Schleiermacher, *On Religion*.
32. Richard Crouter, introduction to Schleiermacher, *On Religion*, xxx.
33. Schleiermacher, *On Religion*, 22.
34. Schleiermacher, *On Religion*, 23.
35. Schleiermacher, *On Religion*, 57, 75.

musical expression for it." In fact, he suggests, "we can well dispense with particular words in church music but not with the singing himself."[36]

To speak of the Christian religion, then, is not first to lay out the central tenets of the Christian faith; it is to evoke the experience of faith itself, the experience of the *Christus praesens*, which later comes to be expressed. Dogma derives from, but is not itself, religion. Some dogmas "are merely abstract expressions of religious intuitions," Schleiermacher writes, "and others are free reflections upon original achievements of the religious sense." In any case, the priority of this religious sense is clear: "Miracles, inspirations, revelations, feelings of the supernatural—one can have much religion without coming into contact with any of these concepts." Still, as he benignly adds, "persons who reflect comparatively about their religion inevitably find concepts in their path and cannot possibly get around them."[37] Reflection is inevitable and appropriate, so long as one recognizes that it is only reflection on the prior feeling that is the essence of religion.

Religion is a firsthand experience. Here Schleiermacher parallels Kant. Whereas Kant exhorts his readers to think for themselves, Schleiermacher celebrates the truly religious who feel for themselves. Whatever the handing down of the Christian faith might entail, it can never render religion secondhand. Schleiermacher acknowledges that nearly everyone will need a mediator, "a leader who awakens his sense of religion from its first slumber and gives him an initial direction. But this is supposed to be merely a passing condition. A person should then see with his own eyes and should himself make a contribution to the treasures of religion; otherwise he deserves no place in its kingdom and also receives none."[38] Mediation is a temporary necessity. All a mediator can do is wake someone up and point him in the right direction. It is then up to the person to see for himself and offer this vision to others. To change metaphors, we might say that the mediator is a midwife, necessary only to facilitate the birth of religion in the soul.[39]

This understanding of religion has far-reaching implications. Consider the question of Scripture: "Every holy writing is merely a mausoleum of

36. Schleiermacher, *Christmas Eve Celebration*, 29, 30. In a letter to his wife, Schleiermacher writes that "in the church, music and singing are the common bond between, and the proof of the emotions stirring, in all, and this community of feeling again heightens the emotions of each individual" (Schleiermacher, *Life of Schleiermacher*, 2:158).

37. Schleiermacher, *On Religion*, 48.

38. Schleiermacher, *On Religion*, 50.

39. Schleiermacher, the eminent Plato translator, echoes Plato's *Meno* on this point. Both question whether something (in Plato's case virtue, in Schleiermacher's religion) can be taught and instead suggest that the most another person can do is play the role of midwife in another's life.

religion, a monument that a great spirit was there that no longer exists; for if it still lived and were active, why would it attach such great importance to the dead letter that can only be a weak reproduction of it? It is not the person who believes in a holy writing who has religion, but only the one who needs none and probably could make one for himself."[40] The most we can expect of holy writings is that they testify to great religious figures of the past. We miss the point entirely if we devote ourselves to a holy book, keeping vigil at a monument to religion, when what we should be doing is carrying the flame of religion in ourselves. If holy writings can offer some inspiration, they run the risk of distracting us from the true business at hand. They are certainly not necessary, and often fatal to religion.

It might seem that such an account would yield a solitary religion, but Schleiermacher insists that religion is inherently social. "Religion hates to be alone," he writes. "When it develops in you, when you realize the first traces of its life, then enter at once into the one and indivisible communion of saints that embraces all religions and in which alone each can prosper."[41] This communion of saints is a community of mutual giving and receiving, in which each person "steps forth to present his own intuition as the object for the rest, to lead them into the region of religion where he is at home and to implant his holy feelings in them; he expresses the universe, and the community follows his inspired speech in holy silence."[42] Schleiermacher rejects a sharp distinction between clergy and laity in favor of a "society of religious people" that is "a priestly people, a perfect republic where each alternately leads and is led."[43]

Religion is historical, too. "Religious people are thoroughly historical; that is not their least praise, but it is also the source of their great misunderstandings."[44] In fact, history is "the highest object of religion," in its inclination to "join the different moments of humanity to one another and . . . divine the spirit in which the whole is directed."[45] Religion is concerned with all that is, being a taste for the infinite and an intuition of the universe, and it seeks to express and communicate itself—hence its historical orientation. But it is also nontransferable. Each of us must feel for ourselves, and all too often, in attending to history, we give over the responsibility for religion to others—hence the misunderstandings.

40. Schleiermacher, On Religion, 50.
41. Schleiermacher, On Religion, 124.
42. Schleiermacher, On Religion, 75.
43. Schleiermacher, On Religion, 77, 76.
44. Schleiermacher, On Religion, 112.
45. Schleiermacher, On Religion, 42.

In any case, we are "born with the religious capacity as with every other," according to Schleiermacher, though it is all too often blocked, buried, or bound.[46] It seems that art and religion find common cause here, in that both seek to awaken people to the infinite. Schleiermacher can conclude that, despite themselves, religion's cultured despisers are "the rescuers and guardians of religion, even though unintentionally so."[47]

All of this might seem far from traditional Christian faith. But while the idiom and tenor of Schleiermacher's writing ("rhapsodic," some scholars call it) change in his mature theological work, many of the features of these early speeches remain. One of the consequences of Kant's commitment to thinking for oneself is that he would consider religion only within the bounds of reason alone.[48] Likewise, Schleiermacher resolved to consider Christian faith within the bounds of feeling alone.

## Starting with Piety

When Schleiermacher turns to Christian doctrine in his *Christian Faith*, he begins with the conviction that "the church is nothing other than a community in relation to piety."[49] As in the *Speeches*, Schleiermacher conceives of piety in terms of feeling: "The piety that constitutes the basis of all ecclesial communities," he writes, "regarded purely in and of itself, is neither a knowing nor a doing but a distinct formation of feeling, or of immediate self-consciousness."[50] Before we reflect on it and form beliefs, before it moves us to action, we experience piety internally as a feeling. The decision of the translators of the new English edition to call the book *Christian Faith* rather than *The Christian Faith* points to the priority of pious feeling over belief for Schleiermacher; his primary interest is in the experience of faith, not the contents of belief. Accordingly, then, doctrines are not extrapolations from Scripture but attempts at "translating internal stirrings of mind and heart into thought" or "conceptions of Christian religious states of mind and heart presented in the form of discourse."[51]

Like Calvin, Schleiermacher eschews speculation in dogmatics, considering it an illicit prying into things that fall outside the purview of Christian theology. He rails against all forms of scholasticism, which intermingles

---

46. Schleiermacher, *On Religion*, 59.
47. Schleiermacher, *On Religion*, 70.
48. See Kant, *Religion within the Bounds of Reason Alone*.
49. Schleiermacher, *Christian Faith* §3.1.
50. Schleiermacher, *Christian Faith* §3.
51. Schleiermacher, *Christian Faith* §13.P.S.; §15.

philosophy and theology and so distracts theology from its proper object. Schleiermacher is clear that theology does not depend on philosophy but proceeds instead from piety; it has no other interests but expressing and examining religious feeling.[52] In sharp contrast to Calvin, though, whose outlawing of speculation is meant to confine dogmatic inquiry to Scripture, Schleiermacher considers the proper study of his dogmatics to be religious feeling *rather than* Scripture. Since its object of inquiry is piety, not Scripture, "dogmatic science has an 'empirical' character that distinguishes it both from a biblical theology and from philosophical speculation."[53] Dogmatics is "empirical" insofar as it examines the (historical, changing) piety of the Christian church as it is expressed in doctrine. Piety finds expression in words, and it arises from words (including the words of Scripture); so we ought not presume a sharp dichotomy between experience and language for Schleiermacher.[54] Like Calvin, and Paul before him, Schleiermacher could proclaim that "faith comes from hearing, and hearing through the word of Christ" (Rom. 10:17). "Christianity has always and everywhere been spread by means of proclamation alone."[55]

To be sure, Schleiermacher does not pit experience against Scripture—but neither does he submit experience to a biblical test. What authority Scripture does have is itself a function of the religious feeling of the earliest Christians. "The Bible is the original interpretation of the Christian feeling," Schleiermacher writes in a letter, "and for this very reason so firmly established that we ought not to attempt more than further to understand and develop it."[56] Schleiermacher's attention to piety does not entail a neglect of Scripture, even if it does change the role the Bible plays in his dogmatics. (We should note that by "Bible," Schleiermacher means the New Testament. The Old Testament "is only a superfluous authority" for dogmatics, not least because Christianity is a new religion, neither a "modification" nor a "reforming continuation" of Judaism; in fact, Christianity "can no more be viewed as a continuation of Judaism than as a continuation of heathenism."[57]) The

52. Schleiermacher, *Christian Faith* §16.P.S.

53. Gerrish, *Continuing the Reformation*, 151.

54. This is one of the chief burdens of Christine Helmer's work on Schleiermacher. Language is, for her, "the vehicle by which Christ is communicated in the church." She goes on to say, "Experiences that refer through words to their subject matter and words that open possibilities for experience—both are the given ingredients of religious life" (*Theology and the End of Doctrine*, 115, 131).

55. Schleiermacher, *Christian Faith* §15.2.

56. Schleiermacher, *Life of Schleiermacher*, 2:282.

57. Schleiermacher, *Christian Faith* §27.3; §12.2. Schleiermacher approaches a Marcionite position here, suggesting that the Old Testament be placed after the New Testament "as an

New Testament is a norm not as a source of doctrine but as the written testimonies of those who first received the impression of Jesus and were taken up into his redemptive life. We should not say that a doctrine "belong[s] to Christianity because it is contained in Scripture—since, on the contrary, it is contained in Scripture only because it belongs to Christianity."[58] And so the New Testament is a norm according to the spirit, not the letter; after all, it too is merely, but really, religious feeling expressed in speech.[59] And thus, the letter of Scripture is revisable.

If "we ought not to attempt more than further to understand and develop" the original interpretation of the Christian feeling, Schleiermacher insists on the latter point: "This right of development, however, I, as a Protestant theologian, will allow no one to defraud me of."[60] On the one hand, even the first Christians who experienced Christ's redemption might not have always expressed their piety with perfect clarity in their writing, so their work might require development. (Didn't Luther suggest as much in adding "alone" to his translation of Rom. 3:28—"by faith alone"?) Furthermore, we are historical creatures, and our consciousness of God will change as we do. So, while we share with the first Christians a piety flowing from Christ the Redeemer, our piety will be shaped by the course of history and the circumstances in which we find ourselves.[61] And precisely because the Christian self-consciousness is ever changing, dogmatics is revisionary.[62] Theology need not be afraid of revising previously held beliefs, because they might have been falsely articulated, or simply obsolete, given our current consciousness of God. Schleiermacher is "liberal" first in this sense, that he claimed a freedom in relation to tradition, a "right of development" that "implied that authorized ecclesiastical doctrines are not irreformable." Brian Gerrish writes that "the dogmatic task, as [Schleiermacher] understood it, included the critique of ancient dogmas and, where necessary, the discarding of them as antiquated."[63] This was a fundamentally *Protestant* impulse, according to Schleiermacher, but whereas Luther and Calvin appealed to the Word of God over against ecclesial tradition, Schleiermacher appealed to "norms from outside the entire Christian heritage" over

appendix, since where it is placed at present does unclearly set forth the presumption that one would have to work through the entire Old Testament in order to get onto the right path to the New Testament" (§132.3).

58. Schleiermacher, *Christian Faith* §128.3.

59. He speaks of "an unevangelical deference to the letter" (*Christian Faith* §135.1).

60. Schleiermacher, *Life of Schleiermacher*, 2:282.

61. Schleiermacher examines specifically Protestant confessions because they give evidence of the current religious consciousness of the Protestant churches.

62. See Gerrish, *Continuing the Reformation*, 13.

63. Gerrish, *Tradition and the Modern World*, 44–45.

against tradition and Scripture.[64] Many of his doctrinal revisions—which are frequently radical—follow from his judgment that the doctrines in their received form do not arise directly from piety.

## What the Heart Knows

What, then, is the content of piety? Schleiermacher begins with a broad account, one not restricted to Christianity: "However diverse they might be, what all the expressions of piety have in common, whereby they are at the same time distinguished from all other feelings—thus the selfsame nature of piety—is this: that we are conscious of ourselves as absolutely dependent or, which intends the same meaning, as being in relation with God."[65] While we experience a relative freedom and a relative dependence with relation to the world—that is, we experience ourselves as partially able to act on and partially acted upon by the world—we experience ourselves as *absolutely* dependent upon another, upon God. This itself is sufficient to supplant all the proofs of God that philosophers and theologians have devised; the minute we are conscious of ourselves as absolutely dependent, we feel that there is a God.[66] And for Schleiermacher, this "'whence' holds the true primary meaning of the term 'God.'"[67] He is the one from whom we are, the one on whom our very being rests at each moment.

God is the omnipotent Creator, the one who has made all there is out of nothing and who continually and perfectly preserves his creation. Our awareness of ourselves as "absolutely dependent" on God "wholly coincides with our discernment that precisely all of this is conditioned and determined by the interconnected process of nature."[68] Divine preservation and natural causation "are the same thing, only regarded from different viewpoints."[69] In a precise sense, this is the best of all possible worlds, as it has been flawlessly created and preserved by God as the arena of redemption. Creation is always already ordered to its end in Christ: "The Christian belief that everything is created with a view to the Redeemer implies that everything is already ordered by means of creation, in both a preparatory and a retrospective way, in relation to the revelation of God in the flesh and for the fullest possible transmission

---

64. Gerrish, *Tradition and the Modern World*, 7. "The problem, for the liberal," Gerrish writes, "is no longer 'Scripture and tradition' but 'tradition (including Scripture) and modernity.'"
65. Schleiermacher, *Christian Faith* §4.
66. Schleiermacher, *Christian Faith* §33.
67. Schleiermacher, *Christian Faith* §4.4.
68. Schleiermacher, *Christian Faith* §46.
69. Schleiermacher, *Christian Faith* §46.2.

of that revelation to the whole of human nature for the purpose of forming the reign of God."[70] This understanding suggests that we "view the divine government of the world only as *one* causality, directed toward but *one* aim." We immediately err when we think of providence as "a special case of divine causality that is somehow simply divorced from its connection with the whole."[71] God wills one thing—redemption.

This conclusion has far-reaching implications within Schleiermacher's theology. Positively, it brokers intellectual peace, allowing us to "establish an eternal covenant between the living Christian faith and completely free, independent scientific inquiry, so that faith does not hinder science and science does not exclude faith."[72] Given God's perfect creation of all there is and creation's absolute dependence on him, there can be no deep conflict between science and religion; we are free to follow the evidence wherever it leads.[73] Negatively, Schleiermacher's doctrine of creation eliminates the possibility of miracles. After all, miracles would seem to compromise divine omnipotence. Rather than testifying to the mighty power of God, they might suggest a lack of foresight on the Creator's part. If a miracle is an emergency intervention in a crisis, we might ask whether God could have avoided the crisis by having done a better job at the outset. Or perhaps he's fallen asleep on the job. "It cannot be religious to think of God as intervening in the world," Gerrish writes, "for this could only mean that, for a fleeting moment at least, the world had slipped out of God's control and taken an unintended course."[74] But in fact, as our knowledge of nature grows, our recourse to miracle shrinks; Schleiermacher suspects that "miracle" is merely a provisional name we have given to occurrences in the world we do not yet understand.[75] For this reason, Schleiermacher concludes that "the most comprehensive exposition regarding divine omnipotence would occur in terms of a conception of the world that would make no use of this notion of miracle at all."[76] Furthermore, appeals for miracles too often neglect the intricacy of natural causation; we fail to

70. Schleiermacher, *Christian Faith* §164.1.
71. Schleiermacher, *Christian Faith* §164.3. "The object of providential care is for him the system, not directly the individual" (Gerrish, *Continuing the Reformation*, 162).
72. Schleiermacher, *On the Glaubenslehre*, 64.
73. See here Plantinga, *Where the Conflict Really Lies*.
74. Gerrish, *Prince of the Church*, 65.
75. Frances Young points to a flaw in this model, or at least to its time-bound character, in light of more recent scientific developments: "'Interventionism' assumes that the self-determined natural order is a closed reality, occasionally disrupted by God poking his finger in, as it were; but the 'clock-work' analogy has long since given way to a recognition of the complexity and plasticity of things, within which the potential influence of the divine Other may not necessarily be ruled out as a hidden factor" (*God's Presence*, 405).
76. Schleiermacher, *Christian Faith* §47.1.

recognize that "every absolute miracle would severely disturb the entire interconnected process of nature."[77]

What, then, becomes of prayer? Schleiermacher is clear that prayer is not meant to influence God's action, much less to change his mind. As the omnipotent Creator, he has already established the world in perfect working order for his redemptive purposes, and as the one on whom we are absolutely dependent, he can in no way be influenced by us, which would imply a mutuality that does not exist.[78] No, prayer does not change God, and it does not change external circumstances; it changes us.[79] In prayer, we become aligned to God, learning to pray, with Jesus, "not my will, but yours, be done" (Luke 22:42). Ultimately, it is impious to seek to disrupt the way things hold together. This view need not suggest a quietism, in which one takes a laissez-faire attitude, but it does suggest a limit to what we might hope for from God. While I can hope and pray for the coming of his kingdom, I cannot and may not desire that his kingdom will come in any other way than naturally, historically. And even this prayer is significant, not because it moves God to bring his kingdom, but because it is an instance of God's doing so, as my heart and mind become aligned to his reign.

Still, we fail, time and again, to live from this feeling of absolute dependence on God. If "piety is a general feature of human life," distinctly Christian piety recognizes "as sin all that has hindered the free development of God-consciousness."[80] While he rejects the notion of a fall (it is not one of "those propositions, which are expressions of our Christian self-consciousness"), Schleiermacher discerns a universal human "susceptibility to sin that is present in [an] individual before any deed of the individual's own" and which "consists of a complete incapacity for good, which incapacity is removed, in turn, only through the influence of redemption."[81] It's no use blaming anyone for this defect; responsibility for sin is shared by all and each. "We are conscious of sin, in part, as grounded in ourselves, and, in part, as having its ground somewhere beyond our own individual existence."[82] Because "original sin is so much the personal fault of every individual who takes part in it," we ought to represent it "as the collective act and collective fault of the

---

77. Schleiermacher, *Christian Faith* §47.2. For this reason, Nathan Hieb suspects that Schleiermacher's system leads to "an implicit rejection of resurrection" ("Precarious Status of Resurrection," 414).

78. See Schleiermacher, *Christian Faith* §147.2.

79. See Gerrish, *Prince of the Church*, 65–66.

80. Schleiermacher, *Christian Faith* §61.4; §66.1.

81. Schleiermacher, *Christian Faith* §72.3; §70.

82. Schleiermacher, *Christian Faith* §69.

human race."[83] It is the fault of all of us and the fault of each of us. Keep in mind that sin, for Schleiermacher, occurs wherever the God-consciousness is hindered. It is a moral category, but it does not merely name transgressions of divine law. It includes any movement away from absolute dependence on God, whether coming in the form of heinous crime or arising from mindless distraction.[84] There truly is none who is righteous, no, not one. It should come as no surprise, then, that "whatever communion with God might exist there rests upon a communication from the Redeemer, and we call this *grace*."[85]

## The Appearance of the Redeemer

The specifically Christian form of piety rests on our experience of Christ the Redeemer. Schleiermacher writes that "the distinctive nature of Christianity consists in the fact that all religious stirrings . . . are referred to the redemption that has occurred through Jesus of Nazareth."[86] This focus leads him to narrow the scope of theology further: "Now, since all Christian piety rests on the appearance of the Redeemer . . . nothing touching upon the Redeemer can be set forth as genuine doctrine that is not tied to his redemptive causality and that does not permit of being traced back to the original and distinctive impression that his actual existence made."[87] Notice the specificity of Schleiermacher's methodological point, which flows from a judgment and supplies a criterion. What the church experiences is redemption (there's the judgment), and so doctrinal claims must remain within the ambit of that redemption (there's the criterion).

Who is the Redeemer, then, and how does he redeem? "The nature of redemption consists in the fact that the previously weak and suppressed God-consciousness in human nature is raised and brought to the point of dominance through Christ's entrance into it and vital influence upon it."[88] This passage captures much of what Schleiermacher has to say on the subject. Human nature has always been conscious of God, but before Christ was born this consciousness was weak, diffuse, and suppressed. It lacked the strength

83. Schleiermacher, *Christian Faith* §71.
84. See Schleiermacher, *Christian Faith* §66.2. At times, Schleiermacher will describe sin in terms of the dominance of the flesh ("that is, the totality of the soul's so-called lower forces") over the spirit, or the "hindering of spirit's determinative force . . . caused by autonomous activity of one's sensory functioning" (§66.2).
85. Schleiermacher, *Christian Faith* §63.
86. Schleiermacher, *Christian Faith* §22.2.
87. Schleiermacher, *Christian Faith* §29.3.
88. Schleiermacher, *Christian Faith* §106.1.

to determine human existence, and we participated in its further compromise by burying it beneath our sensory preoccupations. In entering and influencing human nature, Christ raised our consciousness of God to the point where it gained dominance, reaching a height it had never before known. Christ completes God's creation of humanity as the "second Adam," in whom God-consciousness is perfect and absolute. He is like us in every way, except for sin, and *just so*—by living from a perfect consciousness of God, in absolute dependence on God in every way—he is "the originator and author of this more complete human life, or the completion of the creation of humanity."[89]

Still, how are we to explain the appearance of the Redeemer? Schleiermacher acknowledges the collective nature of sin, which thwarts the development of God-consciousness in humanity. He recognizes that "an unfettered strength of God-consciousness in Jesus cannot be conceived on the basis of the collective life of sin, because sin is naturally propagated in that collective life. Rather, Jesus can have become as strong in his God-consciousness as he himself made evident, only apart from the collective life of sin." While he refuses to call this a miracle and sees no reason to posit a virgin birth, Schleiermacher does write that the appearance of the Redeemer came about through "an initiating divine activity as being something supernatural, but, at the same time," he adds, "we posit a vital human receptivity by virtue of which the supernatural activity can then become something historically natural."[90] Jesus's life required an initial divine activity, but "from birth onward his strengths would gradually have unfolded and would have formed in their appearance from a null-point on to proficiencies in the order natural to humankind." Even Christ's God-consciousness developed gradually, though it always reigned over his self-consciousness.[91] All this is an instance of "the maxim that underlies our presentation throughout—that the beginning of the reign of God is supernatural but becomes natural as soon as it appears."[92] And so the Redeemer's appearance is not "*absolutely* supernatural," in that it is "grounded in the original equipment of human nature" and "prepared by

---

89. Schleiermacher, *Christian Faith* §89.1.

90. Schleiermacher, *Christian Faith* §88.4. See *Christian Faith* §97.2 for Schleiermacher's discussion of the supernatural origin of Christ as it relates to Mary's virginity.

91. Schleiermacher, *Christian Faith* §93.3. Kevin Hector writes, "Jesus was born not with an absolutely powerful God-consciousness, therefore, but with a sufficiently powerful one—sufficiently powerful, that is, to outpace the development of his sensible consciousness" (*Theological Project of Modernism*, 114). This developmental orientation is in keeping with Schleiermacher's keen opposition to any docetic diminishing of the full humanity of Christ. On this concern, see Kelsey, *Schleiermacher's Preaching*, 104.

92. Schleiermacher, *Christian Faith* §13.1. Kevin Vander Schel reads Schleiermacher's theology through the lens of this maxim in his excellent *Embedded Grace*.

all that had preceded it" in such a way that Christ appeared "in the fullness of time."[93] All that preceded Christ prepared for him, and all that followed him was influenced by him.

Because redemption is a matter of Christ's elevating human nature by "tak[ing] up persons of faith into the strength of his God-consciousness," what matters for redemption is that he lived throughout his life in the strength of that God-consciousness.[94] Christ redeemed us, that is, by living a sinless life, ever open and receptive to God, and drawing us into that life. To live without sin is to live in absolute dependence on God, and Jesus's sinless perfection "consists simply in a pure will that is oriented to the reign of God."[95] In the New Testament, redemption is frequently tied to the death of Christ, usually recalling the sacrifice for sins in the Old Testament (see Gal. 3:13; Eph. 1:7; Heb. 9:12, 15). But for Schleiermacher, it is as he lives his life that Christ redeems us. Catherine Kelsey captures this beautifully:

> What did Christ *do* that results in our redemption? He made his own inner life visible, a life in which every impulse was motivated by the divine will, a life in which his relationship with God took up, processed, and directed every physical input and every thought and action. In making his inner life visible, he evoked our receptivity to being taken up into that same relationship with God. Finally, he secured all those who are taken up into this relationship into a community, a physical presence for one another and for the world. The redeemed now experience blessedness.[96]

Christ redeems by living in the strength of his God-consciousness and proclaiming himself as the way, the truth, and the life that God has introduced in the world for our redemption.[97] The death of Jesus is, strictly speaking, irrelevant to redemption. Or to put it differently, Jesus died not in order to redeem us but as a consequence of his redemptive life, as lived out in the face of those who opposed the reign of God.[98]

---

93. Schleiermacher, *Christian Faith* §13.1 (emphasis added). Abraham Kunnuthara draws attention to the natural rather than arbitrary time of Christ's appearing in light of Gal. 4:4 in *God's Work in History*, 25.

94. Schleiermacher, *Christian Faith* §100.

95. Schleiermacher, *Christian Faith* §122.3.

96. Kelsey, *Thinking about Christ with Schleiermacher*, 70.

97. Christ's self-proclamation is the "*one* source from which all Christian doctrine is derived" (Schleiermacher, *Christian Faith* §19.P.S.). Christ proclaims himself as the one who "inaugurates a higher life, and in [whose redemptive activity] the relation to God becomes the principle of human living" (Vander Schel, *Embedded Grace*, 162).

98. See Kelsey, *Schleiermacher's Preaching*, 60. This is reflected in the paucity of sermons that Schleiermacher preached on the death (and resurrection) of Jesus. Of 185 sermons on

Recall that only those claims that can be traced back to Jesus's "redemptive causality" can be put forth as genuine doctrine. Since Jesus's "redemptive causality" is limited to his sinless life lived in the strength of his God-consciousness, this limitation narrows the scope of Christology considerably. The preexistence, death, resurrection, ascension, and return of Christ cannot, then, and do not belong to Christian doctrine. Schleiermacher denies Christ's preexistence, and he suggests that "the facts regarding Christ's resurrection and ascension and the prediction of his return to judge cannot be set forth as genuine components of the doctrine of his person."[99] Because we can know the Redeemer apart from these facts, "the correct impression of Christ can exist, and also did so, without taking any notice of these factual claims."[100] After all, if we believe, as Schleiermacher does, that people were redeemed during Jesus's life and ministry, we could not suppose that a knowledge of his death or resurrection was necessary to experience that redemption.[101] And so, Schleiermacher concludes (with reference to the resurrection and ascension) that "our faith in Christ and our living communion with him would be the same even if we had no knowledge" of these facts or if they were different.[102] To which we can only reply with Paul: "If Christ has not been raised, then our preaching is in vain and your faith is in vain" (1 Cor. 15:14).

## The Influence of the Redeemer

Recall Schleiermacher's claim that "the nature of redemption consists in the fact that the previously weak and suppressed God-consciousness in human nature is raised and brought to the point of dominance through Christ's entrance into it and vital influence upon it."[103] We have considered Christ's entrance into the world, his redeeming life and teaching, but how does he influence the world?

---

the Synoptic Gospels, 146 cover the time between Jesus's baptism and arrest (DeVries, *Jesus Christ*, 79).
    99. Schleiermacher, *Christian Faith* §99.
    100. Schleiermacher, *Christian Faith* §99.1.
    101. See Kelsey, *Thinking about Christ with Schleiermacher*, 11, 65.
    102. Schleiermacher, *Christian Faith* §170.3. And so Hieb judges that "the historicity of the resurrection while not denied is dispensable within Schleiermacher's doctrine of redemption" ("Precarious Status of Resurrection," 403). Dawn DeVries writes that Easter "has less to do with an empty tomb or a resuscitated corpse than with the living presence of the Redeemer in the lives of his own." In his *Life of Jesus*, Schleiermacher "mantains that Jesus did not really die, but only lapsed into a coma-like state from which he recovered because of the strength of his God-consciousness" (Dawn DeVries, commenting on Schleiermacher in *Servant of the Word*, 79, n. 1).
    103. Schleiermacher, *Christian Faith* §106.1.

Although "influence" seems a tepid term, for Schleiermacher the influence of Christ is stronger than first appears. It is central to the redemptive work of Christ and is the way in which we are taken up into that work: "In Christianity the redemptive influence of its founder is what is originative, and the community persists only under this presupposition and only as communication and spreading of that redemptive activity takes place."[104] The redemptive influence of Christ is the basis of the church, and the church exists to spread that influence—that is, Christ's *continuing* influence is as important for the life of the church as his initial influence on his disciples. Christ's relationship to members of the community he founded is unique among the religions. Moses and Muhammad were "elevated out of the crowd of equal or less different human beings, arbitrarily as it were, and what they have received as divine teaching and rule for life is received no less for themselves than it is received for others." But "within Christianity all other persons stand in contrast to Christ, viewed as the sole Redeemer and as the Redeemer for all and as one who is not thought to have been in need of redemption in any way, at any time."[105] Whereas Moses and Muhammad recede behind the teaching and rule of life they bring, Jesus remains central to Christian piety. And the uniqueness of Christ, who stood in no need of redemption, signals the unique relationship he has with Christians. The Christian life is lived under the influence of Christ. Schleiermacher writes that "being-continually-and-receptively-open-to-the-influence-Christ-makes-on-one and being-continually-active-with-that-desire-for-the-reign-of-God together comprise the new human being's life-process."[106]

Again, though, how does he do it? How does the Redeemer exert a continuing vital influence on human nature? Schleiermacher insists here, too, on his controlling maxim of the supernatural-becoming-natural. Jesus developed naturally, even if his origin was supernatural. His influence, too, is natural and historical.[107] Schleiermacher seeks to steer between two extremes with this maxim, as it is applied to Christ's influence. On the one hand, he wants to avoid a magical account of things (associated with "supernaturalism") that "dissolves all conformity to nature in the continuing action of Christ," so that Christ's influence is immediate and in no way "dependent on the establishment of a communal body."[108] Christ's influence "becomes magical

<hr>

104. Schleiermacher, *Christian Faith* §11.4.
105. Schleiermacher, *Christian Faith* §11.4.
106. Schleiermacher, *Christian Faith* §112.1.
107. "Likewise, in his origin Christ is supernatural, but he also becomes natural, as a genuine human being. The Holy Spirit and the Christian church can be treated in the same way" (Schleiermacher, *On the Glaubenslehre*, 89).
108. Schleiermacher, *Christian Faith* §101.3; §100.2.

as soon as it is not transmitted through community of life with Christ," and "from its origin onward the efficacious action of Christ is to be thought of as taking place within this historical form of nature."[109] On the other hand, Schleiermacher seeks to avoid an empirical account of things (associated with "rationalism") that "posits the same efficacious action entirely on a level with that found in ordinary sense perception, [and] thus does not lay a foundation for any supernatural origin and for any distinctiveness that would differentiate it."[110] Here Christ's influence is evacuated into the church, with the church being understood strictly as a community like any other. Thus Christ is no different from any other influential figure in the past.

Reflecting back on the first edition of *Christian Faith*, Schleiermacher wrote to his friend Dr. Lücke, "I would have wished to construct the work so that at every point the reader would be made aware that the verse John 1:14 ['The Word became flesh and dwelt among us'] is the basic text for all dogmatics, just as it should be for the conduct of the ministry as a whole."[111] John 1:14 is, for Schleiermacher, a biblical correlate for his maxim, so that the Word becoming flesh entails that "the divine really does work redemptively in and through natural conditions and not otherwise."[112] Christ, "as well as his entire efficacious action, stands under the law of historical development, and that development is completed through its gradual spread outward from the point of his appearance over the whole of humanity."[113] A question arises here, though: Can we really speak of the Redeemer's ongoing work if it can occur only through natural conditions? At times, this position seems difficult to maintain. "For us now, however," he writes, "instead of his personal efficacious action there is only the efficacious action of his community, insofar as the picture of him still present in the Scriptures has likewise originated and endures only through this community." While he goes on to claim that "this working of the community to bring forth the same faith is also simply the working of that personal perfection of Jesus himself," this might be simply wishful thinking.[114] After all, "we have nothing more to expect from the direct personal influences of Christ," and "these influences of Christ cannot proceed from him directly" today.[115]

One way to look at the question of how Christ continues to influence his community after his earthly life is by considering the role of the Spirit. The

109. Schleiermacher, *Christian Faith* §101.3; §101.4.
110. Schleiermacher, *Christian Faith* §101.3.
111. Schleiermacher, *On the Glaubenslehre*, 59.
112. Tice, *Schleiermacher*, 64.
113. Schleiermacher, *Christian Faith* §89.2.
114. Schleiermacher, *Christian Faith* §88.2.
115. Schleiermacher, *Christian Faith* §127.2.

Johannine Jesus tells his disciples that it is to their advantage that he departs, because after he departs he will send "the Spirit of truth," who "will guide [them] into all the truth" (John 16:13). Schleiermacher discerns a parallel between Christ and the church, in that in both God indwells human nature. (The difference is that in Christ, God dwells individually, while in the church, God dwells corporately.) "The Holy Spirit is the uniting of the divine being with human nature in the form of the common spirit that animates the collective life of faithful persons," Schleiermacher writes.[116] As a "common spirit," this one enlivens and represents the essential character of this community; in this sense it resembles the "spirit" of any corporate body. But the Spirit is also the indwelling God who, by indwelling his people, conforms them to Christ. "In its purity and fullness the Christian church, being animated by the Holy Spirit, is formed as the perfect image of the Redeemer; every regenerate person is a complementary, constituent part of this community."[117] It is this common spirit in which the church is "the bearer and perpetuator of the redemption brought about through Christ."[118]

In light of the way in which the church is "formed as the perfect image of the Redeemer," Richard Niebuhr has argued that it is better to describe Schleiermacher as a "Christo-morphic" theologian than as a "Christocentric" one.[119] Schleiermacher's account of the supernatural-becoming-natural is one in which the Christian community and indeed all of history are molded into the shape of Christ. Just as Christ's life was permeated by his God-consciousness, so will the life of God's people and, eventually, all of humanity be. The emphasis on Christ's form (*morphē*) draws our attention to Christ as the ideal of humanity, the one from whom humanity takes its cues. More needs to be said, though, for a mold can be used to cast a sculpture and then tossed aside. In Schleiermacher's account, the mold continues—somehow—to influence those who have been cast in his image. Consider, by contrast, three exemplary historical figures: Socrates, Francis of Assisi, and Rosa Parks. They are all influential, each in different ways. And they are all dead. Despite the powerful influence each of these people exerts, we would hardly describe them as living and active today in the communities that look to them for inspiration. "Influence," as Schleiermacher understands it, seems to require Christ to be personally present, to be himself active in the ongoing molding of people in his image.

And so, at times Schleiermacher attributes the work of grace directly to Christ. "Christ is alone active in conversion and the individual is simply in

116. Schleiermacher, *Christian Faith* §123.
117. Schleiermacher, *Christian Faith* §125.
118. Schleiermacher, *Christian Faith* §170.1.
119. Niebuhr, *Schleiermacher on Christ and Religion*, 212.

the condition of living receptivity," he writes.[120] At other times, Schleiermacher speaks of this grace being mediated in the church, which is "the bearer and perpetuator of the redemption brought about through Christ."[121] In a discussion of Christ's kingly office Schleiermacher writes that "his spiritual presence is still mediated today through the written word and by the picture of his nature and work laid down within it. Even today, however, his governing influence is not, as it were, a merely mediated and derivative one on that account."[122] Even more strongly, Schleiermacher writes that "today Christ's self-presentation is conveyed by those who proclaim him, though since they are appropriated by him as his instruments and consequently the activity of proclamation proceeds from him, this activity is always essentially his own."[123] This wording sounds like a classic Reformed account of Christ's presence mediated by Word and church. We enter community with Christ as we encounter the church, but in saying this we must be clear that "in no way would Christ retain a passive stance therewith and stay in the shadows over against the church."[124] Schleiermacher seems keen to avoid any eclipse of Christ by the church in writing that "just as Christ is a successor to no one in the communal body governed by him, but he is the sole founder of it, he too has no successor and no surrogate within that communal body." But whereas Calvin might appeal to the risen and ascended Lord, who continues to reign over his church in the world, Schleiermacher continues differently: "That is to say, just as he exercises his dominion by means of ordinances that originate in him, and he himself has declared them to be sufficient, so it all comes down to their correct application."[125] It seems that Schleiermacher wants to preserve a robust account of Christ's presence and action in the church, but without tying this closely to the doctrines of resurrection and ascension. Puzzlingly, he claims that "the spiritual presence promised by [Jesus] and everything that he says about his perpetual influence on those surviving him is mediated by nothing originating from these two factual claims [i.e., the claims that Jesus was raised from the dead and ascended to the right hand of the Father]."[126] Despite Schleiermacher's antispeculative claim that resurrection is not something that

---

120. Schleiermacher, *Christian Faith* §112.2.

121. Schleiermacher, *Christian Faith* §170.1.

122. Schleiermacher, *Christian Faith* §105.1. And so, even if the reading and preaching of Scripture cannot serve as a doctrinal source, it can serve as the instrument through which Christ communicates his perfection and blessedness and so serve "as part of the redeeming work of Jesus Christ" (Nimmo, "Schleiermacher on Scripture," 76).

123. Schleiermacher, *Christian Faith* §108.5.

124. Schleiermacher, *Christian Faith* §127.2.

125. Schleiermacher, *Christian Faith* §105.1.

126. Schleiermacher, *Christian Faith* §99.1.

we can directly infer from piety, the Christian consciousness of redemption seems to imply just this conclusion, that the Redeemer who is present and active in the church is so as the risen and ascended Jesus.

## But Is Jesus *God*?

In doubting the deity of Christ, Schleiermacher lost the faith of his youth. And yet, he cherished the Redeemer throughout his life and wrote a magnificent account of Christian faith. What became, then, of this earlier doubt? Does Schleiermacher, finally, believe that our Redeemer is God?

In order to redeem, Jesus must be like us in every way without sin—that is, he must live in and from "an absolutely strong God-consciousness."[127] Schleiermacher goes on to say that "to attribute an absolutely strong God-consciousness to Christ and to ascribe to him a being of God in him are entirely one and the same thing."[128] To discern Jesus's perfect receptivity to God, his utter openness to the divine will, just *is* to discern God in Christ. What are we to make of this claim?

It is surprisingly difficult to determine whether Schleiermacher believes Jesus is God. Scholars are divided.[129] On the one hand, he subjects traditional formulations of Christian doctrine to incisive critique. Considering the hypostatic union, he quickly ferrets out the linguistic difficulties with terms like "nature" and "person," exposing the logical muddle that threatens in (particularly Chalcedonian) language. In keeping with his desire to purify theology of scholasticism, Schleiermacher suggests the avoidance of expressions like "divine nature" and "duality of natures in the same person."[130] He finds the attribution of divine names to Christ in Scripture ambiguous, pointing out that it is difficult "to distinguish the utterances of a deep reverence that is not in the proper sense divine from strict devotion." And those divine activities, such as creation and preservation, seem to indicate Christ's divinity is "ascribed to Christ only in such a way that it must remain doubtful whether

127. Schleiermacher, *Christian Faith* §89.2.
128. Schleiermacher, *Christian Faith* §94.2.
129. Terrence Tice says he doesn't (*Schleiermacher*, 37); Kevin Hector says he does ("Actualism and Incarnation"). Tice and Hector can be seen as two ends of a spectrum along which scholars place Schleiermacher in relation to the tradition. Tice celebrates Schleiermacher's truly liberal theology, free from traditional constraints, whereas Hector finds in Schleiermacher a postmetaphysical theology that is far more amenable to traditional commitments than Schleiermacher himself realized. We might situate Brian Gerrish somewhere between the two, as he sets Schleiermacher in the context of Reformed theology as one who continued the Reformation.
130. Schleiermacher, *Christian Faith* §96.3.

he is not to be effective cause only insofar as he is final cause."[131] Perhaps it is not that all things were created *by* Jesus, but that they were created *for* him.

On the other hand, Christ is utterly unique among human beings, dignified precisely by the divine presence within him. That absolute strength of Jesus's God-consciousness "must be regarded to be a steady living presence" and thus a "true" or "actual being of God in him."[132] Already in the *Speeches* Schleiermacher can speak of this presence in terms of Christ's "divinity": "The consciousness of the uniqueness of his religiousness, of the originality of his view, and of its power to communicate itself and arouse religion was at the same time the consciousness of his office as mediator and of his divinity."[133] At times, Schleiermacher points to biblical precedent. While he resolutely refuses to speak of Jesus's "divine nature," he nevertheless refers to "the being of God in the Redeemer . . . as his innermost primary strength, from which all his activity proceeds and which links all the elements of his life together."[134] He concludes that "if this expression departs greatly from the former scholastic language, nonetheless it rests in equal measure on the Pauline expression 'God was in Christ' and on the Johannine expression 'The Word became flesh,' for 'word' is the activity of God expressed in the form of consciousness and 'flesh' is the general designation for what is organic."[135] The question seems to be whether Schleiermacher objects to the truth claim that Jesus is God or (only) to the traditional metaphysical explanations for how this is so.[136]

131. Schleiermacher, *Christian Faith* §99.P.S. He makes the same move in an 1832 study of Col. 1:15–20, where "he conceives the role of the historical Jesus in creation in a way that avoids claiming Jesus' preexistence. . . . All is dependent on Christ, not as the mediator of creation, but as its consummation" (Helmer, "Consummation of Reality," 121, 122).

132. Schleiermacher, *Christian Faith* §96.3; §94.

133. Schleiermacher, *On Religion*, 120.

134. Schleiermacher, *Christian Faith* §96.3. Similarly, he speaks of "God-consciousness in [Christ's] self-consciousness as determining every element of his life steadily and exclusively" and of "this complete indwelling of Supreme Being as [Christ's] distinctive nature and his innermost self" (§94.2).

135. Schleiermacher, *Christian Faith* §96.3. Note that even here Schleiermacher avoids any suggestion that the preexistent second person of the Trinity is the Word who became flesh. "The word become flesh is God's word spoken and enacted in Christ, not a preexistent part of the Godhead become incarnate" (Tice, *Schleiermacher*, 76).

136. Hector argues for the latter alternative on the basis of Schleiermacher's actualism, concluding that he holds a surprisingly high Christology, one amenable to more traditional aspects of Christology (like preexistence) than Schleiermacher realized. See Hector, "Actualism and Incarnation." Helmer asks, "Is it true that only one type of metaphysic can establish the parameters required for a true exposition of doctrine?" (*Theology and the End of Doctrine*, 142). Her point is well taken, though the burden of proof falls on those who would introduce a new metaphysic in which to convey the truths of the faith. Schleiermacher rejects the metaphysics of Nicaea of Chalcedon, but he fails to retain their insight into the deliverance of the Scriptures *and* the experience of the early Christians, that "the Word was with God, and the Word *was* God" (John 1:1, my emphasis).

Schleiermacher's genuine love for Jesus makes this a particularly difficult question to answer, but I am convinced that, in the end, Schleiermacher did not believe that Jesus is God. This is something of a cumulative case. It begins with the early letter to his father in which he writes, "I cannot believe that He, who called Himself the Son of Man, was the true, eternal God."[137] This is a strong denial, and as far as I can see Schleiermacher never recants. Secondly, while we have no reason to doubt the sincerity of his exegesis, its deflationary effect further evinces a reverence of Jesus that stops short of identifying him as God. Finally, Schleiermacher's quiet avoidance of Jesus-worship, no matter how often he expresses affection for the Redeemer, suggests a radical revision of the Christian faith: We worship God and celebrate his work in Christ, but we do not worship Christ himself.[138] This seems to leave Jesus on the side of humanity, no matter how much we reverence him and no matter that God uniquely and completely indwells him.[139] And thus it fails to do justice to John's vision:

> And I heard every creature in heaven and on earth and under the earth and in the sea, and all that is in them, saying,
>
> > "To him who sits on the throne and to the Lamb
> > Be blessing and honor and glory and might forever and ever." (Rev. 5:13)

In its praise, all of creation witnesses to this one who is *with* God *as* God (see John 1:1).

We can test this conclusion against the Gospel of John, Schleiermacher's favorite gospel.[140] At times, the Johannine Jesus beautifully exemplifies Schleiermacher's account of a strong God-consciousness: "I can do nothing on my

137. Schleiermacher, *Life of Schleiermacher*, 1:46.

138. In *God's Work in History*, Kunnuthara points out that "one would not see any reference or allusion to worship of either Jesus or the Holy Spirit in his writing" (45). "One may find in Schleiermacher's sermons expressions that may mislead one to think there is endorsement for Jesus-worship," but this typically "means only utmost respect and nothing more" (45, n. 8). "Schleiermacher does not use even *die Gottheit* [divinity] for Jesus, unless it is in the sense of being a carrier of the divine activity. For him, 'divinity' denotes God's active presence in human consciousness. . . . The perfect humanity and divinity are roughly identical in Jesus; they are only two respects of thinking almost the same thing from two different angles" (45–46).

139. I agree with David Law's judgment that, for Schleiermacher, "Christ does not share in the very being of God, but is a human being who is wholly centred on God. 'Divinity' is a circumlocution for a quality of Jesus' human existence, rather than an ontological statement about the character of his being" (*Kierkegaard's Kenotic Christology*, 36). Thanks to George Hunsinger for this reference. This seems to be the case in Scheiermacher's sermon "The Redeemer: Both Human and Divine" (*Servant of the Word*, 36–42).

140. Here I recognize that I am not following Schleiermacher's methodology but am subjecting his claim to a biblical criterion, to which I can only reply that his method is not mine. Also note Kelsey's remark that, though it was his favorite gospel, "Schleiermacher regularly

own. As I hear, I judge, and my judgment is just, because I do not seek my own will, but the will of him who sent me" (John 5:30). But despite the continual deference of Jesus to the one he called Father, he claims a startling equality with him, a claim that leads to his death. The Father "has given all judgment to the Son," Jesus says, "that all may honor the Son, just as they honor the Father" (5:22). As we have seen, Schleiermacher suspects the biblical language of "honoring" to fall short of attributing deity to Jesus, but the strict parallel between the honor accorded to Father and Son here ("just as") suggests that we view the honor given to both in the same light. "This was why the Jews were seeking all the more to kill him," the evangelist writes. "Not only was he breaking the Sabbath, but he was even calling God his own Father, making himself equal to God" (5:18). The upshot of these statements of Jesus is that, as Son, Jesus has an utterly unique relationship with the Father. He is the Father's *only* Son, and just so he is (the "Jews" were right on this score) equal to God. While it indeed seems Jesus has a perfect, undiluted, unimpeded God-consciousness, this is not enough to establish his *equality* with God and the *in principle* (not just in fact) unique character of his relationship with God as the only Son of the Father (cf. 3:16).

## A Pietist of a Higher Order?

In drawing together some of the strands of Schleiermacher's life, Gerrish writes that "if religion was the center of Schleiermacher's feeling, it took the quite specific form of a *Heilandsliebe* ('love of the Savior'), given to him from beyond anything the human spirit could generate for itself. At least, that was Schleiermacher's own judgment: the fact that he took the unusual risk of subjecting so delicate an experience to critical scrutiny was what made him, as he said of himself, a 'pietist (*Herrnhuter*) of a higher order.'"[141] Schleiermacher's spiritual achievement is truly remarkable. An inveterate questioner and a true genius, he managed to navigate a minefield of doubt and arrive at the far side with a deep love for Jesus. And even then, rather than intellectually retreating to the warm hearth of piety, he brought out all the tools of criticism to bear on the religion of the heart. Another Romantic, William Wordsworth, wrote that "we murder to dissect," implying that the division and separation that comes with criticism is an inherently death-dealing activity.[142] But somehow,

---

interpreted John in contradiction to some of the text's strongest themes" (*Schleiermacher's Preaching*, 103).

141. Gerrish, *Continuing the Reformation*, 149.

142. This line is from Wordsworth's poem "The Tables Turned," available at https://www.poetryfoundation.org/poems/45557/the-tables-turned.

Schleiermacher was able to delight and dissect, delight and dissect. Gerrish again: "Although estrangement from the orthodox doctrines, begun even before he entered the seminary, culminated in a systematic critique of dogma, everything in the *Glaubenslehre* still hung on the picture of the Savior and its compelling attraction."[143]

But for all his love of the Redeemer, Schleiermacher did him an injustice. I referred earlier to Schleiermacher's retention of Pietism's Jesus-piety, but this judgment needs to be qualified. Schleiermacher certainly retained a sense of the importance and uniqueness of Jesus. Jesus was the source of his piety, in that he traced the Christian self-consciousness back to the feelings stirred by the impression made by Christ. But we must be cautious in attributing to him a Jesus-piety in the vein of the Pietists. They worshiped the crucified Christ; Schleiermacher only (but really) loved the one in whom God has redeemed the world. If he confidently proclaimed that God was in Christ, he quietly avoided the worship of Jesus, and that makes all the difference.

143. Gerrish, *Continuing the Reformation*, 164.

# 11

## "THE HAPPIEST THEOLOGIAN OF OUR AGE"

*Karl Barth on the One Word*
*of God That We Have to Hear*

When the German news magazine *Der Spiegel* ran a story on Karl Barth at Christmas 1959, the seventy-three-year-old suggested a headline: "A Joyful Partisan of the Good God."[1] Here was an old man, declining in health, who had lived through two world wars and the death of a child, whose theological and political convictions and often brazen communication left him isolated (one book he simply titled *Nein!*), whose household was riven by disloyalty (chiefly his own)—and the first adjective he finds at hand to describe himself is "joyful." On all accounts, it was an apt description. "But what shall we call him?" one person asked at a memorial for Barth. "We can . . . call him the happiest theologian of our age. He was a joyful man, a man of humour." The speaker continues: "Barth's humour is of the 'nevertheless' kind, like Mozart's music, in which the shadows of death and the dark hues of pain and suffering are not absent, but are nevertheless bathed in a radiance and harmony that sing praises to the goodness of God's creation."[2]

Barth adored Mozart. He may have been more influenced by Mozart, even theologically, than by any postbiblical writer, puckishly suggesting the composer be considered for beatification.[3] In Mozart, he found someone able to see the

1. Busch, *Karl Barth*, 440.
2. Martin Rumscheidt, "Epilogue," in Barth, *Fragments Grave and Gay*, 124, 126.
3. Barth, *Letters, 1961–1968*, 285, 316.

whole, to delight in it, and to do so precisely by not taking any of it too seriously. He lamented that "we Swiss lack the Mozartean element, the calm joyfulness so badly needed now in a torn and divided world. We lack the ability to see ourselves in our own relativity—it is that from which true peace comes."[4] It would be easy to misread Barth here. His is not a cautious Stoicism, in which one resigns oneself to one's insignificance; nor is it a callous indifference to suffering. No, his calm joy springs from having heard God's triumphant "Yes!" to sinful humanity in Christ, a victorious "nevertheless" in the face of sin and death.

Contrast Barth's delight in Mozart with his concern about Billy Graham. The two met twice in 1960, and Barth initially was favorably impressed. But Barth was shocked after hearing him preach at St. Jakob Stadium: "I was quite horrified. He acted like a madman and what he presented was certainly not the gospel. . . . It was the gospel at gun-point. . . . He preached the law, not a message to make one happy. He wanted to terrify people. Threats—they always make an impression. People would much rather be terrified than be pleased. The more one heats up hell for them, the more they come running."[5] With desperate urgency, Graham threatened bad news more than he announced good news.[6] Instead of Mozart's calm joy in the light of his relativity, Graham stirred up a feverish fear of hell and emphasized the ultimacy of human decision. Barth wanted nothing to do with this, having come to know a God whose Word alone is decisive and who has only one thing to say to sinful humanity—Yes. Barth's "entire life revolved around [this] single word," which carried with it no conditions, no "Yes, if . . ." or "Yes, but . . ."[7] Because of this unmitigated, unambiguous, unwavering Yes, Barth went about his work with the joy of one who knows that his work is only his work, that it is not the work of God in Christ, and that it never need become that.

### The Life of Barth[8]

It was not always so. Barth studied with the greatest liberal Protestant theologians of his age, and they inducted him into a theology that took a baroque

---

4. Barth, *Fragments Grave and Gay*, 52–53.

5. Barth, quoted in Busch, *Karl Barth*, 446.

6. Contrast this with Rumscheidt's remark that Barth's theology "is marked by the syllable *eu* ['good'] of the word *euangelion* ['gospel' or 'good news']" ("Epilogue," in Barth, *Fragments Grave and Gay*, 126).

7. "His entire life revolved around a single word: the Yes that God says to himself—the Yes that (because he says it to himself ) he says also to the human race. . . . Karl Barth brought the Word of God to light as the Word Yes. That was his accomplishment" (Jüngel, *Karl Barth*, 18).

8. For detailed discussion of Barth's life, see Busch, *Karl Barth*.

interest in the believer's experience of God. In his shock at the method and message of Billy Graham, Barth shows us just how far he has come from his early education.

Barth's theological vocation came early. His father, Fritz, was a pastor and professor, and Karl decided on the eve of his confirmation that he would be a theologian.[9] Barth was born in Basel, Switzerland, and studied at Bern, Berlin (where he met Adolf von Harnack, with whom he later sparred), Tübingen, and Marburg (where he met Wilhelm Herrmann). The foundation of his education was Kant's critical philosophy and Friedrich Schleiermacher's analysis of religion and emphasis on religious experience. But Herrmann won his heart. Barth writes, "I . . . found my first theological refuge in Herrmann's *Ethics*. . . . I absorbed Herrmann through every pore."[10] Though he would later reject much of Herrmann's theological liberalism, much of his teacher's influence remained, including Herrmann's preoccupation with Schleiermacher (Herrmann "once told his students that Schleiermacher's *On Religion* was the most important work to have appeared since the writing of the New Testament") and, "above all, Herrmann's vibrant Christocentrism."[11]

After being ordained by his father in 1908, Barth served for two years as suffragan pastor of the German Reformed congregation in Geneva, where we met his wife, Nelly, a member of his confirmation class. In 1911 he became a pastor in the largely industrial village of Safenwil. "In the class conflict which I saw concretely before me in my congregation, I was touched for the first time by the real problems of real life," he recalls.[12] In his ten years in Safenwil, Barth helped form three trade unions and joined the Social Democrats, after which the workers in town called him "comrade pastor."[13]

World War I changed everything. Barth's theological mentors were "hopelessly compromised by their submission to the ideology of war"—and so were the socialists—suggesting the poverty of their approaches to the world's problems.[14] While Barth kept his radical political commitments for life, his most radical move was not political but exegetical. During the war years, he feverishly studied and preached on Scripture and encountered there a

9. Busch, *Karl Barth*, 31.
10. From an autobiographical sketch in the faculty album of the Faculty of Evangelical Theology at Münster in 1927, in Barth and Bultmann, *Karl Barth–Rudolf Bultmann Letters*, 152–53.
11. Mangina, *Karl Barth*, 9.
12. From an autobiographical sketch in the faculty album of the Faculty of Evangelical Theology at Münster in 1927, in Barth and Bultmann, *Karl Barth–Rudolf Bultmann Letters*, 154.
13. Busch, *Karl Barth*, 103, 82.
14. From an autobiographical sketch in the faculty album of the Faculty of Evangelical Theology at Münster in 1927, in Barth and Bultmann, *Karl Barth–Rudolf Bultmann Letters*, 154.

revolutionary God who called the whole world into question. Barth shocked the world in 1919 with a breathless commentary on Romans, the fruit of his tilling the soil of Scripture in Safenwil.

On the strength of the first edition of his Romans commentary (the second, thoroughly revised edition is the more famous), Barth was invited to take up an academic post in Göttingen in 1921. This opportunity gave him the chance to be "talking and arguing not only with books, but with people."[15] Barth knew himself to be woefully underprepared for the task of lecturing, and he spent much of the 1920s devoting himself to studying Scripture and the Reformed tradition, often working late into the night to finish lectures for the next morning. In addition to his standard theological lectures, he gave exegetical lectures on Ephesians, James, Philippians, the Sermon on the Mount, the Gospel of John, Colossians, and Galatians, and he offered seminars on a number of significant Protestant theologians and the Reformed confessions. Around 1929, Charlotte von Kirschbaum became his collaborator and, vexing as it was to those around him (his marriage had been difficult, and "Lollo" had become a true helpmate), a part of his household.[16]

Barth moved to Bonn in 1930, and in the 1930s he began work on his monumental *Church Dogmatics* ("Moby Dick," as he came to call it—the German edition is big and white) and reentered the political fray. He was convinced that his primary work was the *Dogmatics*, evincing the "calm joyfulness" of this man who confidently proclaimed the victory of Jesus. Because God has revealed himself and reconciled us to himself in Christ, it is left to us only, but really, to witness to the one, true God. But because God has spoken in Christ, we cannot listen to any other purported words of God—including the "revelation" being claimed for Adolf Hitler. Already in 1931 Barth had "characterized Fascism as a religion, 'with its deep-rooted, dogmatic ideas about one thing, national reality, its appeal to foundations which are not foundations at all, and its emergence as sheer power.'"[17] In 1934 Barth took the lead in writing the Barmen Declaration, which confesses: "Jesus Christ, as he is attested for us in Holy Scripture, is the one Word of God which we have to hear and which we have to trust and obey in life and in death. We reject the false doctrine, as though the church could and would have to ac-

15. Barth, quoted in Busch, *Karl Barth*, 132.

16. "Without her dedication and activity," Barth writes, "the whole of the middle period of my life and work would have been unthinkable" (Barth, "Circular Letter to Those Who Congratulated Barth on His Eighty-Second Birthday," in *Letters, 1961–1968*, 297). On the fraught nature of the arrangement, as revealed in correspondence, see Tietz, "Karl Barth and Charlotte von Kirschbaum."

17. Busch, *Karl Barth*, 218.

knowledge as a source of its proclamation, apart from and besides this one Word of God, still other events and powers, figures and truths, as God's revelation."[18] Eventually, Barth was dismissed from Bonn, only to be offered a chair at Basel the next day.

The bulk of Barth's remaining years were taken up in teaching and writing his massive *Church Dogmatics*. He had given up a prior attempt at writing a "Christian Dogmatics." The change in name signaled his recognition "that dogmatics is not a 'free' science. It is bound to the sphere of the church, the only place where it is possible and meaningful."[19] The unfinished *Dogmatics* (fittingly, eschatology, what Barth called the doctrine of redemption, had been left untouched) was "nine times as long as Calvin's *Institutes* and almost twice as long as the *Summa* of Thomas Aquinas," requiring astounding productivity on Barth's part.[20] In the midst of this writing, Barth actively spoke out against German Christianity and, later, against anti-Communism and atomic weapons. He reported for military service at age fifty-four, and in his late sixties and early seventies preached regularly in Basel prison. And Barth kept up long fraternal fights with Schleiermacher and Roman Catholicism.[21] After the Second Vatican Council, he even frequently attended the Bruder Klaus Catholic Church.[22] Barth died on December 10, 1968.

### And Never the Twain Shall Meet

In the nineteenth century, theologians became distracted by the problems and possibilities of human knowing and experience of God. While the answers to the questions of the Enlightenment varied widely, they shared a fatal preoccupation with the human subject. But this was exactly the wrong way to go

18. The Barmen Declaration, thesis 1, cited in Busch, *Barmen Theses Then and Now*, 19.
19. Barth, quoted in Busch, *Karl Barth*, 211.
20. Busch, *Karl Barth*, 486.
21. It is important to underscore that these fights were fraternal. For all his sharp critique of Schleiermacher, Barth was a patient, careful, sympathetic reader of the father of modern theology; and he continued to come back to him over the years as a voice to which we would do well to listen, imagining further conversations with him in heaven. See Barth, *Theology of Schleiermacher*, 277, and the entire "Concluding Unscientific Postscript on Schleiermacher" (261–79). Barth had still more sympathy for Roman Catholicism, preferring it to the Protestantism on offer in his day. See D. Stephen Long's account of Barth's theological friendship with von Balthasar in *Saving Karl Barth*. Invited to the Second Vatican Council, Barth was unable to attend due to illness, but he studied the documents carefully and prepared a list of questions for discussion during a weeklong trip to the Vatican. When he asked Pope Paul VI if it was true that the stress in "*fratres sejuncti*" ("separated brethren," as Roman Catholics refer to Protestants) ought fall on "fratres," Paul "seemed to agree" (Barth, *Ad Limina Apostolorum*, 15).
22. See Long, *Saving Karl Barth*, 285.

about things, Barth realized. It led into a cul-de-sac, and it certainly could not yield knowledge of God. "Schleiermacher's reversal of theology into anthropology" was only one case of modern theology's "cancerous subjectivism."[23]

During his pastorate in Safenwil, Barth had two epiphanies. In 1914 a group of leading German intellectuals—including many of his teachers—endorsed the Kaiser's war policy, and Barth saw clearly the vulnerability of the liberal Protestantism that he had made his own. If this was what the dream of "the Fatherhood of God and the Brotherhood of Man" led to, Barth wanted no part in it. In the wake of such theological impotence, Barth realized that God and the world could no longer be correlated; no longer could it be presumed that the state stands in service of the kingdom of God. Ludwig Feuerbach was right in his suspicion that modern theologians were "planning on an undercover apotheosis of man."[24]

The nineteenth century had founded its theological work on the bedrock of religion, but Barth suspected that this was to build a house on sand. If Schleiermacher rejoiced in the already-religious character of religion's cultured despisers, Barth argued that religion is, at best, an ambiguous reality. In an early essay, he writes that "the religious feeling can just as well distract people from the question of God as it can lead them to it. Religion and a sense for God have never meant the same thing."[25] It gets worse: "Jesus simply has nothing to do with religion."[26] Again: "Religion must die. In God we are rid of it."[27] Such statements could easily have led Barth into a religious individualism and, later, to a heterodox sectarianism in which the individual is the final arbiter of truth. But Barth's concern in critiquing religion was not to preserve the individual; it was to clear the way for an encounter with the living God. If anything good can be said for religion, it is that it marks the (dead) end on our way to God. "Religion, as the final human possibility, commands us to halt. Religion brings us to the place where we must wait, in order that God may confront us—on the other side of the frontier of religion."[28]

23. Barth, *Christliche Dogmatic im Entwurf*, 86, cited in Busch, *Karl Barth and the Pietists*, 265. The description of this as a "cancerous subjectivism" is from T. Torrance, *Karl Barth*, 31. Later in life, Barth suggested that, in a different time, one might attempt a legitimate "theology of the third article, in other words, a theology predominantly and decisively of the Holy Spirit." And he wondered whether this wasn't what Schleiermacher was up to, something of which he "was scarcely conscious, but which might actually have been the legitimate concern dominating even his theological activity" (Barth, *Theology of Schleiermacher*, 278).

24. Barth, "Introductory Essay," xxii.
25. Barth, *Word of God and Theology*, 76.
26. Barth, *Word of God and Theology*, 96.
27. Barth, *Epistle to the Romans*, 238.
28. Barth, *Epistle to the Romans*, 242.

Barth's second epiphany came as he read and preached through the Bible week by week. With the wide-eyed wonder of discovery, Barth writes in 1917 that "*a new world* stands in the Bible. God! God's lordship! God's honor! God's inconceivable love! Not the history of humanity but the history of God. . . . 'God' is the content of the Bible!"[29] Why was this so surprising? It might seem fairly obvious that the Bible is about God, but for Barth this basic claim meant a revolution in theology as it had been done in the previous 150 years. Barth characterized the eighteenth century as the age of "absolute man."[30] "What other age has dared to make architecture of its inmost heart to the extent that this one did? But this was an age which simply had to, for its inmost heart was precisely this idea of man as one taking hold of everything about him and subjecting it to his will."[31] This insight held true across the theological spectrum throughout the nineteenth century. Liberal Protestantism subjected the Christian faith to the acids of criticism, but just as corrosive was the fascination that warmhearted Christians had with their own piety. Both rationalists and pietists, Barth charges, "devalued the objective elements in the Christian creed over against its subjective elements." What is real is what is experienced. Barth goes on: "The real birth of Christ is in our hearts; his real and saving death is that which we see accomplished in ourselves, that which we have to accomplish ourselves; his real resurrection is his triumph in us as those who believe in him."[32] The great Reformation emphasis on the *Christus pro nobis*, "Christ for us," has collapsed in on itself. Christ is now no more than who he is for us, and who he is for us is measured with reference to his subjective effect in us. Note where reality is located—"in our hearts," "in ourselves," "in us." The center of theological gravity has shifted from the historical incarnation, crucifixion, and resurrection of Christ to their repetition or realization in us. Perhaps, even, those prior events are only signs of the thing that happens when Christ enters our hearts. Seen this way, Schleiermacher and the revivalist Charles Finney are scarcely distinguishable. "Especially if one notes the unheard-of way in which revivalist theology led men to occupy themselves with themselves," Barth writes, "the question arises whether this is not even to be regarded as the topmost summit of modern theological anthropology."[33] That is not a compliment.

When Barth discovered the strange world within the Bible, he saw with stark clarity the alternative: he could continue speaking of humanity, or he

29. Barth, *Word of God and Theology*, 26.
30. Barth, *Protestant Theology in the Nineteenth Century*, 22–23.
31. Barth, *Protestant Theology in the Nineteenth Century*, 42–43.
32. Barth, *Protestant Theology in the Nineteenth Century*, 100.
33. Barth, *Protestant Theology in the Nineteenth Century*, 501.

could begin speaking of God. He could no longer pretend that, in speaking of humanity, he was doing justice to the God of the Bible. Barth staked his claim:

> We are concerned here with God. Not with religion, but with the move-
> ment that proceeds from God, with our being moved by him. Hallowed be
> thy name! Thy kingdom come! Thy will be done! What we call "religious
> experience" is a completely derived, secondary, broken form of the divine.
> Even in the highest and purest instances, it is form and not content. . . . For
> far too long, the Church has directed all of its activities toward the cultiva-
> tion of all kinds of piety. Today, we would like to turn our attention entirely
> away from this form.[34]

To speak of God—to be, that is, a theo-logian—Barth would have to find a new starting point, beginning not with the human attempt to reach God but with God's movement toward humanity. In fact, the first thing Barth learned about God is that whoever he is, he is not the pinnacle of humanity, not the end of humanity's highest hopes, that he is not in any way even *like* humanity. In his thunderous commentary on Romans, Barth writes: "The Gospel proclaims a God utterly distinct from men."[35] Ever one to eschew the kind of system that might domesticate this "Wholly Other" God, he sug-gests, "If I have a system, it is limited to a recognition of what Kierkegaard called the 'infinite qualitative distinction' between time and eternity, and to my regarding this as possessing negative as well as positive significance: 'God is in heaven, and thou art on earth.'"[36] God and humanity can in no way be compared. They are qualitatively, not quantitatively, distinct and so cannot be placed at extreme ends of a scale of measurement, and they are infinitely so, so that one cannot even imagine the sheer otherness of God. In the Romans commentary, sin just is our failure to abide by this distinction. "As an event, sin is that interchanging of God and man, that exalting of men to divinity or depressing God to humanity, by which we seek to justify and fortify and establish ourselves."[37]

Given this infinite qualitative distinction, there can be no way for human-ity to ascend to God. "There is no way to God from our position, not even a negative way [*via negativa*]. There is no '*via dialectica*' or '*paradoxa.*' If then a way were to be found, the god who stands at the end of the human way will

34. Barth, *Word of God and Theology*, 43.
35. Barth, *Epistle to the Romans*, 28.
36. Barth, *Epistle to the Romans*, 10 (in the preface to the second edition, published in 1921; the quotation at the end is from Eccles. 5:2).
37. Barth, *Epistle to the Romans*, 190.

have ceased being God."[38] Feuerbach was right: theologians had found their way to god, but the god they had found had ceased to be God. Here Barth is consistent: not even his own dialectical theology, in which he moved back and forth between affirmations and negations about God in an effort to evoke at once his transcendence and the insufficiency of human language to comprehend him—not even that could lead Barth to God. The theologian—and not only the theologian but the Christian, too—faces a crisis: "As theologians, we ought to speak of God. But we are humans and as such cannot speak of God. We ought to do both, to know the 'ought' and the 'not able to,' and precisely in this way give God the glory."[39]

How, then, might we do something that we are not able to do? To answer this requires a change of direction. Instead of us making our way to God, God makes his way to us. "Faith and revelation are the clear rejection of a way from humans to God's grace, love, and life. Both words say that here we are only considering the way of God to humans. But between these two words, stand two other words—and this is the innermost core of Pauline-Reformation theology. They are Jesus Christ."[40] We have no capacity to speak of God. Our best attempts to do so will careen into idolatry, and so will be failed attempts. Theologians can do their work only if God has made his way to them, revealing himself to them in Christ and giving them eyes to see the revelation of Christ by the Spirit. But before the good news of God's coming near resolves our theological crisis, it sets us in an even more acute one, a soteriological crisis. Before it is good news, the gospel of Jesus Christ is bad news. "Grace is the KRISIS from death to life. . . . The Gospel of Christ is a shattering disturbance, an assault which brings everything into question."[41] It is "not a truth among other truths. Rather, it sets a question-mark against all truths."[42] All those things we take for granted, those things by which we navigate and which establish us comfortably in the world, are put on trial and judged. We are undone, in order that we may be made new. Barth puts it bluntly: "To believe in Jesus is the most hazardous of all hazards."[43]

Barth's Romans commentary seemed itself to be "an assault which brings everything into question." Its radical eschatology of crisis brought religion, piety, and the church into question. Its method, in which Barth sought to hear the living voice of Paul with minimal attention to the results of historical

---

38. Barth, *Word of God and Theology*, 166.
39. Barth, *Word of God and Theology*, 177 (emphasis removed).
40. Barth, *Word of God and Theology*, 168.
41. Barth, *Epistle to the Romans*, 225.
42. Barth, *Epistle to the Romans*, 35.
43. Barth, *Epistle to the Romans*, 99.

criticism, brought academic theology into question. Karl Adam said the commentary "fell like a bomb on the playground of the theologians."[44] The apt metaphor evokes the demolition work that marks Barth's early theology. If Schleiermacher was "vague on the point that speaking of God means something *other than* speaking about the human in a somewhat higher pitch," Barth would speak of God in his confrontation with humanity, by speaking of the collapse and destruction of humanity at the coming of God.[45] The judgment of God does not prolong but does away with history.[46] The church is "a crater formed by the explosion of a shell and seeks to be no more than a void in which the Gospel reveals itself."[47] And faith, that darling of the nineteenth century, is "a void, an obeisance before that which we can never be, or do, or possess."[48] All that is left of religion is the mark of its destruction. It seems that, to speak of God, Barth has found it necessary to speak of One who is other than, and in a profound way *against*, humanity, One whose coming undoes us.

## God Speaks

Theology, as we have seen, is humanly impossible, but with God all things are possible. We cannot speak of God, but we must speak of God, and because he has spoken to us, we may speak of God. Accordingly, Barth acknowledges only one "criterion of dogmatics"—the Word of God.[49] The Word of God is not mere shorthand for Scripture. There are three forms of God's Word—divine revelation, the Bible, and proclamation. Revelation is "God's Word in an absolute sense apart from any becoming, the event of God's Word in whose power the Bible and proclamation become God's Word."[50] The Bible and proclamation are not "God's Word to a lesser degree," but "the same Word of God in its relation to revelation."[51] If, then, Jesus Christ, the eternal Word, is God's self-revelation, the Bible and proclamation become the Word of God as the Spirit uses them to open our eyes to the revelation of Christ. "It is God's revelation which decides what true reality is," and so it is fitting that

44. Adam wrote this in the Roman Catholic monthly *Das Hochland* in June 1926; cited in Mangina, *Karl Barth*, 26, n. 5.
45. Barth, *Word of God and Theology*, 183.
46. Barth, *Epistle to the Romans*, 77.
47. Barth, *Epistle to the Romans*, 36.
48. Barth, *Epistle to the Romans*, 88.
49. Barth, *CD* I/1, 43.
50. Barth, *CD* I/1, 290.
51. Barth, *CD* I/1, 304.

God's Word would be the sole criterion for dogmatics.[52] God reveals himself as Lord, and he *remains* Lord in his revelation; he is Subject before and as he is object. As Lord, he gives himself to be known and enables us to know him. The Holy Spirit "is God Himself to the extent that He can not only come to man but also be in man, and thus open up man and make him capable and ready for Himself, and thus achieve His revelation in him."[53]

This narrow gate restricts theological method even as it empowers human speech. Nothing else may determine our knowledge of God, and we need nothing else to know God. Barth exhibited a severe allergy to anything that seemed to drift from devotion to divine revelation by smuggling in purported knowledge of God from elsewhere. He scorned "natural theology" in many forms for its assumption that we can have some knowledge of God on the basis of unaided human reason. The Lord of all hardly needs help, and so Barth rejects any "point of contact" that might enable God to be known by us as idolatry—or worse. The search for vestiges of the Trinity in nature is "an ancient Trojan horse."[54] The *analogia entis*, or analogy of being, which modern Roman Catholics used to link God and the world, is "the invention of anti-Christ."[55] Christian apologetics issues from "anxiety concerning the victory of the gospel."[56] And when his erstwhile friend Emil Brunner posits a "point of contact" in the human person, persisting in spite of sin, Barth writes a tirade titled simply "*Nein!*"[57] Each of these ventures in natural theology was intended as a modest attempt to account for how humans are fit for knowledge of God. Still, Christoph Schwöbel is right: "Natural theology confuses what is constituted *by* human beings with what is constituted *for* human beings, and in this way consistently conflates what human beings can do and what only God can do and has done."[58] Natural theology amounts to a loosing of theology from its Lord, a failure to listen attentively to the one Word of God that we must hear. The rule is simple: "God precedes and man follows." So "there is no 'a priori' human knowledge of God," but only a "relative theology: relative to God's revelation."[59]

Some wondered whether this wasn't all a bit naive. Barth and Rudolf Bultmann exchanged letters over four decades, and Bultmann, who was an ally of Barth in many ways, chided Barth for "falling prey to an outdated

52. Barth, *CD* II/1, 531.
53. Barth, *CD* I/1, 450.
54. Barth, *CD* I/1, 336.
55. Barth, *CD* I/1, xiii.
56. Barth, *Epistle to the Romans*, 35.
57. Brunner and Barth, *Natural Theology*.
58. Schwöbel, "Theology," 32.
59. Barth, *Faith of the Church*, 33.

philosophy" in seeking to free theology from its philosophical captivity.[60] Barth acknowledged the risk his "gypsylike" approach ran, but he insisted that his "hands were already full in trying to *say* something very specific," and so he didn't have time to worry about philosophical precision or consistency.[61] Instead, he would take whatever lay to hand and unapologetically use terms and categories (frequently recasting them in the process) to his theological ends.

The good news is that "revelation grants *courage* to language," allowing even shopworn and certainly inadequate speech to do its job, and so revelation is more than enough for us to speak of God.[62] Prayer helps, too. Barth wrote a small book on Anselm in 1931 that he regarded as pivotal for the *Church Dogmatics*. "Anselm speaks about God while speaking to him," and he shows that "the whole theological inquiry is intended to be understood and carried through in prayer. In prayer and surely that means—by presupposing in the most positive manner conceivable the object of the inquiry, his Presence and his Authority for the course and success of the inquiry concerning him."[63]

### What You See Is What You Get

Barth begins each long section of the *Church Dogmatics* with a *Leitsatz*, a brief paragraph that concisely lays out what follows. When he turns to the reality of God, he writes: "God is who He is in the act of His revelation. God seeks and creates fellowship between Himself and us, and therefore He loves us. But He is this loving God without us as Father, Son and Holy Spirit, in the freedom of the Lord, who has His life from Himself."[64] That first sentence summarizes much of what Barth will say in his doctrine of God. Who is God? Whoever he is, he is the one he is in the act of his revelation. He is the one who reveals himself as himself by himself, the Father manifesting himself in the Son and giving us the eyes to see him for who he is by the Spirit. A number of commitments are hidden in this sentence: the first is that, when God reveals, God reveals himself. All revelation, according to Barth, is self-revelation. This means that there is no other God behind or beyond the God who reveals himself. What you see is what you get.

60. Bultmann to Barth in a letter dated June 8, 1928, in Barth and Bultmann, *Karl Barth–Rudolf Bultmann Letters*, 38.
61. Barth to Bultmann in a letter dated June 12, 1928, in Barth and Bultmann, *Karl Barth–Rudolf Bultmann Letters*, 41.
62. Jüngel, *God's Being Is in Becoming*, 24.
63. Barth, *Anselm*, 102, 150–51.
64. Barth, *CD* II/1, 257.

Notice, too, Barth's actualist accent. Instead of describing who God is in terms of a certain kind of being, Barth immediately speaks of God's being in terms of action. Who is God? He is who he is in what he does. "To its very deepest depths God's Godhead consists in the fact that it is an event—not any event, not events in general, but the event of His action, in which we have a share in God's revelation."[65] This is strange language. It's hard to make sense of God's being *as* event. God is active, sure, but can we say that his very being is action? Doesn't there need to be a being who acts if there is to be action at all?

In the twentieth century, following Georg Hegel's lead, process theology suggested that God is in a continual state of becoming. The trouble with this view is that it calls into question God's perfection and makes creation necessary, so that God becomes in tandem with the world.[66] While a lively debate rages on about whether Barth was developing a revisionist metaphysics, and if so, to what extent, we can safely say that the heart of Barth's concern was to honor the living God in his description of God's being-in-act. "Our subject is God and not being," he writes, "or being only as the being of God." This is the point. If we are to talk of God's being, we must not assume "a concept of being that is common, neutral and free to choose, but . . . one which is from the first filled out in a quite definite way. And this concretion cannot take place arbitrarily, but only from the Word of God."[67] Whereas modern theology evinced an antimetaphysical bias, concerning itself with soteriology but not wanting to talk about being at all, much of scholastic theology (both medieval and Protestant) operated with an unbaptized doctrine of God, talking about being at length before considering how who God is in his Word might determine his being.[68] For Barth, the being of God can be defined only with reference to God's self-revelation. In the sentence "God is," the subject determines the predicate. This means—and note the rigor with which Barth will continue to insist on the proper order of subject and predicate to honor the revelation of God in Christ—that even the notion of "act" operative in the doctrine of God must be "filled out in a quite definite way." Barth will affirm with Thomas that God is *actus purus*, but he gives this further precision: "*Actus purus* is not sufficient as a description of God. To it there must

---

65. Barth, *CD* II/1, 263.

66. The initial resemblance between Barth and process theology can be seen in, e.g., the title of Eberhard Jüngel's book, *God's Being Is in Becoming: The Trinitarian Being of God in the Theology of Karl Barth*. For a comparison of Barth and a leading process theologian, and an assurance that this was *not* what Barth was doing, see Gunton, *Being and Becoming*.

67. Barth, *CD* II/1, 260–61.

68. See Barth, *CD* II/1, 259–60, where Barth spots two errors in Melanchthon that he seeks to avoid in his own work.

be added at least '*et singularis.*'"[69] Only God is pure act, and God is pure act in a singular, unparalleled way; he is sui generis.

Barth goes out of his way to highlight the singularity of the being-in-act of God. Consider just a few examples of how the subject defines the predicate in his exposition of the divine perfections. In speaking of divine immutability (or constancy, as he prefers to call it), Barth writes that "His constancy consists in the fact that He is always the same in every change."[70] Of course, to be immutable is, at least etymologically, *not* to change. In this dialectical form (God changes; God does not change), Barth evokes in readers a recognition that they had assumed that for God to be immutable he couldn't change. But God is *so* constant, Barth seems to be saying, that he can remain the same even as he changes. Such wording threatens to bend language so far that it breaks. And yet, it also seems to be a faithful, if paradoxical, redescription of John 1:14: "The Word became flesh." The unswerving faithfulness of God does not lead to rigidity, with God frozen in his own immutability, for "as the immutable He is the living God and He possesses a mobility and elasticity which is no less divine than His perseverance."[71]

Or consider divine omnipotence. Barth wisely points out that "to define Him in terms of power in itself has as its consequence, not merely a neutralisation of the concept of God, but its perversion into its opposite. Power in itself is not merely neutral. Power in itself is evil. . . . If power by itself were the omnipotence of God it would mean that God was evil, that He was the spirit of revolution and tyranny par excellence."[72] But God is not defined by power; power is defined by God.[73] "Power in itself" is tyrannical, a lording over others that stands in stark contrast to the Lord, who became a servant. But "power in itself" is not even, properly speaking, power at all. After all, Barth writes, "It is God's revelation which decides what true reality is," and in Christ God has revealed his power in weakness and service.[74]

Barth sums up who God is in the act of revelation by saying that God is the one who loves in freedom.

> God loves us. And because we can trust His revelation as the revelation of His own being He is in Himself the One who loves. As such He is completely knowable to us. But He loves us in His freedom. And because here too we can

69. Barth, *CD* II/1, 264.
70. Barth, *CD* II/1, 496.
71. Barth, *CD* II/1, 496.
72. Barth, *CD* II/1, 524.
73. "The relation between subject and predicate is an irreversible one when it is a matter of God's perfections" (Barth, *CD* II/1, 448).
74. Barth, *CD* II/1, 531.

trust His revelation as a self-revelation, He is in Himself sovereignly free. He is therefore completely unknowable to us. That He loves us and that He does so in His freedom are both true in the grace of His revelation. If His revelation is His truth, He is truly both in unity and difference: the One who loves in freedom. It is His very being to be both, not in separation but in unity, yet not in the dissolution but in the distinctiveness of this duality. And this duality as the being of the one God necessarily forms the content of the doctrine of His perfection.[75]

Notice the way divine love and freedom shape each other. God loves us in freedom, which means he can love us without needing us and that his freedom is oriented to our good rather than being merely something to keep him aloof from us. Barth's preference to speak of God as "the One who loves in freedom" rather than, say, "the One who loves and is free" underscores the unity of these two organizing divine perfections.[76] To speak of God's love, one must speak of his freedom, and to speak of his freedom, one must speak of his love. And yet, there is a real difference between the two. God's being is "to be both . . . in unity . . . but in the distinctiveness of this duality."

That said, God's perfections do not represent different sides of him, as if he were internally conflicted. Mercy and righteousness do not compete in the divine life; they embrace. As Barth writes at length on the divine perfections, he continues to display the ways in which they together display the life of God. They are "the letters of the divine Word. It becomes a Word only through the sequence and unity of these letters."[77] As one learns the ABCs of the divine perfections, one learns to hear the Word, whose content is an exposition in time of the eternal life of God. Barth affirms the doctrine of divine simplicity, according to which God has no parts and "every individual perfection in God is nothing but God Himself and therefore nothing but every other divine perfection."[78] But he suspects the tradition of having falsely exalted simplicity and insists on a "continual recognition and confirmation of the plenitude and richness of this one being of God."[79] Barth would have all talk of the divine perfections "move in a circle around the one but infinitely rich being of God, whose simplicity is abundance itself and whose abundance is simplicity itself."[80]

75. Barth, CD II/1, 343.
76. He will go on to organize all of the divine perfections, in contrasting pairs, under the rubric of the perfections of the divine loving and the perfections of the divine freedom.
77. Barth, CD II/1, 327.
78. Barth, CD II/1, 333.
79. Barth, CD II/1, 331.
80. Barth, CD II/1, 406.

At times, Barth's eagerness to find no discrepancy between God as he is in himself and God as he in his self-revelation leads him to questionable claims. Consider the perfection of mercy, which Barth pairs with righteousness. "God the Father, Son and Holy Spirit is merciful in Himself," Barth writes.[81] While it is easy to imagine God as both subject and object of love, the lover and the beloved, it is more difficult to imagine God as an object of mercy. If, as Barth writes, the "mercy of God lies in His readiness to share in sympathy the distress of another," how could we speak of mercy as belonging to God apart from creation?[82] Surely God can't suffer distress and stand in need of another to share it with him. Does the claim that mercy is one of the divine perfections, then, suggest the necessity of creation, even an eternal creation? Perhaps the language of "readiness" serves to bridge the gap by showing how God's mercy to sinners is grounded in the life of God without requiring creation for God to be God. If so, we would then have to ask whether "readiness" can comport with God as *actus purus et singularis*. "Readiness" is not yet the language of act and might suggest a potential in God ill fitting with Barth's doctrine of God.

In any case, Barth will not countenance any God who is less or other than the one we meet in Christ, the man of sorrows, acquainted with grief.[83] This is the same Lord who passed before Moses on Sinai and proclaimed his name: "The LORD, the LORD, a God merciful and gracious, slow to anger, and abounding in steadfast love and faithfulness, keeping steadfast love for thousands, forgiving iniquity and transgression and sin, but who will by no means clear the guilty, visiting the iniquity of the fathers on the children and the children's children, to the third and fourth generation" (Exod. 34:6–7). Barth acknowledges what is regularly, often disturbingly, on view in Scripture, that "the personal God has a heart. He can feel, and be affected." So far, so good. Barth proceeds: "He is not impassible."[84] Here, he appears to depart abruptly and sharply from the tradition's consensus that God does not suffer. Note that Barth does not bluntly say that God suffers; he says that God is not impassible, that he is not incapable of suffering. Recall the proper order of subject and predicate. If the tail is not to wag the dog, we must allow the divine subject to determine the content of its predicate, whether we say that "God suffers" or "God cannot suffer." Barth continues:

81. Barth, *CD* II/1, 372.
82. Barth, *CD* II/1, 369.
83. Rob Price puzzles over Barth's treatment of divine mercy and points to Barth's pastoral urgency in *Letters of the Divine Word*, 67–72.
84. Barth, *CD* II/1, 370.

He is not impassible. He cannot be moved from outside by an extraneous power. But this does not mean that He is not capable of moving Himself. No, God is moved and stirred, yet not like ourselves in powerlessness, but in His own free power, in His innermost being: moved and touched by Himself, i.e., open, ready, inclined (*propensus*) to compassion with another's suffering and therefore to assistance, impelled to take the initiative to relieve this distress. God finds no suffering in Himself. And no cause outside God can cause Him suffering if he does not will it so. But it is, in fact, a question of sympathy with the suffering of another in the full scope of God's own personal freedom.[85]

Divine impassibility historically meant that God could not suffer. Often, theologians conflate the two senses in which one can suffer: one can either experience negative emotions or events or one can be acted upon, in the older English sense of suffering the actions of another. (The King James Version of Mark 10:14 reads, "Suffer the little children to come unto me.") With the tradition, Barth affirms that God cannot be moved by another. But, he continues, this does not imply that he cannot be moved at all; he can move himself. He can "move" and "stir" and "touch" himself to relieve another's distress, and this is not an expression of his powerlessness but of "His own free power." This is who he is, the Lord gracious and compassionate. And if God can suffer with another in her distress, then he is "not impassible." Or if he is, "The impassibility of God cannot in any case mean that it is impossible for Him really to feel compassion. . . . It is always a question, no more and no less, of the heart, the innermost being of God. This is not closed but open to feel the distress of man. God cannot be moved from outside, but from inside His own being He shares it in sympathetic communion."[86]

Barth affirms what the doctrine of impassibility traditionally affirmed—that, as *actus purus*, as the living God, God cannot be moved by another, cannot be the object of another's actions but remains the lordly subject in all he is and does—but in so doing Barth orients this point to the One who in freedom *loves*. What does God do with his freedom? He gives himself in love to his creation.

## A Question Answered: Barth on Election

If I want to get a rise out of my students, I tell them that if they don't believe in election and predestination, they aren't sufficiently Christian. Some protest;

---

85. Barth, *CD* II/1, 370.
86. Barth, *CD* II/1, 371.

after all, most students at our Christian university are Arminian evangelicals, whether or not they've heard the term. I insist, however, that biblical Christians must believe in election and predestination, even if they needn't be Calvinists. God "chose [there's election] us in him before [and there's predestination] the foundation of the world, that we should be holy and blameless before him" (Eph. 1:4).

Still, for most of my students, the doctrine of election remains at best peripheral, at worst an unsettling piece of very bad news. Even if they are confident in their own election, they wonder about their friends; they wonder, too, about people around the world who know nothing of the God and Father of our Lord Jesus Christ. It is this anxious wondering that saddens Barth. He discerns a fatal abstraction at the heart of traditional accounts of election. They treat both the subject (the electing God) and the object (the elected person) of predestination as unknown quantities. "In the sharpest contrast to this view our thesis that the eternal will of God is the election of Jesus Christ means that we deny the existence of any such twofold mystery."[87] Central to Barth's account is that election is not an unknowable mystery but one that has been revealed in Christ. He proclaims that "predestination is not hidden but disclosed. God is the self-revealing God, and as such He is the electing God."[88] Therefore, "we are not led into the void when we ask concerning the divine election, concerning that eternal will which predetermines and overrules both time and all that is in time. Fundamentally, this question is not unanswerable."[89] In fact, this question—*Who is elect?* Or perhaps, *Am I elect?*—has already been answered. Christ is the elect one, and in Christ I learn that I too am elect.

For this reason, Barth can write: "The doctrine of election is the sum of the Gospel because of all words that can be said or heard it is the best: that God elects man; that God is for man too [and not just in and for himself] the One who loves in freedom."[90] The doctrine of predestination "is not a mixed message of joy and terror, salvation and damnation. Originally and finally it is not dialectical but non-dialectical. It does not proclaim in the same breath both good and evil, both help and destruction, both life and death. . . . In substance, therefore, the first and last word is Yes and not No."[91] There is no hedging of bets, no rider, no qualification, or caveat. Election is God's "altogether Yes" and so "the very essence of all

87. Barth, *CD* II/2, 146.
88. Barth, *CD* II/2, 156.
89. Barth, *CD* II/2, 159.
90. Barth, *CD* II/2, 3.
91. Barth, *CD* II/2, 13.

good news."[92] "The election of grace is the sum of the Gospel—we must put it as pointedly as that."[93]

In a daring innovation, Barth inserts election into the doctrine of God. He recognizes that he is doing something new. Others had championed the doctrine of election, others had seen the importance of election being in Christ, but none had given it such prominence; certainly none had included it within the doctrine of God. In placing election within the doctrine of God rather than, say, the doctrine of creation, Barth testifies that God is none other than the One who elects himself for fellowship with humanity. Election is a word about God before it is a word about humanity. "It is part of the doctrine of God because originally God's election of man is a predestination not merely of man but of Himself."[94] God just *is* the One who elects. Does this suggest that election somehow precedes or constitutes God's very being, so that what he chooses is logically prior to who he is? That conclusion would seem to be pressing too far, as there has to be someone to do the electing. But recall that God has his perfect being-in-act. At the very least, Barth wants to press God's election of himself as far as possible into the eternal life of God, writing that "in Himself, in the primal and basic decision in which He wills to be and actually is God, in the mystery of what takes place from and to all eternity within Himself, within His triune being, God is none other than the One who in His Son or Word elects Himself, and in and with Himself elects His people."[95] God is who he is in the decision "in which He wills to be and actually is God." The Triune God is "none other" than the One who elects himself in his Son. Speaking of Jesus Christ, Barth writes that "He is the beginning of God before which there is no other beginning apart from that of God within Himself. Except, then, for God Himself, nothing can derive from any other source or look back to any other starting-point. . . . Before Him and without Him and beside Him God does not, then, elect or will anything."[96]

Echoing John 1:1, Barth declares that Jesus Christ, who was born just over two thousand years ago, is the beginning of God's ways with the world. He is the one with and through whom God does all that he does.

> In the beginning, before time and space as we know them, before creation, before there was any reality distinct from God which could be the object of the love of God or the setting for His acts of freedom, God anticipated and

92. Barth, *CD* II/2, 13, 14.
93. Barth, *CD* II/2, 13.
94. Barth, *CD* II/2, 3.
95. Barth, *CD* II/2, 76.
96. Barth, *CD* II/2, 94.

determined within Himself (in the power of His love and freedom, of His knowing and willing) that the goal and meaning of all His dealings with the as yet non-existent universe should be the fact that in His Son He would be gracious towards man, uniting Himself with him. . . . This choice was in the beginning. As the subject and object of this choice, Jesus Christ was at the beginning. He was not at the beginning of God, for God has indeed no beginning. But He was at the beginning of all things, at the beginning of God's dealings with the reality which is distinct from Himself. Jesus Christ was the choice or election of God in respect of this reality.[97]

The whole point of creation is Jesus Christ. God created in order that he might be gracious toward humanity in Christ. Jesus is the primary object of God's choosing. He is also the subject of this choice. Somehow, the man born two thousand years ago is himself the God who "before time and space as we know them" determined all this. As strange as this way of putting it is, it is no stranger than Paul's claim that "by him all things were created" and that "he is before all things, and in him all things hold together" (Col. 1:16–17).

Barth sums things up: "In its simplest and most comprehensive form the dogma of predestination consists, then, in the assertion that the divine predestination is the election of Jesus Christ." Since election refers to both an elector and an elected, he divides this claim into two—"that Jesus Christ is the electing God, and that He is also elected man."[98]

Jesus Christ is the electing God. We must not ask concerning any other but Him. In no depth of the Godhead shall we encounter any other but Him. There is no such thing as Godhead in itself. Godhead is always the Godhead of the Father, the Son and the Holy Spirit. . . . There is no such thing as a *decretum absolutum* [absolute decree]. There is no such thing as a will of God apart from the will of Jesus Christ. Thus Jesus Christ is not only the *manifestatio* [manifestation] and *speculum nostrae praedestinationis* [mirror of our predestination]. . . . Jesus Christ reveals to us our election as an election which is made by Him, by His will which is also the will of God.[99]

The Reformed tradition spoke of an "absolute decree" in which God decided in eternity whom he would elect to salvation and whom to damnation. This formulation could breed endless doubts and fears about one's own election, and it suggested the question of whether the death and resurrection of

97. Barth, *CD* II/2, 102.
98. Barth, *CD* II/2, 103.
99. Barth, *CD* II/2, 115.

Jesus reliably displayed the character of God. Might there not be a God behind Jesus, and might he not be anything but merciful? Barth advocates "replacing the doctrine of the *decretum absolutum* by that of the Word which was in the beginning with God," insisting that if God speaks for himself, we would do well to listen to what he says.[100] The God who elects is none other than Jesus Christ. There is no God behind God-with-us. In fact, to look for a God beside, behind, or above Jesus Christ is to succumb to idolatry, by refusing God as he has given himself to be known in his self-revelation in Christ. As there is no God behind Jesus, there is no will of God apart from his will. Christ is not just the will of God (though he is this); he is the willing God.

Barth goes far beyond an account of election in Christ that would speak of Christ instrumentally, as the one in whom or in light of whom believers are elect to salvation. Christ should be "thought of not merely as the executive instrument of the divine dealings with man ordained in the election but as the Subject of the election itself."[101] Barth reads the Pauline "in Christ" not only instrumentally but also agentially: "From the very beginning (from eternity itself), there are no other elect together with or apart from Him, but, as Eph. 1:4 tells us, only 'in' Him. 'In Him' does not simply mean with Him, together with Him, in His company. Nor does it mean only through Him, by means of that which He as elected man can be and do for them. 'In Him' means in His person, in His will, in His own divine choice, in the basic decision of God which He fulfils over against every man."[102]

Jesus Christ is, then, the electing God. He is also the elected man. What does such a formulation mean?

> It tells us that before all created reality, before all being and becoming in time, before time itself, in the pre-temporal eternity of God, the eternal divine decision as such has as its object and content the existence of this one created being, the man Jesus of Nazareth, and the work of this man in His life and death, His humiliation and exaltation, His obedience and merit. It tells us further that in and with the existence of this man the eternal divine decision has as its object and content the execution of the divine covenant with man, the salvation of all men. . . . Jesus Christ, then, is not merely one of the elect but the elect of God.[103]

---

100. Barth, *CD* II/2, 114. "The Son of Man was from all eternity the object of the election of Father, Son and Holy Spirit. And the reality of this eternal being together of God and man is a concrete decree. It has as its content one name and one person. This decree is Jesus Christ, and for this very reason it cannot be a *decretum absolutum*" (II/2, 158).

101. Barth, *CD* II/2, 67.

102. Barth, *CD* II/2, 116–17.

103. Barth, *CD* II/2, 116.

Creation was made for Christ. As Barth puts it in volume 3 of the *Dogmatics*, the covenant is the "internal basis" of creation, the reason for creating in the first place. What God chose from all eternity—rather, *whom* God chose—is Jesus Christ, in his life, death, and resurrection, as the fulfillment of the covenant God would make with humanity.

Barth can speak, with the Reformed tradition, of double predestination, but not in terms of two subsets of humanity with two different eschatological destinations. Rather, "in the election of Jesus Christ which is the eternal will of God, God has ascribed to man the former, election, salvation and life; and to Himself He has ascribed the latter, reprobation, perdition and death."[104] Instead of predestining some for salvation and others for reprobation, God elects humanity in Christ for salvation and himself in Christ for reprobation. It is no longer a question of whether God will save or damn a particular person; indeed, in Christ, God reveals that this was *never* a question. God's first, last, and unequivocal word to humanity in Christ is, "Yes!" It is a word of affirmation, of life, of blessing and salvation. "We are no longer free, then, to think of God's eternal election as bifurcating into a rightward and a leftward election. There is a leftward election. But God willed that the object of this election should be Himself and not man."[105] There is still a "No" spoken, but "it is not a No spoken against man."[106] There is still damnation and rejection, but God has taken our damnation and rejection and made it his own, giving us in exchange his blessed life.[107]

Clearly, the election of Jesus Christ has far-reaching implications for humanity. But whereas traditional discussions of election take up the individual as their center of concern, Barth takes up Christ. Election's "direct and proper object is not individuals generally, but one individual—and only in Him the people called and united by Him, and only in that people individuals in general in their private relationships with God."[108] This is the order: Christ → the community → the individual. First, Christ is the elect one. His people, Israel and the Christian community, are elect by, in, and with him, as are individuals—indeed, all individuals. The rhetorical effect of reading hundreds of pages on the doctrine of election before getting to the election of individuals is to induct readers into a radical reconstrual of the purposes and ways of God. Slowly, readers cease to see themselves as the center of God's purposes and come instead to see Christ. For Barth, individuals generally are peripheral,

104. Barth, *CD* II/2, 163.
105. Barth, *CD* II/2, 172.
106. Barth, *CD* II/2, 166.
107. See Barth, *CD* II/2, 164.
108. Barth, *CD* II/2, 43.

in the strict sense; they do not lie in the center of God's gracious election. As the electing God, Jesus Christ elects these others "in His own humanity." But "His election is the original and all-inclusive election."[109]

Before moving on to Barth's magisterial doctrine of reconciliation, a brief word about the universal reach of election is warranted. Barth is clear that *all* of humanity is elect in Christ. The only difference between believers and nonbelievers is that the former *know* they are elect in Christ and joyfully witness to the truth of Christ. Does this position imply universalism? Barth resists such a move, believing it would foreclose on the divine freedom to assume that all people will be saved in the end. But Christians ought to hope and pray for such to be the case, he believes.[110] If Barth is a universalist, he is so for the best of reasons—because he believes that Christ really did take our place in his life, death, and resurrection, remaking sinful humanity in his image. Over against the emphasis on the piety and subjective experience that so worried him in the nineteenth century, Barth trumpeted the great objectivity of the gospel. Jesus Christ, not my pious feeling or even my faith, is the measure of reality. If everything has objectively changed in Christ, then, well, everything has changed.

## The Prodigal Son

"In Christ God was reconciling the world to himself, not counting their trespasses against them, and entrusting to us the ministry of reconciliation" (2 Cor. 5:19). As Barth reads Scripture—and in this, for all of his adjustments, he is deeply Reformed—at the heart of God's ways with the world lies the covenant.[111] The covenant is a fellowship with mutual obligations, but one initiated entirely from God's side. In its most basic form, the covenant names the relationship established in God's promise, "I will be your God, and you shall be my people."[112] Notice that God does not ask Israel if they would like to be his people. He tells him that this will be so, and this is a promise rather than a threat because it is good news. In the radical asymmetry of the relationship, this is a covenant of grace, as God stoops to an unworthy humanity. And it is all the more so in light of the sorry history of humanity's failure to keep the covenant. "And if the essence of God as the God of man is His grace,

---

109. Barth, CD II/2, 117.
110. See Barth, CD IV/3.1, 477–78.
111. See Barth's miniature biblical theology of covenant (one of the many exegetical asides that refute accusations that Barth plays fast and loose with Scripture) in Barth, CD IV/1, 22–34.
112. Barth references Jer. 7:23; 11:4; 30:22; 31:33; 32:38; Ezek. 36:28 (CD IV/1, 22).

then the essence of men as His people, that which is proper to and demanded of them in covenant with God, is simply their thanks."[113] "The grace of God calls for this modest but active return."[114] It is modest—hardly commensurate with the gift of grace, a faint echo of the rousing song of God's love—but still active—the fitting, proper response of humanity in joyful gratitude. This is not just what it is to be God's faithful covenant partner; it is what it is to be *human*. The covenant is decisive, being "the internal basis of creation," so that "'ye shall be my people' means that it is proper to you and required of you in your being, life and activity to correspond to the fact that in My being, life and activity for you I am your God."[115]

God keeps his promises. He is an ever-true covenant partner, never wavering in his steadfast commitment to his people. We, however, are another story, a tired, repetitive story of brief faithfulness followed by temptation, complaint, idolatry, ruin, and repentance, until the cycle begins again. Like addicts, we vow next time will be different. But it never is.

Until Jesus Christ. "In Him man keeps and maintains the same faithfulness to God that God had never ceased to maintain and keep to him."[116] Jesus Christ fulfills the covenant from both sides. He is God keeping covenant with us by restoring fellowship in his incarnation, death, and resurrection. He is also—and this is unprecedented—us keeping fellowship with God. Finally, someone has lived a life and died a death in which the promise "you shall be my people" is perfectly realized. Just so, in the fulfillment of the covenant, we are reconciled to God, and atonement is made. "The new man who keeps the covenant has been born and is alive and revealed. Therefore we have peace with God—without any uncertainty. This alteration in the human situation has already taken place. This being is self-contained. It does not have to be reached or created. It has already come and cannot be removed. . . . This is the mystery of the man reconciled to God in Jesus Christ."[117]

The language of this passage suggests that Barth has Ephesians 2:13–16 in mind. There, Paul describes the cross as the site of new creation, where Jews and Gentiles are reconciled to God and one another and made into "one new man." The central point, and the heartbeat of Barth's theology, is that the great alteration "has already taken place." Nothing remains to be done. "His death was the death of all: quite independently of their attitude or response to this event, not only when the proclamation of it comes to them and is received

113. Barth, *CD* IV/1, 42.
114. Barth, *CD* IV/1, 43.
115. Barth, *CD* IV/1, 42.
116. Barth, *CD* IV/1, 89.
117. Barth, *CD* IV/1, 90.

and accepted by them, not only in virtue of the effect of certain ecclesiastical institutions and activities, not only in the dark process of their taking up the cross, certainly not only in certain sacramental or mystical or even existential repetitions or reflections or applications of the event of the cross." No, Barth protests, the cross "needs no completion or re-presentation." What's done is done. Anything further "should attest this event but only attest it."[118] Barth has in his sights the kind of piety that seems more concerned that Christ should be born in our hearts than that he be born in a manger. Such piety, though rightly concerned that the affections be awakened by Christ, can easily trade devotion to the God-man for fascination with the vagaries of religious emotion.

Barth seeks to take Paul's language of dying and rising with Christ as seriously as possible, but whereas Paul refers to our having died and risen with Christ when we repented, believed, and were baptized, Barth looks back further. We died and rose with Christ when Christ died and rose—all of humanity did.[119] "[God] has acted, therefore, without us and against us and for us, as a free subject in Jesus Christ. . . . What He has done is not just something which applies to us and is intended for us, a proffered opportunity and possibility. In it He has actually taken us, embraced us, as it were surrounded us, seized us from behind and turned us back again to Himself."[120]

The good news is not a once-in-a-lifetime offer. It is an announcement of something that has already happened. God has made us new. Our sins have been forgiven. We have been reconciled to God in Christ. Therefore, "the history of Jesus Christ, precisely, that is my history! It is closer to me than the various events of my own life."[121] Our lives are hidden with Christ in God, and Christ *is* our life (see Col. 3:3–4). "In Jesus Christ, God gives us his life and takes ours. Our life becomes his concern and his life becomes our concern. Whether we are sinners is no longer our concern, nor is it any longer our business."[122] This explains something of Barth's discomfort with Billy Graham's evangelistic methods. As Eberhard Busch writes, "This truth is not expressed as 'Accept it, otherwise it is not real for you,' but as 'Because it is real for you too, accept it!'"[123]

---

118. Barth, *CD* IV/1, 295–96.
119. George Hunsinger writes: "When God comes to humanity in the history of Jesus Christ, humanity at the same time is brought to God in that history objectively. It is not faith which incorporates humanity into Jesus Christ. Faith is rather the acknowledgement of a mysterious incorporation already objectively accomplished on humanity's behalf" (*How to Read Karl Barth*, 37).
120. Barth, *CD* IV/1, 88–89.
121. Barth, *Faith of the Church*, 97.
122. Barth, *Faith of the Church*, 155.
123. Busch, *Karl Barth and the Pietists*, 303.

Most simply put, the doctrine of reconciliation can be summed up in a name—Emmanuel. Jesus Christ is "God with us," which means, too, that he is "us with God." But it is misleading to think of this as a state of affairs. Barth describes Emmanuel not as a state but as a history, unfurling a vast, textured, inclusive narrative Christology. He takes the various parts of traditional accounts of Christology and reworks them, composing a symphony of reconciliation. The person and work of Christ are inextricable, and "the being of Jesus Christ, the unity of being of the living God and this living man takes place in the event of the concrete existence of this man. It is a being, but a being in a history"—and so it is best to speak of "His active person or His personal work."[124] The two natures and two states of Christ are combined, so that in Christ "humanity is exalted humanity just as Godhead is humiliated Godhead."[125] The two states aren't stages, in which the suffering servant lives his earthly life and then is exalted in the resurrection, but two "sides or directions or forms of that which took place in Jesus Christ for the reconciliation of man with God."[126] Moreover, Barth counterintuitively applies the states, such that it is not God but humanity who is exalted. Still, while this may be counterintuitive, it is fitting: "In Him God Himself humiliated Himself—not in any disloyalty but in a supreme loyalty to His divine being (revealing it in a way which marks it off from all other gods)."[127] Barth treats the three offices of Christ under the rubric of "The Lord as Servant" (priest), "The Servant as Lord" (king), and "The True Witness" (prophet). Finally, Barth sets his narrative Christology against the backdrop of the parable of the prodigal son. I will pick out just a couple salient features of Barth's breathtaking doctrine of reconciliation below.

Consider, to begin with, the way in which God is with us, according to Barth. In Christ, God draws near to us as the Lord who is a servant. How does he serve? By making his way into the far country and there taking our place. In becoming flesh, the eternal Son becomes the prodigal son: "The way of the Son of God into the far country, i.e., into the lowliness of creaturely being, of being as man, into unity and solidarity with sinful and therefore perishing humanity, the way of His incarnation is as such the activation, the demonstration, the revelation of His deity, His divine Sonship."[128] Barth will have no truck with theologies that find in Jesus's identification with sinners

124. Barth, CD IV/1, 126, 128.
125. Barth, CD IV/1, 131.
126. Barth, CD IV/1, 133.
127. Barth, CD IV/1, 134.
128. Barth, CD IV/1, 211. Note that the younger son in Jesus's parable travels to "a far country" where "he squandered his property in reckless living" (Luke 15:13).

a threat to his deity. No, this identification is the very revelation of his deity, the way in which God *is* in Christ. As a result, Barth doesn't shrink back from the implications of Christ's having taken on our plight: "His is a creaturely, human and even sinful essence. It is flesh with all the weakness of flesh."[129] Creaturely, human: yes—but sinful? What does Barth mean by this?

> That the Word became "flesh" means that the Son of God made His own the situation of man in the sense that with him He faced the impossible in all its power, that He faced the dreadful possibility of ingratitude, disobedience, unfaithfulness, pride, cowardice and deceit, that He knew it as well as He did Himself, that He came to closer grips with it than any other man. He had to achieve His freedom and obedience as a link in the chain of an enslaved and disobedient humanity. . . . He was not immune from sin. He did not commit it, but He was not immune from it. In this respect, too, He became the brother of man. He did not float over the human situation like a being of a completely different kind.[130]

Jesus could free us from sin only as part of "an enslaved and disobedient humanity." He was tempted "in every respect" as we are, "yet without sin" (Heb. 4:15). "His condition was no different from ours. He took our flesh, the nature of man as he comes from the fall. . . . His sinlessness was not therefore His condition. It was the act of His being in which He defeated temptation in His condition which is ours, in the flesh."[131] Barth seems to imply here that Christ was peccable—he was able to sin. Or rather, he emphasizes that the sinlessness of Jesus does not name an inherent (in)capacity, his inability to sin, but a history of faithfulness in which he never gives himself over to sin. His sinlessness was not a given, but rather something achieved over the course of Jesus's temptations as he trusted the Father in the Spirit.

In his faithful obedience to the Father, the sinless Jesus takes on the sins of the world, becoming "the unrighteous amongst those who can no longer be so because He was and is for them."[132] Barth writes that "in His own person He has made an end of us as sinners and therefore of sin itself by going to death as the One who took our place as sinners. . . . He has removed us sinners and sin, negated us, cancelled us out."[133] We do not evade judgment, as if all God's threats hurled at covenant breakers were bluffs. "Everything happened

---

129. Barth, *CD* IV/2, 96.
130. Barth, *CD* IV/1, 215–16.
131. Barth, *CD* IV/1, 258–59. On Jesus's temptations, in the wilderness and Gethsemane, see 259–73.
132. Barth, *CD* IV/1, 237.
133. Barth, *CD* IV/1, 253.

to us exactly as it had to happen," Barth insists, "but because God willed to execute His judgment on us in His Son it all happened in His person, as His accusation and condemnation and destruction. He judged, and it was the Judge who was judged, who let Himself be judged."[134]

That is how God is with us in Christ—in humiliation. Everything else Barth will say about reconciliation from this angle derives from the obedience of the Son of God. We may not like it—and Barth understands sin precisely as our proud refusal of this divine condescension—but all of humanity is determined by this servant-king.

The second salient point to mention about Barth's doctrine of reconciliation complements the first: if in Christ God is with us in humility, in Christ we are with God in exaltation. The life, death, and resurrection of Jesus are the way of the Son of God into the far country; they are also, and just so, the homecoming of the Son of Man.[135] In the parable of the prodigal son (Luke 15:11–24), the younger son returns to his father's house in shame, only to be met by a jubilant father who falls on his son, embraces him, and throws him a lavish party to celebrate his return. Barth clarifies that this is not deification, a making God, but an exaltation of humanity to fellowship with God.[136] It is an active fellowship, in which God gives humanity in Christ a share in his work. Of sanctification in Christ, Barth writes that "sanctification means exaltation, but because it is exaltation in fellowship with the One who came to serve it is exaltation to the lowliness in which He served and still serves, and rules as He serves."[137] The "divine Yes [is] echoed by the royal man Jesus," and in him we too answer God's glorious affirmation with one of our own.[138]

Barth is clear that in Christ "the homecoming of the Son of Man has already taken place."[139] Humanity is no longer wandering in the far country, but in Christ we have found our way home. This conclusion follows from the assumption of humanity in the incarnation: "What God the Son assumed into unity with Himself and His divine being was and is—in a specific individual form elected and prepared for this purpose—not merely "a man" but the *humanum*, the being and essence, the nature and kind, which is that of all men, which characterises them all as men, and distinguishes them from other creatures."[140] Because the Son assumed human being as such, "His incarnation

---

134. Barth, *CD* IV/1, 222.
135. See Barth, *CD* IV/2, 20–154.
136. Barth, *CD* IV/2, 117.
137. Barth, *CD* IV/2, 691.
138. Barth, *CD* IV/2, 180.
139. Barth, *CD* IV/2, 117.
140. Barth, *CD* IV/2, 48.

signifies the promise of the basic alteration and determination of what we all are as men. In Jesus Christ it is not merely one man, but the *humanum* of all men, which is posited and exalted as such to unity with God."[141] He describes what took place in Christ as "the new impression of humanity as such."[142]

We are back again at the question of what remains for us to do, given the expansiveness of Christ. Quite a lot, it turns out. For even if the question of humanity has been answered in Christ, even if those who were lost have been found in him, the prodigal son returned, sinners forgiven, the dead raised, nevertheless there is work to do. We have been exalted to fellowship with our Lord the servant and are invited to join him outside the camp (see Heb. 13:13). We have been given a direction, summoned by Christ "to act as the men we are, in real freedom."[143] We are not "reduced to mere spectators" but "are made free for Him. . . . This one thing does not mean the extinguishing of our humanity, but its establishment."[144] The people of God are "those who know that this is all that remains to us, but that it does remain to us" to witness to Emmanuel with joy and gratitude.

## The Humanity of God

Barth once snarled that one cannot speak of God simply by speaking of humanity "in a somewhat higher pitch."[145] He later remembered the iconoclasm of those early days: "How we cleared things away! And we did almost nothing but clear away!"[146] "We viewed this 'wholly other' in isolation, abstracted and absolutized, and set it over against man, this miserable wretch—not to say boxed his ears with it—in such fashion that it continually showed greater similarity to the deity of the God of the philosophers than to the deity of the God of Abraham, Isaac, and Jacob."[147]

In retrospect, Barth sees how close his theological iconoclasm came to idolatry, setting up a false god (that of the philosophers, the abstract "wholly other") in the place of the one, true God of Abraham, Isaac, and Jacob, the God and Father of our Lord Jesus Christ. If Barth continued throughout his career to uphold the magisterial freedom and glory of God, he nevertheless acknowledged that the one, true God can even become a man. He is not so

141. Barth, *CD* IV/2, 49.
142. Barth, *CD* IV/2, 519.
143. Barth, *CD* IV/2, 362.
144. Barth, *CD* IV/1, 14–15.
145. Barth, *Word of God and Theology*, 183.
146. Barth, *Humanity of God*, 43.
147. Barth, *Humanity of God*, 45.

other that he cannot become one of us; or better, his otherness is seen precisely in the loving freedom in which he becomes one of us. And so, Barth ends his career by confessing that, in order to speak properly of God, one *must* speak of humanity: "It is precisely God's *deity* which, rightly understood, includes his *humanity*." He continues: "How do we come to know that? What permits and requires this statement? It is a *Christological* statement, or rather one grounded in and to be unfolded from Christology."[148] It is not that Barth has given up his earlier insistence on God as wholly other or that he has softened in his old age, trading in a radically transcendent God for a kinder, gentler version. Rather, he has consistently meditated on the God he first met in the strange world of the Bible, the God "who looks on the earth and it trembles, who touches the mountains and they smoke" (Ps. 104:32), who formed Leviathan to play in the seas (v. 26), and whose glory has shone in the face of Christ (2 Cor. 4:6). Barth would confess, "There is none like you, O Lord"—and he would add in the same breath that this same one was "made like his brothers in every respect" (Heb. 2:17). For Barth, it was always Christ.

148. Barth, *Humanity of God*, 46.

# BIBLIOGRAPHY

Allen, Michael, and Scott R. Swain. *Reformed Catholicity: The Promise of Retrieval for Theology and Biblical Interpretation*. Grand Rapids: Baker Academic, 2015.

Allen, R. Michael. *The Christ's Faith: A Dogmatic Account*. New York: T&T Clark, 2009.

Althaus, Paul. *The Theology of Martin Luther*. Translated by Robert C. Schultz. Philadelphia: Fortress, 1966.

Anatolios, Khaled. *Athanasius: The Coherence of His Thought*. New York: Routledge, 1998.

———. *Retrieving Nicaea: The Development and Meaning of Trinitarian Doctrine*. Grand Rapids: Baker Academic, 2011.

Anselm of Canterbury. *Anselm of Canterbury: The Major Works*. Edited by Brian Davies and G. R. Evans. Oxford: Oxford University Press, 2008.

Athanasius. *Letters to Serapion on the Holy Spirit*. In *Works on the Spirit: Athanasius and Didymus the Blind*. Translated by Mark DelCogliano, Andrew Radde-Gallwitz, and Lewis Ayres. Crestwood, NY: St. Vladimir's Seminary Press, 2011.

———. *On the Incarnation*. Translated and edited by A Religious of C.S.M.V. Crestwood, NY: St. Vladimir's Seminary Press, 1993.

———. *Select Works and Letters*. In vol. 4 of *Nicene and Post-Nicene Fathers*, Series 2. Edited by Archibald Robertson. New York: Christian Literature Company, 1892.

Augustine. *City of God*. Translated by Henry Bettenson. New York: Penguin Books, 1984.

———. *Confessions*. Translated by Henry Chadwick. Oxford: Oxford University Press, 2009.

———. *Enchiridion on Faith, Hope, and Love*. Translated by J. B. Shaw. Washington, DC: Regnery, 1996.

———. *Expositions of the Psalms, 1–32*. Translated by Maria Boulding. Edited by John E. Rotelle. Hyde Park, NY: New City Press, 2000.

———. *Homilies on the Gospel of John 1–40*. Translated by Edmund Hill. Edited by Allan D. Fitzgerald. Hyde Park, NY: New City Press, 2009.

———. *On Christian Teaching*. Translated by R. P. H. Green. Oxford: Oxford University Press, 1999.

———. *Selected Writings on Grace and Pelagianism*. Translated by Roland Teske. Edited by Boniface Ramsey. Hyde Park, NY: New City Press, 2011.

———. *The Trinity*. Translated by Edmund Hill. Edited by John E. Rotelle. Hyde Park, NY: New City Press, 1991.

Aulén, Gustaf. *Christus Victor: An Historical Study of the Three Main Types of the Idea of the Atonement*. Translated by A. G. Herbert. New York: Collier Books, 1986.

Ayres, Lewis. *Nicaea and Its Legacy: An Approach to Fourth-Century Trinitarian Theology*. New York: Oxford University Press, 2004.

Badcock, Gary D. *The House Where God Lives: Renewing the Doctrine of the Church for Today*. Grand Rapids: Eerdmans, 2009.

Bainton, Roland H. *Here I Stand: A Life of Martin Luther*. London: Hodder & Stoughton, 1952.

Balthasar, Hans Urs von. *The Glory of the Lord*. Vol. 2, *Clerical Styles*. Edinburgh: T&T Clark, 1985.

Barnes, Timothy. *Athanasius and Constantius: Theology and Politics in the Constantinian Empire*. Cambridge, MA: Harvard University Press, 1993.

———. *Constantine and Eusebius*. Cambridge, MA: Harvard University Press, 1981.

Barth, Karl. *Ad Limina Apostolorum: An Appraisal of Vatican II*. Translated by Keith R. Crim. Richmond: John Knox Press, 1968.

———. *Anselm: Fides Quaerens Intellectum; Anselm's Proof of the Existence of God in the Context of His Theological Scheme*. Translated by Ian W. Robertson. 2nd ed. London: SCM, 1960.

———. *Church Dogmatics*. Translated and edited by G. W. Bromiley and T. F. Torrance. 13 vols. Edinburgh: T&T Clark, 1956–75.

———. *The Epistle to the Romans*. Translated by Edwyn C. Hoskyns. 6th ed. Oxford: Oxford University Press, 1933.

———. *Evangelical Theology: An Introduction*. Translated by Grover Foley. Grand Rapids: Eerdmans, 1963.

———. *The Faith of the Church: A Commentary on the Apostles' Creed according to Calvin's Catechism*. Translated by Gabriel Vahanian. New York: Living Age Books, 1958.

———. *Fragments Grave and Gay*. Translated by Eric Mosbacher. Edited by Martin Rumscheidt. London: Collins, 1971.

————. *The Humanity of God*. Translated by John Newton Thomas and Thomas Wieser. Louisville: Westminster John Knox, 1960.

————. "Introductory Essay." In *The Essence of Christianity*, by Ludwig Feuerbach, translated by George Eliot, x–xxxii. New York: Harper & Row, 1957.

————. *Letters, 1961–1968*. Translated by Geoffrey W. Bromiley. Edited by Jürgen Fangmeier and Hinrich Stoevesandt. Edinburgh: T&T Clark, 1981.

————. *Protestant Theology in the Nineteenth Century: Its Background and History*. Translated by Brian Cozens and John Bowden. Grand Rapids: Eerdmans, 2002.

————. *The Theology of Schleiermacher*. Translated by G. W. Bromiley. Edited by Dietrich Ritschl. Grand Rapids: Eerdmans, 1982.

————. *The Word of God and Theology*. Translated by Amy Marga. New York: T&T Clark, 2011.

Barth, Karl, and Rudolf Bultmann. *Karl Barth–Rudolf Bultmann Letters, 1922–1966*. Translated by Geoffrey W. Bromiley. Edited by Bernd Jaspert and Geoffrey W. Bromiley. Edinburgh: T&T Clark, 1982.

Bauerschmidt, Frederick Christian. *Thomas Aquinas: Faith, Reason, and Following Christ*. Oxford: Oxford University Press, 2013.

Bayer, Oswald. *Theology the Lutheran Way*. Translated and edited by Jeffrey G. Silcock and Mark C. Mattes. Grand Rapids: Eerdmans, 2007.

Beale, G. K. *The Temple and the Church's Mission: A Biblical Theology of the Dwelling Place of God*. Downers Grove, IL: IVP Academic, 2004.

Behr, John. *Formation of Christian Theology*. Vol. 1, *The Way to Nicaea*. Crestwood, NY: St. Vladimir's Seminary Press, 2001.

————. *Formation of Christian Theology*. Vol. 2, *The Nicene Faith*. Crestwood, NY: St. Vladimir's Seminary Press, 2004.

————. *Irenaeus of Lyons: Identifying Christianity*. Oxford: Oxford University Press, 2013.

Bergquist, Anders. "Gnosticism: Can People Be Saved by Acquiring Secret Knowledge?" In Quash and Ward, *Heresies and How to Avoid Them*, 102–12.

Billings, J. Todd. *Calvin, Participation, and the Gift: The Activity of Believers in Union with Christ*. Oxford: Oxford University Press, 2007.

————. *The Word of God for the People of God: An Entryway to the Theological Interpretation of Scripture*. Grand Rapids: Eerdmans, 2010.

Bird, Michael F., and Preston M. Sprinkle, eds. *The Faith of Jesus Christ: Exegetical, Biblical, and Theological Studies*. Peabody, MA: Hendrickson, 2009.

Bonhoeffer, Dietrich, and Maria von Wedemeyer. *Love Letters from Cell 92: The Correspondence between Dietrich Bonhoeffer and Maria von Wedemeyer*. Translated by John Brownjohn. Edited by Ruth-Alice von Bismarck and Ulrich Kabitz. Nashville: Abingdon, 1995.

Boulton, Matthew Myer. *Life in God: John Calvin, Practical Formation, and the Future of Protestant Theology*. Grand Rapids: Eerdmans, 2011.

Bouwsma, William J. *John Calvin: A Sixteenth-Century Portrait*. New York: Oxford University Press, 1988.

Brakke, David. *Athanasius and Asceticism*. Baltimore: Johns Hopkins University Press, 1985.

Brecht, Martin. *Martin Luther: His Road to Reformation, 1483–1521*. Translated by James L. Schaaf. Minneapolis: Fortress, 1985.

———. *Martin Luther: Shaping and Defining the Reformation, 1521–1532*. Translated by James L. Schaaf. Minneapolis: Fortress, 1990.

———. *Martin Luther: The Preservation of the Church, 1532–1546*. Translated by James L. Schaaf. Minneapolis: Fortress, 1993.

Brown, Joanne C., and Carole R. Bohn, eds. *Christianity, Patriarchy, and Abuse*. New York: Pilgrim, 1989.

Brown, Peter. *Augustine of Hippo: A Biography*. London: Faber & Faber, 2000.

Brunner, Emil. *The Mediator: A Study of the Central Doctrine of the Christian Faith*. Translated by Olive Wyon. Philadelphia: Westminster, 1947.

Brunner, Emil, and Karl Barth. *Natural Theology: Comprising "Nature and Grace" by Professor Dr. Emil Brunner and the Reply "No!" by Dr. Karl Barth*. Translated by Peter Fraenkel. Eugene, OR: Wipf & Stock, 2002.

Burrell, David B. "Act of Creation with Its Theological Consequences." In *Aquinas on Doctrine*, edited by Thomas Weinandy, Daniel Keating, and John Yocum, 27–44. New York: T&T Clark, 2004.

———. "Analogy, Creation, and Theological Language." In Van Nieuwenhove and Wawrykow, *Theology of Thomas Aquinas*, 77–98.

Busch, Eberhard. *The Barmen Theses Then and Now*. Translated by Darrell and Judith Guder. Grand Rapids: Eerdmans, 2010.

———. *Karl Barth and the Pietists: The Young Karl Barth's Critique of Pietism and Its Response*. Translated by Daniel W. Bloesch. Downers Grove, IL: InterVarsity, 2004.

———. *Karl Barth: His Life from Letters and Autobiographical Texts*. Translated by John Bowden. Grand Rapids: Eerdmans, 1994.

Butin, Philip Walker. *Revelation, Redemption, and Response: Calvin's Trinitarian Understanding of the Divine-Human Relationship*. Oxford: Oxford University Press, 1995.

Calvin, John. *Calvin's Commentaries*. Translated by the Calvin Translation Society. Edited by John King et al. 22 vols. Edinburgh, 1843–55. Reprint, Grand Rapids: Baker, 2009.

———. *Institutes of the Christian Religion*. Translated by Ford Lewis Battles. Edited by John T. McNeill. 2 vols. Louisville: Westminster John Knox, 1960.

Canlis, Julie. *Calvin's Ladder: A Spiritual Theology of Ascent and Ascension.* Grand Rapids: Eerdmans, 2010.

Carson, D. A. *Exegetical Fallacies.* 2nd ed. Grand Rapids: Baker Academic, 1996.

Cary, Phillip. "Why Luther Is Not Quite Protestant: The Logic of Faith in a Sacramental Promise." *Pro Ecclesia* 14 (2005): 447–86.

Catholic Church. *Catechism of the Catholic Church.* 2nd ed. Vatican: Libreria Editrice Vaticana, 2012.

Cavadini, John C. "Augustine's Homiletic Meteorology." *Church Life: A Journal for the New Evangelization* 1 (2012): 65–71.

Cessario, Romanus. *A Short History of Thomism.* Washington, DC: Catholic University of America Press, 2005.

Chadwick, Henry. *Augustine.* Oxford: Oxford University Press, 1986.

Chenu, Marie-Dominique. *Aquinas and His Role in Theology.* Translated by Paul Philibert. Collegeville, MN: Liturgical Press, 2002.

Chesterton, G. K. *Orthodoxy.* In vol. 1 of *The Collected Works of G. K. Chesterton.* San Francisco: Ignatius Press, 1986.

———. *What's Wrong with the World.* In vol. 4 of *The Collected Works of G. K. Chesterton.* San Francisco: Ignatius Press, 1987.

———. *St. Thomas Aquinas.* London: Hodder & Stoughton, 1933.

Clark, Mary T. *Augustine.* New York: Continuum, 1994.

Crisp, Oliver. *Divinity and Humanity: The Incarnation Reconsidered.* Cambridge: Cambridge University Press, 2007.

———. *God Incarnate: Explorations in Christology.* New York: T&T Clark, 2007.

———. *Jonathan Edwards on God and Creation.* New York: Oxford University Press, 2012.

———. "Jonathan Edwards's Ontology: A Critique of Sang Hyun Lee's Dispositional Account of Edwardsian Metaphysics." *Religious Studies* 46 (2010): 1–20.

Daley, Brian E. "A Humble Mediator: The Distinctive Elements in Saint Augustine's Christology." *Word and Spirit* 9 (1987): 100–117.

Daniel, Stephen H. "Edwards' Occasionalism." In Schweitzer, *Jonathan Edwards as Contemporary,* 1–14.

Dante Alighieri. *Paradise.* Translated by Anthony Esolen. New York: Modern Library, 2007.

Davies, Brian. *The Thought of Thomas Aquinas.* Oxford: Clarendon, 1992.

Decosimo, David. *Ethics as a Work of Charity: Thomas Aquinas and Pagan Virtue.* Stanford, CA: Stanford University Press, 2014.

Descartes, René. *Meditations on First Philosophy.* Edited and translated by John Cottingham. Cambridge: Cambridge University Press, 1996.

DeVries, Dawn. *Jesus Christ in the Preaching of Calvin and Schleiermacher.* Louisville: Westminster John Knox, 1996.

Dillard, Annie. *An American Childhood*. New York: Harper & Row, 1989.

———. *Pilgrim at Tinker Creek*. New York: HarperCollins, 1974.

———. *The Writing Life*. New York: HarperPerennial, 1989.

Dulles, Avery. *A History of Apologetics*. San Francisco: Ignatius, 2005.

Edwards, Jonathan. *The Works of Jonathan Edwards*. Edited by Perry Miller, John E. Smith, and Harry S. Stout. 26 vols. New Haven: Yale University Press, 1957–2008.

———. *The Works of Jonathan Edwards Online*. http://edwards.yale.edu.

Emery, Gilles. "Trinity and Creation." In Van Nieuwenhove and Wawrykow, *Theology of Thomas Aquinas*, 58–76.

Eusebius. *The History of the Church from Christ to Constantine*. Translated by G. A. Williamson. Revised and edited by Andrew Louth. New York: Penguin, 1989.

Evans, G. R. *Anselm*. New York: Continuum, 1989.

Farrow, Douglas. *Ascension and Ecclesia: On the Significance of the Doctrine of the Ascension for Ecclesiology and Christian Cosmology*. Edinburgh: T&T Clark, 1999.

Filoramo, Giovanni. *A History of Gnosticism*. Translated by Anthony Alcock. Cambridge, MA: Blackwell, 1990.

Forde, Gerhard O. *Where God Meets Man: Luther's Down-to-Earth Approach to the Gospel*. Minneapolis: Augsburg, 1972.

Gavrilyuk, Paul L. *The Suffering of the Impassible God: The Dialectics of Patristic Thought*. Oxford: Oxford University Press, 2004.

Gerrish, B. A. *Continuing the Reformation: Essays on Modern Religious Thought*. Chicago: University of Chicago Press, 1993.

———. *A Prince of the Church: Schleiermacher and the Beginnings of Modern Theology*. Philadelphia: Fortress, 1984.

———. *Tradition and the Modern World: Reformed Theology in the Nineteenth Century*. Chicago: University of Chicago Press, 1978.

Golitzin, Alexander. *Mystagogy: A Monastic Reading of Dionysius Areopagita*. Edited by Bogdan G. Bucur. Collegeville, MN: Liturgical Press, 2013.

Gordon, Bruce. *Calvin*. New Haven: Yale University Press, 2009.

Gregory of Nazianzus. *On God and Christ: The Five Theological Orations and Two Letters to Cledonius*. Translated by Lionel Wickham. New York: St. Vladimir's Seminary Press, 2002.

Gregory of Nyssa. *Catechetical Oration*. Translated by Cyril C. Richardson. In *Christology of the Later Fathers*, edited by Edward R. Hardy, 268–325. Louisville: Westminster John Knox, 1954.

———. *The Life of Moses*. Translated by Abraham Malherbe. New York: Paulist Press, 1978.

Griffiths, Paul J. *Intellectual Appetite: A Theological Grammar*. Washington, DC: Catholic University of America Press, 2009.

Gunton, Colin E. *The Actuality of Atonement: A Study of Metaphor, Rationality, and the Christian Tradition*. New York: T&T Clark, 1998.

———. *Being and Becoming: The Doctrine of God in Charles Hartshorne and Karl Barth*. London: SCM, 2001.

———. *Father, Son, and Holy Spirit: Toward a Fully Trinitarian Theology*. New York: T&T Clark, 2003.

———. *The Triune Creator: A Historical and Systematic Study*. Grand Rapids: Eerdmans, 1998.

Gwynn, David. *Athanasius of Alexandria: Bishop, Theologian, Ascetic, Father*. New York: Oxford University Press, 2012.

Hadot, Pierre. *Philosophy as a Way of Life: Spiritual Exercises from Socrates to Foucault*. Malden, MA: Blackwell, 1995.

Hart, David Bentley. *The Beauty of the Infinite: The Aesthetics of Christian Truth*. Grand Rapids: Eerdmans, 2004.

Hart, Trevor. "Irenaeus, Recapitulation, and Physical Redemption." In *Christ in Our Place: The Humanity of God in Christ for the Reconciliation of the World; Essays Presented to Professor James Torrance*, edited by Trevor A. Hart and Daniel P. Thimell, 152–81. Allison Park, PA: Pickwick, 1989.

Hays, Richard. *The Faith of Jesus Christ: The Narrative Substructure of Galatians 3:1–4:11*. 2nd ed. Grand Rapids: Eerdmans, 2001.

Healy, Nicholas M. *Church, World, and the Christian Life: Practical-Prophetic Ecclesiology*. Cambridge: Cambridge University Press, 2000.

Heaney, Seamus. *Poems, 1965–1975*. New York: Farrar, Straus & Giroux, 1980.

Hector, Kevin W. "Actualism and Incarnation: The High Christology of Friedrich Schleiermacher." *International Journal of Systematic Theology* 8 (2006): 307–22.

———. *The Theological Project of Modernism: Faith and the Conditions of Mineness*. Oxford: Oxford University Press, 2015.

Helmer, Christine. "The Consummation of Reality: Soteriological Metaphysics in Schleiermacher's Interpretation of Colossians 1:15–20." In *Biblical Interpretation: History, Context, and Reality*, edited by C. Helmer and T. G. Petrey, 113–32. Atlanta: Society of Biblical Literature, 2005.

———. *Theology and the End of Doctrine*. Louisville: Westminster John Knox, 2014.

Hieb, Nathan D. "The Precarious Status of Resurrection in Friedrich Schleiermacher's *Glaubenslehre*." *International Journal of Systematic Theology* 9 (2007): 398–414.

Hodge, Charles. *Systematic Theology*. Vol. 1. Grand Rapids: Eerdmans, 1970.

Hogg, David S. *Anselm of Canterbury: The Beauty of Theology*. Burlington, VT: Ashgate, 2004.

Holmes, Stephen R. "Does Jonathan Edwards Use a Dispositional Ontology? A Response to Sang Hyun Lee." In *Jonathan Edwards: Philosophical Theologian*, edited by Paul Helm and Oliver D. Crisp, 99–114. Aldershot, UK: Ashgate, 2003.

———. "A Simple Salvation? Soteriology and the Perfections of God." In *God of Salvation: Soteriology in Theological Perspective*, edited by Ivor J. Davidson and Murray A. Rae, 35–46. Burlington, VT: Ashgate, 2011.

Hunsinger, George. *How to Read Karl Barth: The Shape of His Theology*. New York: Oxford University Press, 1993.

Irenaeus of Lyons. *Against Heresies*. Edited by Alexander Roberts, James Donaldson, and A. Cleveland Coxe. N.p.: Ex Fontibus, 2010.

———. *On the Apostolic Preaching*. Translated by John Behr. Crestwood, NY: St. Vladimir's Seminary Press, 1997.

Jacobs, Alan. *Looking Before and After: Testimony and the Christian Life*. Grand Rapids: Eerdmans, 2008.

———. *Original Sin: A Cultural History*. San Francisco: HarperOne, 2008.

———. *A Theology of Reading: The Hermeneutics of Love*. Boulder, CO: Westview, 2001.

Jenson, Matt. *The Gravity of Sin: Augustine, Luther, and Barth on* homo incurvatus in se. New York: T&T Clark, 2007.

———. "'Where the Spirit of the Lord Is, There Is Freedom': Barth on Ecclesial Agency." *Pro Ecclesia* 24 (2015): 517–37.

Jenson, Matt, and David Wilhite. *The Church: A Guide for the Perplexed*. New York: T&T Clark, 2010.

Jenson, Robert W. *Canon and Creed*. Louisville: Westminster John Knox, 2010.

———. *Systematic Theology*. Vol. 1, *The Triune God*. Oxford: Oxford University Press, 1997.

———. *The Triune Identity: God according to the Gospel*. Eugene, OR: Wipf & Stock, 2002.

Jüngel, Eberhard. *God's Being Is in Becoming: The Trinitarian Being of God in the Theology of Karl Barth*. Translated by John Webster. Edinburgh: T&T Clark, 2001.

———. *Karl Barth: A Theological Legacy*. Translated by Garrett E. Paul. Philadelphia: Westminster, 1986.

Kant, Immanuel. "An Answer to the Question: What Is Enlightenment?" In *Practical Philosophy*, translated and edited by Mary J. Gregor, 15–22. Cambridge: Cambridge University Press, 1996.

Kaufman, Peter Iver. "Redeeming Politics: Augustine's Cities of God." In *The City of God: A Collection of Critical Essays*, edited by Dorothy F. Donnelly, 75–91. New York: Peter Lang, 1995.

Kelly, J. N. D. *Early Christian Doctrines*. 5th ed. New York: Continuum, 1977.

Kelsey, Catherine L. *Schleiermacher's Preaching, Dogmatics, and Biblical Criticism: The Interpretation of Jesus in the Gospel of John*. Eugene, OR: Pickwick, 2007.

———. *Thinking about Christ with Schleiermacher*. Louisville: Westminster John Knox, 2003.

Keshgegian, Flora A. "The Scandal of the Cross: Revisiting Anselm and His Feminist Critics." *Anglican Theological Review* 82 (2000): 475–92.

Kierkegaard, Søren. *Philosophical Fragments / Johannes Climacus*. Edited and translated by Howard V. Hong and Edna H. Hong. Princeton: Princeton University Press, 1985.

King, Karen. *What Is Gnosticism?* Cambridge, MA: Harvard University Press, 2003.

Kolb, Robert. *Martin Luther: Confessor of the Faith*. Oxford: Oxford University Press, 2009.

Kruszelnicki, Karl S. "Ostrich Head in Sand." *ABC Science*, November 2, 2006. http://www.abc.net.au/science/articles/2006/11/02/1777947.htm.

Kunnuthara, Abraham Varghese. *Schleiermacher on Christian Consciousness of God's Work in History*. Eugene, OR: Pickwick, 2008.

Kuyper, Abraham. "Sphere Sovereignty." In *Abraham Kuyper: A Centennial Reader*, edited by James Bratt, 461–90. Grand Rapids: Eerdmans, 1998.

Law, David R. *Kierkegaard's Kenotic Christology*. Oxford: Oxford University Press, 2013.

Leclercq, Jean. *The Love of Learning and the Desire for God: A Study of Monastic Culture*. Translated by Catharine Misrahi. New York: Fordham University Press, 1961.

Lee, Sang Hyun. "God's Relation to the World." In *The Princeton Companion to Jonathan Edwards*, edited by Sang Hyun Lee, 59–71. Princeton: Princeton University Press, 2005.

———. "Jonathan Edwards's Dispositional Conception of the Trinity: A Resource for Contemporary Reformed Theology." In *Toward the Future of Reformed Theology: Tasks, Topics, Traditions*, edited by David Willis and Michael Welker, 444–55. Grand Rapids: Eerdmans, 1999.

———. *The Philosophical Theology of Jonathan Edwards*. Princeton: Princeton University Press, 2000.

Leith, John C., ed. *Creeds of the Churches*. 3rd ed. Louisville: Westminster John Knox, 1982.

Leithart, Peter J. *Athanasius*. Grand Rapids: Baker Academic, 2011.

Letham, Robert. *The Holy Trinity: In Scripture, History, Theology, and Worship*. Phillipsburg, NJ: P&R, 2004.

Lewis, C. S. *Mere Christianity*. New York: Macmillan, 1960.

Lohse, Bernhard. *Martin Luther's Theology: Its Historical and Systematic Development*. Edited and translated by Roy A. Harrisville. Minneapolis: Fortress, 1999.

Long, D. Stephen. *Saving Karl Barth: Hans Urs von Balthasar's Preoccupation*. Minneapolis: Fortress, 2014.

Louth, Andrew. *Denys the Areopagite*. Wilton, CT: Morehouse-Barlow, 1989.

———. *The Origins of the Christian Mystical Tradition: From Plato to Denys*. Oxford: Clarendon, 1981.

Luther, Martin. *The Complete Sermons of Martin Luther*. Grand Rapids: Baker Books, 2000.

———. *Large Catechism*. In *The Book of Concord: The Confessions of the Evangelical Lutheran Church*, translated and edited by Theodore G. Tappert, 357–461. Philadelphia: Fortress, 1959.

———. *Luther's Works*. American ed. Edited by J. Pelikan and H. Lehmann. 55 vols. St. Louis: Concordia; Philadelphia: Fortress Press, 1955–86.

———. *The Schmalkald Articles*. In *Luther's Theological Testament: The Schmalkald Articles*, by William R. Russell, 117–52. Minneapolis: Fortress, 1995.

Mangina, Joseph L. *Karl Barth: Theologian of Christian Witness*. Louisville: Westminster John Knox, 2004.

Mannermaa, Tuomo. *Christ Present in Faith: Luther's View of Justification*. Edited by Kirsi Stjerna. Minneapolis: Fortress, 2005.

Marsden, George M. *Jonathan Edwards: A Life*. New Haven: Yale University Press, 2003.

———. *A Short Life of Jonathan Edwards*. Grand Rapids: Eerdmans, 2008.

McCall, Thomas H. *Forsaken: The Trinity and the Cross, and Why It Matters*. Downers Grove, IL: InterVarsity, 2012.

McClymond, Michael J. "Hearing the Symphony: A Critique of Some Critics of Sang Lee's and Amy Pauw's Accounts of Jonathan Edwards' 'View of God.'" In Schweitzer, *Jonathan Edwards as Contemporary*, 67–92.

McClymond, Michael J., and Gerald R. McDermott. *The Theology of Jonathan Edwards*. Oxford: Oxford University Press, 2012.

McDermott, Gerald R. *Jonathan Edwards Confronts the Gods: Christian Theology, Enlightenment Religion, and Non-Christian Faiths*. Oxford: Oxford University Press, 2000.

———. "Jonathan Edwards, John Henry Newman, and Karl Barth: Is a Typological View of Reality Legitimate?" In *The Ecumenical Edwards: Jonathan Edwards and the Theologians*, edited by Kyle C. Strobel, 149–66. Burlington, VT: Ashgate, 2015.

McGinnis, Andrew M. *The Son of God Beyond the Flesh: A Historical and Theological Study of the Extra Calvinisticum*. London and New York: Bloomsbury T&T Clark, 2014.

McGrath, Alister E. *Luther's Theology of the Cross: Martin Luther's Theological Breakthrough*. Oxford: Blackwell, 1985.

McLoughlin, William G., Jr. *Modern Revivalism: Charles Grandison Finney to Billy Graham*. Eugene, OR: Wipf & Stock, 2004.

Miles, Margaret R. "Happiness in Motion: Desire and Delight." In *Rereading Historical Theology: Before, During, and After Augustine*, 34–51. Eugene, OR: Cascade Books, 2008.

Milton, John. *Paradise Lost*. In *John Milton: The Major Works*, edited by Stephen Orgel and Jonathan Goldberg, 355–618. New York: Oxford University Press, 1991.

Minear, Paul S. *Images of the Church in the New Testament*. Louisville: Westminster John Knox, 2004.

Morris, Thomas V. *The Logic of God Incarnate*. Ithaca, NY: Cornell University Press, 1986.

Mosser, Carl. "The Earliest Patristic Interpretations of Psalm 82, Jewish Antecedents, and the Origin of Christian Deification." *Journal of Theological Studies* 56 (2005): 30–73.

Muller, Richard A. *The Unaccommodated Calvin: Studies in the Foundation of a Theological Tradition*. New York: Oxford University Press, 2000.

Newman, John Henry. *The Idea of a University*. Edited by Frank M. Turner. New Haven: Yale University Press, 1996.

Niebuhr, Richard R. *Schleiermacher on Christ and Religion*. New York: Scribner, 1964.

Nietzsche, Friedrich. *On the Genealogy of Morals*. In *On the Genealogy of Morals and Ecce Homo*, translated by Walter Kaufmann and R. J. Hollingdale, edited by Walter Kaufmann. New York: Vintage, 1989.

Nimmo, Paul T. "Schleiermacher on Scripture and the Work of Jesus Christ." *International Journal of Systematic Theology* 31 (2015): 60–90.

Norris, R. A., Jr. *God and World in Early Christian Theology: A Study in Justin Martyr, Irenaeus, Tertullian, and Origen*. New York: Seabury Press, 1965.

Oberman, Heiko A. *The Harvest of Medieval Theology: Gabriel Biel and Late Medieval Nominalism*. Durham, NC: Labyrinth, 1983.

———. *Luther: Man between God and the Devil*. Translated by Eileen Walliser-Schwarzbart. London: Image Books, 1992.

O'Donovan, Oliver. *The Problem of Self-Love in St. Augustine*. New Haven: Yale University Press, 1980.

———. *Resurrection and Moral Order: An Outline for Evangelical Ethics*. 2nd ed. Grand Rapids: Eerdmans, 1994.

———. "*Usus* and *Fruitio* in Augustine, *De Doctrina Christiana I*." *Journal of Theological Studies* 3 (1982): 361–97.

———. *The Word in Small Boats: Sermons from Oxford*. Edited by Andy Draycott. Grand Rapids: Eerdmans, 2010.

O'Meara, Thomas F. *Thomas Aquinas Theologian*. Notre Dame, IN: University of Notre Dame Press, 1997.

Osborn, Eric. *Irenaeus of Lyons*. Cambridge: Cambridge University Press, 2001.

Owen, John. *Communion with the Triune God*. Edited by Kelly M. Kapic and Justin Taylor. Wheaton: Crossway, 2007.

*Oxford Dictionary of the Christian Church*. Edited by F. L. Cross and E. A. Livingstone. 3rd ed. Oxford: Oxford University Press, 2005.

Packer, J. I. *Knowing God*. Downers Grove, IL: InterVarsity, 1993.

Pauw, Amy Plantinga. *The Supreme Harmony of All: The Trinitarian Theology of Jonathan Edwards*. Grand Rapids: Eerdmans, 2002.

Perrin, Nicholas. *Jesus the Temple*. Grand Rapids: Baker Academic, 2010.

Pieper, Josef. *The Silence of St. Thomas*. Translated by John Murray and Daniel O'Connor. South Bend, IN: St. Augustine's Press, 1957.

Plantinga, Alvin. *Where the Conflict Really Lies: Science, Religion, and Naturalism*. Oxford: Oxford University Press, 2011.

Plotinus. *Enneads*. Translated by A. H. Armstrong. 7 vols. Loeb Classical Library. Cambridge, MA: Harvard University Press, 1966–88.

Price, Robert B. *Letters of the Divine Word: The Perfections of God in Karl Barth's Church Dogmatics*. New York: T&T Clark, 2011.

Pseudo-Dionysius. *Pseudo-Dionysius: The Complete Works*. Translated by Colm Luibheid and Paul Rorem. New York: Paulist Press, 1987.

Quash, Ben, and Michael Ward, eds. *Heresies and How to Avoid Them: Why It Matters What Christians Believe*. Peabody, MA: Hendrickson, 2007.

Radner, Ephraim. *Time and the Word: Figural Reading of the Christian Scriptures*. Grand Rapids: Eerdmans, 2016.

Redeker, Martin. *Schleiermacher: Life and Thought*. Translated by John Wallhausser. Philadelphia: Fortress, 1973.

Rhodes, Ben. "The Spirit of Fellowship: Karl Barth's Pneumatology and Doctrine of Sanctification." PhD diss., University of Aberdeen, 2012.

Riordan, William. *Divine Light: The Theology of Denys the Areopagite*. San Francisco: Ignatius, 2008.

Roberts, Robert C. *Spiritual Emotions: A Psychology of Christian Virtues*. Grand Rapids: Eerdmans, 2007.

Rogers, Eugene F., Jr. *After the Spirit: A Constructive Pneumatology from Resources outside the Modern West*. Grand Rapids: Eerdmans, 2005.

Rorem, Paul. *The Dionysian Mystical Theology*. Minneapolis: Fortress, 2015.

———. *Pseudo-Dionysius: A Commentary on the Texts and an Introduction to Their Influence*. New York: Oxford University Press, 1993.

Roukema, Riemer. "The Good Samaritan in Ancient Christianity." *Vigiliae Christianae* 58 (2004): 56–74.

Rupp, Gordon. *The Righteousness of God: Luther Studies*. London: Hodder & Stoughton, 1953.

Sanders, Fred. *The Image of the Immanent Trinity: Rahner's Rule and the Theological Interpretation of Scripture*. New York: Peter Lang, 2005.

Sauter, Gerhard. *Eschatological Rationality: Theological Issues in Focus*. Grand Rapids: Baker, 1996.

Schleiermacher, Friedrich. *Christian Faith*. Translated by Terrence N. Tice, Catherine L. Kelsey, and Edwina Lawler. Edited by Catherine L. Kelsey and Terrence N. Tice. 2 vols. Louisville: Westminster John Knox, 2016.

———. *Christmas Eve Celebration: A Dialogue*. Edited and translated by Terrence N. Tice. Eugene, OR: Cascade Books, 2010.

———. *The Life of Schleiermacher as Unfolded in His Autobiography and Letters*. Translated by Frederica Rowan. 2 vols. London: Smith, Elder, 1860.

———. *On Religion: Speeches to Its Culture Despisers*. Translated and edited by Richard Crouter. Cambridge: Cambridge University Press, 1988.

———. *On the Glaubenslehre: Two Letters to Dr. Lücke*. Translated by James Duke and Francis Fiorenza. Ann Arbor, MI: Scholars Press, 1981.

———. *Servant of the Word: Selected Sermons of Friedrich Schleiermacher*. Translated by Dawn DeVries. Philadelphia: Fortress, 1987.

Schweitzer, Don, ed. *Jonathan Edwards as Contemporary: Essays in Honor of Sang Hyun Lee*. New York: Peter Lang, 2010.

Schwöbel, Christoph. "Theology." In *The Cambridge Companion to Karl Barth*, edited by John Webster, 17–36. Cambridge: Cambridge University Press, 2000.

Smail, Tom. *The Giving Gift: The Holy Spirit in Person*. London: Darton, Longman & Todd, 1994.

Smith, James K. A. *Desiring the Kingdom: Worship, Worldview, and Cultural Formation*. Grand Rapids: Baker Academic, 2009.

Soulen, R. Kendall. *The Divine Name(s) and the Holy Trinity*. Vol. 1, *Distinguishing the Voices*. Louisville: Westminster John Knox, 2011.

Southern, R. W. *Saint Anselm: A Portrait in a Landscape*. Cambridge: Cambridge University Press, 1990.

Spohn, William C. "Finding God in All Things: Jonathan Edwards and Ignatius Loyola." In *Finding God in All Things: Essays in Honor of Michael J. Buckley, S.J.*, edited by Michael J. Himes and Stephen J. Pope, 244–61. New York: Crossroad, 1996.

Stang, Charles. *Apophasis and Pseudonymity in Dionysius the Areopagite*. Oxford: Oxford University Press, 2012.

Steinmetz, David C. *Luther and Staupitz: An Essay in the Intellectual Origins of the Protestant Reformation*. Durham, NC: Duke University Press, 1980.

Stewart-Kroeker, Sarah. *Pilgrimage as Moral and Aesthetic Formation in Augustine's Thought*. Oxford: Oxford University Press, 2017.

Strobel, Kyle C. *Jonathan Edwards's Theology: A Reinterpretation*. New York: T&T Clark, 2013.

Sweeney, Douglas A. *Jonathan Edwards and the Ministry of the Word: A Model of Faith and Thought*. Downers Grove, IL: IVP Academic, 2009.

Tanner, Kathryn. *Christ the Key*. Cambridge: Cambridge University Press, 2010.

————. *Jesus, Humanity and the Trinity: A Brief Systematic Theology*. Edinburgh: T&T Clark, 2001.

Thomas Aquinas. *Commentary on the Gospel of John, Chapters 1–5*. Translated by Fabian Larcher and James A. Weisheipl. Edited by Daniel Keating and Matthew Levering. Washington, DC: Catholic University of America Press, 2010.

————. *Commentary on the Gospel of John, Chapters 13–21*. Translated by Fabian Larcher and James A. Weisheipl. Edited by Daniel Keating and Matthew Levering. Washington, DC: Catholic University of America Press, 2010.

————. *Summa contra gentiles*. Translated by Anton C. Pegis, James F. Anderson, Vernon J. Bourke, and Charles J. O'Neil. 5 vols. Notre Dame, IN: University of Notre Dame Press, 1975.

————. *Summa theologica* (or *Summa theologiae*, which is slightly more common and which I use throughout). Translated by Fathers of the English Dominican Province. 5 vols. Allen, TX: Christian Classics, 1981.

Tice, Terrence N. *Schleiermacher*. Nashville: Abingdon, 2006.

Tietz, Christiane. "Karl Barth and Charlotte von Kirschbaum." *Theology Today* 74 (July 2017): 86–111.

Tilby, Angela. "Marcionism: Can Christians Dispense with the God of the Old Testament?" In Quash and Ward, *Heresies and How to Avoid Them*, 73–80.

Torrance, James B. "The Vicarious Humanity of Christ." In *The Incarnation: Ecumenical Studies in the Nicene-Constantinopolitan Creed, A.D. 381*, edited by Thomas F. Torrance, 127–46. Edinburgh: Handsel Press, 1981.

————. *Worship, Community, and the Triune God of Grace*. Downers Grove, IL: InterVarsity, 1996.

Torrance, T. F. *Karl Barth: An Introduction to His Early Theology, 1910–1931*. Edinburgh: T&T Clark, 1962.

————. *The Mediation of Christ*. Rev. ed. Colorado Springs: Helmers & Howard, 1992.

————. *Space, Time, and Incarnation*. Edinburgh: T&T Clark, 1997.

Torrell, Jean-Pierre. *Aquinas's Summa: Background, Structure, and Reception*. Translated by Benedict M. Guevin. Washington, DC: Catholic University of America Press, 2005.

————. *Saint Thomas Aquinas*. Vol. 1, *The Person and His Work*. Translated by Robert Royal. Rev. ed. Washington, DC: Catholic University of America Press, 2005.

————. *Saint Thomas Aquinas*. Vol. 2, *Spiritual Master*. Translated by Robert Royal. Washington, DC: Catholic University of America Press, 2003.

Treier, Daniel J. *Introducing Theological Interpretation of Scripture: Recovering a Christian Practice*. Grand Rapids: Baker Academic, 2008.

Vander Schel, Kevin M. *Embedded Grace: Christ, History, and the Reign of God in Schleiermacher's Dogmatics*. Minneapolis: Fortress, 2013.

Vanhoozer, Kevin. *The Drama of Doctrine: A Canonical-Linguistic Approach to Christian Theology*. Louisville: Westminster John Knox, 2005.

Van Nieuwenhove, Rik, and Joseph Wawrykow, eds. *The Theology of Thomas Aquinas*. Notre Dame, IN: University of Notre Dame Press, 2005.

Velde, Rudi A., te. "Evil, Sin, and Death: Thomas Aquinas on Original Sin." In Van Nieuwenhove and Wawrykow, *Theology of Thomas Aquinas*, 143–66.

Visser, Sandra, and Thomas Williams. *Anselm*. New York: Oxford University Press, 2009.

Wainwright, Geoffrey. *Doxology: The Praise of God in Worship, Doctrine, and Life*. New York: Oxford University Press, 1980.

Watson, Philip. *Let God Be God! An Interpretation of the Theology of Martin Luther*. Philadelphia: Muhlenberg Press, 1947.

Wawrykow, Joseph P. *God's Grace and Human Action: "Merit" in the Theology of Thomas Aquinas*. Notre Dame, IN: University of Notre Dame Press, 1995.

———. "Grace." In Van Nieuwenhove and Wawrykow, *Theology of Thomas Aquinas*, 192–221.

———. "John Calvin and Condign Merit." *Archiv für Reformationsgeschichte* 83 (1992): 73–90.

———. *The Westminster Handbook to Thomas Aquinas*. Louisville: Westminster John Knox, 2005.

Webster, John. *Confessing God: Essays in Christian Dogmatics II*. Edinburgh: T&T Clark, 2005.

———. "Theologies of Retrieval." In *The Oxford Handbook of Systematic Theology*, edited by John Webster, Kathryn Tanner, and Iain Torrance, 583–99. Oxford: Oxford University Press, 2007.

———. *Word and Church: Essays in Church Dogmatics*. New York: T&T Clark, 2006.

Weinandy, Thomas G. *Athanasius: A Theological Introduction*. Burlington, VT: Ashgate, 2007.

———. *Does God Suffer?* Notre Dame, IN: University of Notre Dame Press, 2000.

Wendel, François. *Calvin: The Origins and Development of His Religious Thought*. Translated by Philip Mairet. London: Collins, 1963.

Werpehowski, William. "Weeping at the Death of Dido: Sorrow, Virtue, and Augustine's Confessions." *Journal of Religious Ethics* 19 (1991): 175–91.

Widdicombe, Peter. *The Fatherhood of God from Origen to Athanasius*. Oxford: Oxford University Press, 2001.

Wilhite, David E. *The Gospel according to Heretics: Discovering Orthodoxy through Early Christological Conflicts*. Grand Rapids: Baker Academic, 2015.

Willard, Dallas. *The Divine Conspiracy: Rediscovering Our Hidden Life in God*. San Francisco: HarperSanFrancisco, 1998.

Williams, Michael Allen. *Rethinking "Gnosticism": An Argument for Dismantling a Dubious Category*. Princeton: Princeton University Press, 1996.

Williams, Rowan. *Arius: Heresy and Tradition*. Rev. ed. Grand Rapids: Eerdmans, 2002.

———. *The Wound of Knowledge: Christian Spirituality from the New Testament to Saint John of the Cross*. Rev. ed. Cambridge, MA: Cowley Publications, 1990.

Williams, Thomas. "Anselm's Quiet Radicalism." *British Journal for the History of Philosophy* 24 (2015): 3–22.

Wilson, Sarah Hinlicky. "The Law of God." *Lutheran Quarterly* 27 (2013): 373–98.

Wright, N. T. *The Climax of the Covenant: Christ and the Law in Pauline Theology*. Edinburgh: T&T Clark, 1991.

———. *The New Testament and the People of God*. Minneapolis: Fortress, 1992.

Wright, Ross McGowan. "Karl Barth's Academic Lectures on Ephesians: Göttingen, 1921–1922: An Original Translation, Annotation, and Analysis." PhD diss., University of St. Andrews, 2007.

Young, Frances. "'Creatio Ex Nihilo': A Context for the Emergence of the Christian Doctrine of Creation." *Scottish Journal of Theology* 44 (1991): 139–52.

———. *God's Presence: A Contemporary Recapitulation of Early Christianity*. New York: Cambridge University Press, 2013.

Zachman, Randall C. *Image and Word in the Theology of John Calvin*. Notre Dame, IN: University of Notre Dame Press, 2007.

Zizioulas, John. *Being as Communion: Studies in Personhood and the Church*. Crestwood, NY: St. Vladimir's Seminary Press, 1985.

# SCRIPTURE INDEX

## Old Testament

### Genesis

1:3  145
6:6  43
22  125

### Exodus

3:13–15  135
3:14  213
3:15  135n28
15:26  28
20:4  199
33:19  213
34:6–7  290

### Leviticus

26:36  173

### Deuteronomy

5:26  135n26

### Joshua

3:10  135n26

### 1 Samuel

17:26  135n26
17:36  135n26

### 2 Kings

19:4  135n26
19:16  135n26

### Job

42:5–6  128

### Psalms

14:1  109
19:1  81, 82
19:3–4  81
27:4  89
34:8  225, 250
42:2  135n26
53:1  109
69:9  45
82:6  27
84:2  135n26
84:5  79
95:7–8  49n94
100:3  118
103:17  213n131
104:26  304
104:32  304
119  180
127:3–5  53
145:2  83
147:7–9  145–46

### Proverbs

8  22
8:22  49n94
9:1  49n94

### Isaiah

37:4  135n26
37:17  135n26

42:8  190
46:1–2  189–90
46:3–4  190
46:5  190
46:7  190
46:9  190
52:13  190
53:4–6  190–91
55:9  43

### Jeremiah

7:23  297n112
10:10  135n26
11:4  297n112
23:36  135n26
29:7  74
30:22  297n112
31:33  297n112
32:38  297n112

### Ezekiel

10:18  41
36:28  297n112
43:1–12  41

### Daniel

6:20  135n26
6:26  135n26

### Hosea

1:10  135n26
5:12  92
8:6  200

## Zechariah

1:3  159n157

## Apocrypha

### Wisdom of Solomon

8:1  147, 147n99

## New Testament

### Matthew

3:16  149
4:1–11  48n90
4:17  170
5:8  97
7:18  186n144
9:13  172n31
11:27  49n94
16:16  135n26
20:28  123
23:37  176n73
26:39  49n94
26:63  135n26

### Mark

1:10  149
1:12–13  48n90
1:15  175n60
2:17  172n31
4:26–29  167
10:14  291
10:45  123
12:28–34  81
13:32  49n94

### Luke

2:52  49n94
3:22  149
4:1–13  48n90
5:32  172n31
13:34  176n73
15:11–24  302
15:13  71, 300n128
22:42  261

### John

1:1  136n34, 271n136, 272, 293
1:3  147n99

1:14  39, 52n116, 136n34,
    267, 288
1:16  46, 150, 151n113
1:18  51, 52n116
1:32  149
2:17  45
3:8  229
3:16  52n116, 137, 208, 273
3:18  52n116
3:35  49n94
5:18  273
5:19  60
5:22  273
5:30  273
6:40  228
7:37  16
9:25  95
10:10b  39
10:18  123
10:30  49n94, 51
12:27  49n94
14:9  51, 202
14:10  49n94
14:23  59
15:5  160n160
15:13–16  163
16:13  268
17:3  39, 49n94, 202

### Acts

14:15  135n26
17:28  90, 184, 239
17:34  87

### Romans

1  169, 197
1–11  186n145
1:19–20  198
1:20  65, 73, 140
1:20–23  198
3:27  219
3:28  258
5  45n68, 82n97
5:5  79
5:12–21  23
6  156
7:17  77
7:20  77
7:24  174
8:15  59

8:26  79
8:29  53
8:32  208
9–11  215
9:15  213
9:26  135n26
10:17  178, 226, 257
11:36  90
12–16  186n145
13:13–14  66

### 1 Corinthians

1  22
1:24  147n99
1:30  175
3:5–9  155
4:7  193, 211
6:11  56
7:31  73
12:4–6  58
12:28  16
15  45n68
15:14  265
15:17  45
15:45  23

### 2 Corinthians

1:22  245
3:3  135n26
3:5  211
4:6  202, 232, 304
5:5  245
5:6  73
5:19  297
6:16  59, 135n26
13:14  58, 209–10, 246n128

### Galatians

2:20  175, 186
3:13  264
3:24  20
4:6  59
4:24  82n97
5:18  20

### Ephesians

1  45n68
1:3  10
1:3–14  23, 215

1:4  292, 295
1:4–5  213
1:7  264
1:10  23
1:14  245
1:17–18  57
2:3  203
2:8–9  213
2:12  203
2:13–16  298
2:14–16  123n98
2:20  15
3:15  52n112
5:2  125
5:30  176
6:17  182

**Philippians**

2:6–7  187
2:9–10  49n94

**Colossians**

1:3  10
1:15–20  59, 271n131
1:16  147n99
1:16–17  294
1:17  90, 144n86
1:21  198, 203
1:27  150n110
3:2  69
3:3–4  299

**1 Timothy**

1:8  189
1:17  227
3:15  13, 135n26
3:16  13
4:10  135n26
6:16  51, 97, 199
6:20  10
6:20–21  5

**Hebrews**

1:3  38, 41n41, 57
1:4  49n94
2:17  205, 304
3:2  49n94
3:12  135n26
4:12  182
4:15  26, 205, 301
5:7–8  44
5:8  205
6:20  92
9:12  264
9:14  135n26
9:15  264
10:14  46
10:19–22  104
10:31  135n26
11:23–29  92n39
12:1  71
12:14  92n41
12:22  135n26

12:29  216
13:13  303

**James**

1:17  193, 215
2:14–17  185
2:26  186

**1 Peter**

1:18  123

**2 Peter**

1:4  27, 163, 243, 245n120

**1 John**

2:22  18n94
4:8  233
4:9  52n116
4:16  138n50
4:19  188

**Revelation**

4:8  228
5:9  123
5:13  272
7:2  135n26
21:2  145
22:17  16

# SUBJECT INDEX

absolute dependence on God, 259–62
Adam
  corruption of, 37
  fall of, 76
Adam, Karl, 284
Adeodatus, 64
adoption, 27, 53, 58, 207
adoptionism, 19
affections, 230–32, 249–50
Albertus Magnus, 131
Alexander of Alexandria, 34–35
Allen, R. Michael, 152n119
Althaus, Paul, 178n93
Ambrose, 64
Anabaptists, 34, 171
*analogia entis*, 285
analogical language, 140
Anatolios, Khaled, 35n5, 40n40, 41, 46n72
angelology, of Denys, 104
Anselm, 107–28, 181, 286
  on the atonement, 117–25
  on the incarnation, 36, 37n15, 117–21
  life of, 111–14
  and prayer, 109
  soteriology of, 116
antichrist, 18, 26n163, 165
Antony, 45, 54–55, 66
apophatic theology, 91, 93, 94–95, 101n93, 103, 134–36, 139
apostolic teaching, 14
Arians, Arianism, 34–36, 57, 59–60
aristocracy, 3
Aristotelianism, 88
Aristotle, 67, 131, 132–33, 177, 186

Arius, 34–35, 47, 51, 55
*Arrested Development* (television program), 31n216
ascent, 29, 92, 100
  in Lord's Supper, 218
assurance, Luther on, 182–85
Athanasius, 33–61, 233
  on divine impassibility, 42–46
  on eternal generation of the Son, 51–53
  on Holy Spirit, 56–59
  on the incarnation, 36–42
  life of, 33–36
  on Son of God, 46–51
  on the Trinity, 58–59
atonement, 107
  *Christus Victor* model, 121
  descriptions of, 121–22
  as "divine child abuse," 117–19, 123–25
  moral influence model, 122
  penal substitution model, 122, 125
  satisfaction model, 121–25
  as ransom, 122–23
Augustine, 34, 63–84, 88, 93, 111, 130
  on creation, 83–84
  exegesis of, 81–82
  on the incarnation, 77
  life of, 64–67
  on love, 67–72, 80–82
  on resurrection, 78
  on salvation, 116
  on sin, 75–77
Aulén, Gustav, 118n57, 121
autopsy, 226

Badcock, Gary D., 151n116
Bainton, Roland, 169, 171
Balthasar, Hans Urs von, 279n21
baptism, 27, 69, 76, 101, 217, 224
Barmen Declaration, 242n106, 278
Barnes, Timothy, 34n2, 35
Barth, Karl, 2, 127, 214, 242, 275–304
    actualism of, 287
    on election, 291–97
    on Holy Spirit, 245
    as joyful, 275–76
    life of, 276–79
    pneumatology of, 242n106
    on reconciliation, 297–303
    universalism of, 297
beatific vision, 139, 141, 246
beauty, 64. *See also* lovely things
beauty of God, 89–90, 97
Behr, John, 23, 39n35
Being in general, 234, 241
Benedictines, 131
Bernard of Clairvaux, 213n131
Bible, as Word of God, 284. *See also* Scripture
Billings, Todd, 211n121, 218n170
blasphemy, of Gnostics, 10–11
Bonaventure, 93
Bonhoeffer, Dietrich, 129n2
Bora, Katherine von, 171
Boulton Matthew Myer, 196n17, 203n63
Bouwsma, William J., 212n122
Brainerd, David, 224
Brown, Peter, 74
Brunner, Emil, 7, 285
Bucer, Martin, 105
Bultmann, Rudolf, 285–86
Burrell, David, 142n72
Busch, Eberhard, 299
Butin, Philip, 211n121

Calvin, John, 193–219, 249, 258, 269
    on descent and ascent, 205n76
    on election, 211–15
    on knowing God and self, 108n6
    life of, 194–97
    on Lord's Supper, 217–19
    on prayer, 215–17
    on speculation, 256–57
Canlis, Julie, 205n76
Caravaggio, 214
Cary, Phil, 183
cataphatic theology, 91, 101n93
Catechism of the Catholic Church, 140–41

catholicity, 2, 17
causality, 145–49, 240
    efficient cause, 208
    final cause, 208
    instrumental cause, 208
    material cause, 208
    *See also* secondary causality
Cavadini, John, 82n96
celestial hierarchy, 97, 102
certainty, 181
Chalcedonian two-natures Christology, 40
charity, 68, 79
Chenu, Marie-Dominique, 131
Chesterton, G. K., 1–2, 129, 168, 241
Christian "heterodoxy," 8n14
Christian humanism, 28
Christian life
    as growth into maturity, 30
    Luther on, 166, 188–89
Christian self-consciousness, 258, 261, 274
*Christus pro nobis*, 281
church
    as bank, 16
    and canonization, 14–15
    Christ as head of, 151
    as "crater" formed by revelation, 284
    as feeling community, 256
    as marked by hearing, 178
    as marked by preaching, 178
    as mystic body of Christ, 151
    as pillar and buttress of the truth, 15–16
    and rules of faith, 13–14
    unifies God's people, 13
    where the Spirit is, 30
church covenant, 223
church discipline, 196
*Church Dogmatics* (Barth), 278–79, 286
clerical abuse, 98
clock-work analogy, 260n75
Coakley, Sara, 4
communion of the saints, 1–2, 101, 255
complacency, about temporal things, 79
confessions, 13
conscience, 182
consent, 232–35
Constantinian settlement, 33–34
continued creation, 239–41
conversion, 229–30
Council of Chalcedon (451), 88, 271n136
Council of Constantinople (381), 56
Council of Nicaea (325), 34–35, 53n118, 57, 88, 271n136

covenant, 209n103, 296, 297–98
*creatio ex nihilo*, 21n115, 236
creation
  Athanasius on, 38–39
  beauties of, 84
  blasphemy against, 11
  consummation of, 145
  dependence on God, 145–46
  Edwards on, 235–36
  goodness of, 21, 69–70, 143–44
  integrity of, in Thomas Aquinas, 133–34
  non-self-sufficiency of, 239
  and redemption, 9, 32, 38
  renewal of, 37, 38
  as theater of God's glory, 198
Creator, blasphemy against, 10
Creator-creature distinction, 139–41
Crisp, Oliver, 42n50, 236n68, 239, 241n97
crucifixion, and recapitulation, 25
curiosity, 200

daily bread, 217
Dante, 100
darkness of unknowing, 93, 96–97
Davies, Brian, 137, 148
de Bure, Idelette, 196
decree, 294–95
deification, 27, 45, 54, 99, 302
deism, 238–39, 246
deliberative will, 156, 158
democracy, and tradition, 1
Denys the Areopagite, 51, 85–105
  background, 87–89
  Christology of, 102–5
  on hierarchy, 95–102
  on knowing and unknowing, 94–95
Descartes, René, 67, 109
descent and ascent, in Calvin, 205n76
devil, Luther on, 182
DeVries, Dawn, 265n102
dialectical theology, 282–83
Dillard, Annie, 4, 182, 241n100
Dionysius. *See* Denys the Areopagite
Diotima, 93
distraction, 83
divine splendor, 96
divinization, 101
dogma, 254
dogmatics
  as revisionary, 258
  and Word of God, 284

Dominicans, 131, 149
Donatists, 65
double grace, 210
double predestination, 157n146, 296

Eadmer, 114
ecclesiastical hierarchy, 97, 98, 102
Edict of Milan, 33
Edwards, Jonathan, 145, 221–46, 249
  and conversion, 225–27
  on holiness, 228
  life of, 221–25
  on religious affections, 230–32
election, 157
  Barth on, 291–97
  Calvin on, 211–15
elitism, 99
emanation, 237n77, 238
embodiment, 9, 41
Emmanuel, 300
emotions, 230n37
enjoyment and use, 72–74
Enlightenment, 252, 279
"enthusiasts," 171
episcopal succession, 15–16
equivocation, 140
eternal life, 45
Eucharist. *See* Lord's Supper
Eusebius, 34
Eve-Mary comparison (Irenaeus), 26, 31n215
evil, as privation of good, 70
excellency, 233
experience, and Scripture, 257

faith
  as apostolic, 17
  as catholic, 17
  formed and unformed, 185
  gazes at Christ, 175–76
  as gift, 179
  as instrumental cause of salvation, 208
  and justification, 187
  and love, 185–89
  relies on promises of God, 183
  trusts Word of God, 180–82
  unity of, 13, 17–20
faith and reason, 107–11, 125–28, 181
false teaching, 6
Farel, Guillaume, 195
Farrow, Douglas, 104n112
Fascism, 278

Father, 46–47, 193–94, 203, 209, 216–17
  unity with the Son, 48–51
feeling, Schleiermacher on, 256–59
Feuerbach, Ludwig, 280, 283
fideism, 107
figural interpretation, 82
Filoramo, Giovanni, 8, 11n29
Finney, Charles, 223, 281
firstborn, 53, 54, 60
first commandment, 242
flesh, 19, 29, 40–42, 218, 267, 300–301
fountain image, 50, 57, 237
Frederick the Wise, 170
freedom of the will, 115
free will, Thomas Aquinas on, 155–59
free-will defense, in Irenaeus, 27
friends of God, 163

Gavrilyuk, Paul, 42–43, 44–45
Gerrish, Brian, 258, 259n64, 260, 270n129, 273, 274
gifts, 153–54
gifts of the Spirit, 244
glory of God, 208
Gnostics, 6, 7, 8–13, 14, 16, 86
God
  as *actus purus*, 287–88, 290, 291
  as being-in-act, 287–88, 293
  as cause of being, 134
  communication of, 237–38
  compassion of, 291
  and creation, 21, 60, 134, 137–38, 141–45, 235–36, 239–41
  as Creator, 17–18
  descent to us in Christ, 93
  devoid of passion, 134
  freedom of, 114–17, 288–91
  goodness in creation, 143–44
  has no potential, 134–35
  holiness of, 228
  humanity of, 303–4
  immutability of, 288
  impassibility of, 42–46, 124, 290–91
  incomprehensibility of, 141
  as living God, 135, 136
  as love, 233
  love of, 78–79, 82, 138, 288–91
  mercy of, 213–14, 290
  and necessity, 114–16, 121
  omnipotence of, 146, 260–61, 288
  righteousness of, 167–70, 191

self-revelation of, 95
  simplicity of, 136–37, 233n54
  suffering of, 290–91
  transcendence of, 51, 60, 90–95, 283, 304
  as "Wholly Other," 282, 284, 304
  *See also* Father; Holy Spirit; Son
God-consciousness, 261–65, 268, 270, 271, 272–73
Golitzin, Alexander, 88n11, 99n78, 101nn86–87, 102–3
good works, Luther on, 188–89
Gordon, Bruce, 195, 197
gospel, Luther on, 174–77
grace, 150–51, 160–61
  cooperative, 161
  habitual, 160–61
  helping, 160–61
  operative, 161
  and sacraments, 152–53
Graham, Billy, Barth on, 276, 277, 299
greed, 68
Gregory of Nazianzus, 26n165, 38n27, 50n106, 92n39
Gregory of Nyssa, 88, 92n39, 93n44
Gunton, Colin, 124
Gwynn, David, 35n5

habit, 153
"half-way covenant," 224
hands of God, 60, 149
  in creation, 21–22
  in redemption, 22–23
happiness, 72
Harnack, Adolf von, 25n157, 277
Hart, David Bentley, 43, 85, 87, 104
Hart, Trevor, 25n157
Heaney, Seamus, 4
heart, 225–26, 231
Hector, Kevin, 263n91, 270n129, 271n136
Hegel, Georg, 237–38, 287
*Heilandsliebe*, 273
Helmer, Christine, 257n54, 271n236
heresy, 9, 10, 13
heretics
  compromise of the incarnation, 18–19
  use of language of Scripture, 48
Herrmann, Wilhelm, 277
Hick, John, 94n52
Hieb, Nathan D., 265n102
hierarchy, Denys on, 95–102
High, Nathan, 261n77

Hitler, Adolf, 278
Hodge, Charles, 53n118
Hogg, David S., 116n44
holiness, 45, 196, 197, 228, 232
Holmes, Steve, 137
Holy Spirit
    and application of salvation, 209–10
    Athanasius on, 56–59
    in creation, 22
    Edwards on, 242–46
    Irenaeus on, 19, 28–31
    makes us lovers of God, 79
    at Pentecost, 149
    and prayer, 216
    Schleiermacher on, 267–68
    sheds light on excellency of Word, 226
homecoming, 73–74, 79
*homoousion*, 56, 59
Hopkins, Gerard Manley, 140
human flourishing, 28
humanism, of Calvin, 194–95
human nature, after Adam, 76–77
humans, as lovers, 67–69
Humboldt, Wilhelm von, 251
Hume, David, 240, 241
Hunsinger, George, 299n119

Iamblichus, 89
idolatry, 83
illumination, 97, 100
image of God, 24, 28, 36n11, 38–39, 141–42,
    155–56
images
    Calvin on, 199–200
    Luther on, 171
imitation of Christ, 122
immortality, and incarnation, 120
imputation of Christ's righteousness, 176–77
incarnation
    Anselm on, 117–21
    Athanasius on, 36–42
    Augustine on, 77
    Barth on, 302–4
    Irenaeus on, 18–19, 24
    and salvation, 45–46
    Thomas Aquinas on, 149
"in Christ," 295
indulgences, 168–69, 170
*Institutes of the Christian Religion* (Calvin),
    196, 197, 203n63, 207, 208–9, 212, 279

introspection, of Anselm, 108
Irenaeus, 5–32, 149
    doctrine of sin, 31–32
    on Gnosticism, 8–13, 86
    on handing on the faith, 13–17
    on hands of God, 21–23
    on Holy Spirit, 19, 28–31
    life of, 6–8
    on recapitulation, 23–27, 116
    on unity of the faith, 13, 17–20

Jacobs, Alan, 80n90, 229–30
Jenson, Robert, 13–14, 56
Jesus Christ
    ascent of, 93
    blasphemy against, 10–11
    body of, 41–42
    deity of, 270–73
    election of, 294
    exaltation of, 302
    as final Adam, 23, 27, 60
    forms faith, 186
    as High Priest, 205
    humanity of, 26
    humiliation of, 301–2
    influence of, 265–70
    mediation of, 103–4
    obedience of, 124, 206
    as pattern of grace, 150–51
    perfect God-consciousness of, 263–64, 270
    and reconciliation, 300–303
    as Redeemer, 262–65, 270
    suffering of, 44–45
    as thread of the Word, 201
    threefold office of, 205, 300
Jews, Luther on, 171
journey of discipleship, 142
Jüngel, Eberhard, 287n66
justice, 115, 117–18
justification, 159, 177, 183, 187, 211
Justin Martyr, 6, 7, 43n55

Kant, Immanuel, 250, 252–54
Kelly, J. N. D., 14n58, 17n80
Kelsey, Catherine, 264, 272n140
Kierkegaard, Søren, 226, 282
King, Karen, 8n12
Kirschbaum, Charlotte von, 278
Kolb, Robert, 175n58
Kunnuthara, Abraham, 264n93, 272n138
Kuyper, Abraham, 173n39

labyrinth, 199, 200, 201
laity, as second-class Christians, 99
Lanfranc, 111, 112–13
Law, David, 272n139
law, Luther on, 173–74
Leclerq, Jean, 111n18
Lee, Sang Hyun, 236n70
Leithart, Peter J., 45, 50n106, 55n130
Lewis, C. S., 26n166, 86
liberal Protestantism, 280–81
libertarian freedom, 115
light image, 50, 57, 237
Lombard, Peter, 131
Long, D. Stephen, 279n21
Lord's Prayer, 180
Lord's Supper
    Calvin on, 217–19
    as "converting ordinance," 224
    Denys on, 99, 101
    Luther on, 179
Louth, Andrew, 100, 101n93
love
    Augustine on, 67–72
    Edwards on, 232
    for God, 68, 72–73, 79, 244
    for neighbor, 68, 188, 232
lovely things, 64, 69, 71, 82–84
Luther, Martin, 3, 85, 103n107, 165–71, 246, 249, 258
    on assurance, 182–85
    life of, 167–72
    on Word of God, 178–82

Mannermaa, Tuomo, 186n148
Marcion, 7, 9–10, 12, 13, 14, 18, 19, 257n57
martyr, 45
Mary, as coredemptrix, 26
Maximus the Confessor, 103n107
means of grace, extends yearning, 80
McClymond, Michael, 227n22, 235, 236n70
McDermott, Gerald, 227n22, 235
McFague, Sally, 94n52
McLoughlin, William, 223
meditation, 254
Melanchthon, Philipp, 204, 287n68
mercy of God, 213–14
    and justice, 117
meritocracy, 3
"Mighty Fortress Is Our God, A" (hymn), 165–66

Miles, Margaret R., 68n30
Milton, John, 172n35
Minear, Paul, 104n111, 151n116
miracles, 147–49, 260
Monica, 64
monotheism, 20–22
Moravian Brethren, 248–49, 250, 274
Morris, Thomas V., 42n50
Moses, 92, 97, 266
Mozart, W. A., 275–76
Muhammad, 266
mysticism, 100
    of Schleiermacher, 249
    of Thomas Aquinas, 130n6

natural theology, Barth on, 285
nature and grace, 162
Neoplatonism, 85, 86, 88–89, 237n77
new creation, 84, 298
Newman, John Henry, 133n18
Newtonian laws of nature, 238, 240, 241n100
Nicene Creed, 19, 117
Niebuhr, Richard, 268
Nietzsche, Friedrich, 28
Norris, Richard, 8n12

obedience, 232
Oberman, Heiko, 167
O'Meara, Thomas, 150, 153–54
"only begotten," 52
ontological argument, 107, 108–9, 112
order of love, 72–73
original sin, 76, 261–62
Osborn, Eric, 24n140

Packer, J. I., 207
panentheism, 86
pantheism, 94n50
partakers of divine nature, 27, 31, 228, 163, 228, 243
passion, 137–38
Patty, Sandi, 38n21
Paul VI (pope), 279n21
Pauw, Amy Plantinga, 229, 233n54
pears episode (Augustine), 75–76
Pelagians, 65
perfection, 97–98, 100
perseverance, 161, 162, 162n177, 213, 245
philosophy, 65–66
Pieper, Josef, 129n2, 132
pietism, of Schleiermacher's youth, 249–50

piety
  Barth on, 245
  Calvin on, 203
  Edwards on, 225
  of Schleiermacher, 273–74
  Schleiermacher on, 246, 256–59
pilgrimage, 73–74, 79, 139, 141
Plato, 133n18, 251, 254n39
Platonism, 65–66, 85, 88
pleasure, 69–70, 71, 73, 84
Pliny, 5
Plotinus, 88
Polycarp, 6, 9n18
Possidius, 67
praise, 63, 84
prayer
  Anselm on, 109, 112
  Barth on, 286
  Calvin on, 215–17
  Denys on, 91
  Luther on, 180–81
  Schleiermacher on, 261
preaching, Luther on, 178
predestination
  Calvin on, 215
  Barth on, 291–92
  Thomas Aquinas on, 157–58
  See also double predestination
preparationism, 229
process theology, 287n66
proclamation, as Word of God, 284
Proclus, 88, 89, 105
prodigal son, parable of, 71
  Augustine on, 71
  Barth on, 300–303
propitiation, 204, 207
providence, 147, 158, 260
Pseudo-Dionysius. See Denys the Areopagite
pseudonyms, 87
punishment, and satisfaction, 124
purification, 97, 100
Puritans, on conversion, 229–30

Quartodeciman controversy, 7
quietism, 261

Radner, Ephraim, 82n95
rationalism, 107, 109
reading, telos of love in, 81
recapitulation, 23–27, 32, 116
reconciliation, Barth on, 297–303

Redeker, Martin, 251
redemption
  Anselm on, 124n100
  Athanasius on, 38
  Calvin on, 206–7
  Luther on, 176, 177
  Schleiermacher on, 262–65
reflective faith, 183
regeneration
  Calvin on, 211
  Edwards on, 243
religion
  as experience, 253–55
  as historical, 255
  as social, 255
Religious Affections (Edwards), 230–32
religious experience, 243, 253–55, 282
religious feeling, 256–59
remanation, 238
repentance
  Luther on, 170
  occurring in Christ, 299
reprobation, 157n146, 214–15
resurrection, Augustine on, 78, 84
revelation
  Athanasius on, 51
  Barth on, 283, 284–89
  Denys on, 93–95
revisionist theology, 94, 95
revival, 222–23
righteousness of God, 167–70, 191
Roberts, Robert, 230n37
Romans commentary (Barth), 283
Rome, fall of, 34
Rorem, Paul, 98n71, 103n107
Roscelin, 109–10, 112, 127
rule of faith, 14
Rumscheidt, Martin, 276n6

Sacramentarians, 171
sacraments
  Calvin on, 217–19
  Luther on, 179
  Thomas Aquinas on, 152–53
salvation
  by faith alone (Luther), 177
  as function of election, 211–13, 296
  as healing (Augustine), 78
  as recapitulation (Irenaeus), 23–27
  as work of God (Luther), 173
salvation in Christ, 208–9

sanctification, 46, 302
satisfaction, and punishment, 124
Sauter, Gerhard, 242
Schleiermacher, Friedrich, 242, 246, 247–74,
    277, 280, 281, 284
  on absolute dependence on God, 259–62
  as "Christo-morphic" theologian, 268
  on deity of Christ, 270–73
  on God-consciousness of Christ, 263–64, 270
  life of, 250–52
  on religious feeling, 256–59
Schwöbel, Christoph, 285
Scripture
  blasphemy against, 11–12
  and experience, 257
  figural readings of, 82
  gives eyes to see God, 201
  theological interpretation of, 52n115
  unity of, 14–15, 25, 32
secondary causality, 147–49, 154–55
Second Vatican Council, 279
seed of religion, 198
self-exile, 71
self-love, 244
sense of deity, 198
sense of divine beauty, 225–28
"sense of the loveliness and beauty of holiness
    and grace," 225–26
Servetus, Michael, 197
simul iustus et peccator, 172
sin
  bondage to, 77
  deceitfulness of, 172
  as diminishment, 70
  as disordered love, 75–77
  guilt of, 37n15
  as hindrance of God-consciousness, 262
  Irenaeus on, 31–32
  as rebellion against God, 204
  and recompense, 119, 120
  unfittingness of, 116–17
Smail, Tom, 2n5
Smith, James K. A., 68
sola fide, 186
solus Christus, 186
Son
  as "becoming," 39–42
  eternal generation of, 51–53
  as God, 47
  incarnation of, 149
  unity with the Father, 48–51

Sonderegger, Katherine, 4
sonship, 27, 54, 55
Soulen, Kendall, 135nn28–29
Southern, R. W., 111, 126n108
spirit-matter dualism, 11
spiritual elitism, 99
splendor, 96
Stang, Charles, 88n9
Staupitz, Johannes von, 184–85n137
Stoddard, Solomon, 221, 222, 224
Stoicism, 83, 276
Strobel, Kyle L., 236n68
suffering, prompts prayer, 216
Summa contra gentiles (Thomas Aquinas), 131
Summa theologiae (Thomas Aquinas), 131, 279
supernaturalism, 266
supersessionism, 19–20

Tanner, Kathryn, 4, 29, 36n11, 239n87, 243
Taylor, Charles, 67
Tertullian, 10
Tetragrammaton, 135nn28–29
thearchy, 96
theodicy, 240n94
Theodosius, 34
theological language, 140
theophanies, 18
theurgy, 88–89
Thomas Aquinas, 40, 86, 129–63, 240, 287
  appropriation of Aristotle, 132–33
  on causality, 145–49
  on God and creation, 134, 137–38, 141–45
  on grace, 160–61
  on integrity of creation, 133–34
  life of, 130–34
  on the Son, 150–54
  on the Spirit, 149–50
Tice, Terrence, 252, 270n129
Tolkien, J. R. R., 86
Torrance, James, 46n75
Torrance, T. F., 46n75, 280n23
Torrell, Jean-Pierre, 133, 162
total depravity, 203n66
trinitarian monotheism, 22
Trinity
  Athanasius on, 58–59
  Augustine on, 72–73
  Calvin on, 208–9
  Edwards on, 238
  and election in Barth, 293
  external acts undivided, 144–45

Thomas Aquinas on, 144–45
vestiges of, 285
tritheism, 233n54
Tropikoi, 57
two cities (Augustine), 68, 69, 74

union with Christ, 26
union with God, 100, 101
universalism, 27, 297
University of Berlin, 251
univocation, 140
Urban II (pope), 113

Valentinians, 10
Valentinus, 10
Vander Schel, Kevin, 263n92
Vanhoozer, Kevin, 57n140
vanity of life, 83
*via affirmativa*, 93. *See also* cataphatic theology
*via negativa*, 93, 94, 282. *See also* apophatic theology
Victor, bishop of Rome, 7
virtue, 234
virtues, 153–54
Visser, Sandra, 109n8, 126

Wawrykow, Joseph, 158, 161
way of causation, 139
way of excellence, 139
way of negation, 141
way of remotion, 139

Webster, John, 229n27
Wendel, François, 194, 197
Wesley, John, 231n41
Westminster Catechism, 225
Whitefield, George, 223
will, Edwards on, 230–31
Willard, Dallas, 45n64
William Rufus (king), 113
Williams, Rowan, 34n2, 35n5, 51
Williams, Thomas, 109n8, 111n16, 126
wisdom of God, inscrutability of, 215
women theologians, 3–4
Word
becomes flesh, 40–42
and creation, 150n109
and grace, 150n109
Word and sacrament, as extrinsic spirituality, 179
Word and Spirit, 56
Word of God
Luther on, 178–82
obedience to, 197
as sole criterion for dogmatics, 284
Wordsworth, William, 273
works of love, 188
works righteousness, 160, 183
World War I, 277–78
wrath of God, 204, 207–8, 214

yearning, 79–80
Young, Frances, 4, 21n115, 260n75

Printed and bound by CPI Group (UK) Ltd, Croydon, CR0 4YY